AF476876

LOST ENGLAND
1870-1930

ALLEN'S.
FOR
PURE
SWEETS
FOR
PURE
SWEETS
ALLEN'S SWEET
VELMA
ICES

LOST ENGLAND
1870-1930

Philip Davies

ATLANTIC PUBLISHING

This is an Atlantic Publishing book
38 Copthorne Road, Croxley Green
Hertfordshire, WD3 4AQ, UK.

Reprinted 2017

Photograph credits, acknowledgements and copyright details– see page 559

A catalogue record for this book is available from the British Library.

ISBN 978 1 909242 79 1

Printed in China

CONTENTS

For Ann

And did those feet in ancient time
Walk upon England's mountains green?
And was the Holy Lamb of God
On England's pleasant pastures seen?

And did the Countenance Divine
Shine forth upon our clouded hills
And was Jerusalem builded here
Among these dark satanic mills?

William Blake

PUBLISHER'S NOTE

The Historic England Collection

Photography was one of the wonders of the Victorian age – the camera captured the way people lived and the image became an eyewitness, a priceless primary source making vivid the lives of our forebears. Lost England, 1870–1930 features a selection of more than 1,300 photographs from the Historic England collection, a matchless archive of nine million images that tell the national story from the middle of the 19th century.

Sifting and organizing pictures for inclusion in the book has presented many challenges. The photographs are arranged in a gazetteer-style, ordered within regions and then by county and town, so the reader is able to experience a geographical tour of England. The county structure of England around 1900 was somewhat different from today and this has presented challenges which the Publishers hope have been overcome with common sense rather than adhering to strict conventions. There are some diversions and deviations because of the editors' desire to include as many photographs as possible with the best quality. Enlarging some pictures to their optimum size sometimes required licence in their sequencing. This approach is driven by the desire to present a visual narrative of this fascinating period in England's history with previously unseen breadth and clarity.

While most of the images are from the extraordinary national asset of Historic England's Archives, other exceptional collections have been drawn on and these are credited at the end of this book.

Can you help?

The Historic England photographic collection has accumulated over decades, with the addition of many archives from a wide variety of sources around the country. The priceless photographic content tells its own visual story, often accompanied by definitive text. But while there is a vast amount of information in the captions in this book, we are conscious that some details about the photographs have been lost over the years. However, with the growing interest in the past – whether from conservation societies, popular genealogy or local history groups – an increasingly important source of information is held by the descendants of the people who grew up and lived in communities across the country a century or more ago and whose local knowledge is retained in today's generation. Where there are omissions, anomalies or mistakes, or simply extra information that would enhance the historical database we would love to hear from you via the website:
www.Lost-England.co.uk
or email to LostEngland@atlanticpublishing.co.uk.

The Publishers would like to thank:
Mike Evans, Anna Eavis, Lindsay Jones, Alyson Rogers and the Archives team at Historic England; John Hudson of Historic England Publishing.

Picture research and caption text: James Alexander, Sarah Rickayzen, Andrew Sergeant, Michael Wilkinson.

INTRODUCTION

THE LOST COUNTRY

Images of England 1870 – 1930

'Into my heart an air that kills
From yon far country blows:
What are those blue remembered hills,
What spires, what farms are those?'

'That is the land of lost content
I see it shining plain,
The happy highways where I went
And cannot come again'

(A E Housman)

For each generation the golden age is always yesterday. Each has its own idealised vision of the past and how it might have been – a romantic evocation of a Lost England. The Victorians were no different. As the 19th century progressed many reacted against the march of the cities and industry by evoking wistful images of an older pre-industrial England, which were expressed in a counter culture, which embraced everything from Pre-Raphaelite painting to the ideals of William Morris and the Arts and Crafts movement. The reality was very different.

Between 1820 and 1914 Britain was transformed on a scale unprecedented in its history. The growth of its economy was little short of miraculous. In 1914, it was a staggeringly wealthy country. Its total overseas investments amounted to £4,000 million, one-fifth of all the capital in the world, generating £200 million a year to their owners, equal to the entire French national budget. After such phenomenal progress, in spite of rising challenges at home and abroad, at the dawn of a new century many looked forward to the future with unadulterated optimism. A glittering new horizon of science and technology beckoned. Many believed that the real golden age lay ahead little knowing that just a few years later such innate optimism would be cruelly shattered by the most catastrophic war in history.

One hundred years earlier England was a very different country.In 1801 London was the only city with a population of more than one million people – more than ten times larger than Liverpool, its nearest rival. One hundred years later there were 30 places with a population of over 100,000, and a further 49 towns with between 50,000 and 100,000 inhabitants. At the outbreak of the First World War, as the pace of urbanisation began to slacken, nearly 80 per cent of Britain's 37 million people lived in urban places – the highest proportion in Europe. This compared with just over a third of its almost 12 million citizens one hundred year earlier. By the beginning of the new century one in five English people lived in London.

The relentless march of urbanisation was one of the defining characteristics of the century. Contemporary observers were astonished at the speed with which once somnolent villages and ancient market towns were engulfed by a tide of development as the great manufacturing cities of the age – Manchester, Liverpool, Birmingham, Leeds, Newcastle and Sheffield – exploded across the fair face of England. John Ruskin, for one, fulminated against the degradation of the English landscape, and his own particular vision of a Lost England, condemning cities as 'spots of dreadful mildew spreading by patches and blotches over the country they consume.'[1]

The reasons for this phenomenal growth have been the subject of much debate, but a key factor was the changing age structure of Britain. In the 1820s almost two thirds of the population were under 30. Fuelled by falling death rates in the early 19th century and an excess of births over deaths in both urban and rural areas, a reservoir of surplus labour was created. People moved out of the villages in search of the jobs which they could no longer provide. But it was in the industrial districts and urban areas where the natural increase in population was most rapid. Britain was in ferment.

Between 1831 and 1901 the number of manufacturing towns in England more than doubled from 412 to 895. Liverpool and Preston, for example, grew fivefold, and Bradford eightfold in the 50 years from 1811. Until the mid century the fastest growing towns were the dynamic centres of the industrial revolution in south Lancashire, west Yorkshire, the Potteries and the West Midlands, but by the 1870s some wholly new industrial towns like Middlesbrough, Barrow-in-Furness and Cardiff had outstripped older, slower growing historic places such as Exeter, Chester, Norwich and York.

Victorian city streets were an assault on the senses. The bustling manufacturing cities looked, smelt and sounded different. They were occupied almost exclusively by the working and middle classes. The wealthier moved out as soon as they could to healthier, higher ground on the periphery, or to comfortable houses in the rural fringe.

In England the prevailing winds usually come from the west. These blew the smoke from thousands of coal fires and factory chimneys across the towns and cities coating everything in a thick black grime, so in most urban areas like London, Manchester, Sheffield and Birmingham, the poorer areas were to be found on the east side.

Atmospheric pollution caused a permanent toxic smog. When the temperature dropped, these caused impenetrable fogs; their miasmatic vapours shrouding the streets in an eerie, ethereal haze muffling the sounds of the surrounding gas-lit city. But the acrid tang of smoke also meant work, prosperity and freedom from want. When the Prince of Wales opened the new Town Hall in Middlesbrough in 1887, the Mayor extolled the smoke. 'If there is one thing more than another that Middlesbrough can be proud of. It is the smoke'. [2]

It was just as bad elsewhere – in London, Leeds, Manchester and Bradford, for instance, where a local satirist wrote:

'How beautiful is the smoke
The Bradford smoke:
Pouring from numberless chimney-stacks,
Condensing and falling in showers of 'blacks'…
… In lane and yard and street;' [3]

In Birmingham and the Black Country billowing blasts of hot air were emitted from the glowing maws of furnaces and foundries; the streets constantly echoing to the dull repetitive pounding of the great steam hammers as they tortured molten metal into the sinews of industrial power punctuated by the shriek of steam as it escaped from hundreds of whistling boilers. The mill towns of Lancashire echoed to the incessant rattle of thousands of cotton spinning machines. Abattoirs and meat markets reeked of blood, offal and discarded entrails. Gas works belched out smoke and fumes across teeming town centres. Tanning and dyeing works stank of human urine and the toxic chemical dyes used in their foul processes. In Wapping and the London Docks the air was pungent with the smell of tobacco and cinnamon, nutmeg and cloves shipped across the world from the colonies. In Limehouse opium-scented air wafted from backstreet houses where those who could pay might briefly escape the squalor of their surroundings into a drug-fuelled stupor.

Workshops and factories worked cheek by jowl alongside terraces of back-to-back housing in London and the industrial cities of the north and Midlands. Everywhere there was the cacophonous clatter of iron wheels on streets of hard granite setts and the rank smell of manure from thousands of horses. Noxious fumes wafted on the air from tallow makers, bone boilers, arsenic and white lead works, and from factories producing lethal dyes, caustic soda, Prussic acid, paint and varnish.

For those toiling in the factories and workshops, work was repetitive, exhausting and often lethal. Overnight those injured or disabled could be consigned to a life of poverty. While successive Factory Acts slowly improved working conditions, there was little awareness of health and safety at work.

Above: 102-104 Bagot Street, Birmingham. Most working class people in Victorian cities lived in insanitary 'back-to-back' dwellings built in dense courts or terraces.

Cutlery grinders and potters were prone to black spit (a form of asthma), chimney sweeps to soot wart, brass founders to 'Monday' fever, and matchmakers to 'phossy jaw,' or facial necrosis. Fashionable emerald -green dresses, shoes and wallpapers were dyed with deadly copper and arsenic-based pigments poisoning those who both made and wore them. The invention of mauvene dye in 1856 may have revolutionised Victorian tastes, but it was manufactured from picric acid, arsenic and other highly toxic chemicals. The mercury used to make shiny top hats all too often drove the hatters insane; hence the phrase 'mad as a hatter.'

The streets of Victorian England were a veritable pandemonium swarming with pedestrians, commuters, costermongers and shoppers all cheek by jowl with street sweepers, beggars, prostitutes and entertainers. Gas had been introduced for street lighting in Pall Mall in 1807, and in Preston in 1816. By the 1860s it was in universal use even in the most squalid courts and alleys, bathing the soot-blackened buildings in a sickly yellow effulgence; a universal visual metaphor for the Victorian city. Entire buildings were sheathed in hand-painted signboards, posters and enamel advertisements offering everything from quack medicines to lemonade. Shopfronts with elegant painted, or gilt and glass fascias, proudly displayed their wares – purveyors of an unparalleled range of consumer goods from Reckitt's Blue to Colman's mustard. This was the age of mass-produced cast iron which enriched England's towns and streets with elaborate railings, coal hole covers, lamp columns, drinking fountains, street urinals and clock towers many of which can be seen in these photographs.

The smells and sounds of Victorian England may have long since vanished, but how it looked is very apparent from the wealth of historic photographs which survive. By providing windows on to a lost world, they offer a direct link to the past. They allow us to travel back through time and gaze at long-lost streets, and look again at the faces of those long since dead: forgotten people frozen in time, their faces captured forever as they stared at the photographer; sometimes, if they moved, little more than ghostly traces left on the glass plate negative. Poignant, moving and profoundly haunting, they are impartial records of things that really happened, and of people who really lived, captured at random moments in time before they retreated from life into history, and before they could be distorted through the eyes of the historian. What could be more evocative as a reminder of the transience of the life and death of cities and places, and, of course, ourselves?

Some of the older people, captured on camera would have looked back themselves at an earlier, pre-industrial world; their own generational memory of a Lost England, a world with buildings and landscapes which would have been as familiar to them as their world is to us. Many of them mourned the loss of that simpler, more agrarian world of their childhoods. In 1942 Clarence Winchester captured this enduring myth of a lost Golden Age, which perpetually haunts each generation, and the melancholic yearning for the loss of the world of childhood.

'Nor shall we ever let the memory go
Of England's greenest fields and tuneful streams
Of ancient inns that bind most ancient dreams
Within their blackest oaks'. [4]

***

The Industrial Revolution in England involved a long process of technological change. In the early part of the 18th century a great deal of industry was located in the countryside – for example stocking weavers in Leicestershire, toolmakers in South Yorkshire, and fustian-weavers in Lancashire, or in small cottage industries, such as nail-making in the West Midlands. Even one hundred years later, the majority of the population still worked on the land.

In 1800 most goods were handmade by individual craftsmen aided by an apprentice or unskilled labourer. Old towns like Sheffield, Leeds and Wolverhampton were established centres for the finishing and marketing of quality goods. As the intensity of labour increased, the thrusting merchants of the new industrial age favoured the economies of scale offered by existing and new urban locations. Specific trades tended to aggregate together. Large firms attracted clusters of local suppliers and customers, which rapidly developed into an elaborate support network.

Right: A Harper, Sons & Bean, Dudley, c1915. The manufacturing towns and cities were fed a continuous stream of industrial fodder as migrants were displaced from the countryside.

As regional specialisation intensified, so too did the demand for transport. In the late 18th century this had been met by an immense investment in a network of metalled roads to maximise the potential of horse-drawn transport. From the 1760s, they were complemented by the first canals. These earned such fantastic dividends for their proprietors that they induced a 'canal mania', which soon turned sour when rampant speculation and war with France threw many into debt. Nonetheless, by the 1820s the sight of huge, horse-drawn canal barges laden with raw materials and merchandise, plus a flourishing coaching industry, proved to many that investment in horse-powered transport had paid off. Trade and manufacture reaped huge benefits. Between 1809 and 1839 the value of exports tripled from £25.4 million to £76 million.

Sustained by a rising population, an economic and social revolution was triggered, driven by a whole variety of different factors, but by far the most significant was the practical application of steam power and technology. Above all else, the wealth of Victorian Britain was built on coal, iron and steam, along with the seemingly insatiable appetite of entrepreneurs to make money, an avaricious quality which appalled many observers, like John Ruskin, who wrote of the city of London in Cestus of Aglaia. 'Ask a great money-maker what he wants to do with his money, – he never knows. He doesn't make it to do anything with it. He gets it only that he may get it ... So all that great foul city of London there, — rattling, growling, smoking, stinking, — a ghastly heap of fermenting brickwork, pouring out poison at every pore – you fancy it is a city of work? Not a street of it!' [5]

The manufacturing towns and cities were fed a continuous stream of industrial fodder as migrants were displaced from the countryside, and, in particular, from Ireland. They tended to be young unmarried people in search of employment. Women sought positions as domestic servants for the rising middle classes, or jobs in textiles, while men looked for

new opportunities in the workshops and factories that were generating unprecedented wealth. In most industrial towns between 5–10 per cent of migrants were poor Irish workers in search of a better life, but there were widespread regional variations. In 1851 in Preston the poor Irish comprised 14 per cent, and in Liverpool over 22 per cent.

The booming industries of Victorian England – textiles, iron, steel and engineering – all required inexhaustible supplies of coal and coke to feed the steam engines powering the country's factories, railways and steamships. From 1850, new pits were opened in virtually every British coalfield to meet their voracious demands. The industry grew at an astonishing rate. By 1880 over 380,000 men were employed in close-knit mining communities in Northumberland and Durham, South Lancashire and Yorkshire, Derbyshire and Nottinghamshire, and South Wales. By 1900 it was 820,000, and by 1913 over 1,128,000. Output more than doubled from around 70 million tons in the 1850s to 153 million tons in 1880 before peaking at 287 million tons in 1913, of which a third was exported to feed emerging foreign industries.

The mining villages of Britain were cohesive communities with tight loyalties; the terraces of solid working class houses built and let by the colliery owners. Many became bastions of the Trade Union movement with considerable political influence at Westminster, but because the whole life of the community revolved around the pit, it made them vulnerable to economic downturns.

Mineral rights were owned by the surface landowner, which generated huge profits for those lucky enough to sit above the great underground seams, but private ownership fostered the development of small firms and local pits which constrained both investment and productivity. Until the First World War, mining remained a labour-intensive 'pick and shovel' industry relying on back-breaking manual work for cutting and primitive haulage. Although the worst abuses of child and female labour were abolished through the Mines Act of 1842, it was a dangerous and strength-sapping job.

Gradually safety measures and ventilation were improved. The industry was slow to utilise new materials, like steel or concrete, for underground pit props, but at surface level machinery was introduced for the screening, sizing and sorting of the coal. As the more easily-worked seams were exhausted, new technology was deployed to allow deep mining and unlock hitherto inaccessible supplies. In Durham they even mined far out under the sea.

However, over-reliance on manual labour meant wages comprised as much as 70 per cent of total costs, so when world consumption eased for the 20 years after 1913, the swollen ranks of miners faced longer hours, reduced wages and lay-offs, which paralysed the mono-cultural mining communities, with major political repercussions. By 1939 the labour force had halved in size; an ageing body of men, whose children sought opportunities elsewhere rather than following their fathers and grandfathers into the pits.

Rudimentary steam locomotives had been used in collieries and quarries since the early 19th century. The technology had been refined and improved by pioneers such as George Stephenson and Richard Trevithick, but this new-fangled innovation was viewed with suspicion, particularly by the entrenched vested interests – the canal companies, Turnpike Trusts, coach proprietors and horse traders, who had invested so much in the canal and road networks. They grossly exaggerated the dangers. Passengers would die of suffocation in the smoke-filled tunnels, they argued, or suffer hideous injuries beneath the deadly iron wheels of the new steaming juggernauts.

Above: Newcastle Central Station, 1894. The wealth of Victorian England was built on coal, iron and steam. Railways were the supreme material achievement of the Victorian age, and they transformed the country.

In 1825 the first railway passenger service began between Stockton and Darlington. Four years later, the famous Rainhill locomotive trials were held, won by Robert Stephenson's Rocket. It achieved astonishing speeds of over 30 miles an hour, demonstrating to all that the railway was the key to the future. A year later the Liverpool and Manchester Railway was opened by the Duke of Wellington, a momentous event marred by the death on the track of the MP William Huskisson. The accident only served to reinforce the prejudices of the hostile vested interests that the new iron roads and their steaming leviathans were lethal, but the momentum was unstoppable. Other railways soon followed, including the world's first trunk routes.

The railway was the supreme material achievement of the Victorian age, bringing food, raw materials and agricultural produce into the pulsating new centres of population and carrying away goods and manufactures from the mills and factories to freight depots and ports across the land at speeds previously thought unnatural.

The Grand Junction Railway linking Birmingham to Manchester was completed in 1837. It was followed a year later by Robert Stephenson's London to Birmingham Railway. Its station at Euston was the first mainline terminus in a capital city anywhere in the world, heralded by the gigantic Euston Arch, a 70ft high Doric propylaeum designed by Philip Hardwick. It was a spectacular symbol for the new railway age.

By 1840 Derby, Nottingham, Leicester and Rugby were linked by the Midland Counties Railway, Brunel's Great Western Railway was well underway, and a line had been completed between London and Southampton. On 13 June 1842 the railways received the royal seal of approval when Queen Victoria made her first rail journey in a purpose-built saloon from Slough to Paddington. Never before in history had a reigning monarch entered a capital city in such a way.

Railway hysteria swept the country. By November 1846, 23 new railway schemes had been laid before parliament in a frenzy of wild speculation. Ironically this appalled many of the great engineers of the day. Brunel wrote 'the whole world is railway mad. I am really sick of hearing proposals made. I wish it were at an end; it would suit my interests and those of my clients perfectly if all railways were stopped for several years to come'.[6] But it was not to be. Legislation was pushed through parliament to ensure that cheap travel was available for all and that trains conformed to national standards of speed and comfort. The same Act compelled the railway companies to allow the new electric telegraph to be carried alongside the iron tracks revolutionising national communications.

By 1850 over 6,000 miles of railway had been completed by armies of navvies (navigators). In less than 20 years some of the remotest areas of the countryside were linked with the thrusting new centres of England's towns and cities. Railways transformed the national economy and triggered a whole new wave of technological progress built on the mass manufacture of capital goods.

By the mid century Britain was the undisputed workshop of the world. In 1851 Britain proclaimed its prosperity to the world at the Great Exhibition in the Crystal Palace in Hyde Park. It was designed by Joseph Paxton, a pioneer of glasshouses and railway structures, who sketched out his initial concept on a piece of blotting paper.

Completed in just nine months, this revolutionary three-storey structure of cast iron and glass covered a vast exhibition space of courts and galleries as a showcase for Britain's goods and merchandise. After it ended, the entire structure was dismantled and re-erected to a modified design at Sydenham in a park embellished with statuary and fountains. These included the world's first dinosaur sculptures designed by Benjamin Waterhouse Hawkins. Pre-dating Darwin's *On the Origin of Species* by six years, they were inaugurated with a celebration dinner inside the iguanadon on New Year's Eve 1853.

The railway network transformed the landscape of Britain. Guided by some of the most gifted engineers of their day, and with breath-taking bravura, lines were thrown across rivers and valleys, marsh and moorlands. They were burrowed in tunnels beneath hills, rivers and mountains, and raised on elevated embankments, bridges and viaducts through the new city centres. This was the heroic age of railway engineering. British engineers using innovative construction techniques led the world.

For his mighty high-level bridge across the Tyne between Gateshead and Newcastle begun in 1846, Robert Stephenson designed a bow and string structure with short spans carried on five huge stone piers conveying road and rail traffic on its two decks. It was to be the last great monument of cast-iron bridge construction because, although cast iron possesses immense strength in compression, it is brittle and fatally weak in tension, a fact well known to the early railway pioneers.

For his subsequent Britannia Bridge across the Menai straits, Stephenson had tests carried out on wrought-iron sections to devise the best form of girder – a hollow rectangular box section made up of small plates and angle irons riveted together and large enough for a train to pass through. The structural components were floated out into the water before being raised into place by powerful steam jacks.

At each end, the bridge was guarded by two brooding lions couchant carved in limestone, later mercilessly lampooned in verse by the Welsh poet John Evans.

'Four fat lions
Without any Hair,
Two on this side
And two over there'.

Opened in March 1850, the revolutionary new construction techniques deployed inspired Stephenson's great rival Isambard Kingdom Brunel for his famous Royal Albert Bridge across the Tamar at Saltash completed in 1859. Other wrought iron bridges followed at Crumlin in 1857, Belah in 1861 and the Severn Bridge in 1879 before steel superseded iron.

In their scale and ambition the engineering structures of the railway age rivalled the awe-inspiring mediaeval cathedrals. The magisterial Ribblehead Viaduct, snaking across the Ribble valley in North Yorkshire, was completed by over 1,000 navvies for the Midland Railway in 1874, but perhaps the greatest achievement of all was the colossal Forth Railway Bridge in Scotland, now a World Heritage Site. Opened in 1890, it was the largest bridge in the world, a spectacular monument to the age of steel, each span over four times wider than Stephenson's entire Britannia Bridge. With the benefit of hindsight, many now see these majestic engineering structures as inextricably part of the poetry of the English landscape, but at the time they were excoriated by John Ruskin, William Morris and others as a blight upon the fair face of England.

As its iron tentacles spread across the land, the expansion of the railway network seemed utterly relentless. Journeys that once would have taken days by stagecoach were cut to a few hours by train. Between 1861 and 1888 mileage grew by 81 per cent, and rail traffic by 180 per cent, particularly freight, which generated between a third and a half more income than pure passenger traffic alone.

By the 1870s more people were travelling by rail than ever before, most of them third class. In the previous 20 years third class ticket sales had risen by 584 per cent. Vast numbers of working class passengers used the network. For many, work no longer necessarily revolved around the place where they were born. The introduction of cheap morning workmen's fares enabled the working man to commute from the periphery, liberating him from the need to live in congested city centres. This stimulated the growth of the outer suburbs. By the end of the century 18,860 miles of track were in operation carrying over 1,100 million passengers at speeds in excess of 70mph, something which seemed unimaginable in the age of the horse-drawn coach just 60 years before.

In the great city centres railway companies competed with each other to build ever more imposing stations as symbols of commercial and civic pride. And it was to architects that they turned to provide a respectable face to the stations, bridges and tunnel entrances to adorn the new railway. Only Brunel insisted on retaining a direct involvement in architectural design. For the magnificent spans of the train shed at Paddington it was he, rather than the company, who appointed Matthew Digby Wyatt to work as his assistant.

Newcastle Central by John Dobson, completed in 1855, was one of the first and finest, with a great curving roof of wrought-iron ribs set behind a handsome stone frontage. At St Pancras, the awe-inspiring parabolic iron vault of the train shed by W H Barlow and R M Ordish was the largest in the world on its completion in 1868, complemented six years later by George Gilbert Scott's romantic Gothic railway hotel, a truly heroic building for the railway age.

When it opened in 1877 with 13 platforms, York was the largest railway station in the world. Designed by Thomas Prosser and William Peachy, architects to the North-Eastern Railway, its three huge curved spans carried on iron arcades of Corinthian columns were regarded as one of the engineering marvels of the time. In Bristol, a new through station was built in the same year at Temple Meads by Matthew Digby Wyatt complementing Brunel's earlier terminus of 1840 with its false hammer-beam roof.

As the century progressed, small, picturesque country stations using local materials in a variety of delightful architectural styles became part of the fabric of the English landscape. Many resembled estate lodges or cottages orné enriched with standardised cast-iron columns, brackets and canopies from company foundries and workshops.

Alongside revolutionary new forms of transport, older methods of movement continued to grow. Rural transport depended heavily on animals and horse drawn vehicles. An extensive network of carriers and car men transported both goods and passengers between outlying villages, market towns and railheads. In the towns and cities, armies of hauliers and costermongers ferried newly arrived goods from the railway depots to shops and markets.

For the aspiring middle classes, private carriage ownership was seen as a status symbol, but after 1870 city centre congestion, the rising costs of feed and stabling, and the ease of rail transport dampened enthusiasm. The ancient coaching inns, which for centuries had provided the only regular service between towns, were dealt a slow and lingering death by the railways. Even by the mid century, they were in terminal decline. Many were converted to hotels, given over to storage and casual stabling,

Above: Bedford, Silver Street, c1900. For the aspiring middle classes, private carriage ownership was seen as a status symbol, but after 1870 city centre congestion, the rising costs of feed and stabling, and the ease of rail transport dampened enthusiasm.

or unceremoniously demolished, their once bustling courtyards rendered obsolete by the sleek, steaming locomotives drawn up alongside the platforms of the nearby station.

In the cities, long distance walking remained a common feature of everyday life. Charles Dickens thought nothing of walking over 20 miles through London every day. Commuters and the poor often had little alternative. Increasingly there was pressure to remove barriers to movement, including tollbooths on the main highways and bridges, as local vestries and municipal corporations took over control. In the countryside there was an intense struggle to retain common land, rural footpaths, bridleways and rights of way in the face of encroachment by landowners.

At strategic sites and junctions, new railway towns sprang up with a single purpose – to service the engineering needs of the network. Swindon, Eastleigh, Ashford and Wolverton owed their very existence to the railway, each lined with unprepossessing terrace houses on a grid plan to serve the adjacent railway engineering works. These were single company towns. A local railway man wrote of Wolverton 'It is a little red brick town composed of 242 little red-brick houses – all running either this way or that way at right angles – three or four tall red-brick chimneys, a number of very large red-brick workshops, six red houses for officers, one red-beer shop, two red public houses and...a substantial red school-room...the whole being built by the order of a Railway Board, at a railway station, by a railway contractor, for railwaymen, railway women and railway children; in short, the round cast iron plate over the door of every house, bearing the letters LNWR is the generic symbol of the town.'[7]

Only at Crewe did the railway company make real efforts to plan long term to create a more integrated community. The town, laid out by the engineer John Locke and the architect John Cunningham was notable for its wide, regular streets, decent building standards and sanitation. In an enlightened exercise in industrial self-interest, the company laid on water, sewerage, gas and refuse collection, and even provided schools, shops, churches, assembly rooms, and policemen.

By 1901 Crewe had swollen almost tenfold in the previous 50 years from 4,500 to 42,074 people driven by the mass manufacture of over 4,000 locomotives for Britain and its expanding Empire. In some older towns, such as Derby, Doncaster and Newton Abbot, the railway added a whole new dimension to their industrial base. Elsewhere, new engineering works sprang up in specialist railway suburbs at Gorton in Manchester, Hunslet in Leeds and Saltley in Birmingham, for instance.

The railways facilitated the expansion of seaside resorts. By 1911 over half the population were visiting the coast for day excursions. Many, of course, had enjoyed success before the railways. For Londoners, access to the Kent coast had been provided by Thames steam packets from Woolwich and Gravesend since the early 1820s; the latter with the oldest cast-iron pier in the world completed in 1834. Pleasure boats plied the coasts of Lancashire and Cheshire from Liverpool.

Royal patronage had boosted the popularity of Worthing and Weymouth in the late 18th century, and also Brighton under the Prince Regent, but, with the arrival of the train, numbers soared. In 1850 more than 70,000 people arrived in Brighton by train in just a single week compared with an annual total of 50,000 by stagecoach only 13 years earlier. When the railway reached Cleethorpes in August 1863, over 30,000 people arrived on the first day alone.

The popularity of the spa persisted well in to the 19th century. After 1840 new railways brought a wave of new development. Matlock and Buxton revived with the support of the Duke of Devonshire and the arrival of the railway in 1863. Tenbury Wells and Droitwich flourished as a spin-off from the Cheshire salt extraction industry, while municipal investment sparked a wave of luxurious new facilities in both Bath and Harrogate whose reputations rivalled those of the sybaritic Continental spas.

New hotels sprang up in the fashionable spa towns to cater for the growing clientele, such as the Queens on Imperial Square in Cheltenham. Completed in 1839 to the designs of R W and C Jearrad, it vaunted an imposing, Corinthian centrepiece, all iced in stucco to match the rest of the town. The Great Western Hydro Hotel in Bristol by R S Pope opened in

Above: The Grand Hotel, Scarborough, designed by Cuthbert Brodrick between 1863–7 in a bombastic French Renaissance style, perched high on a cliff overlooking the North Sea.

the same year. Its warm, cold and vapour baths were intended to serve the Atlantic Steamship Line and Brunel's impending railway link to London.

From the mid century onwards, a whole new era of railway hotels began with P C Hardwick's Great Western Hotel in 1853 at Paddington, which offered over 150 rooms. Paddington was followed in 1862 by the Grosvenor Hotel at Victoria, a massive pile with curved mansard roofs in French Second Empire style, which in turn set the tone for the development of the adjacent Grosvenor Gardens. Other luxury hotels soon followed at the principal London termini, notably E M Barry's two set pieces – Cannon Street in 1861, and then Charing Cross in 1864, complete with a replica of the mediaeval Eleanor Cross on the forecourt. Gilbert Scott's St Pancras Hotel, finished in 1874 in a romantic High Victorian Gothic style, set a new benchmark of opulence at a total cost of over £1 million.

Outside the capital, there was steady growth in the seaside towns such as Dover, Bournemouth and Torquay, but the real tour de force was the aptly named Grand in Scarborough, designed by Cuthbert Brodrick between 1863–7 in a bombastic French Renaissance style. Perched high on a cliff overlooking the North Sea, it dominates the town.

By 1871 the 50 towns officially classified as seaside resorts had grown by over 20 per cent, but there was widespread regional variation. Although the railway had reached Cornwall in 1859, its tourism potential remained unexploited until well after the First World War. In the south-west, only Torquay flourished. It quadrupled in size between 1841 and 1901 as a genteel all year round resort.

This was the age of the seaside promenade pier, which became a hugely popular feature of many of the emerging resorts. The earliest was completed at Ryde in 1814, but others soon followed around the coast of Britain from Clevedon and Cleethorpes to Brighton and Blackpool, which boasted three. At Margate in 1853 the doyen of pier design, Eugenius

Birch, built the first screw-pile pier in Britain. Over the next 30 years he was responsible for building another 13 including Brighton West Pier, Aberystwyth, Eastbourne, Bournemouth and the splendid Birnbeck Pier at Weston-super-Mare.

Aided by their micro-climates, new middle-class resorts, like Bournemouth and Eastbourne, also enjoyed a longer season, something which working class resorts, like Southend and Blackpool, were unable to offer, the latter dependent on the 'wakes' or holiday weeks of the Lancashire textile trade when whole factories closed and the mill towns emptied for the seaside.

By the 1870s the introduction of Bank Holidays gave the working classes time for leisure. With the increase in real wages and the growth of savings in friendly societies and holiday clubs, factory workers were able to take advantage of block bookings and cheap lodging houses, all too often ruled by the archetypal seaside landlady. Strong links developed between particular resorts and their hinterland. Prestonians preferred Blackpool, while the 'middling comfortable' artisans of Manchester opted for Southport.

For many Blackpool offered a world far removed from the daily drudgery of the factory and mill. There were winter gardens, music halls, three piers, ballrooms and theatres and the jaw-dropping Blackpool Tower rising over 500 feet above the panoramic sweep of Morecambe Bay. In 1861 some 135,000 people arrived in Blackpool by train. By 1879 it was 1 million, and by 1914 over 4 million. Those affronted by its vulgarity retreated to Lytham St Annes, or Southport, which had become a middle-class resort and commuter town for Liverpool. Successful Lancashire business men fled to their own commodious houses in the Lake District and Cheshire, their Yorkshire counterparts opting for second homes in Scarborough and Harrogate.

Some towns, such as Bridlington and Weston-super-Mare, initially tried to resist the railway, but eventually they too succumbed. Conversely, more entrepreneurial landowners, like Lord Burlington in Eastbourne, actively campaigned for links. Nearby Brighton embraced it, but resisted pressure to cater for the London working class. It invested heavily in two new piers built in 1866 and 1896, and top-end hotels aimed at enticing the aspirational nouveaux riches from the attractions of the French Riviera, and the spas of Central Europe. The Grand Hotel by John Whichcord, completed in 1864, set a new benchmark for opulence, only to be exceeded in 1888 by the nearby Metropole both of which can be seen in the photographs.

Below: The Victoria Pier, Blackpool. The promenade pier was a popular feature of many emerging seaside resorts.

Luxury hotels in central city locations became a common feature of English life. In London, the Langham, designed by John Giles and opened in 1865, terminated the vista from Portland Place. The Russell (1898) and Imperial Hotels (1911) by Fitzroy Doll, clad in fiery red terracotta, occupied most of the eastern side of Russell Square in Bloomsbury, while the Carlton (1891) and the Savoy (1889), both the product of Cesar Ritz, the Swiss hotelier and entrepreneur, offered the latest modern conveniences, including bedrooms with bathrooms. In Piccadilly, the Ritz, the acme of sophistication, was completed by Mewès and Davis in1906 with a Parisian-style arcade to the frontage. It was one of London's first steel-framed buildings. Outside London, perhaps the last gasp of the hotel boom was the Midland Hotel in Manchester by Charles Trubshaw, finally completed in blood red brick and terracotta in 1917.

If there was a loser in the relentless pace of urbanisation, it was the small market towns of less than 10,000 people, particularly those bypassed by the railways. Rural depopulation decreased demand for local crafts and services, and cottage industries atrophied in the face of mass industrial production.

The railway accelerated the pace of other changes too. Before the advent of a national rail network, time was marked differently across the country. National railway timetables necessitated the use of a universal time throughout England. In 1880 Greenwich mean time was made the legal national standard. Four years later at the International Meridian Conference, Greenwich was adopted as the global meridian for longitude. Some of the photographs in this book show the prominence of clocks and clock towers in central locations in town and market squares, such as Aylesbury, Newbury, Penrith and Blackburn at once proclaiming national standard time and burgeoning civic pride.

One casualty in the relentless drive towards standardisation was the gradual erosion of regional identities, traditions and dialects. When the radical Newcastle MP John Cowen made his debut in parliament in 1874, his speeches, delivered in a broad Geordie brogue, were simply not understood. As late as 1890, Gladstone's gruff Lancashire accent raised eyebrows when he spoke in Oxford. Even within individual neighbourhoods, local trades often had their own distinctive patois which was incomprehensible to others. The old provincial character of England with its peculiar local traditions, intense loyalties and nuances of speech was being consigned to history as a more homogeneous national culture emerged, and 'correct' received pronunciation was inculcated into the speech of the younger generation.

Above: Manchester Piccadilly, c1880. In just 20 years between 1831 and 1851 Manchester's population increased from 182,016 to over 300,000. The fortunes generated from the textile trade and industry financed a fabulous array of public buildings and institutions.

The story of the development of Victorian cities in the 19th century is one of provincial diversity as separate provincial cultures evolved in their own distinctive ways with different administrative systems and social structures before they conformed gradually to a national standard. Birmingham, for instance, was quite unlike Liverpool, Sheffield or Hull. Some grew naturally out of their older 18th century life; others out of the vigorous energies of the new merchants and industrialists, but as John Marshall, the successful Leeds flax master, wrote, 'the first effects of newly acquired wealth are always seen in the buildings of a town'.

Manchester has been dubbed the 'shock city' of the Victorian age. Together with its satellite towns, like St Helens, Rochdale and Oldham, it generated a massive amount of the wealth of Victorian England. When Alexis de Tocqueville visited in 1835 he was appalled at the 'homes of vice and poverty, which surround the huge palaces of industry and clasp them in their hideous folds'. In Manchester 'humanity attains its most complete development and its most brutish; here civilisation works its miracles, and civilised man is turned back almost into a savage', but, he concluded, 'it is in the middle of this vile cesspool that the greatest stream of human industry flows out to fertilise the entire universe. From this filthy sewer flows pure gold.'[8]

As early as the beginning of the 18th century, Manchester boasted a well-established, textiles industry with over 30,000 home-based spinners and weavers producing high quality goods, but one hundred years later a wave of ground-breaking technological inventions in spinning, weaving and dyeing transformed what was once a cottage activity into Britain's biggest industry. Textiles became the main pillar of British exports and one of its largest employers. Their growth propelled both Manchester and Liverpool to the forefront of British cities.

Manchester was peculiarly well-placed to capitalise on the new industry. In 1761 the Duke of Bridgewater's canal had reached Castlefield. Soon raw cotton was being imported through the port of Liverpool via the Mersey and Irwell Navigation canal system. With its mild damp climate so well-suited to the spinning of fragile raw cotton threads, its plentiful supplies of water and coal to power the new machinery, and an excellent network of canals and later railways, Manchester developed into the main distribution centre for raw cotton and spun yarn.

Richard Arkwright built the first great cotton mill in the town in 1780. Its tall brick chimney was the first of many that would come to dominate the skyline. Similar mills soon spread across the town and into the surrounding areas. Surrounded by bleaching and dyeing works, engineering workshops and foundries, these huge vertiginous buildings looming six or seven storeys above the surrounding area were revolutionary. They transformed the landscape. Manchester became 'Cottonopolis,' and King Cotton reigned supreme.

A critical mass of experienced iron founders, engineers and brilliant scientists propelled the town into the forefront of technological innovation. Ancoats and Chorlton-on-Medlock were dominated by tightly packed mills and factories clad in hard red-brick around innovative cast-iron and fireproof structures with forests of chimneys taller than church spires. By the 1820s Ancoats was one of the most intensely industrialised sites in the world with iron foundries, glass works and a welter of other industries cheek by jowl with the great spinning mills.

Foreign visitors were overwhelmed by the sublime majesty of it all. In 1844 the French writer Leon Faucher was amazed at the 'breathing of vast machines, sending forth fire and smoke through their tall chimneys, and offering up to the heavens, as it were in token of homage, the sighs of that Labour which God has imposed upon man.' [9]

In just 20 years between 1831 and 1851 Manchester's population increased from 182,016 to over 300,000. The fortunes generated from the textile trade and industry financed a fabulous array of public buildings and institutions. Prominent among these was the superb Free Trade Hall designed by Edward Walters between 1853 and 1856, which celebrated Manchester's leading role in the fight for free trade and the abolition of the Corn Laws.

Grand classical buildings, such as Charles Barry's Athaeneum, set a trend for the city centre, most notably Walters' magnificent Manchester and Salford Bank of 1862 in full-blown cinquecento style.

As the gravitational centre around which a galaxy of satellite towns revolved, it was commerce and trade that drove the form of the city centre as much as industry. This generated demand for city centre warehouses close to the Manchester Exchange. Some were shipping warehouses for storage and export, but others were akin to showrooms where goods could be displayed and inspected for the domestic market.

One of the hallmarks of Manchester's development was the way in which these commercial warehouses were adapted to an array of architectural styles. Edward Walters introduced the Renaissance palazzo. Others soon employed fashionable Gothic styles in polychrome brick and stone, but, more than any other architect, it was Alfred Waterhouse who was responsible for conferring his own distinctive style on the city. This was influenced by the desire for a more 'correct' form of Gothic architecture adumbrated by John Ruskin.

The most conspicuous example is the magnificent Town Hall, completed in 1877, then the world's most expensive public building, a romantic tour de force in High Victorian Gothic style with a clock tower soaring over 280 feet above the city. It was one of the most important Victorian buildings in the country. Inside, is the Great Hall, spanned by a hammer beam roof and with walls painted with stunning frescoes depicting scientific progress by Ford Madox Brown.

As the city prospered civic improvements enhanced the centre. Piccadilly was laid out as an esplanade by Joseph Paxton in 1854 with fine public statuary. Albert Square followed eight years later with a huge memorial to Prince Albert by Thomas Worthington. For the next 20 years the city centre witnessed a frenzy of new building as shops, offices and a new generation of warehouses arose in popular Italianate and Gothic styles.

By 1884 there were over 1,600 firms engaged in spinning and weaving or both, the vast majority family firms and partnerships. Although the machinery changed little, there had been great increases in efficiency through the application of steam power to weaving. After 1900 electricity was introduced slowly, but trade continued to expand powering a new boom in spinning. In just two years, between 1905 and 1907, 95 new mills were built alongside the older mills, many with over 100,000 spindles, ten times more than their predecessors, increasing spinning capacity by over one fifth.

With its over reliance on Liverpool as its gateway to the world, trade was slowly strangled by the excessive dock usage fees charged, so a bold new enterprise was launched to give the city direct access to the sea to enable it to export its manufactured goods directly. The brainchild of Daniel Adamson, a local industrialist, the Manchester Ship Canal was one of the most ambitious engineering operations of the Victorian age. It allowed ocean-going ships to sail right into the heart of Salford.

Begun in 1887, more than 11,000 men were employed in this massive feat of engineering. As the photographs show, it involved cutting a canal 26 feet deep by 170 feet wide for almost 35 miles to the sea and then removing over 53 million cubic yards of material. No less than five railway lines, including the main line from Euston, needed to be raised 75 feet above the canal. The local River Gowy was diverted beneath the canal in iron siphons, and the world-famous Barton aqueduct replaced by a new technical marvel – the Barton Swing aqueduct, the only example of its kind in the world.

Opened in 1894, the Ship Canal was a stupendous piece of infrastructure very much the equal of the staggering Forth Rail Bridge completed four years earlier. The writer W M Acworth believed that it 'is probably safe to say that, never since the world began has so much been done in so short a space of time to change the face of Nature over five-and-thirty miles of country.' [10]

Although initially trade was slow, tonnage grew steadily from 1.8 million tons in 1896 to 5 million in 1907, and then 7 million thirty years later. The link revitalised Manchester's economy. The banks of the canal were lined with new industries, oil refineries and the world's first industrial estate at Trafford Park, which was complete with its own private freight railway system and shipping line.

By 1900 the Manchester city region was the ninth most populous place on earth, attracting modern industries such as chemicals, electrical engineering and cars to replace the declining cotton mills, which had given the city its world-wide reputation. It had evolved into the business capital of a whole constellation of smaller surrounding textile towns, such as Bolton, Rochdale, and Oldham. By 1931 its population reached its all-time peak of 766,311 before entering into a steep decline as the textile industry collapsed in the face of foreign competition and the doleful effects of the Great Depression.

Just 35 miles to the east, Liverpool owed its prosperity to its position on the Mersey estuary and its domination of the Atlantic trade routes. Its first enclosed wet dock, Old Dock, which opened in 1715, soon became the focus for rapid development east of the city centre. Major improvements to the turnpikes in the early 18th century, followed by the formation of an extensive network of canals, linked the nascent town to nearby coalfields at Worsley and St Helens, and ushered in a period of phenomenal expansion.

By 1800 four additional wet docks had been completed, handling one sixth of the tonnage of all English ports, primarily because of the town's pivotal role in the Atlantic slave trade. Liverpool captains shipped manufactured goods, like copper and brass from Staffordshire, guns from Birmingham and Lancashire textiles to West Africa where they were traded for slaves. These were then shipped to the West Indies, Brazil and the Americas and sold for handsome profits before the ships returned to Liverpool laden with sugar, tobacco, coffee, cotton and molasses.

Abolition of the slave trade in 1807 made little difference to the town's economy as it was heavily engaged in the shipping of many other commodities. Soon it exploited its strategic position to eclipse Bristol as the primary focus for trans-Atlantic trade. The town and docks continued to flourish aided by the arrival of the Liverpool & Manchester railway in 1830, with its terminus at Lime Street opened in 1836.

A series of handsome Greek Revival buildings was erected, including a fine new Custom House on the site of the original Old Dock, designed by John Foster. However, the greatest symbol of Liverpool's civic ambition was the construction of the magnificent St George's Hall, a combination of law courts and concert hall completed in the 1840s. It resembled a great Roman temple at the heart of the city; a neo-classical masterpiece, designed by a young architect Harvey Lonsdale Elmes and subsequently lauded by Pevsner as 'one of the finest neo-Grecian buildings in the world'.

Gradually, around this civic forum a group of new public buildings was erected for cultural and educational purposes, including in 1857 the William Brown Library and Museum by Thomas Allom, the Picton Reading Room in 1874, the Walker Art Gallery, completed a year later, the Sessions House in 1882, and the College of Technology by E W Mountford, many of which are illustrated here.

By the mid century the port had expanded further with ranges of monumental dock buildings; the best of them designed by Jesse Hartley – austere, brick classical warehouses raised on massive granite piers; powerful symbols of the town's mercantile might. Others soon followed for specific commodities, including an impressive array of Italianate-style grain warehouses at Waterloo Dock, completed in 1868.

It was a town bustling with the demands of commerce and trade thronging with merchants, sea captains, investors and entrepreneurs all eager to make their fortunes. Its serried ranks of dock buildings stretched over five and a half miles along the banks of the Mersey. From a population of just 78,000 in 1801, 50 years later it was the largest British town outside London with over 376,000 people.

Its streets were lined with opulent offices, banks, insurance and shipping companies, many designed in classical Florentine or Venetian styles in a conscious echo of the palazzi of the merchant princes of the Italian Renaissance. In 1845–48 a branch of the Bank of England opened. In 1864 at Oriel Chambers in Water Street, the little-known local architect Peter Ellis designed one of the earliest examples of a curtain-wall building with faceted glass bays wrapped around an iron-framed structure; the precursor of the modern curtain-wall office.

In 1880 Liverpool was raised to city status, and widely regarded as the second city of the British Empire. Rebuilding continued unabated for insurance companies, such as the British and Foreign Marine Insurance Company, shipping companies, like The White Star Line, and public buildings, such as the General Post Office and City Education Offices. In sharp contrast to the stone classical palaces of the mercantile and shipping companies, from the 1880s exuberant High Victorian Gothic and Romanesque buildings in blood-red brick and terracotta were introduced, most notably by Alfred Waterhouse, for insurance offices in the city centre, but also at the Royal Infirmary, and the Victoria Building at University College.

In the early 20th century three huge buildings were erected on the waterfront which were to become internationally recognised icons of the city, completed ironically just as its prosperity was beginning to wane. Known as the 'Three Graces', the first, begun in 1903 and designed by Sir Arnold Thornely and F B Hobbs, was for the Mersey Docks and Harbour Board. The second, the Royal Liver Building, raised between 1908 and 1911, was a gigantic concrete-framed office block designed by Walter Aubrey Thomas on an American scale. Climbing 320 feet over the river, it was the tallest building in Europe at the time. In 1916 the trio

Left: The offices of the White Star Line, Liverpool, 1898.
Opposite: Although Bristol lost out to Liverpool in the race to dominate trans-Atlantic trade, the city continued to expand.

was completed by the Cunard Building in a restrained classical style by Willink and Thicknesse, artfully inserted between the two leviathans on either side.

At virtually the same time, a competition was held for a new Anglican cathedral on high ground overlooking the city on what was the site of the old St James's cemetery. The winner was the young Giles Gilbert Scott. The foundation stone was laid in 1904. Five years later Scott revised the design completely, before work was curtailed by the First World War, and then bomb damage in the Second World War. This last great work of the Gothic Revival was only completed in 1979.

Unlike upstart Liverpool, Bristol had been a city as early as 1542. A booming trade in wool, fish and grain across the Irish Sea, and further afield to Spain, Portugal and Iceland, had laid firm foundations for its future growth. Its narrow streets, filled with overhanging mediaeval timber-framed houses, were complemented in the 18th century by elegant stone terraces built outside the city walls on the old town marsh. These were occupied by prosperous businessmen and merchants, many of whom thrived on the profits of the slave trade. Queen Square, completed in 1727, was quite the equal of the urbane squares of London.

Everything stood in favour of Bristol becoming the prime port for trans-Atlantic trade. In 1841 Isambard Kingdom Brunel's Great Western Railway arrived at Temple Meads opening up a fast route to London, but the city's geography remained a constant constraint. Even after a floating harbour was completed in 1809, the long passage up the Avon Gorge discouraged trade, and war with France disrupted its maritime commerce; problems which Liverpool exploited to its own advantage.

Spanning the gorge was a major challenge too. The Clifton Suspension Bridge, one of the iconic buildings of the Victorian age, took almost 30 years to come to fruition. Designed by Brunel, construction began in 1836 only to be interrupted seven years later when it ran out of money. It was not finished until five years after Brunel's death in 1864.

Brunel played a key role in the expansion of shipbuilding. A new generation of mighty steamships was built in the city, in particular, his two titans – the *Great Western* in 1837 – followed in 1844 by the *Great Britain*. Designed for the Bristol-New York service, it was the longest passenger ship in the world.

However, in spite of all its advantages and innovations, after a period of rapid growth, by the 1840s the city's economy began to stagnate in the face of competition from Liverpool and other emerging industrial towns. By the mid century, after a radical, if protracted, reconstruction of the port, it started to recover and grow steadily with a diversified economy based on small family firms. These engaged in a wide range of production including sugar, shipping, iron-foundries, soap making, leather works, glass and ceramics.

In August 1869, the *Bristol Times and Mirror* noted 'our ancient and well-beloved city is getting on in the world; and…in spite of business depression and various discouragements which beset commercial affairs at present, we are in a state of vigorous life and progressive advancement… we cannot, perhaps, expect to compete with Liverpool, with its enormous manufacturing background of Lancashire and Cheshire. Onward movement is the order of the day, and our good city is resolved not to be a laggard in the competitive race'. [11]

Although Bristol lost out to arriviste Liverpool in the race to dominate trans-Atlantic trade, with the development of newer industries such as printing, paper, tobacco, chocolate and foodstuffs, the city continued to expand, however, at nothing like the rate of the great manufacturing towns of the Midlands and north. The same newspaper noted in 1870 'a steady forward, not flashy, spirit of enterprise growing up amongst us. While the old firms are more than holding their own, new ones are settling in the city and a healthy and competitive activity is producing results of which we have substantial proof in the new and splendid houses and villas that girdle our town'. [12]

That proof was only too evident in the elegant new detached and semi-detached villas, which were springing up in Italianate style. The Guildhall of 1843–46 and Charles Cockerell's Bank of England branch office were notable early public buildings, but with the recovery of the local economy from the 1860s, civic enhancement gathered momentum.

Colston Hall completed in 1873, provided the city with a major concert and meeting hall, but the most distinctive contribution was a sequence of commercial and industrial buildings designed in what has come to be known as 'Bristol Byzantine', a generic term embracing a variety of richly detailed Italian Gothic styles. These conferred a very strong local identity, and consciously evoked the symbolism and mercantile prowess of the city states of the Italian Renaissance.

By 1901 Bristol had swelled to 330,000 people from just 68,800 a century earlier. Its steady growth continued into the 20th century with the opening of the Royal Edward Dock in 1908 and the foundation of its university a year later. With its reputation for embracing innovation and new technology, Bristol was a pioneer of the aviation industry. Boosted by the demands of the First World War, it soon became the city's largest industry. The original British and Colonial Aeroplane Company expanded from its early home in two converted tram sheds at Filton into one of Britain's most important aircraft companies designing and making engines and airframes for both military and civilian uses.

If Manchester was the 'shock city' of the Victorian age, then Birmingham can rightly be regarded as the cradle of the Industrial Revolution. It was here in the late 18th century that Matthew Boulton and James Watt developed the industrial steam engine. The city became a centre of innovation in science, technology, philosophy and medicine. In a series of bold innovations Boulton and Watt established how steam power could be used efficiently to generate the rotary motion necessary to drive manufacturing machinery.

As early as the 16th century Birmingham had a flourishing trade in leather tanning and textiles, but gradually it became known for its iron goods capitalising on its close connections with the Black Country. From the 1760s the town rapidly became the centre of an intricate network of canals. By 1830 their aqueous tentacles had spread across 130 miles linking Birmingham with the Black Country serving a maze of wharves and basins which facilitated the transport of manufactured goods to the rest of the country and beyond. It was the city's proud boast that it had more miles of canals than Venice.

By the early 19th century, manufacturing was well-established, but dispersed in small workshops and foundries. These produced an ever more dazzling array of products – guns, knives, locks, buttons, buckles, brassware, nails, jewellery, snuff boxes, toys and metal goods of all kinds. Birmingham was renowned as 'the city of a thousand trades.'

Its earlier transport links were reinforced by the railways. In 1837 the Grand Junction Railway linked the city with Manchester and Liverpool. A year later it was connected to London, and with the opening of Birmingham New Street station in 1854, it became a central node of the British railway system.

By the 1860s the city was a hive of business activity as both traditional specialised industries and larger factories began to reap greater economies of scale. Some older industries were clearly in decline. Over 600 million gilt buttons were still being produced each year, but as fashions changed, the industry employed just a third of the number which it had 30 years earlier. Other newer trades, like umbrella manufacture, cycles and electroplating sprang up in their place facilitated by a stable banking and insurance system out of which grew Lloyd's (from Taylor and Lloyd's founded in 1765), the Midland Bank (from the Birmingham and Midland 1836), and the Municipal Savings Bank, later the Trustee Savings Bank, founded by Neville Chamberlain.

Industries tended to aggregate in specific neighbourhoods. Using local supplies of hard water, the 'Vinegar Quarter' grew up around Aston Cross concentrating on brewing and comestibles – such as vinegar, sauce making and Bird's custard. By 1860 the famous 'Jewellery Quarter' employed over 20,000 people in specialist gold and silver trades working out of small, domestic premises and workshops.

In the 'Gun Quarter' this clustering of trades was even more pronounced as individual components – literally locks, stocks and barrels – were produced by separate specialists and then brought together to be assembled. With the formation of Birmingham Small Arms (BSA) in 1861, the craft assembly process in small domestic workshops was complemented by mechanisation in larger, purpose-built factories. BSA soon diversified to produce cycles and later motor bikes. Nonetheless small craft workshops, often family run, remained a distinctive feature of the city's economy encouraging much lower levels of unionised activity than in other great industrial cities.

Some of the city's larger manufacturers concentrated in new purpose-built factories in Smethwick. The huge new Cornwall Works set up in 1855 by the Tangye brothers produced hydraulic machinery. Chance brothers, which specialised in sheet glass and optics, supplied over 1 million square feet of glass for the Crystal Palace. Chamberlain and Nettlefold was the

Below: Birmingham Small Arms Company, 1917. Birmingham was dubbed 'the workshop of the world'.

Above: The Great Hall of the Victoria Law Courts, Birmingham, 1891. The chandeliers were the first outside London to be lit by electricity.

country's largest producer of screws alongside the Patent Nut and Bolt Company, both of which mutated into GKN by 1902.

Birmingham really did seem like the workshop of the world, manufacturing an astonishing array of goods for a global market. Joseph Gillott dominated the world's demand for steel pen nibs. Its largely female workforce produced over 14 million per week. Nearby, Elkington's pioneered silver and bronze electro-plating for a huge range of products from cutlery to public statues. Webster and Horsfall developed from a specialised maker of piano wire into the innovative producer of everything from umbrella frames and needles to the colossal undersea transatlantic telegraph cable, which used 30,000 miles of finely honed, durable wire.

With the development of electric power, new industries sprang up. These perpetuated the city's reputation for dynamism and innovation. Joseph Lucas specialised in lamps for the cycle and car industries. Kynoch's (later ICI Metals) progressed from percussion caps to brass castings, paper, soap, railway signals, gas engines and steel and copper tubing. In 1919 it introduced the zip fastener to Europe.

In the first two decades of the 20th century, manufacturers seized the opportunities offered by the new automobile industry. The first Austin car rolled off the production line at Longbridge in 1906. Four years later it employed over a thousand workers. The Dunlop Rubber Company established its enormous works at Fort Dunlop in 1916 supplying rubber tyres and hoses to the fledgling car industry. Designed by Sidney Stott and W W Gibbings, it remains a famous Birmingham landmark to this day, albeit converted to new uses.

The wealth this generated was invested in a host of municipal improvements and public buildings, which expressed local civic pride. In 1838 the town gained its Borough charter. A huge new Greek Revival Market Hall with a capacious iron roof was raised between 1831 and 1835 designed by Charles Edge, but by far the grandest was the Town Hall, a magnificent Roman-style temple based on the design of the Temple of Castor and Pollux in Rome designed by two, young and relatively unknown architects, Joseph Hansom and Edward Welch. Intended as a venue for the Birmingham Music Festival, it was one of the first great town halls of the period. Faced in Anglesey marble over a brick core, it was begun in 1832, and opened two years later, but was not fully completed until 1849, by which time Hansom, the designer of the Hansom cab, had gone bankrupt. Elsewhere, the famous King Edward's School, founded in 1552, was rebuilt by Charles Barry in Tudor Gothic style between 1833 and 1837. Pugin's St Chad's Cathedral followed two years later creating a new city landmark.

By the 1860s the centre of the city was being transformed by the great citadels of banking, commerce and insurance. Splendid new buildings arose, usually in fashionable Italian classical styles, such as H R Yeoville Thomason's Union Club in Colmore Row, and Chatwin's 1864 palazzo for the Birmingham Joint Stock Bank in Temple Row West, but although many fine groups of buildings were commissioned privately, it was the city fathers who wrought the greatest changes.

One of the great drivers of Birmingham's civic renaissance, and its transformation into England's second city, was the development of 'the Civic Gospel'. This was an evangelical movement for positive municipal action first articulated by George Dawson, a visionary preacher in a city with a strong non-conformist tradition. He argued that 'a town is a solemn organism through which should flow, and in which should be shaped, all the highest, loftiest and truest of man's intellectual and moral nature'. [13] His colleague H W Crosskey extolled 'the glories of Florence and of the other cities of Italy in the Middle Ages,' that 'suggest that Birmingham, too, might become the home of a noble literature and art'. [14]

This moral crusade was soon taken up and echoed by others, most notably Joseph Chamberlain, the dynamic Lord Mayor. In just three years between 1873 and 1876 he transformed what had been a sclerotic municipal borough into a model of enlightened local government underpinned by Christian principles. Old fashioned laissez-faire attitudes were swept aside on a wave of civic improvements.

Under Chamberlain's Improvement Scheme of 1875, local water and gas companies were taken over and run by the Corporation. Some of the poorest slums were eradicated. Corporation Street, cut in 1878, designed to demolish a whole area of slum housing, was conceived as a broad Parisian-style boulevard lined with an eclectic mix of commercial buildings. John Bright Street followed from 1882.

A splendid new Council House was erected to form a civic centre close to the Town Hall. After much wrangling over the design, it was completed in 1874, a handsome classical range by the architect H R Yeoville Thomason, symbolically crowned by a pediment containing a figure of Britannia receiving the manufactures of Birmingham. Almost immediately, it was extended between 1881 and 1885 to form a new Art Gallery and Museum and offices for the newly municipalised Gas Corporation.

In 1880 the Chamberlain Memorial was raised – an elegant Gothic spire enriched with fountains and mosaics to pay tribute to the achievements of Joseph Chamberlain as Councillor and Mayor. His achievements were legion, and characteristically, he was not backward in announcing them.

In 1892 he wrote 'During a little over half a century the town has been transformed and ennobled. Formerly it was badly lighted, imperfectly guarded and only partially drained; there were few public buildings and few important streets…But now, great public edifices; not unworthy of a midland metropolis have risen in every side. Wide arteries of communication have opened up. Rookeries and squalid courts have given way to fine streets and open places. The roads are well paved, well kept, well lighted and well-cleansed.' [15]

Elsewhere across the city plush new civic buildings arose, including over 30 Board Schools built between 1871–83. Many new buildings were clad in modish red brick or plum red terracotta, like the splendid School of Art designed by Martin and Chamberlain in 1885. Perhaps grandest of all, were the High Victorian Gothic Victoria Law Courts by Sir Aston Webb and Ingress Bell, opened with a great civic fanfare by the Prince and Princess of Wales on 21 July 1891.

Alongside the new civic and commercial buildings, Birmingham became celebrated for its elegant shopping arcades, and vibrant music halls, which animated its once dour city centre with swanky new entertainment venues. With its strong non-conformist and temperance tradition, Birmingham led the movement for public-house reform. Riotous street corner pubs in the city centre, which were often havens of drunkenness and petty crime, were displaced by genteel Arts and Crafts buildings strategically placed at suburban road junctions, which conjured up their own particular vision of a Lost England – Brewers Tudor.

As a result of the municipal and moral activism promoted by the Civic Gospel, by the early 1880s Birmingham was widely regarded as being 'the best governed city in the world.' What made it so effective was the readiness with which the great landowners and captains of industry were prepared to fund public amenities, such as the Art Gallery, and open spaces, like Adderley Park in 1856.

As the photographs bear witness, by the early 20th century Birmingham was a city of great beauty with a magnificent heritage of opulent Victorian buildings. Unfortunately, the extensive damage it suffered during the Second World War was compounded by idealistic post-war planning, systematic comprehensive redevelopment of the city centre and a new Inner Ring Road, which acted as a concrete ligature around the once vibrant heart of the city. The City Engineer and Surveyor, Herbert Manzoni, airily dismissed any objections commenting in 1957 that there was 'little of real worth in our architecture'. The result was the catastrophic evisceration of one of England's finest Victorian cities. Neither he nor his modernist associates had learned anything either from the civic gospel, or the more enlightened attitudes of his predecessors about the building of sustainable communities.

Some of these earlier pioneers took direct responsibility for the social well-being of their workers. At Hays Mills Joseph Horsfall endowed a church for the community and built a school for the children of his workforce.

The Cadbury family had been established in Birmingham since the 1820s. Devout Devon Quakers, and leaders of the Temperance movement, they took their social responsibility as employers seriously. In June 1878 the firm acquired a new site for a factory between Stirchley and Selly Oak perfectly placed beside the Worcester and Birmingham Canal for supplies of milk, and the Midland railway for bulk cocoa.

Fifteen years later the company purchased an adjacent site of 120 acres to build a model community for its employees to alleviate the 'evils which arise from the insanitary and insufficient accommodation supplied to large numbers of the working classes, and of securing to the workers in factories some of the advantages of outdoor village life'. [16] George Cadbury was a devout Quaker who believed in 'feeding the hungry, giving drink to the thirsty and taking in the stranger'. Determined to address the twin evils of poor housing and drink, Cadbury became a developer inspired by the ideal of a model community.

Much influenced by the social and aesthetic ideals of William Morris, the Arts and Crafts and Garden City movements, Bournville and other similar model communities were an attempt to reconcile the industrial future with a romantic image of a Lost England. In truth, this had never existed, but the idealistic dream exerted a powerful sway over many who felt alienated by the relentless march of urbanisation.

It was essentially a rural vision and a radical departure from the grid plan which characterised so many of the large conurbations. There were no pubs, but culs-de sac, closes, winding lanes, grass verges and generous open spaces all disposed around an estate layout of 1894 planned by the Quaker surveyor, Alfred Pickard Walker. Horticulture was seen as the ideal antidote to slum-dwelling drunkenness. The houses, designed by William Alexander Harvey, were grouped into short terraces set in generous gardens with a natural focus around the shopping centre. There were primary schools, a College of Arts and Crafts, a parish church and a Friends' Meeting House.

Below: Mock Tudor homes in Port Sunlight model village, which was built by Lever Brothers to house the workers in their soap factory.

Bournville showed how enlightened patronage coupled with sensitive planning and polite, reticent architecture could create highly desirable communities. It was a huge success. In 1904 the local death rate was 6.9 per thousand compared with 19 per thousand in the city. It became a compelling model for the subsequent development of Garden Cities and Suburbs across the country.

Steam may have been the driving force of the new industrial age, but it relied on the marriage of coal and iron ore to create the industrial infrastructure that propelled Britain into the world's greatest power. Nowhere was this more evident, or more devastating for the environment, than in the Black Country of the West Midlands, which became the manufacturing heartland of the economy. Here the combination of a huge coal seam, and large deposits of ironstone, fireclay and limestone provided ready-made resources for the iron industry. The earlier development of the canal network, the introduction of steam power, and the growth of the rail network provided a highly-efficient transport system, which enabled the Black Country to become the epicentre of the greatest iron-producing district in Britain, and one of the largest in the world.

Many were appalled by the environmental degradation. At a time when much of rural England resembled a pastoral idyll unsullied by industry and mass manufacturing, the Black Country offered an apocalyptic vision of hell. The landscape boiled under a cloud of belching smoke and fire from myriad furnaces punctuated by vast heaps of discarded slag from the coking process required to feed their unquenchable appetites. This, rather than Lancashire, was the England of William Blake's dark, satanic mills.

James Nasmyth wrote of the nightmare scene in 1883: 'The earth seems to have been torn inside out. Its entrails are strewn about; nearly the entire surface of the ground is covered with cinder-heaps and mounds of scoria. The coal, which has been drawn from below ground, is blazing on the surface. The district is crowded with iron furnaces, puddling furnaces and coal-pit engine furnaces. By day and by night the country is glowing with fire…The grass parched and killed by the vapours of sulphureous acid thrown out by the chimneys; and every herbaceous object was of a ghastly grey – the emblem of vegetable death. Vulcan had driven out Ceres.'

Wandering through the works and foundries he watched in a mixture of awe and horror as he saw the 'white-hot iron run out of the furnaces … spun…into bars and iron ribbands' and heard the sounds of 'the ponderous hammers and clanking rolling mills' while the workmen seemed 'to run about amidst the flames as in a pandemonium…' [17]

The whole process was astonishingly wasteful. Ninety per cent of the heat from the iron furnaces was lost. Until the 1880s and the introduction of coke ovens, raw coal was reduced to coke by burning on the surface, which accounted for the nightmare images of blazing fires noted by so many who visited the region. It was also laborious. While cast iron could be produced direct from the blast furnace, most of the output was pig iron, which needed to be re-melted in puddling furnaces and then forged under the hammer for conversion into the wrought iron required for the pistons, paddle-shafts, boilers, rails and bridges of the industrial economy. 'None of this would have been possible if it had not been for the titanic labours of those fierce, white-eyed men whom Nasmyth saw leaping about like fiends amid the flames of their furnaces.' [18]

Situated half way between Birmingham and Manchester, North Staffordshire had been the home of English pottery manufacture since the 17th century. The local abundance of coal and clay supported a flourishing local business in earthenware production. By 1800 there were over 300 pot works scattered across the area. With the construction of the Trent and Mersey Canal in 1777, china clay was imported direct from Cornwall, which prompted a massive expansion of the manufacture of bone china and cream ware. Through a combination of meticulous research and innovative design, family firms, such as Royal Doulton, Spode, Wedgwood and Minton, became world-famous brands producing everything from fine china for the royal houses of Europe to floor tiles for the far-flung offices of Empire.

By the 1870s there were over 4,000 bottle kilns disgorging a permanent haze of smoke and toxic fumes. This blocked out the sun from the six dispersed towns of the region, and caused a fearfully high death rate from respiratory diseases and lead poisoning. The blighted industrial landscape they created was quite the equal of the nearby Black Country or the West Midlands, fuelling nascent environmental concerns.

By 1900 the Potteries had become the centre of the world's production of ceramics. Over 500 pot works were in operation each employing between 100 and 400 workers. Eventually, in 1910, the fiercely competitive polycentric towns of the Potteries – Hanley, Burslem, Longton, Fenton and Tunstall set aside their rivalry and joined with Stoke to form the County Borough of Stoke-on-Trent with a combined population of over 240,000.

South Yorkshire had been a centre of the domestic cloth-making industry since the Middle Ages. Its economy too was transformed by the Industrial Revolution, in particular, the opening of the Leeds–Liverpool Canal in 1777, and the establishment of a vibrant new engineering industry in Hunslet and Holbeck, which produced machine tools, steam engines and structural iron work. Within ten years, large new cloth mills, like those at Armley, rebuilt in 1788, were replacing domestic-based weaving and spinning.

In 1806 John Marshall opened a new flax spinning mill in Leeds using an innovative fireproof construction of cast-iron columns, beams and brick vaults, which he had pioneered ten years earlier at Ditherington Flax Mill, Shrewsbury, the oldest iron-framed building in the world. It was a huge success. Between 1838 and 1843 he built a vast new single storey mill using a similar structural system with glass domes at Temple Mills – all executed in full-blown Egyptian style by the architect Joseph Bonomi.

With a flourishing flax trade and an innovative engineering industry, Leeds grew from a medium-sized town of 53,000 in 1801 into the fourth largest city in England bursting with almost 430,000 people a century later. The introduction of an elected town council ushered in a period of progressive civic government. It commissioned a whole series of grand new public buildings to assert Leeds' claim to be the 'Capital of the North' in the face of its intense rivalry with Bradford.

The Town Hall, designed by Cuthbert Brodrick in an exuberant French neo-classical style, was built between 1852–58. It was one of the finest of all Victorian town halls. Its tall crowning clock tower, grand Corinthian order and imposing central hall were a powerful declaration of civic ambition. Other fine edifices followed including the Corn Exchange of 1860, also by Brodrick, and the reconstruction of Leeds General Infirmary by George Gilbert Scott between 1863 and 1868 in High Victorian Gothic style using richly-textured polychrome brick, a material which was utilised on many city churches of the period.

Perhaps most emblematic of the city's vibrant commercial life was the great concentration of grand cloth warehouses which surrounded the original Cloth Hall, (now sadly demolished). These incorporated storage, offices, showrooms and often manufacturing in a single building. Designed in a riotous mixture of styles, the most exotic was the spectacular Hispano-Moorish factory and warehouse designed by Thomas Ambler in 1878 for John Barran, a local magnate, who made his fortune through mechanising the cutting of cloth for the clothing trade.

T R Harding's Tower Works at Holbeck was built to make steel pins for the carding and combing processes used in the textile industry. It made its own very distinctive contribution to the city skyline with three spectacular chimneys. The original, completed in 1866, was modelled on Giotto's campanile in Florence; the tallest and most ornate, added in 1899, was inspired by the Torre dei Lamberti in Verona, and the third, completed in 1919, echoed the towers of the Tuscan houses of San Gimignano.

As the city evolved into the regional centre for banking and insurance, magnificent groups of Italianate, classical and Victorian Gothic buildings arose, including a provincial branch of the Bank of England. Its moonlit, rain-soaked streets of grand commercial buildings and warehouses were immortalised by the Leeds artist John Atkinson Grimshaw in a series of evocative paintings, which bear witness to the unlikely romantic grandeur of the city centre.

One of the most striking characteristics of the city was the development of numerous shopping arcades along Briggate where the narrow mediaeval burgage plots lent themselves to the creation of covered, top-lit spaces lined with shops. The grandest – the County and Cross Arcades – were carved out of the old shambles between 1898 and 1904. They were enriched with lustrous faience and mosaics using Burmantofts terracotta made locally by the Leeds Fireclay Company. By the late 19th century terracotta and faience in a variety of fiery yellow, pink, red and orange hues were employed widely across the city, notably on Alfred Waterhouse's Prudential Assurance building, and the Yorkshire Penny Bank, both completed in 1894.

Like its great rival Leeds, Bradford was a mediaeval wool town, but in the 19th century it exploded into the world centre of the worsted textile industry – 'Worstedopolis'. Helped by the construction of the Bradford Canal in 1774, Bradford was a thriving industrial centre with a booming iron industry utilising local iron ore deposits to make heavy armaments, locomotive parts and ornamental iron work to adorn the street and houses of the region. The tangle of mediaeval streets in the city centre was soon surrounded to the west by concentrations of wool warehouses, and to the east by those for yarn and finished products ready for shipment by rail.

By the 1850s rapid industrialisation and uncontrolled factory building had created such a degree of urban squalor that measures were taken by the Street Improvement Committee to reconstruct the city centre to match its rivals. Almost all of the work was executed by just one local architectural practice – Lockwood and Martin.

Bradford's population mushroomed from just 13,000 in 1801 to 104,000 by 1851 before soaring to 280,000 fifty years later. It engulfed smaller surrounding townships like Manningham and Horton, and achieved city status in 1897.

One of its largest mills, the Lister Mills, was built at Manningham in 1871 for the industrialist and inventor, Samuel Cunliffe-Lister, later Baron Masham. This converted silk waste into luxurious velvets, carpets and imitation sealskin. The huge Italianate complex designed by Andrews and Pepper employed over 5,000 people. Dominating the skyline, it comprised two massive blocks with an ornamental chimney designed as a campanile rocketing skywards at one end.

A unique feature of the Bradford worsted trade was the role played by a small, but influential group of enterprising German merchants, who created an enclave of handsome mid 19th-century warehouses in Little Germany, many of which were built by Lockwood and Martin. It was German Jews active in the cloth trade, who financed St George's Hall (1851–53), the grand new concert and meeting hall as one of the first projects for the rebuilding of the core of the inner city. This was followed seven years later by the Wool Exchange, and then in 1873, the great tour de force – the magnificent High Victorian Gothic Town Hall with its facade enriched by statues of each of the rulers of England, and a spectacular clock tower inspired by the Palazzo Vecchio in Florence, towering 220ft over the town.

While Leeds and Bradford dominated the cloth trade, Halifax also boasted a long history of textile making. Its Piece Hall, an elegant arcaded quadrangle of honey-coloured freestone, was designed in 1779 for the sale of produce by local woollen handloom weavers, but in the 19th century the town became the home of one of the world's largest carpet manufacturers. At the colossal Dean Clough Mills in the Hebble valley between 1841and 1870 John Crossley and Sons erected a phalanx of mills extending over 1,250,000 sq ft with their own railway sidings connected to the main line for the export of carpets all over Britain and the world.

Sheffield had a long-established reputation as a specialist centre for cutlery, knives and high quality metalwork, but by the 17th century it was notorious for the appalling pollution emanating from the furnaces and coal fires used for smelting. The problem was only exacerbated by steam power and the smoke which belched from thousands of industrial chimneys, and which coated the city with sulphurous pollution. Following a boom during and after the Napoleonic Wars, by the mid 19th century larger firms began to move in alongside older traditional trades, like cutlery making.

Spear and Jackson established their Aetna Works in 1837, Cammell's followed in 1845, and then John Brown, which in 1858 introduced the Bessemer steel making process. The factory buildings usually followed a similar pattern – a three-storey street frontage containing the offices with the furnaces, forges and workshops around a central rear courtyard.

Industrial giants, like John Brown and Cammells, were soon operating the newer Siemens open-hearth process to produce bulk steel for heavy engineering and armour plating for the Navy, while Vickers concentrated on producing guns and armaments. Smaller light trades continued to mass produce cutlery, but increasingly they concentrated on special steels, alloys for machine tools, silverware and surgical instruments. Shortly after Sheffield became a city in 1893, its population reached half a million from just 46,000 a century before.

The town was slow in developing a commercial and civic centre, but the Council began an ambitious programme of civic improvements in 1875 culminating in a splendid new Town Hall by E W Mountford. This provided a landmark around which the centre was reconstructed. Streets were widened and new thoroughfares built to create a linear commercial area at the heart of the town with frontages of grand new buildings for the banks, offices and institutions, so characteristic of England's northern manufacturing towns.

By the 1890s terracotta, faience and glazed brick was in common use in an effort to resist the dreadful atmospheric pollution, which caused such a high local death rate and turned the buildings black. Royal Exchange Buildings, The White Building in Fitzalan Square and other Sheffield landmarks boasted fine glazed brick or faience facades often embellished with nacreous polychrome interiors. However, by the early 20th century, other than their front offices, the vast industrial buildings erected along the Don valley had degenerated into little more than utilitarian sheds. In common with other manufacturing towns of the Midlands and the North, the wealthy moved westward out of the city away from the pollution to genteel houses and villas at Nether Edge, or the Broomhall estate.

In the north-east, at the centre of perhaps the oldest industrial region in the country, Newcastle was an ancient Roman settlement and port established beside a convenient bridging point over the steep valley of the River Tyne. By the 18th century it had become a centre of the printing industry, as well as the world's leading producer of glass using sand from ballast taken from boats in the Tyne. Surrounded by huge coal fields, which provided a limitless source of fuel for the domestic and industrial needs of London and the towns of the east coast, Newcastle was one of the powerhouses of the Industrial Revolution.

Above: Cammell Laird and Company, 1913. Two men operate the armour plate-rolling machine.
Opposite: Leeds General Infirmary, Great George Street, 1895.

In the 1820s George and Robert Stephenson established the world's first locomotive works in the city building engines for the burgeoning railway industry, including the famous Rocket. A local pottery industry, Maling, established by French Huguenots, relocated from Sunderland in 1817 and soon expanded into an enormous factory complex. Using mechanized mass production rather than hand-made techniques, it became one of the world's biggest producers of pottery.

The export of coal fostered the growth of the shipbuilding industry. By 1800 Newcastle had developed from producing colliers and wooden coastal vessels into one of the largest shipbuilding regions in the country. This nurtured the development of other forms of heavy engineering. The invention of the steam turbine by Charles Parsons revolutionized ship propulsion and provided a whole new momentum to the industry.

Some of the most advanced warships and passenger vessels of their day were built on Tyneside. In 1847 at Elswick, just west of the city, William Armstrong established a huge new armaments factory, a military-industrial complex producing massive hydraulic cranes and heavy guns for the army and navy. It was here that the formidable dreadnoughts of the Royal Navy had their guns fitted before being commissioned into the Fleet to patrol the oceans of the world.

Newcastle combined a strong sense of tradition with all the ambition and swashbuckling self-confidence of the Victorian age. Much of the centre of the town had been transformed early in the century with dignity and grace. Between 1831 and 1841 the builder–developer Richard Grainger and the architect John Dobson created a unified composition of elegant stone-faced classical buildings, which rivalled the best creations of Bath, Edinburgh and Nash's Regent Street. Gladstone considered the gently curving Grey Street to be 'the finest street in England'.

The terraces of Grainger Town were soon complemented by Dobson's impressive railway station; a paean of praise to the new age of progress with the railway boldly carried into the city across Robert Stephenson's High-Level Bridge. In 1854 a huge fire on the Gateshead side jumped the river and swept through the warren of old riverfront alleys and timber-framed buildings clustered close to the river, which were soon replaced by groups of handsome new commercial and office buildings.

Newcastle continued to grow – from 100,000 people in 1851 to over 210,000 fifty years later. By then its earlier ebullience had begun to subside, although shipbuilding continued to flourish. Britain remained pre-eminent producing over 60 per cent of the world's total tonnage, much of it on Tyneside and the Clyde.

In contrast, Nottingham, which like Newcastle was an older industrial town, was hamstrung by the lack of an effective Enclosure Act. It was fortunate to have its own high-pressure mains water system installed as early as 1831 by the engineer Thomas Hawksley. This reduced the risk of cholera, but the overcrowded streets and courts of the town centre were deemed to be more appalling than anything to be found in any of the slums of the northern manufacturing towns.

With the eventual passing of an Enclosure Act in 1845, Nottingham was transformed virtually overnight as factories, warehouses and offices sprang up on a surge of redevelopment. Unfortunately, unlike Dobson's plan for Newcastle, there was little co-ordination or overall plan, driving a local newspaper editor to lament 'a man may ask what sort of exhibition this New Nottingham will make when its irregular streets are fully occupied by their equally irregular edifices'.[19]

The town had an illustrious history of hosiery and stocking manufacture and, in particular, lace-making, which became increasingly mechanized. By the early 19th century there were over 1,400 net manufacturers making lace. Initially this was from distinctive houses with long, horizontal attic windows to maximize the light, but later it operated on a global scale from a cluster of handsome seven and eight storey red-brick industrial buildings in the Lace Market, such as the Adams Building, designed by the prolific local architect T C Hine, which opened in 1855.

By 1900 many of the warehouses, banks and offices of the city centre had been rebuilt in red brick and terracotta in what became popularly known as 'Northern Renaissance' style echoing the mediaeval precedents of Flanders and the Low Countries. More eccentric and eclectic flourishes were offered by the local architect Fothergill Watson using a frenetic mixture of carved ornamental details, gables and pyramidal-capped dormers for a variety of clients, including the Temperance Albert Hall, offices for the Nottingham and Nottinghamshire bank, and the *Nottingham Daily Express*. An example of his distinctive eclectic style can be seen in the photographs of Newark.

However, Nottingham's prosperity was sustained not by its old industries, like hosiery and framework knitting, which were stagnating by the 1920s, but by new industries which had begun to concentrate there from the 1890s, including the chemical industry, light engineering firms like Raleigh bicycles, Player's tobacco, Viyella fabrics and pharmaceuticals in the form of Boots the Chemist.

By the 1880s the railways and new electric tram systems fuelled the growth of suburban settlements on the fringes of the main towns. London, Birmingham, Manchester and other great conurbations spilled over and engulfed surrounding residential and satellite towns. In the ten years between 1881 and 1891 the counties with the highest population growth were Middlesex with 51 per cent, Essex with 38 per cent, Glamorgan with 34 per cent, Surrey with 24 per cent, and Monmouthshire and Durham each with 17 per cent. Of the fastest growing towns, four out of the top six were around the London periphery. Leyton grew by 133 per cent, Willesden by 122 per cent, Tottenham by 95 per cent and West Ham by 59 per cent, the same level of growth as Rhondda in South Wales.

At the same time, some older towns such as Norwich, Coventry, Leicester, Derby and Northampton underwent a resurgence as new industries moved in to exploit surplus skilled labour displaced by declining crafts and agricultural unemployment. Northampton specialised in boots and shoes, Leicester in hosiery, Luton in hats, Peterborough in brick-making, and Batley and Dewsbury in 'shoddy,' the recycling and reworking of second-hand rags into blankets and uniforms.

One of the most distinctive features of the Victorian age was the process by which prevailing laissez-faire attitudes were slowly moderated and then replaced by concerted philanthropic and municipal intervention. Three years after the passage of the Great Reform Act in 1832, the Municipal Reform Act transferred power from a narrow oligarchy of remote vested interests to 175 municipal corporations governed by elected councils.

In 1848 the Health of Towns Act was the start of a process to force the new municipalities to improve sewerage, housing, hospitals and burial grounds. As the century wore on, further major administrative changes were made under the Local Government Acts of 1882, 1888 and 1894, together with a mass of national legislation covering paving, lighting, gas, water, railways, bridges, trams, canals, housing and public health.

Municipal intervention changed the face of Britain's towns and cities on a scale never seen before. In the process, it bequeathed a legacy of stunning public buildings which would enrich the lives of all their citizens. These were designed in a range of styles from classical, Gothic and Renaissance Free style to late 19th century eclecticism and Edwardian Baroque. Rivalry between Victorian towns and cities was intense. Municipal patriotism was expressed in lavish displays of local civic pride. Nowhere was this more evident than in the development of the town hall. It was the ultimate statement of municipal status and ambition. As each town vied to outdo its neighbours, competition created magnificent new focal points around which other public buildings coalesced.

The town halls and civic buildings of the early Victorian period, such as Birmingham Town Hall by Joseph Hansom and St George's Hall in Liverpool by H L Elmes were powerful statements of civic ambition dressed in the classical language of antiquity. Such lessons were not lost on other towns as they grew in wealth and status. Manchester turned to Charles Barry and neo-Renaissance classicism for its Royal Institution, completed in 1835, and for the Athenaeum of 1837. Edward Walters' cinquecento Free Trade Hall of 1853 was perhaps the ultimate expression of the style before the town turned to Gothic. Not to be outdone by its rivals, in 1853 Leeds commissioned its grand new town hall from Cuthbert Brodrick, the gifted young architect from Hull, who left his own indelible impression on the town.

By the 1860s the battle of the styles was at its height. Aspiring young Gothicists vied with the classical establishment for a slice of the action. Strongly influenced by Pugin and Ruskin, and their own interpretations of mediaeval precedents in Flanders, Italy and Germany, they produced stunning new focal points in the manufacturing towns of England.

At Northampton in 1860, Edward Godwin designed a richly modelled polychrome town hall with ornamental sculpture depicting the town's history and industry. Chester, Plymouth, Middlesbrough, Rochdale, Wakefield and Bradford all followed suit with magnificent Gothic town halls from some of the most gifted architects of their day.

Below: The Harris Art Gallery and Museum, Preston, c1920. Raised high on a podium, this powerful gallery and museum building was opened in 1880 and named after its benefactor, Edmund Robert Harris, a local lawyer whose bequest of £300,000 made its construction possible.

Driven by its desire to emulate Liverpool, Manchester adopted the Gothic style with a vengeance. Outside Waterhouse's great Gothic Town Hall, Thomas Worthington's huge canopied memorial to Prince Albert pre-dated the Albert Memorial in London. In London, Gothic reached its apogee for public buildings with the erection of George Edmund Street's monumental complex for the Law Courts in Fleet Street between 1874 and 1882.

As the century drew to a close, some of the more progressive architects explored a creative intermingling of styles for monumental public buildings. Pragmatic eclecticism replaced architectural dogma. In London, for instance, in 1881 Waterhouse's Natural History Museum in yellow and grey terracotta superimposed Romanesque elevations on to a fairly free Renaissance form. In Sheffield the new town hall of 1897 by E W Mountford successfully combined a soaring cupola-crowned clock tower with a medley of English, French and Flemish nuances.

Others reacted against the lack of discipline inherent in these diverse Free styles and opted for a bombastic version of Baroque revival, such as Colchester Town Hall, of 1898–1902, by John Belcher, and several of the new Town Halls for the London boroughs; Deptford (1900–03) by Lanchester and Rickards and Woolwich by Alfred Brumwell Thomas, completed in 1906, among the most conspicuous examples.

Exuding power, stability and civilising values, civic classicism in all its diverse forms, from neo-classical and Palladian to Edwardian Baroque and Beaux Arts, remained a popular style for monumental public buildings well into the mid 20th century, for instance, at Halifax by Charles Barry in 1863, at Bolton in 1873 and Portsmouth Guildhall in 1890, both by William Hill, at County Hall for the London County Council, which was built in phases from 1912 by Ralph Knott, and at Luton in 1934.

***

For all the explosive energy unleashed by the railways and the growth of the cities, large parts of the country appeared to remain untrammelled by the relentless pace of change. Many of the photographs in this book portray a vision of rural England as a timeless pastoral idyll; small farms set in a patchwork of fields punctuated by ancient timber-framed houses and church spires. But this is misleading. The truth was rather different. In the first half of the 19th century English agriculture went through a revolution, which transformed the face of England and propelled the Industrial Revolution.

Traditionally, village agriculture involved common grazing alongside an open field system with the strip cultivation of commonly owned arable land in a two or three course rotation. In the 18th century the work of enlightened landlords such as Thomas Coke of Norfolk, and the introduction of the Norfolk system of four-course rotation and high farming, greatly increased crop and livestock yields. The planting of different types of crops such as turnips, lucerne and clover restored plant nutrients and improved fertility.

Above: Farm workers near Hellidon, Northamptonshire, harvesting with a horse-drawn Hornsby Reaper in 1902. The Agricultural Revolution in Britain was a long process of gradual improvement.

The General Enclosure Acts of 1836, 1840 and 1845 accelerated the long-standing process of enclosing land and eliminated what remained of the old peasant proprietors by encouraging large-scale investment in land drainage and improved breeds of animals and plants. Fields were enclosed with hedgerows, which can be seen in some of these photographs. Far from being part of a timeless English landscape, most were new, transforming the face of the English countryside. Many villagers were left without common land or grazing rights. Fewer farmers and labourers were needed to work the land, which triggered massive resettlement as redundant labourers drifted to the towns, or the colonies, in search of work.

In the early 1840s a severe economic depression set in. The condition of the working classes was so bad that riots broke out. In this period, known as 'The Hungry Forties', the working classes organized politically into trade unions. The People's Charter of 1838 demanded universal suffrage, but in spite of all the agitation not one of the Chartists' demands was ever met.

By 1850 high farming methods had become widespread boosting productivity and helping to feed the rapidly growing urban population. Large farms of 200 acres or more were commonplace, particularly in the south-east. As a result, British agricultural output was one third higher than that of France, and twice that of Russia, which retained a system based on serfdom. Since 1815 the Corn Laws had protected British grain prices by imposing tariffs on imports of foreign grain, but in 1846 these were abolished in the interests of free trade. For the poor, food immediately became cheaper. Many farmers feared an immediate deluge of cheap foreign grain. Although it did not materialise for some time, they switched to animal husbandry.

Ironically, as the pictures in this book bear witness, long after steam power had been applied to industrial manufacture and transport, British farming still relied almost exclusively on the horse. Mechanisation was slow to arrive. The threshing machine, invented in 1787 by Andrew Meikle, a Scottish millwright, slowly spread throughout the corn-growing counties of England, but it faced fierce resistance, and even riots, from farm labourers whose livelihoods were threatened.

Gradually cast and wrought iron replaced wood and stone for ploughs and farm implements. In 1803 Robert Ransome had introduced an experimental ploughshare of chilled cast iron from his foundry in Ipswich, with a point that was able to withstand continuous abrasion. By the early 1840s British agricultural engineers were mass producing iron-framed ploughs, harrows, seed drills, chaff cutters and barn machinery, but traction still depended on horse power. From 1863 Pirie's plough boosted productivity by allowing one man with two or three horses to replace two men with four horses.

It was not until 1845 that Clayton and Shuttleworth of Lincoln produced portable steam engines for agricultural use on a commercial scale. By 1856 they had built over two thousand, but only the largest and most prosperous farmers could afford them. Later they produced a mobile, self-moving engine, but for most farmers living on the edge of profitability, the horse remained cheaper and more efficient. Over the next 20 years a whole host of small rural iron companies, mainly in the east of England, produced a range of mobile traction engines. Increasingly, travelling teams of threshers toured the country with steam engines hiring out their labour, which prompted the famous Red Flag Act of 1865 which restricted speeds to four miles an hour.

The first commercial, petrol-driven tractor was introduced in 1902. Six years later Saunderson's of Bedford introduced a lighter four-wheel design, but at the outbreak of the First World War there were still over one million horses working the land, more than there had been over 30 years earlier.

The Agricultural Revolution in Britain was a long process of gradual improvement. By the mid 19th century new farming methods, the selective breeding of cattle, mechanisation and improved husbandry all combined to support a population far in excess of earlier levels helping to sustain Britain's industrial supremacy. Although agriculture grew until 1860, it then went in to a period of sustained decline. One by one English produce was undercut by cheap overseas imports. The story of British agriculture from 1860–1910 is one of shrinkage and adjustment in the face of ruinous foreign competition.

With the abolition of the Corn Laws, and rapid improvements in international shipping, free trade exposed British farmers to the full rigours of foreign competition. The economic development of the wider world may have acted as a powerful stimulant for British industrial products and manufacturing, but for grain farmers it was a disaster. The introduction of the steamship devastated British agriculture. In the ten years from 1873–83 the cost of shipping grain from Chicago to Liverpool fell by a third. In the 20 years from 1864, imports of Australian wool doubled, and then doubled again, throwing sheep farming into disarray.

Between 1873 and 1896 the British economy entered the Great Depression. While manufacturing suffered badly, agricultural fortunes collapsed in the face of falling prices and the import of cheap grain. In the 30 years from 1870 permanent pasture increased by 4.6 million acres as once arable land was taken out of production and put under grass. By 1890 the total area under the plough had been cut by over a third in less than 20 years.

Unfortunately, those who switched from corn to cattle were hit yet again. As techniques of refrigeration improved, huge quantities of meat were imported from Australia, New Zealand, the USA and Argentina in fast new steamships undercutting home produce.

As agricultural wages fell, increasingly the countryside became depopulated. Between 1850 and 1880 the number of poor agricultural labourers fell by 20 per cent as they poured in to the new industrial towns in search of work. In 1841 almost a quarter of the population had been employed in agriculture or fisheries. By 1911 it was just 8 per cent.

As farmers fell into arrears with their rents, landlords' incomes fell, and capital for improvements in both farming practice and the buildings slumped. Rural poverty became widespread, worse in many cases than the slums of the great cities, on which so much attention has been focused.

Most tenant farmers and agricultural labourers lived in old cottages and farm buildings, which had changed little in the past two centuries with few, if any, modern facilities. Built in local materials like weatherboarding, stone and slate, wattle and daub or cob and thatch, these ancient vernacular buildings varied widely around the country. As the Great Depression and foreign competition delivered blow after blow, the very fabric of the countryside decayed. Buildings were neglected. Barns and farm workers' cottages crumbled, their poor condition only too evident in some of the photographs.

Ancient mills, which had ground corn for centuries fell out of use, and were either abandoned, demolished, or converted to new uses. With the collapse of the market in grain, the great mediaeval barns with their spectacular timber roofs, which had for so long been one of the glories of the English countryside, became redundant, or were allowed to fall into ruin by impecunious farmers, who often could not even afford to demolish them.

The agricultural sector embraced a wide range of produce not just grains, grasses and root crops, but meat, wool, dairy produce, fruit and vegetables. Not all farmers were affected equally badly. In many parts of the country they adjusted pragmatically by switching produce. Patterns of farming became much more flexible. Cash crops like potatoes, cabbages, peas and beans could be readily marketed in the nearest towns, while various legislative changes encouraged the spread of market gardening in the Thames Valley, East Anglia and the Fens.

The booming urban population fuelled demand for dairy products, fruit and vegetables. Many Scots took over farms in East Anglia and introduced their own economical ideas of dairy farming. The dairy industry thrived supplying milk by railway to the towns and cities. By 1900 one fifth of all farm output was dairy produce, of which milk was by far the greatest product.

The appearance of the countryside changed as large areas of land were given over to vegetable gardens to serve the insatiable demands of the towns and cities. The acreage of fruit orchards increased extensively in Worcestershire, Cambridgeshire and Essex close to newly established jam factories. In the Lea Valley and parts of Kent, glasshouses produced tomatoes, which for the first time ceased to be a rich man's food.

Scientific advances in veterinary surgery, soil science and pesticides began to translate into tangible improvements on the land. The increasing use of artificial fertilisers freed farmers from the tyranny of crop rotation. The pioneering Rothamsted Research Station had experimented with the use of organic and inorganic fertilisers to improve crop yields since 1843. By the 1890s the import of guano and phosphates from Chile and elsewhere improved yields for those arable farms still in production.

Petrol engines increasingly mechanised a whole range of mundane jobs from pumping water to lifting ricks, but even as late as the 1930s, oxen were still drawing ploughs alongside tractors in Oxfordshire, and hand flails were commonplace on the small farms of rural Essex.

By 1920 Britain had become an essentially urban nation. Uniquely among the major world economies, it relied on imports for over half of its food.

Many of the same trends applied to forestry. During the Napoleonic Wars English hardwood was seen as a crucial national resource for sustaining the wooden-walled navy. Landowners tended to replant accordingly, but with the use of coke rather than charcoal for iron smelting, and the advent of iron steamships, demand for timber declined.

By 1900 Britain was almost totally reliant on imports of softwoods and most hardwoods from Russia, Scandinavia and the Empire. In the First World War the government woke up to the strategic weakness of relying so heavily on imported supplies. A huge reforestation programme began. Upland areas of the country were swathed in vast, impenetrable conifer plantations planted in dense blocks. By displacing traditional native species, like oak, elm, ash and beech, they eradicated a great deal of the biodiversity of the land they cloaked; a long-term environmental issue, which is still being addressed today.

The way of life of coastal communities and fishing techniques had changed little over the centuries. For generations sea fishing had existed in many coastal areas as a seasonal activity often supplementing farming incomes. Seaweed and shellfish were harvested from the seashore.

Until 1850, while smoked or salted fish could be procured in inland areas, it tended to be too expensive for mass consumption. Away from the coast, fresh fish was virtually unknown. By the mid 19th century, like so many other aspects of English life, this was revolutionised by the railways,

Above: Newlyn, Cornwall, 1907. Special types of buildings gave fishing towns and villages a very distinctive character.

facilitated by the use of ice from domestic ice houses, but also in much greater quantities imported from Norway.

Suddenly regular supplies of fresh fish could be delivered across the country. Demand soared, and the nation's diet changed. Between 1860 and 1890 catches at Grimsby alone mushroomed from 450 tons to over 60,000 tons per year. More than twelve trains a day were needed just to distribute the town's catches across a huge arc of the country. By 1910 the average city-dwelling Englishman was eating 30 pounds of fish a year, and fish and chips had become a staple of the working man's diet.

The fishing industry soon concentrated into a number of ports, in particular Hull, Grimsby, Whitby, Lowestoft and Aberdeen on the North Sea, and Fleetwood on the Atlantic coast; each operating large, deep-sea fleets of steam-driven trawlers. Often developed in conjunction with the railway companies, new infrastructure, such as fish processing works, markets, ice factories and shipping and insurance offices soon surrounded the harbours. Lavish new public buildings, banks and shipping offices, which expressed local civic pride and celebrated the wealth generated from the sea, transformed the centres of Hull and Grimsby.

Special types of buildings gave fishing villages and towns a very distinctive character. Pilchard fishing in Mount's Bay, Cornwall was associated with double-storeyed stone buildings with living accommodation above fish-processing cellars. At Hastings, tall timber net-drying sheds were built on the foreshore, where they remain a distinctive historic feature of the town today, the oldest dating from the 16th century.

Gradually, smaller fishing ports such as Weymouth, St Ives, Lyme Regis, Mevagissey and Yarmouth, which operated fishing smacks and sailing boats from old harbours around the coastline, were marginalised as fishing became industrialised. By the early 20th century many turned to capitalising on their quaint way of life as seaside destinations for tourists.

***

Society in Victorian England was highly stratified by class and culture. At the top were the ancient families of the landed aristocracy. In 1871 over half the land in England was owned by just 7,400 people, and a quarter by just 1,200, mostly peers and titled families. The largest estates were in the north and west rather than the congested south-east.

As owners of the land on which the railways, canals, factories and towns were built, many great aristocrats had reinforced their landed wealth through shrewd investment in the Industrial Revolution, in particular, the Dukes of Sutherland in the Potteries, the Earls of Dudley and Dartmouth in the Black Country, the Calthorpes in Birmingham, and the Dukes of Devonshire in Barrow-in-Furness. Others used their landed wealth to recast their family seats into something more imposing and palatable to current tastes than their customary reticent Georgian boxes.

Highclere Castle, Hampshire, for instance, the setting for the popular television series Downton Abbey, was remodelled by Charles Barry into a neo-Elizabethan extravaganza between 1839 and 1842 for the Earl of Carnarvon. Between 1870 and 1883 the Duke of Westminster's seat at Eaton Hall in Cheshire was reworked by Alfred Waterhouse into a gigantic Gothic ducal palace complete with one of his characteristic clock towers alongside the private family chapel.

Ensconced in their ancient seats and country houses, older aristocratic families, like the Cecils, Lansdownes, Devonshires, Norfolks and Northumberlands, dominated the political system and continued to hold the levers of power and social influence well into the early 20th century. In the 1880s half of all MPs came from families with over 2,000 acres. One sixth had hereditary titles. The nobility held more than half the appointments in both the Liberal and Conservative cabinets, including occupying the post of Foreign Secretary continuously from 1868–1905.

In spite of the frenetic pace of urbanisation and industrialisation, large parts of Victorian England still remained inherently feudal infused with underlying notions of a natural and divine order of things. 'Providence has ordained the different orders and gradations into which the human family is divided, and it is right and necessary that it should be maintained', wrote the great Victorian architect George Gilbert Scott. 'Wealth must always bring its responsibilities, but a landed proprietor is especially in a responsible position. He is the natural head of his parish or district – in which he should be looked up to as the bond of union between the classes.' [20]

Widely dispersed across their landed estates, the aristocracy was a rural elite at the pinnacle of a complex social network with duties and responsibilities expressed in the ideal of noblesse oblige. Traditionally drawing their income from farming and the land, they developed a very personal, close-knit personal relationship with their tenant farmers and estate workers.

With its proximity to Court and the sophisticated salons of the rich and powerful, London dominated national life and the social scene throughout the century. Provincial society was considered restricted and gauche. The great aristocratic families only tended to come together in London during the Season, which coincided with the sitting of parliament and usually ran from February until late June. Many maintained a large London house specifically for the purpose. These were concentrated in Mayfair, like Devonshire House, Lansdowne House and Chesterfield House, or close to the Court in St James's, like Norfolk House, Bridgewater House and Lancaster House. When the houses were not in use they were rented out to the aspirant, non-landed super-rich, but by the 1920s they had become an expensive liability and most were sold off to avaricious developers.

Life for the fortunate 7,000 or so revolved around an endless series of balls and soirees, where the sons and daughters of the landed gentry could be introduced and hopefully matched up with the new wealth of the rising manufacturing and industrial classes. The Season culminated in Queen Charlotte's Ball where nervous young debutantes were presented at Court. For the hereditary nobility it was a chance to attract new blood, and a golden opportunity for wealthy, socially ambitious mothers eager to offer a hefty dowry in exchange for a title.

The political strength and social influence of the aristocracy were supported by county society. This was also rigidly hierarchical. It embraced the lesser gentry in their smaller mansions, who were strong in eastern England, the Welsh borders and the Cotswolds, and who enjoyed an income of between £1,000 – £10,000 per annum. The squirearchy owned between 1,000 and 3,000 acres, and most commonly lived in the south and south-east. Highly respected, both formed the backbone of rural English life with their own social calendar, the highlight of which was the Hunt Ball.

Beneath them were subtle gradations of precedence from Lord Lieutenant and master of the foxhounds to bishop, colonel of the yeomanry and MP, and then dean, archdeacon and justices of the peace. Scattered across England in their manor houses and village rectories, each resided in their own scaled-down models of the country house ideal.

Next in the social hierarchy came the City bankers and merchants, and the manufacturers and industrialists, who had made their fortunes in finance and insurance, and trades as diverse as textiles, property development, newspapers, pharmaceuticals and retailing. Riches were generated not just in London, but by business magnates right across the country, particularly in the large conurbations of the Midlands and North. Shipping fortunes were made in the north-west and north-east, while in Yorkshire and the south-west the captains of industry thrived. Industries at the heart of the Industrial Revolution were also great wealth makers – shipbuilding, iron and steel, cotton and foodstuffs. The Quaker Cadbury clan maintained enormous wealth and influence in Birmingham, as did Jeremiah Colman, the mustard baron, in East Anglia, the Pilkingtons in glass, and the Guinness and Wills families in brewing and tobacco.

Socially, the City of London was well-integrated into the upper echelons of society. Its bankers and merchants were closer to the landed elite than the industrial magnates of the north. Although the capital was the centre for banking with names like the Rothschilds, Barings and Sterns, other important trades flourished there too. Department store owners like William Whiteley, property developers like the Cubitts, Sir Blundell Maples of Maples Stores, and newspaper proprietors, such as Alfred Harmsworth, all made their fortunes in the capital. The great brewing families of Bass, Allsopp and Guinness were all elevated to the peerage, as was the Northumberland arms manufacturer, Sir William Armstrong.

Once the Victorian industrialist, or self-made man, had acquired a fortune, those who sought to aspire to the landed gentry looked for a suitable match and / or built their own country houses, which became such a hallmark of Victorian England. The 1860s and 70s were the high water mark for country house building before the slump in agriculture and foreign competition began to hit rents.

Between 1835 and 1889 over 500 houses, each with their own substantial estates, were remodelled or built anew for the wealthy nouveaux riches. The Arcadian landscape of England was enriched, and also occasionally blighted, by a whole range of large houses in a variety of fashionable styles of the day – initially Greek, Roman and Italianate, but later High Victorian Gothic, Elizabethan, Queen Anne revival and Arts and Crafts.

By the late 19th century French Renaissance had become popular too, a style often associated with nouveaux riches excess. Perhaps the most conspicuous, and incongruous, example being the vast Bowes Museum on its hilltop site outside Barnard Castle. Completed in 1896, and built by John Bowes of Streatlam Castle for his wife as a house, gallery and museum, it was modelled on the French hotel de ville in Le Havre.

The great cotton, brewing, iron and wool barons vied with Jewish financiers and builders in unadulterated ambition, extravagance, and often eccentricity.

Below: In the 1840s Edward Bulwer-Lytton transformed Knebworth from a red-brick Tudor house into flamboyant Victorian fantasy.

Wyfold Court, Oxfordshire, built between 1872 and 1876, for the Lancashire cotton magnate Edward Hermon by George Somers Clarke was a riot of flamboyant French Gothic enriched with fashionable structural polychromy. Rendcomb, a classical pile designed by P C Hardwick between 1863 and 1865, was built over the road between Cirencester and Cheltenham for the Jewish bullion dealer Sir Francis Goldsmid complete with a gigantic statue of King Saul in the vestibule. Perhaps most bizarre of all was Witley Park in Surrey, built by the fraudster Whitaker Wright in the 1890s with a glass-domed billiard room submerged beneath the waters of his lake.

While the visual expressions differed, the underlying impulse remained the same. The upwardly mobile, self-made man sought recognition and status by assuming the apparel of the aristocracy, albeit with the latest conveniences. Typical was Tyntesfield, outside Bristol, a rambling, eclectic Gothic pile. It was remodelled from a much smaller, earlier house by the Gibbs family between 1863–65, whose fortune had come from merchant banking and the guano trade. Designed by John Norton, it was thoroughly modern with a hot air heating system, its own gasometers for lighting the house, stables and lodges, and two water wheels, which pumped water to reservoirs which supplied the house. Fire hydrants were located around the inside and the kitchen was roofed with the latest fireproof construction. A splendid chapel, designed by Sir Arthur Blomfield, modelled on Saint Chapelle in Paris, was added in 1873–75, and electricity and a hydraulic lift were added in the 1880s.

At the other end of the country at Rothbury in Northumberland, Cragside epitomised the progressive, late 19th century country house. Perched on the side of a steep hill, overlooking the river Coquet, it was built for Sir William Armstrong, the greatest of the Victorian armaments manufacturers between 1869 and 1884.

A modest original lodge was expanded enormously in all directions by the architect Richard Norman Shaw. It too was innovative using the latest technology. In 1870 water from one of the estate's lakes was used to drive a hydraulic engine which powered a lift, the central heating, laundry machines and even a kitchen rotisserie from what was the world's first hydro-electric power station. Lamps made by Armstrong's friend, Joseph Swan, the pioneer of electricity, were installed in 1880, making Cragside the first house in England, and possibly the world, to be fitted with electric light. Cragside was described by a contemporary paper as 'truly the palace of a modern magician'. The King of Siam, the Shah of Persia and the Crown Prince of Afghanistan all paid a visit and departed astonished. It was an extraordinary combination of innovative, late Victorian technology all wrapped up in a romantic, nostalgic vision of a Lost England replete with half-timbered gables, crenelated parapets, oriel windows and towering chimneystacks.

The Victorian country house encapsulated English life in microcosm. Most followed a similar pattern with a clear segregation between the family, guests and servants. This dictated their internal spatial layout and plan. Even within the family there was separation between male and female preserves and rooms for the children. The smoking room and billiard room were regarded as exclusive male retreats.

Some of the largest houses, like Thoresby Hall in Northamptonshire, employed over 40 indoor and outdoor staff, in strict hierarchical fashion. Each member of staff was acutely aware of their own status from the lowest scullery maid or footman to the housekeeper and butler, but all took great pride in their responsibilities and willingly accepted the discipline and authority as part of what was perceived as the natural order of things.

The middle classes were predominantly urban, and, like the wealthy and the poor, also had their own subtle gradations of class and status. At the top of the heap was the 'exclusive' middle class; merchants, industrialists, bankers, army and naval officers, and the clergy. Professionals, such as lawyers, and doctors, formed tightly knit local elites. Living in comfortable detached and semi-detached villas in the wealthier parts of England's towns and cities, or the urban-rural fringe, they enjoyed the fruits of rising wealth and status.

Even amongst the wealthy middle class, there were bewildering levels of snobbery. Country surgeons and doctors, for instance, were looked down upon and often had to use the tradesman's entrance. Mrs Marrable in Trollope's *The Vicar of Bullhampton* had an idea that the son of a gentleman '...should earn his income as a clergyman, or as a barrister, or as a soldier or as a sailor. Those were the professions intended for gentlemen. She would not absolutely say that a physician was not a gentleman...But she would never allow to physic the same absolute privileges which, in her eyes, belonged to law and the church...But she had no doubt that when a man touched trade or commerce in any way he was doing that which was not the work of a gentleman'. [21]

Irrespective of class, the Victorians were obsessed with respectability – with what was 'proper' behaviour. Self-identity was determined not just by age or gender, but by education, earnings, family size and background, intelligence and accent. To the lower middle classes respectability meant deference to one's superiors. To the artisan, it meant self-reliance and independence, values of self-help, and the Victorian work ethic advocated by Samuel Smiles.

The lower middle classes – the white-collar workers, travelling salesmen and armies of clerks – prided themselves on their merit and respectability. Satirised in 1892 as the Pooters in George and Weedon Grossmith's *The Diary of a Nobody*, they felt insecure at the rapid pace of change both in office functions and also at the increasing employment of women. The outer suburbs of the great conurbations were lined with respectable semi-detached villas and terrace houses, each with their own gardens, each of which housed respectably genteel families of Pooters.

Occupying a central middle class niche of their own in towns and villages all over the country were the shopkeepers, and shop assistants. By 1891 there were over 1.1 million of them, comprising over 9 per cent of the working population trading from large retailing outlets to small neighbourhood corner shops.

Across all classes the home was where wealth, status and respectability were displayed not just in their architecture, but also in their interiors and domestic furnishings. As can be seen in the photographs, many towns still retained mediaeval timber-framed houses and weather boarded buildings, but the most commonplace form of town housing was the terrace town house. This had been perfected in the 18th century in London, Bath and other Georgian cities. Contracts were drawn up between landowners and speculative builders, and regulated by the leasehold system. Whole neighbourhoods were laid out on this basis with individual houses subordinated to the overall composition. This continued throughout the 19th century in a variety of materials and architectural styles.

Wherever possible local materials were used to minimise the cost of transport, like knapped flint and brick in areas without stone, but with the expansion of the railway network materials began to be transported much more easily around the country, eroding local distinctiveness. The terrace houses of Liverpool, for instance, were built almost entirely in Welsh red brick from Ruabon. Welsh slate, granite and building stone all became much more widely available across England.

In the early Victorian period classical styles were the most fashionable for domestic and public buildings utilising an architectural vocabulary drawn from Greek and Roman precedents. Its language of symmetry and laws of proportion evoked the values of classical antiquity, which found ready acceptance in a society which respected natural order. The continuation of this Georgian tradition can be seen in John Dobson's planning and designs for Grainger Town in Newcastle, or in Thomas Cubitt's development of Belgrave Square in London, and his work at Kemp Town in Brighton. The inspiration continued well into the mid century in the growing suburbs of London and the provincial conurbations.

One of the more popular forms of suburban development was the semi-detached house which became popular following John Nash's early picturesque compositions at Park Village, Regent's Park, in the 1820s. These provided a model which was soon taken up on the outskirts of towns across the country, often faced in stucco with projecting porches, moulded stucco architraves, and simple classical details.

Stucco remained popular well in to the 1870s, but under the influence of Pugin and Ruskin, Gothic styles became more popular. From the 1850s many of the great new public buildings, like St Pancras Station and the University Museum in Oxford used structural polychromy with bands of contrasting brick to striking effect. This fashion soon percolated into domestic architecture – in the villas of North Oxford, for instance, and houses for the prosperous middle classes, which were arising in all the main towns in the 1860s and 70s.

By the end of the century the residential streets of the major towns and cities were lined with terraces which were essentially elaborations of the Georgian terrace form, albeit enriched with larger rear extensions containing sculleries, kitchens and bathrooms. Most were set back from the street behind a basement well enclosed by ornamental cast iron railings, or sometimes a short front garden, with the entrance approached by a tiled path, or short flight of steps. Inside, the parlour, or drawing room, and the dining room occupied the principal ground floor with the bedrooms on the upper floors and services at the rear.

Above: King's Parade, Cambridge, c1890. Although many towns still retained mediaeval timber-framed buildings, the most common form of urban housing was the terrace town house.

From the 1860s a reaction set in against mass-produced, speculative housing and the widespread use of machine-made fittings and details. This reflected a deeper unease at the impact of industrialisation and urbanisation. In art the pre-Raphaelite movement looked back to what they believed was a purer form of art depicting achingly romantic themes from English history, Arthurian legend and the Renaissance. In architecture, the Arts and Crafts movement advocated a new aesthetic approach in all fields of design seeking truth in simplicity.

In 1859, at the Red House in Bexleyheath, Philip Webb designed a new house for William Morris, which encapsulated this new ideal with oriel windows, gables, a turret and tower-capped garden well; the interiors enriched with stained glass and tiles designed by Morris and his acolytes. It triggered a whole new school of domestic architecture reinterpreting the vernacular precedents of the past and utilising the built forms of an older, Lost England for the needs of a new age. Soon this 'Old English Revival' was taken up by others, influencing the form and layout of the new Garden Suburbs and cities of the period.

Architects like C F A Voysey and Mackay Hugh Baillie Scott took the traditional harling of Cumbria, and redeployed it as white painted roughcast with horizontal windows of leaded lights, low ceilings and angled outside walls to striking effect.

Sir Edwin Lutyens, an architectural genius and the most gifted English architect since Wren, took inspiration from a whole range of past precedents from 16th century vernacular to 17th century Baroque and transmuted them into wholly unique compositions often in conjunction with the gifted landscape designer Gertrude Jekyll. His commissions ranged from grand country houses, like Heathcote near Ilkley and Castle Drogo at Drewsteignton, to the remodelling of Lindisfarne Castle and the planning of Hampstead Garden Suburb and New Delhi.

By the late 19th century a style known as Queen Anne revival marked a significant departure from established norms. Characterised by picturesque juxtapositions of bay windows and gables, sash windows, tile hanging and beautifully crafted panels of soft rubbed red brick, it too was intended to conjure up an idyllic vision of a Lost England.

From 20 years or so from the 1880s, Norman Shaw's work at Bedford Park was taken up and reworked with varying degrees of success by speculative builders for middle class housing. Large, red brick houses with porches, wooden verandas, tile hung gables and white painted sashes became a familiar sight in the suburbs of London, in places like Swiss Cottage and Hampstead, in Surrey and the Home Counties, and around other large towns and cities. Sinuous art nouveau patterns of stained glass became popular for front doors with paths and floors of decorative encaustic tiles, which were produced in huge quantities from the 1870s onwards by Minton and the ceramics factories of the Potteries.

Flats were commonly associated with philanthropic housing for the respectable working classes, but from the 1850s onwards large blocks began to appear on a speculative basis in and around Victoria Street in London. Queen Anne's Mansions designed by the London School Board architect E R Robson between 1876 and 1888 was an early example – a colossal brick block rising over 14 storeys. Others soon followed. Over a seven-year period from 1879 a phalanx of tall, red brick blocks was raised alongside the Royal Albert Hall by Norman Shaw in an accomplished and elegant Queen Anne style. These offered completely new perspectives on high-density, urban living.

In 1884 Archer and Green completed Whitehall Court towering over the Victoria Embankment Gardens in the shadow of the Palace of Westminster with a romantic skyline of turrets and cupolas, which enriched the picturesque skyline in long views from Hyde Park. Flats were here to stay.

***

By 1900 it was very clear that while England may be the richest country in the world, millions of its people did not have any stake in the profits of its commercial and industrial success. The rapid pace of urbanisation had sucked in millions from the countryside and abroad in search of a living wage and employment, but consigned them to conditions of appalling squalor. Almost one third of all English people were crowded into poorly built dwellings in insanitary districts, their lives blighted by poverty, ill health, disease and early death.

This had been very evident for decades. In 1845 the young Benjamin Disraeli, the future Tory Prime Minister, shared the same concerns at the condition of the poor as the Chartists, public health reformers and early socialists. In his novel Sybil, or The Two Nations, published just a year after Friedrich Engels's discourse on The Condition of the Working Class in

Above: Newcastle: picturesque squalor. In 1900 almost one third of the population of England lived in poorly built dwellings in insanitary districts, their lives blighted by poverty, ill health, disease.

England, he wrote scathingly of 'The Two Nations between whom there is no intercourse and no sympathy.'

In the early Victorian city before the connection was made between dirt and disease, typhus, typhoid, tuberculosis, cholera, diphtheria, smallpox and scarlet fever stalked the streets and alleys of England. Life expectancy varied enormously across the country between classes and districts. Industrialisation and urbanisation reversed improvements in life expectancy which had been growing steadily over the previous one hundred years. Shockingly, in 1842 the average life expectancy for a manual labourer was just 15 years in Liverpool, 17 years in Manchester and 19 years in Leeds. For professionals, the corresponding figures were 35, 38 and 44 years. By contrast, in rural Rutland the figure for professionals was 52 years. In the same year, out of a total of 350,000 deaths in England, 140,000 were of children under 5 years old. The life chances of a slum dweller in early Victorian England were the lowest since the Black Death 500 years earlier.

By the early 19th century, the expanding population and high death rates precipitated a national burial crisis. Old mediaeval burial grounds overflowed with rotting corpses and became breeding grounds for disease. It was common for bodies to be exhumed and dismembered to create fresh burial space. Coffins were sold for firewood and human bones as fertiliser. The smell from the gases and effluvia of decomposing cadavers was appalling. In one case worshippers attending church were forced to cover their mouths and noses to prevent their inhalation. On returning home, they found themselves covered in 'body bugs.'

To address the matter, vast new private cemeteries were created around the major cities. In London alone, Kensal Green opened in 1832 followed by West Norwood in 1836, Highgate in 1839, Abney Park, Brompton and Nunhead in 1840, and Tower Hamlets a year later. Under the Burial Act of 1852 another nine were planned. Two years later the London Necropolis Railway opened a railway line to carry cadavers and mourners from London to what was then the largest cemetery in the world at Brookwood in Surrey. By the end of the century, there had been substantial improvements in public health, but average life expectancy for all classes still varied widely – just 30 years in Liverpool compared with 42 years in Newcastle and a national average of 46 years. In London the average age of death in the West End was 55. In the East End it was 30.

The poor had the worst food. In the absence of any system of quality control, food and drink were adulterated. Bread was whitened with ground bones, alum or plaster of Paris, tea with black lead, coffee with mangel-wurzel and acorns, vinegar with sulphuric acid, beer with green vitriol, and milk with water and chalk. The Food and Drugs Act of 1860 introduced a modicum of control, but only very limited inspection. However, by the 1870s once bacterial contamination and lead poisoning had been eliminated from the canning process, tinned meat and fruit began to offer a reliable source of nutritious food for mass consumption.

As the great cities of Victorian England grew, so the poor were driven into the least salubrious places, districts which were unknown to the vast majority of the middle classes. These were alien neighbourhoods comparable to darkest corners of Africa, where respectable people, and quite often the police, simply did not venture.

There was a common pattern in most towns and cities. All too often the poor were confined to low-lying areas susceptible to damp and flooding, for instance, along the rivers Irwell and Medlock in Manchester, or the Don valley in Sheffield. London's Millbank was notorious for its flooding. As late as 1928, 14 people drowned when the Thames burst its banks.

It was also common for the poor to occupy marginal land like spaces sandwiched between railway lines as they carved their way through the cities in areas such as Somers Town in London and Little Ireland in Manchester.

In 1899 the Quaker Seebohm Rowntree carried out a massive house-to-house survey of York. He concluded that over a quarter of the population was living in primary or secondary poverty. Low wages accounted for 52 per cent, large families 22 per cent and the death of the chief wage earner 15.6 per cent. A few years earlier Charles Booth had come to similar conclusions in London where he estimated that more than a third of Londoners – 1,800,000 – lived below the poverty line with a further 1 million with just a week's wages between respectability and pauperism. The highest concentration of poverty in London – 68 per cent – was in Bankside, between Blackfriars and London Bridge. In Greenwich it was 65 per cent.

The poor, of course, were not a homogeneous, amorphous mass, but highly stratified with subtle distinctions between the status of the respectable or worthy poor, the working poor, the casual or seasonal labourer, and the destitute.

In some towns almshouses provided a refuge for widows and the respectable poor. The workhouse was intended for the destitute. It was to be feared and avoided unless truly desperate. To discourage the able-bodied poor from applying, the regime was harsh with soul-destroying work like crushing bones for fertiliser, or picking oakum with a nail (hence the euphemism 'spike' for the workhouse), but they provided a safety net for those who really were in need.

In most large towns the workhouse was a conspicuous local landmark and a familiar part of the English landscape, often two storey classical ranges grouped around a central courtyard. The first wave, erected after the Poor Law Act of 1834, resembled panopticon prison buildings of the period; 'pauper bastilles', forbidding cruciform blocks shut behind high walls with separate work and exercise yards, many designed by the architect Sampson Kempthorne.

After savage criticism by the Poor Law inspectors of both the system and the buildings, between 1840-70 a new generation was built in a variety of architectural styles from Italianate and Elizabethan to Gothic. Over 150 were erected in and around England's towns and cities. These were huge rambling edifices with attenuated wings of long corridors containing wards in which men, women and children were separated, such as Winson Green in Birmingham erected in 1852 with accommodation for over 1,600 inmates.

After 1870 a further wave of improvements took place with workhouse infirmaries designed more like the Nightingale wards of military hospitals with parallel blocks of pavilions and lines of huge windows providing light and ventilation to the wards. The first, and one of the largest, erected in 1855 at Chorlton in Lancashire, soon became the new model. Others, like the Manchester Union infirmary followed usually with a chapel attached. Conditions inside the workhouse, where there was food, basic medical care and free education for children, were often preferable to a life of poverty outside. By the early 20th century the workhouse had tended to become a final refuge for the elderly and sick. In 1900 about 30 per cent of the entire population over 70 lived out their last days there where they received free medical care in the infirmary.

Closely allied to the workhouse were asylums catering for the mentally ill. Colney Hatch in Middlesex, designed by Samuel Daukes and opened in 1850, had a central block crowned by a large dome and elongated wings which were longer than the Crystal Palace, as well as its own dedicated railway sidings serving over 3,500 inmates. The grandest of all, the Royal Holloway Sanatorium at Virginia Water in Surrey, was completed between 1871 and 1884 for one hundred middle-class patients. The gift of Thomas Holloway, who had made a fortune from patent medicines, it was designed by WH Crossland in full-blown Gothic style complete with an imposing turreted tower and a Great Hall covered by a magnificent hammer beam roof.

The problems of urban life such as health, sanitation, housing and public order, which were usually associated with the new industrial towns, were often just as bad, if not worse, in the older communities, such as cathedral cities like Norwich, Exeter and Canterbury. Some of the least healthy places in the country were to be found in the timeworn quarters of the old towns, districts which had been ravaged by cholera outbreaks. Exeter was particularly badly hit by the cholera outbreak of 1832, York in 1849, and Newcastle in 1854. All the moral problems of the urban underworld, of the dangerous classes, were as present in these older towns as they were in the new, even if their scale was much smaller. Prostitution was as evident in Salisbury as it was in Manchester, as was rioting.

In 1899 the journalist Robert Blatchford wrote of a voyage of discovery into the heart of working class Manchester, a place which had so appalled Friedrich Engels over 50 years before. Whole areas were subsumed with filth, broken pavements, rubbish, and stagnant pools of water, which were a breeding ground for disease. He saw 'miles of narrow, murky streets, the involuted labyrinths of courts and passages and covered ways, where a devilish ingenuity seems to have striven with success to shut out light and air.'[22] By the 1880s many of the middle classes of Manchester had fled the city for the leafy environs of Cheshire to the south. The city centre, inner ring and Salford had become a virtual ghetto for the poor.

Some of the worst evils could be found in the cellar houses of the northern industrial cities. These were basement dwellings built beneath mean terraced houses. A single foul, unventilated cellar could house a family of eight or nine poor people. In the 1860s one fifth of the population of Liverpool lived in cellar houses in 3,273 foetid courts in conditions of appalling degradation. The city's Medical Officer of Health noted that 'fluid matter' from communal privies on the ground floor oozed into the cellars. Elsewhere the cellar floors were so wet that their residents had to walk on doors which were taken off their hinges and laid flat on bricks.

Above: Barefoot urchins. The plight of the destitute homeless was worst of all. Forced to sleep outdoors, as winter approached their death rate increased from exposure, malnutrition and suicide.

Thirty years later, many had been closed down with no provision for re-housing, their occupants pushed out exacerbating conditions in surrounding areas as they crowded into neighbouring districts to start a further downward spiral of squalor and distress. Similar houses could be found right across the north, particularly, in Manchester, Leeds and the seaports, where cellars of 'penny hangs' were patronised by drunken sailors. Here the keeper suspended ropes breast high between the basement walls. Overnight lodgers would drape their bodies over these until dawn when the ends were unfastened and an insensible mass of humanity would collapse in a heap on to the urine-soaked floor.

However, for the urban poor the most commonplace form of housing across a great swathe of England was the back-to-back terrace. In the 1840s they comprised over 70 per cent of the total housing stock of Manchester, Birmingham, Liverpool, Leeds, Nottingham and Huddersfield. They were common too in the poor areas of London like Somers Town, Shoreditch, Whitechapel and Bankside. As late as 1914 in Handsworth, Small Heath, Aston and Ladywood in Birmingham's inner city, there were still over 6,000 courts surrounded by over 43,000 back-to-backs, the last of which were only demolished in the late 1960s.

Back-to-back houses maximised the number of dwellings which could be crammed on to a small plot of land reaping handsome rental returns for unscrupulous slum landlords. Jerry-built houses were thrown up for short-term gain with little concern for their poor unfortunate occupants. These were the most vulnerable who could afford no more, usually unskilled, seasonal workers, the chronically-ill, and those who were but a step away from the workhouse, or life on the streets.

Shoddily-built, badly-drained, and devoid of light and sun, even when new many were unfit for human habitation. Most followed a common pattern with a terrace of dwellings running at right angles to the street, their backs separated from a parallel range of houses or factory by a wafer-thin wall just one brick thick. Access was through a narrow tunnel entry or covered way beneath another terrace of houses facing the roadway. The courtyard, usually sunless and often whitewashed, contained shared facilities for dozens of families with communal washhouses, privies, ashcans and miskins for rubbish, and usually a lone standpipe for water, and perhaps a solitary gas lamp. Some can be seen in the photographs of Ancoats and Birmingham, for instance.

Back-to-backs were just one room deep and about 15 feet square sometimes over a cellar. Inside, the ground floor had a multi-purpose scullery which acted as a kitchen, living room, dining room and workshop. Food was cooked on an open fire or rudimentary range, and the floors were covered with sacking or rags. Up a steep set of stairs were usually two bedrooms, although in Birmingham some had three storeys each with a single room. Bedrooms might be shared by five or six people plagued by rats, bugs and fleas. When someone died it was common practice for the body to be laid out in the tiny ground floor room for up to a week, often with a saucer of onions to disguise the smell of rotting flesh, until such time as the family could take time off work on a Sunday for burial.

Variations of these types could be found in different regions. In Newcastle, Tyneside flats were the commonest form of speculative rental housing where a single two-bay wide house formed two homes each with its own front door – one for the lower floor, which opened directly into the front room, and the other to the stairs to the upper flat, with a shared back yard containing an outhouse privy and a coal store serviced by a rear lane of granite setts for the removal of night soil and refuse.

In Sheffield, where back-to-backs were proscribed, a distinctive form of terraced house evolved rising in steps across the steep slopes of the town, each with two rooms on the ground floor separated by a lateral central staircase with backyards shared between groups of houses and privies lined up along the back wall. There was no service road; access and servicing all being conducted via a narrow tunnel entry on to the street.

In Hull, courtyards in the Old Town were initially infilled by two-storey, one-up, one-down, court housing. After an 1854 bylaw prohibited tunnel entrances and specified a maximum length of 120ft and a minimum width of 20ft, a distinctive cul-de-sac court form emerged with terraces set at right angles to the main road, many with front and rear gardens.

Slightly better than the back-to-backs were the two-up, two-down terrace through houses, which can still be found in virtually all the towns and cities in England. These offered accommodation for single families. Unattached at the rear, and often with a small yard, each had a small front living room, tiny rear kitchen and two small bedrooms above. While some were well-built, all too many were poorly constructed and planned. As they fell in to multiple occupation as one room tenements, or lodging houses, they rapidly deteriorated.

Common lodging houses, where a bed could be obtained for a nightly rent in a communal dormitory, were close to the bottom of the heap. Just one step away from the workhouse casual wards, they provided a nightly refuge for the outcast poor who might otherwise be forced to sleep on the streets. In 1851 and 1853 legislation was passed which regulated lodging houses and set minimum standards, but legal lodging houses tended to be more expensive. This pushed the destitute and most vulnerable into illegal lodgings where as many as 15 men, women and children might be forced to share the floor in a single small room without any partitions or separation. Sexual immorality and abuse were commonplace. Prostitutes lay alongside drunken men and traumatised children. In London in 1900, over 900,000 people relied on over 11,000 lodging, or doss houses. A further 300,000 lived in one-room tenements.

In Macclesfield the newly convened Board of Health visited a typical lodging house and found 188 people lodged in four cottages with a single small yard and just two privies. In the yard were a number of occupied shacks. In one 'lay a woman in the pains of labour; by her side lay a man apparently asleep, and ten other men, women and children'. Behind, in a back space 'used as a receptacle for the filth of the house, lay three little children in some shavings' Above 'lay six women and children on the floor, and in the front room were four beds on the floor, filled with men, women and children varying from 2 to 6 a bed'. [23]

The plight of the destitute homeless was worst of all. Each night thousands were forced to sleep on park benches, or huddle together in doorways for warmth. As winter approached, the death rate increased, either from suicide for those who could take no more, or from exposure and malnutrition.

As the social geography of England's towns and cities mutated, once-grand houses in the inner city, occupied just a couple of generations previously by wealthy merchants and the middle classes, fell into multiple occupation. Entire districts became rookeries as old decrepit houses were occupied by the most dissolute and criminal classes in areas like All Saints in Newcastle, and the rookeries of London rendered notorious by Dickens – Seven Dials, St Giles, Saffron Hill and Jacob's Island in Bermondsey.

As wholesale clearances penetrated the densely packed rookeries and ancient districts, it was not just the fabric of the city, but the lives of its poorest inhabitants that were violated; tossed aside with their precious few possessions and bundles of old rags, like so much human rubbish. It was an unfortunate irony that however well-intended, the demolition of slum areas simply exacerbated the overall problem by shifting those displaced elsewhere to begin again the same downward spiral of environmental degradation.

Until the later 19th century, when the scientific link was proven between dirt and disease, the concept of environmental health was alien to most Victorian minds. It took the efforts of Medical Officers of Health and sanitary reformers like Edwin Chadwick and Southwood Smith for concerted action to make any headway. It was commonly believed that diseases such as cholera, smallpox and diphtheria were miasmatic, and that people contracted them from breathing in vitiated air from the fumes of decomposing rubbish and excrement. Such fumes could roll out of the slums of the inner city and infect the middle classes. In *Dombey and Son*, Dickens wrote: 'if the noxious particles that rise from vitiated air were palpable to the sight, we should see them lowering in a dense black cloud above such haunts, and rolling slowly on to corrupt the better portions of the town'. [24]

The squalor and smell of the rookeries and tenements was equated with moral pestilence. Olfactory sensibilities were acute. Smell was an aspect of class discrimination and associated with outsiders or ethnic minorities. The 'great unwashed' were commonly believed to be filthy, impious, depraved, murderous and drunk. The health of the poor was inextricably linked to their morality. Unless the cities were cleaned, the people could not be cleansed of their sins – hence the popular Victorian belief that cleanliness was next to godliness.

Southwood Smith wrote 'A clean, fresh and well-ordered house exercises over its inmates a moral, no less than a physical influence, and has a direct tendency to make members of the family sober, peaceable, and considerate of the feelings and happiness of each other' whereas for the dweller of a hovel 'the connection is obvious between the constant indulgence of appetites and passions of this class, and the formation of habits of idleness, dishonesty, debauchery, and violence; in a word the training to every kind of degree of brutality and ruffianism'.[25]

Given such popular perceptions, not surprisingly, the respectable poor placed great weight on the cleanliness of their homes both inside and out to distinguish themselves from the lowest orders; hence the common sight of working class women scrubbing the entrance steps of their terrace houses with donkey stones.

William Booth, the founder of the Salvation Army, estimated that there were 3 million people who were living in 'such conditions of misery and destitution, vice and crime, as put them outside the limits of civilised society.'[26] This underclass, or residuum, terrified the middle classes and authorities. They were feared not just because they might infect the worthy poor, but because they might actually foment revolution, as had happened in France. With uncanny prescience, George Sims wrote in 1886 'This mighty mob of famished, diseased, and filthy helots is getting dangerous, physically, morally, politically dangerous ... and it may do the state mischief if it is not looked to in time'.[27] A month later, the mob, mainly homeless poor, descended upon Trafalgar Square, rioted and promptly occupied St James's Park.

The semi-criminal underclass indulged in a bewildering spectrum of criminal activities. There were footpads and garrotters, cracksmen and pickpockets, shofulmen (counterfeiters) and palmers (shoplifters) and widespread casual prostitution. Worst of all were the baby farmers; women who took in illegitimate children for an exorbitant fee, insured and then murdered them for rich pickings. In 1860, in London alone, 226 infants under the age of two were recorded as having died by foul play. This was just the tip of the iceberg. Many infant corpses were never recovered. The gruesome Jack the Ripper murders in Whitechapel of 1888 were famously depicted by John Tenniel in Punch as 'The Nemesis of Neglect'; a hideous phantom brandishing a butcher's knife hovering over the Whitechapel slums.

In the working class areas of the big cities territorial street gangs, or hooligans, fought each other viciously for control. Distinguished by their clothing, in Manchester they were called scuttlers. Typical were the 'Bengal Tigers' who hailed from a maze of slum streets near Bengal Street in Ancoats. In Birmingham they were the 'Peaky Blinders', or 'sloggers'. In the capital there were Jewish, Italian and Irish gangs. Territorial control of the criminal underworld remains a feature of urban life today.

The poorest slums of the great cities were where new arrivals congregated. By far the largest group of immigrants were the Irish, who, as British citizens, were no more foreign than someone from Yorkshire or Scotland, but they were treated as semi-barbaric, rebellious aliens. They had been coming for centuries, but following the failure of the potato crop in the late 1840s the steady stream became a deluge. By 1854 between 1.5 and 2 million left Ireland for England, America and the colonies.

Stigmatised as illiterate, sub-human drunks and criminals with houses 'not even fit for pigsties', they tended to be semi-skilled, or unskilled labourers, who sought manual jobs – the heavy-lifting jobs of the British economy constructing the railways, and working in the docks, factories and mines, which underpinned the wealth of the country. 'Ireland is pouring in to the cities and even into the villages, wrote *The Times* at the height of the potato famine 'a fetid mass of famine, nakedness, dirt and fever'.

In the first five months of 1849, over 300,000 arrived in Liverpool – then a town of 250,000. Typhus was known popularly as 'the Irish fever'. By 1861 there were 805,717 Irish in the country crowding in to the already teeming slums of Birmingham, the West Midlands and the mill towns of Lancashire, provoking anti-Irish riots in Cardiff, Wigan, Preston, Blackburn and Oldham. Over 170,000 could be found in London. The St Giles's rookery was known as Little Dublin, and the area south of the Oxford Road in Manchester, sandwiched between the river and the railway, 'Little Ireland'. As the century wore on and demands for Irish independence grew, Fenian outrages added fuel to the flames of communal tensions.

Not all Irish were poor emigrés who gravitated to the big cities, there were sizeable communities in the port towns and Cornish tin mines, and in smaller towns like Carlisle, Derby, Plymouth, Hull and Colchester.

Contrary to the prejudiced stereotype, nearly half of all Irish immigrants found skilled or professional work. In Stafford, over five hundred developed a local shoemaking trade. Alongside respectable butchers, grocers, milliners and publicans, there were successful lawyers, merchants and traders.

Perhaps most illustrious of all was Thomas Barnardo, born an Irish Jew, who became a Christian evangelist. By the time of his death in 1905 he had saved over 60,000 street urchins from appalling squalor. As the generations passed, the Irish inter-married and became increasingly assimilated into mainstream British life.

After the Irish the next largest ethnic minority were the Ashkenazi Jews. With the assassination of Czar Alexander II in 1881, a wave of Jewish immigration took place as they fled westward from the anti-semitic pogroms of Eastern Europe. Between 1881 and 1914 around 150,000 settled in Britain gravitating to Whitechapel in London, Leylands in Leeds and Redbank in Manchester, all of which had a tradition of textiles, tailoring and the sweated trades making furniture and shoes. Jewish pedlars collected, repaired and then reworked rags in to second-hand clothes. All three districts became Jewish ghettos. Yiddish was widely spoken. Synagogues, shuls, soup kitchens, mikvahs and bakeries soon sprang up to service the needs of the new arrivals.

The other sizeable community was the Italians, who arrived in increasing numbers in the wake of the upheavals caused by Italian unification. In 1861 there were just 5,000. By 1901 there were over 20,000, of whom half lived in London, mostly concentrated in Little Italy in Clerkenwell, but there were also concentrations in Manchester, Liverpool, Leeds, Hull and Sheffield.

Above: Labourers using a hand-cranked crane work at Edge Hill cuttings on the approach to the London and North Western Railway's Liverpool Lime Street station, c1882.

The earliest arrivals were often urchins brought over by a padrone to play the barrel organ, which led many to complain about their interminable noise. In 1856 *The Times* thundered, 'It is impossible to exaggerate the nuisance…We endure them simply as idle people endure dirt and vermin … It is an evil which threatens to make London unendurable.'[28] But in the wake of the musicians came small traders and ice cream makers opening cafes and delicatessens, specialist craftsmen skilled in marble and mosaics, and armies of bakers and waiters. In 1884 a modern Italian Hospital opened in Queen Square, Bloomsbury.

Not all Italian immigrants were deemed a nuisance. In 1896 Guglielmo Marconi demonstrated his new-fangled radio from the roof of the Post Office in St Martin's Lane. Five years later the first radio message was sent across the Atlantic, ushering in a new age of electronic communications.

Large ports, such as London, Southampton and Liverpool, accommodated a wide range of seamen from around the world who stamped their own particular identities on the maritime communities around Britain's coast. There were Seamens' missions for Swedes, Finns and Norwegians in the London Docks, and a Strangers' Home for Asiatics, Africans and South Sea Islanders close to the West India Docks. Bengalis, Indians, Malays and Lascars could be found in Southampton, Bristol, Hull, South Shields and Cardiff. There were small Chinese communities in Chinatown in Limehouse and in Liverpool. In 1889 England's first Islamic mosque appeared in Woking. Founded by a German-Hungarian Oriental academic, it brought an exotic echo of Moghul India to the woodlands of Surrey.

As first generation pioneer immigrants settled in, they attracted friends, families and business contacts in a chain of migration to form newly emerging colonies. In Bradford's Little Germany, as the textile merchants flourished and their status increased, they integrated socially with wealthy English families, and in turn drew in a group of lower status Germans, like pork butchers to serve their culinary needs. In London, by 1914 there were over 30,000 Germans clustered around Fitzrovia where Charlotte Street was dubbed 'Charlottenstrasse'.

In the absence of decisive action by the local vestries, the greatest help for the poor and disadvantaged often came from philanthropic individuals and organisations who dedicated themselves to alleviating poor housing conditions, particularly in London. Bodies such as the Artisans, Labourers and General Dwellings Company, the Society for Improving the Condition of the Labouring Classes, and the Four Per Cent Industrial Dwellings Company led by example, providing comfortable and sanitary dwellings for the 'deserving poor' usually for a 4 or 5 per cent return on their investment thereby, in typical Victorian fashion, happily marrying philanthropic endeavour to a decent financial return.

In 1862 the American philanthropist George Peabody donated £150,000 'to ameliorate the condition of the poor and needy…and to promote their comfort and happiness' through the erection of model dwellings in London. The first estate opened in Spitalfields in 1864. Over the next 30 years, others followed, eradicating some of the worst areas of slum housing in the capital. Their tall, austere blocks became a distinctive feature of the urban townscape lamented by some, like George Gissing, as sheer, monolithic blocks, unbroken by ornament and for their 'row upon row of windows in the mud coloured surface', but they offered infinitely better living conditions for those fortunate enough to be re-housed in them.

They could be found outside London too, in Manchester and Newcastle for instance, but in the Midlands and North it was the enlightened industrialists who frequently led the way by providing model housing and social amenities for their workers; a long tradition that could be traced back to Richard Arkwright's village at Cromford, Derbyshire, as early as 1771, and Robert Owen's New Lanark founded in 1783.

Outside Halifax, Copley and Akroydon, model villages built by the textile industrialist Edward Akroyd, employed the architects George Gilbert Scott and W H Crossland to create a hierarchy of house types for different classes and a Working Men's College for self-improvement. Others arose around Bolton – New Eagley and Egerton, financed by the Ashworth family, and Robert Gardner's settlement at Barrow Bridge. Price's Candle Company built another at Bromborough Pool Village near Liverpool.

Perhaps the most famous early example was Saltaire, at Shipley near Bradford. This integrated model community was built by Sir Titus Salt from 1850 onwards to the designs of Lockwood and Mawson to support his vast textile mill alongside the Leeds and Liverpool Canal. In addition to robust, well-appointed stone houses each with running water, there were bath-houses, a church, schools, a library and concert hall, a billiard room, laboratory, hospital and gymnasium.

In the later 19th century the imperative of sanitary reform and the social ideal of alleviating the condition of the working classes were elided with the pursuit of the picturesque and new thinking about town planning promoted by Ebenezer Howard and the Garden City and Garden Suburb movement. As the suburbs of London and the industrial conurbations of England expanded with the spread of the railway and tram systems, so new model communities arose uniting the two aspirations.

The first, Bedford Park at Turnham Green, with houses by Norman Shaw, was predominantly a middle class suburb, but the idea was soon taken up to build integrated mixed communities of all classes. Bournville, built by the Cadburys outside Birmingham, began in 1894. Port Sunlight outside Liverpool was begun even earlier, in 1888, guided by the enlightened patronage of the Lever brothers. Both made ample provision for community buildings, the latter with the splendid Lady Lever Art Gallery designed in 1913, but not completed until after the Great War in 1922.

Victorian England was the heyday of the public house and music hall, two of the few pleasures open to the poor. They were everywhere. London had one pub for every 345 persons, Sheffield one for every 176. This was the age of the gin palace with dazzling interiors of glittering tiles, mirrors and etched glass lit by sizzling gasoliers. Outside, monstrous lanterns suspended from sinuous tentacles of ironwork draped above mahogany frontages of gilded glass enticed the poor into an intoxicating world far removed from their usual drudgery. Chronic alcoholism was endemic. As drink was seen as one of the greatest evils for the poor, so the model communities begun in the early years of the 20th century, like Letchworth and Welwyn Garden Cities and Hampstead Garden Suburb, excluded pubs. Gardening, allotments, parks and open spaces were offered as a healthy alternative to alcohol.

With their sylvan houses and whimsical terraces inspired by English vernacular precedents, all artfully disposed in curving tree-lined roads, these model communities evoked an idealised, and romantic vision of communities of the past; a Lost England, which only ever existed in some abstract chamber of the mind, but which nonetheless exerted a very powerful sway over the national consciousness. It was the same imperative that encouraged the wealthy entrepreneur and merchant to flee the city in favour of an Arcadian life in the country. Man may have made the town, but God made the country.

Throughout the 19th century, England's cities were in a permanent state of flux as older tightly-knit streets of insanitary houses were swept aside in favour of newer, broader thoroughfares lined with taller buildings. Some began to question what was being lost – an older England – as ancient timber-framed houses and historic buildings disappeared. As the mid century approached, one commentator noted 'the old street architecture of Leicester is rapidly vanishing...the greater part of the half-timbered lath-and-plaster houses, remarkable for their grotesque gables and picturesque appearance, have given place to plainer but more convenient dwellings.' [29] And it was not just Leicester, but right across the country.

Above: Butcher Row, Coventry, 1889. A picturesque range of timber-framed buildings which was demolished in 1936.
Opposite: The three glass pavilions at Sheffield Botanical Gardens, founded by the Sheffield Botanical and Horticultural Society in the 1830s.

In an article published in 1885 on 'Some London Clearings' the narrator wrote of the creation of a new thoroughfare through Soho – Shaftesbury Avenue. 'Now no more shall domestic fires burn in those snug fireplaces... for here is an end of it all in a heap of old bricks and some ragged rafters.' Like a voyeur, he watched as 'the old street, half of which has been lopped away, has a curious blinking aspect...full day light streaming in where once was convenient gloom and obscurity'. [30]

As the pace of change accelerated, the preservation of historic buildings became a popular cause for the educated middle classes, and those interested in new ideas of town planning and philanthropy. Increasingly people were dismayed to see so much of their familiar landscape changing, particularly ancient buildings, like coaching inns and mediaeval houses, which had conferred a sense of local identity for centuries.

As early as 1875 the Society for Photographing Relics of Old London was formed by a group of enthusiasts. They left a priceless record of a vanishing Lost England. In 1877 the Society for the Protection of Old Buildings was founded by William Morris, Philip Webb and others, who were appalled at proposals for the radical 'restoration' of Tewkesbury Abbey and other mediaeval churches and cathedrals by the great architects of their day. In 1893-94 the National Trust for Places of Historic Interest and Natural beauty was formed, the brainchild of the social reformer and housing pioneer, Octavia Hill along with Robert Hunter and Canon Hardwicke Rawnsley. It was the birth of the long and noble struggle for the architectural conservation of the genuine fabric of England's past; the true Lost England.

Philanthropic bodies played a crucial role in advancing sanitary improvements in many areas other than housing. One of the most important was the public drinking fountain movement, which mobilised the support of prominent public figures to make a practical contribution by providing hundreds of free, fresh drinking fountains for the urban poor. Ironically it was the great brewing families of Hanbury and Buxton who became stalwarts of the movement rather than the Temperance movement, which initially viewed it with distrust.

The Metropolitan Free Drinking Fountain Association was founded in 1859 by Samuel Gurney, the nephew of the great prison reformer Elizabeth Fry. Its first fountain was opened amid scenes of great public rejoicing in the same month at St Sepulchre's, Snow Hill in London. There was a strong evangelical element. Water was a symbol of purity and Christian piety. Many were inscribed with uplifting biblical quotations to encourage the sober poor to remain so. Others soon followed across the country. Patrons and towns vied with each other to provide ever more elaborate designs, often incorporating other street furniture like gas lamps and public clocks, some of which can be seen in many of the photographs, for instance in Dudley, Henley, Mansfield and Peterborough.

It was commonplace for horses to be driven to death, or for cattle to be driven to market on the hoof without any water for two or three days at the height of summer. From its inception, the Association worked closely with the RSPCA. In 1867 it changed its name to the Metropolitan Drinking Fountain and Cattle Trough Association, and attracted powerful sponsorship for fountains and horse troughs. By 1885 over 50,000 horses drank from London troughs alone – the filling stations of their day.

The expansion of the towns and cities of the Midlands and the North coupled with growing awareness of the importance of sanitation and free fresh drinking water generated unprecedented demands for reliable sources of water, which could no longer be addressed by insanitary communal pipes, pumps and conduits. In 1881 a massive new masonry dam was constructed at Vyrnwy in Wales to supply Liverpool. By the time of its completion over eleven years later, it was a fifth of a mile long and 144 feet high holding back a reservoir of over 12 billion gallons of water, the largest artificial lake in Europe. Manchester and Birmingham soon followed suit.

Manchester utilised Lake Thirlmere in the Lake District with a masonry dam completed in 1894. In 1896 Birmingham commenced an ambitious 20-year plan for a series of dams in the Elan valley in central Wales. Designed by the engineer James Mansergh, water was conducted across country by gravity via a piped aqueduct 73 miles long. Bristol, notorious as one of the dirtiest cities in England, tapped supplies from the Mendips in the late 1840s, but a reliable supply was only achieved in the 1870s at which point the death rate plummeted.

As well as supplies of free, fresh water, great weight was placed on the importance of ventilation and access to fresh air. The Victorian open spaces movement had two primary aims – the first was to create parks for the masses in densely populated districts; the second was to preserve commons and countryside from encroachment. Philanthropy joined with municipal enterprise to humanize the urban environment.

Here, as all too often, it was pressure groups that led the way. The Manchester and Salford Sanitary Association was established as early as 1852, the Commons Preservation Society in 1865, the Kyrle Society in 1875 and the Metropolitan Public Gardens Association in 1885. Local open spaces societies campaigned for recreation grounds in overcrowded working class areas, for the conversion of disused burial grounds and wasteland into small parks, and for the multiple use of school playgrounds outside school hours.

Public parks were one of the major achievements of the later 19th century. They left a distinctive mark on the townscape of England. They were also a popular focus for civic monuments, memorials, bandstands, fountains and statuary. Perhaps the most ambitious of these was the colossal Ashton Memorial in Williamson Park, Lancaster, known as the Taj Mahal of the North. Erected in 1906–09, it towers over the surrounding town and countryside, the gift of Lord Ashton, the son of James Williamson, the park donor, who made his fortune from linoleum.

By the 1870s most major conurbations had public parks, many the gift of private philanthropists. Birmingham had a chain of seven on its outskirts, Manchester had three and Bradford five. It was not just the big cities. Smaller towns all over England, like Grimsby, Sunderland, Barnsley and Darlington all took great pride in creating their own civic parks.

In Liverpool public parks were the focus for the development of the residential suburbs. The first, the initiative of the philanthropist, Richard Vaughan Yates, was Prince's Park laid out by Joseph Paxton and James Pennethorne from 1842. The Council soon adopted the idea and a belt of new parks followed notably Wavertree Park in 1856 and Shiel Park in 1862.

Under the Liverpool Improvement Act three much bigger projects were started: Stanley Park, Newsham Park and, the most ambitious of all, Sefton Park, the largest creation in the country since Regent's Park.

The underlying driver for a great deal of philanthropic activity was a deeply held belief in Christian duty towards those less fortunate. The Church had a profound influence on all aspects of Victorian life setting social and moral conventions, and inspiring philanthropic activity and missionary work at home and overseas. It provided a discipline for individual thought and personal behaviour. The evangelical spirit, with its emphasis on proselytising zeal and individual salvation, permeated all denominations, particularly the non-conformists. Its pervasive influence is only too evident in photographs of the period where the church spire and town tabernacle are common features of towns and cities all over the country.

Many Anglican churches were ancient buildings which had stood on their sites for centuries, but as England urbanised there was a huge demand for new places of worship for all denominations. The situation was worst in London and the industrial districts of those provincial towns and cities into which a tide of humanity had flowed in massive numbers.

Cities were seen as immoral places, rife with disorder, drunkenness and sin. The 1851 census shocked the nation when it revealed that almost half of the working class had not visited church the previous Sunday, and of those that had, over half did so outside the Church of England. The situation challenged all denominations, and all responded with a vigorous programme of church building. Organised religion underwent a huge revival.

The Salvation Army, founded in 1865 by William Booth, reached out beyond the churches to the dispossessed in the slums. By the end of the century, upper and middle class pioneers set up Settlement Houses in the worst areas to preach the social gospel. The first at Toynbee Hall in Whitechapel attempted to combat social problems like poor housing and drunkenness. It was no coincidence that this inspired its founders, Samuel and Henrietta Barnett, to put their social idealism into practice by founding a model community at Hampstead Garden Suburb with housing for all classes, educational institutions, allotments and no pubs.

In 1876 a parliamentary report recorded that since 1840 7,144 Anglican churches had been restored and 1,727 new churches built at a staggering total cost of over £25 million. The non-conformist churches – the Congregationalists, Baptists and Methodists – registered even more impressive figures, the latter building over 10,000 chapels in the 50 years from 1801. As a result of this great revival in religion, Victorian architects left an indelible stamp on almost every city, town and village in England.

The Church was united only by its diversity. After the Catholic Relief Act of 1791, Catholic worship was no longer illegal. With the removal of many legal and constitutional restrictions in 1829, Roman Catholicism underwent a revival in its old strongholds in Lancashire and north-west England, particularly amongst the immigrant Irish and Italian communities.

Emancipation triggered the construction of a wave of new churches. Many of the earliest were quite simple, but as the century progressed Catholic churches became richer and more extravagant. The prime mover in this was A W N Pugin, a febrile Catholic convert, who had a profound impact on the architecture of the age. He, like so many others, reacted against the industrial revolution and harked back to a Lost England of the Middle Ages as the source of 'truth.' He regarded classical buildings as 'pagan', and advocated a return to authentic Gothic architecture where craftsmen and artists could work in harmony to create magnificent new buildings for the sacred celebration of the Mass.

Above: The Primitive Methodist Chapel, Monkwearmouth. More than 10,000 Methodist chapels were built in the 50 years from 1801.

Pugin produced over 100 buildings, many of them churches in Early English and then Decorated or Middle Pointed style. St Mary's, Derby, Pugin's first major parish church, was intended to cater for the huge influx of Irish immigrants. At its opening in 1838, it was described by the Bishop as 'the most magnificent thing that Catholics have yet done in modern times in this country' and it 'would not have done dishonour to Rome'. [31]

St Chad's in Birmingham, erected in 1839–41, was the first Roman Catholic cathedral to be built in Britain since the Reformation. Pugin chose a rather curious offering, with twin spires resembling a Baltic church of the Hanseatic League. Perhaps more typical was St Augustine's Abbey, Ramsgate, which Pugin designed and funded. Just two years after its completion, he was buried beneath it in 1852, exhausted from overwork and periodic bouts of insanity.

However, not all Catholics accepted Pugin's fanatical obsession with Gothic. By the end of the century two of the country's most important

Catholic churches departed from the Puginian norm – Brompton Oratory, by the little-known architect Herbert Gribble, was designed in Roman classical style, and in 1895–1903 Westminster Cathedral was executed in a neo-Byzantine style by John Francis Bentley with a glorious campanile, which towered over neighbouring Victoria and cocked a snook at nearby Westminster Abbey.

Influenced by Pugin and the ideals of the Cambridge Camden Society, which were propagated through its journal *The Ecclesiologist*, the Anglican church also enthusiastically embraced the passion for Gothic architecture, and a revival of its mediaeval splendour. In the 1840s, as demand soared, new churches arose in a whole variety of styles. St Peter's, Leamington Spa, for instance, commenced in 1844 was modelled on Cologne and Regensburg cathedrals. Perpendicular was the most popular. As the Ecclesiologists gained ground, by the mid century pressure grew for a more 'correct' style. One of its chief proponents was George Gilbert Scott, who worked on hundreds of designs for churches both at home and abroad. Typical of his work was All Souls, Haley Hill, Halifax, which he completed in 1859, and which he regarded as his best church, a perfect juxtaposition of its component parts, its great spire piercing the heavens in a paean of praise to both God and the Gothic revival.

From the mid century until the 1870s a series of gifted architects each made their own inimitable contribution to a style which came to be known as High Victorian Gothic, and which bequeathed a legacy of spectacular church buildings across England.

At All Saints, Margaret Street, in Marylebone, William Butterfield devoted nine years of his life to the construction of a model church for the Ecclesiological Society on a cramped city centre site marked by a tall, thin tower and spire. The design incorporated the latest thinking using structural polychromy of banded and diapered red brick (popularly referred to as 'streaky bacon'). The interior was decorated with dazzling patterns of multi-coloured glazed tiles and red, black and grey bricks inspired by the brightly coloured decoration of the mediaeval cathedrals, which had been whitewashed or destroyed following the Reformation.

George Edmund Street, the architect of London's Law Courts, developed the style further from early works, such as St James the Less in Pimlico in 1859 and St Philip and St James in Oxford through provincial churches, like the superb All Saints' Clifton completed in 1864, to his magnificent tour de force at St Mary Magdalene, Paddington with its pencil-thin banded brick spire completed in 1873.

William White and S S Teulon each offered their own highly individual renditions, the latter in a strongly muscular Gothic idiom at St Stephen's, Rosslyn Hill in Hampstead, and at St Mark's Silvertown. James Brooks met the need for tall, well-lit town churches with large unobstructed spaces by producing a whole chain of buildings in the poorer areas of the capital, particularly London's East End. His contemporary John Loughborough Pearson designed two of the most iconic buildings of the period, both with interiors characterised by lofty stone and brick vaults carried on delicate thin shafts of stonework. The first, St Augustine's Kilburn, was begun in 1871, but only completed in 1898, its slender tower and spire, a local landmark visible for miles around. Truro Cathedral, built in phases between 1880-1910, revelled in the verticality of the composition with a central spire over the crossing and two subordinate towers at its western end.

By the end of the century, tastes had changed. George Frederick Bodley explored a return to early English Gothic before the Arts and Crafts movement began to permeate church design, most notably in the exquisite internal decoration at Holy Trinity, Sloane Street, by John Dando Sedding. This wonderful interior was enriched with stained glass by Burne-Jones and William Morris and gorgeous fittings by some of the leading sculptors of the day, including F W Pomeroy and Hamo Thorneycroft.

In sharp contrast to the lavish buildings and interiors of the Catholic and Anglican churches, non-conformist church buildings hailed from a very different tradition. In the Puritan heartlands of Wales and East Anglia, Baptist and Methodist chapels were regarded simply as preaching boxes. They were deliberately plain and unadorned. Often classical in style, usually they followed a similar pattern with galleries on three sides carried on iron pillars with the fourth side containing an organ and pulpit from which the sermon was given.

There were exceptions to this convention. Gothic was deployed by the Methodists, and in particular, the Congregationalists. Its most notable exponent was John James who designed exuberant Gothic churches in Halifax, Barnsley and Sheffield in the 1850s, which were virtually indistinguishable from their Anglican counterparts. By the last decades of the century there was greater freedom of expression with the emphasis on creating large unobstructed central spaces, and barn-like interiors, like James Cubitt's Union Chapel in Islington.

***

One of the biggest drivers of social mobility was the landmark Education Act of 1870, which provided for universal elementary education. It spawned a whole new building type which became a familiar hallmark of late Victorian England. Before 1870 children were educated, if at all, in a variety of different ways depending on their social class and where they lived. For the middle and upper classes education was often at home by family members or governesses.

In the middle decades of the century the growing wealth of the middle classes created demand for new public schools. These modelled themselves on their older rivals highlighting the three principal tenets advocated by Thomas Arnold, the headmaster of Rugby school – religious principles, gentlemanly conduct and intellectual ability.

Among the most notable, Lancing College near Shoreham was begun in 1854 in Gothic style to the designs of R C Carpenter using local stone and flint. Work was continued after his death by his son and William Slater. The monumental chapel perched high upon the Sussex Downs, (the largest school chapel in the world), was only finally completed in 1978.

Clifton, founded in 1862 outside Bristol, also followed the Gothic style favoured by many of the new Anglican public boarding schools with buildings by Charles Hansom. Marlborough, founded in 1843, was extended around the original house by Edward Blore from 1844 onwards in William and Mary style, while Wellington was founded in 1853 as a national memorial to the recently deceased Iron Duke. John Shaw, the architect of Christ's Hospital School in the City of London, created a grand, symmetrical composition in full-blown Wrenaissance style complete with elaborate French mansards.

The expansion of the Victorian education system was responsible for the invention and codification of organised games as an integral part of character building. With increased leisure time, cricket and rugby became popular spectator sports, and their grounds part of the urban townscape. Football was popular at both ends of the social spectrum. It was played both in the public schools and in the working class districts of the manufacturing towns of the north and Midlands. Clubs sprang up all over the country. The Football Association was founded in London in 1863 and the Football League in 1888. The oldest League club, Notts County, was inaugurated in 1866 followed shortly after by Sheffield Wednesday, Aston Villa in 1874, Everton in 1878, Manchester United in 1885 and Woolwich Arsenal in 1886. Bramall Lane, Sheffield, the oldest football stadium, was opened in 1855, Deepdale at Preston North End in 1875, and St James's Park, Newcastle, where it towers over the city skyline, in 1880.

For the majority of children in country areas, village schools, often endowed by a local squire or benefactor, offered rudimentary teaching in reading, writing and arithmetic. Some older towns had endowed grammar schools, which operated from a variety of building types. They provided a decent education for the children of the aspiring middle classes and aped the uniforms and social mores of the public schools, which catered for those who could afford the fees. In parallel were private schools, and a large number of church schools from a variety of different denominations. At the other end of the spectrum, in the working class areas of the cities, the dame school offered basic teaching, and in the slum areas, the ragged school or workhouse. Where there were deficiencies, the 1870 Act specified that a school board should be set up, which gave rise to the birth of the Board School.

Architecturally, these lofty citadels of learning, symbolically rising above their surroundings, became a common sight above the townscapes of England's urban areas. To Sherlock Holmes in 'The Naval Treaty', they were: 'Lighthouses, my boy! Beacons of the future! Capsules, with hundreds of bright little seeds in each, out of which will spring the wiser, better England of the future'. [31]

Most had separate entrances and playgrounds for girls and boys. There was widespread regional variation. In London they were usually tall, gabled edifices in Queen Anne style faced in red and yellow brick or terracotta with large windows for light and ventilation; many designed by E R Robson, the architect to the Board. In Bristol they opted for Gothic or Tudor styles with a large central hall surrounded by single storey blocks, but it was in Sheffield that a highly distinctive local style emerged to the designs of the Board's architects Charles John Innocent and Thomas Brown. Over a period of 30 years 39 Board schools were erected locally in English Domestic Gothic style faced in rugged local stone and with classrooms arranged around a central hall. In Nottingham a local Renaissance style gradually emerged in red brick whereas in Leeds Italianate and Gothic styles were preferred.

The Education Act of 1870, and its successor in 1902, provided real momentum not only to elementary education, but to the foundation of new voluntary educational institutions, such as Mechanics Institutes, Literary Societies and Reading Rooms, many of which offered lectures and evening classes for working men and women.

Between the 1880s and the Great War there was a huge enthusiasm for free public libraries. Any town worth its salt built its own, aided in no small part by Andrew Carnegie, a Scots philanthropist, who made a fortune in the United States, and who endowed 380 libraries across Britain.

Architecturally, public libraries rivalled the great Town Halls. They offered an opportunity to express civic pride in a medley of exuberant styles. In Liverpool, the magnificent Picton Reading Room by Cornelius Sherlock was added to the existing library in 1879 in the form of a huge classical rotunda. In Nottingham, the public library formed just one element of a much wider civic composition for the University College and museum, all executed in Ancaster stone in High Victorian Gothic style to the designs of the Bradford architects Lockwood and Mawson between 1877 and 1881.

This educational revolution demanded a massive increase in schoolteachers, which offered real opportunities for social advancement for self-educated working men as pupil-teachers, and also for gifted women. By 1888 women filled two-thirds of all teaching posts. By the end of the century alongside the major educational institutions were popular youth movements, which inculcated more muscular pursuits – the Boys' Brigade, the Church Lads' Brigade and, of course, the Boy Scouts, founded by Baden Powell in 1907. The Girl Guides followed a year later.

The universities too flourished. In 1900 just 20,000 students graduated from British universities, many from Scottish institutions, such as Edinburgh, Glasgow and St Andrews. Outside of Oxford and Cambridge, there was only a handful of universities in England, but between the late 19th century and the Great War various provincial institutions developed into civic universities. These placed a strong emphasis on the practical application of knowledge and on the scientific and technical skills demanded by industry, medicine and engineering.

Birmingham, which evolved from the Mason Science College and an earlier Medical School, achieved university status in 1900. Three years later it was followed by Liverpool and the Victoria University of Manchester. Leeds grew out of its earlier School of Medicine in 1904, Sheffield from its Medical School in 1905, and Bristol out of the existing University College in 1909. All boasted fine new buildings. The Victoria Building at the University of Liverpool, completed in High Victorian Gothic in 1892 to the designs of Alfred Waterhouse, was faced in hard red brick which became a lasting eponym for the new wave of provincial universities.

The thirst for education and self-improvement was aided by a revolution in communications and information. By the 1840s the railways had transformed the postal service and replaced the old network of mail

Above: Mason University College, Birmingham, established as a college of science by Josiah Mason in 1880, was intended to train graduates to serve local industry.

coaches. Rowland Hill's Penny Post had been established in 1840 and the first pillar boxes, advocated by the future novelist Anthony Trollope, were cast for use in St Helier, Jersey in 1853. An early fluted box can be seen in the photograph of Bridge Street, Chester. Pillar boxes soon became a distinctive feature of the English townscape stamping far-flung provincial communities with the badge of national sovereignty. A whole series of different designs emerged, including the famous hexagonal Penfold box, which was the standard issue from 1866 until 1879 before a reversion to cylindrical designs. By the 1870s city centres enjoyed up to six collections and deliveries a day.

The telegraph had existed in various forms since early in the century. After various refinements, it spread rapidly alongside the railway network, and later across the world by virtue of the trans-oceanic cable systems, of which two thirds were operated by British companies. Britain was connected to America in 1866, to India in 1870, to Australia by 1872 and across the Pacific by 1902. The international telegram soon became a common method of communication, and the national network of telegraph poles and wires a familiar part of the English landscape.

With the abolition of taxes on newspapers and improvements in technology, there was a massive growth in the circulation of newspapers and journals. In 1846 there had been just 14 newspapers. By 1890 there were over 180 including new national titles such as the *Daily Telegraph* and the *Standard* distributed nationally by the railways. As a result, London's daily papers reached Birmingham by 7.30 am, and York by 10am. In 1890 the *Daily Graphic* was the first to feature photographs on its pages followed in 1904 by the *Daily Mirror.*

By 1900, although the telephone was still regarded as something of a novelty, the first public telephone kiosks were appearing on the streets in a variety of novel guises. In 1926 Sir Giles Gilbert Scott designed the K2 kiosk, a national standard design modelled on the tomb of Sir John Soane, which soon became a familiar and cherished national icon. By 1930 there were almost one and a half million personal telephones in offices and households across the country providing instant communication nationwide. Once isolated communities could be informed instantly about news from the wider world; a process which only accelerated with the first live public radio broadcasts from the Marconi factory in Chelmsford in 1920 and the foundation of the BBC two years later.

Advances in education, rights for women and new opportunities for employment in schools and offices slowly transformed prospects for women. Their role in Victorian England was closely related to their class and circumstances, and the prevailing doctrine of 'separate spheres'.

Men and women had fundamentally different roles in society. This influenced everything from individual social and sexual behaviour to the layout of country houses where there were separate domains for men and women. Women were seen as fragile and dependent on, and subordinate to, men. Their role as 'the angel of the house' was to focus entirely on the home and children. For the accomplished, intelligent women whose households were run by servants, and whose husbands were absent, it was a suffocating and isolated existence. Their lives could be stultifyingly boring.

At the other end of the spectrum, for the poor 'submerged tenth' or unfortunate 'fallen' woman, the reality was far worse. In 1890 William Booth wrote: 'The bastard of a harlot, born in a brothel, suckled on gin, and familiar from earliest infancy with all the bestialities of debauch, violated before she is 12, and driven out on to the streets by her mother a year or two later, what chance is there for such a girl in this world...I say nothing of the next?...And with boys it is almost as bad'.[33] In London the girls of the Woolwich 'Dusthole' survived by trawling through the local refuse heap. William Booth was appalled at what he found there. 'The women living and following their dreadful business in this neighbourhood are so degraded that even abandoned men will refuse to accompany them home. Soldiers are forbidden to enter the place, or to go down the street, on pain of 25 days' imprisonment; pickets are stationed at either end to prevent this.'[34]

Under the Contagious Diseases Acts, in some ports and garrison towns women could be taken off the streets, subjected to forcible examination, brought before a magistrate and hospitalised if they were found to have venereal disease. In London alone in 1890 it was estimated that there were over 50,000 prostitutes on the streets from those plying the top end of the market in Hyde Park to the destitute poor seeking pennies to pay for a bed or a floor for the night in a doss house.

When a woman married everything she owned belonged to her husband. Anything she acquired during the marriage became his also, even if he deserted her. A husband could seek to have his conjugal rights enforced in the courts, or deny access to their children. Their inability to own property had crucial political repercussions as it debarred women from the vote, so the movement for rights for women was linked closely to the fight for women's suffrage.

Progress was slow. In 1870 the Married Women's Property Act allowed women to control any wages they earned. Twelve years later it was extended, and after a vigorous campaign the Contagious Diseases Acts were repealed in 1886. Women over 30 did not receive the vote until 1918, and they did not achieve electoral parity with men until 1928.

Usually upper class girls were educated at home by a governess, and then schooled into how to run a household before coming out for the London Season in their late teens in search of a suitable husband. For the middle classes, the obsession with respectability ensured that girls had a long controlled childhood before receiving education privately, or, from the 1850s, either at academic secondary schools, like Cheltenham College or North London Collegiate, or at day, or boarding schools.

Until the 1860s middle class women were expected to marry and not to work, but as the century progressed new opportunities opened up, particularly for those who remained single – initially as governesses, but with the spread of the telephone, and then the typewriter, as clerks in offices, retail assistants or as school teachers. By 1910 over 150,000 women were employed as female clerks from a mere 19 in 1851.

In 1907 Mrs Frank Stephens published helpful hints to girls about to marry in 'How to Manage a Home'. She advised that 'a hungry man should never be worried. If anything unpleasant has to be told him, it is best to wait until he has a good meal.' 'The unsatisfactory wife… always craving amusement, never satisfied' was duly admonished but, in a sign that times were changing, she pointed out with breath-taking condescension that 'it is now quite possible for a woman of ordinary intelligence to earn a comfortable livelihood for herself.'

By the early 20th century things had improved enormously. In 1908 Mario Borsa, an Italian visitor, was astonished to see 'shopgirls, milliners, dress makers, typists, stenographers, cashiers of large and small houses of business, telegraph and telephone girls…able to wander alone at night from one end of London to the other, spending all their money in gadding about, on sixpenny novels, on magazines, and above all on the theatre'. [35]

Working class women had very different expectations. Children usually started work within the household at six or seven. After the 1870 Education Act, this increased to 12 or 14, following which girls might enter a local workshop or factory, or take work as seamstresses, or perhaps in lace or dress making. In July 1888 the strike of 1400 match girls at the Bryant and May match factory at Bromley-by-Bow in London's East End was a landmark in the development of working women's rights. Toiling 14 hours a day and at severe risk of 'phossy jaw' from working with white phosphorus, their success was a major inspiration to other unskilled workers and boosted the rise of a new trade unionism.

However, by far the largest number of women entered domestic service. By the 1880s one third of all women between the ages of 15 and 21 were employed as servants; over 2 million in total.

***

By the last decade of the 19th century Britain's industrial and commercial pre-eminence were being challenged as other nations industrialised and modernised, particularly the United States, Germany and France. There was widespread concern that the country's industry was stagnating, but this should not be overstated. In the 1880s Britain still produced twice as much steel as Germany and three times more than France. It produced more pig iron than all the major European nations combined. Its output of coal was twice that of Germany and eight times greater than France.

Below: Women shred fruit at Frank Cooper's marmalade factory in Oxford, c1900.

One reason for the growing perception of stagnation was the export of capital overseas rather than its re-investment in new equipment and machinery in Britain's factories. Profitable opportunities in new and distant lands offered very appealing returns on investment. Only about a third of this went within the formal British Empire, particularly India. Much more went to Britain's wider informal commercial empire, and into building new infrastructure abroad, like railways in the United States, Argentina, Japan and Russia, which in turn offered the prospect of opening up rich new markets.

And it was not just capital that flowed abroad. Between 1881 and 1890 over 3.2 million people emigrated from Britain and Ireland, a staggering 9.3 per cent of the population. Over 12 per cent went to Australia and New Zealand, just over 10 per cent to Canada, and 70 per cent to the United States. In the first ten years of the new century, a further 1.5 million Britons emigrated, more than half within the Empire – mostly to Canada, Australia, New Zealand, and the newly pacified South Africa. This diaspora of English speaking people and capital may have sown the seeds of global power and influence, but it also weakened the pool of domestic labour and disposable capital.

In 1897 when Queen Victoria celebrated her Diamond Jubilee, Britain's wealth and power seemed unassailable. Its huge naval dockyards at Portsmouth, Chatham and Plymouth lay at the heart of a vast military-industrial complex, which spanned the globe. A ring of massive Palmerston forts had been built in the 1860s to protect Portsmouth from potential cross-Channel attack by the French. Woolwich Arsenal, the Royal Small Arms factory at Enfield, Armstrong's factories in Elswick and Vickers in Sheffield all produced a formidable array of advanced weaponry to enforce the Pax Britannica.

At the huge naval review at Spithead on 26 June 1897, the Royal Navy displayed a formidable array of 21 battleships and over 50 cruisers supported by dozens and dozens of gunboats and destroyers in lines seven miles long. Not one was taken from service on foreign stations. It was the largest assembly of naval power in the world's history. The British fleet was greater than the combined strength of all the other great powers. Just over three years later, on 2 February 1901, at the funeral of Queen Victoria troops from across the Empire, as well as most of the crowned heads of Europe marched through the streets of London to pay homage to the dead Queen. It was the symbolic end of an era.

Both events bore eloquent testimony to Britain's imperial might, but for much of the 19th century the colonies were seen as an encumbrance. Disraeli spoke of 'these wretched colonies' and referred to them as a 'millstone round our necks.' They required expensive garrisons and guard ships for no great economic advantage for the heavy outlay involved.

The Empire was an agglomeration of overseas territories acquired at different points in time for a whole variety of different reasons, in what Lord Acton has described as 'a fit of absence of mind.' By the 1880s large areas of the Empire already enjoyed responsible self-government including Canada, Newfoundland, New Zealand, the Australian colonies and Cape Colony. Many thought Ireland would follow.

However, from 1870 perspectives began to change as European powers jostled for their own overseas colonies sparking an international rivalry that triggered the scramble for Africa, and the acquisition of yet more distant new lands and commitments from Fiji and New Guinea to East Africa and Nigeria. Trade did not follow the flag, but the flag could create the peace and stability conducive to free and fair trade for all

One of the great achievements of Victorian England was the spread of English-speaking peoples, institutions, law and culture throughout the world. That this occurred was due to the astounding levels of wealth Britain accumulated through its industrial and commercial supremacy during the period in which the photographs in this book were taken.

It was to stand the country in good stead for the challenges of the 20th century. In spite of all the tensions at home and competition from abroad, Britain remained a global colossus. In 1939 London was the largest city in the world. It was its largest port handling twice the tonnage of Liverpool in its heyday. It financed half the world's trade, while the volume of its manufacturing output exceeded that of any of the industrial cities of the North and Midlands. The capital lay at the heart of the largest Empire the world had ever seen.

Together with its Empire and Commonwealth, Britain was the only great power to fight two world wars from beginning to end and emerge on the winning side. One hundred years after the Great War, its economy is the fifth largest in the world and its people enjoy unparalleled levels of prosperity.

The concept of a Golden Age, and of a Lost England, is a fanciful, but perpetually beguiling chimera refracted through a prism of nostalgia for a world which never existed, except in some nostalgic country of the heart. Victorian and Edwardian England was as beset with its own social tensions and economic problems as any other period in history, but the energy, self-confidence, suffering and sacrifice of its people laid the foundations for the freedoms and prosperity we enjoy today.

'The past is a foreign country; they do things differently there,' [36] wrote the novelist L P Hartley in 1953. For many who look at the photographs in this book, they are looking at a world their parents, or grandparents knew. A great deal does not look that foreign or different. Much seems tantalisingly familiar, but equally there is much that is poignantly remote. Today we are infinitely better off than our forefathers with levels of prosperity, health, opportunity and life expectancy, which they could never have imagined.

The photographs in this book offer a unique window on the past. They help us to understand the world they record. Embrace the past with remembrance, but the future with optimism. Look back, but don't stare.

Philip Davies

BON MARCHÉ
BON MARCHÉ
BON MARCHE
THE AVONDALE
CAFÉ RESTAURANT
THE AVONDALE
LADIES' & GENTLEMENS
DINING ROOMS
THE AVONDALE
CAFÉ RESTAURANT
LIVERPOOL CLERKS' CAFÉ C° L^{TD}
THE AVONDALE
CAFÉ RESTAURANT
LUNCHEON & DINING ROOMS

LOST ENGLAND
1870-1930

Southport Pier, c1900

NORTH WEST

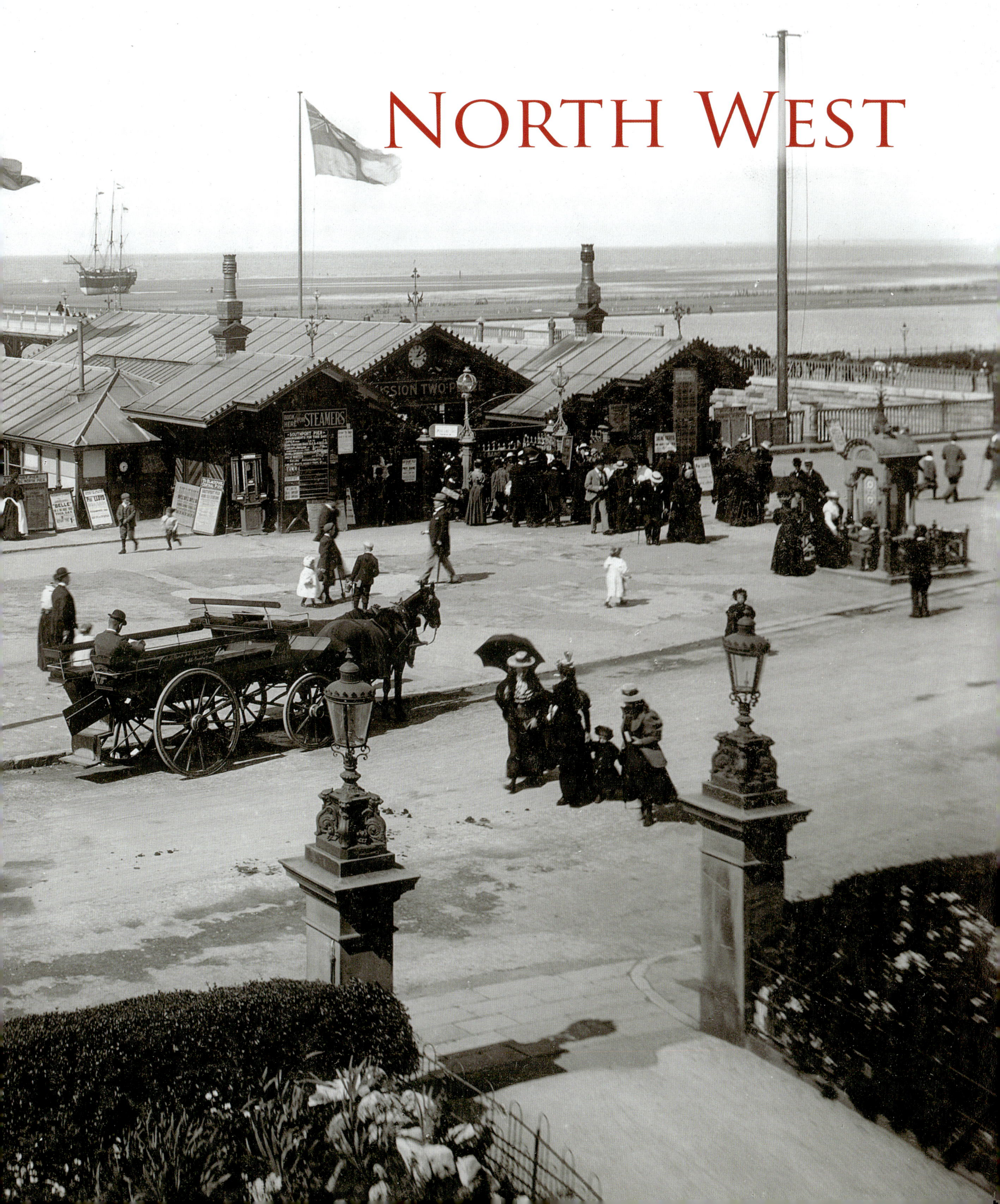

THE CROSS

Opposite top right: The Cross, Chester, 1895
View from the Cross, looking south-east towards the corner of Eastgate and Bridge Street. The Cross takes its name from the High Cross, an historic monument that stood on this spot until 1646, when it was destroyed with Protestant fervour during the Civil War. The finely carved sandstone cross was laden with mediaeval significance, and was a site of proclamation as well as the dispensing of justice; to emphasise the ceremonial importance, the top part was gilded in 1603. The Cross was returned to its current location when parts of the city were pedestrianised in 1986.

Opposite below: 6 Lower Bridge Street, 1887
View south-west towards the Falcon Inn and neighbouring buildings. The Falcon was the town house of Sir Richard Grosvenor during the Civil War and licensed as an inn in the 18th century before its life as a temperance hotel and 'Cocoa House' around 1879.

Opposite top left: 45–49 Bridge Street, c1890
This group of three buildings includes two four-storey jettied houses with shop premises at street level; 51–55 Bridge Street Row are at first-storey level. The Rows of Chester are essentially upper-storey streets running as galleries above ground level. The timbered buildings' ancient character is not always what it appears to be: many were rebuilt in the Victorian period – including these, in 1891.

Cheshire

CHESTER

Top: Watergate Street, c1890
View westwards towards what looks like a bridge but is actually the Watergate. The red sandstone ashlar structure replaced the mediaeval gate around 1790 and was designed by Joseph Turner for the City Council to keep the continuity of the City Walls. Chester remains one of the best-preserved walled cities in Britain. Apart from a short section around County Hall, the walls are complete – a circuit of almost two miles.

Above: Eastgate, 1887
View eastwards towards the grand colonnaded front of the Grosvenor Hotel, with the Eastgate on the left. The intricately wrought clock mounted on the Eastgate today was conceived as a homage to Queen Victoria and was unveiled, to mixed reactions, on her 80th birthday in May 1899.

A. JONES

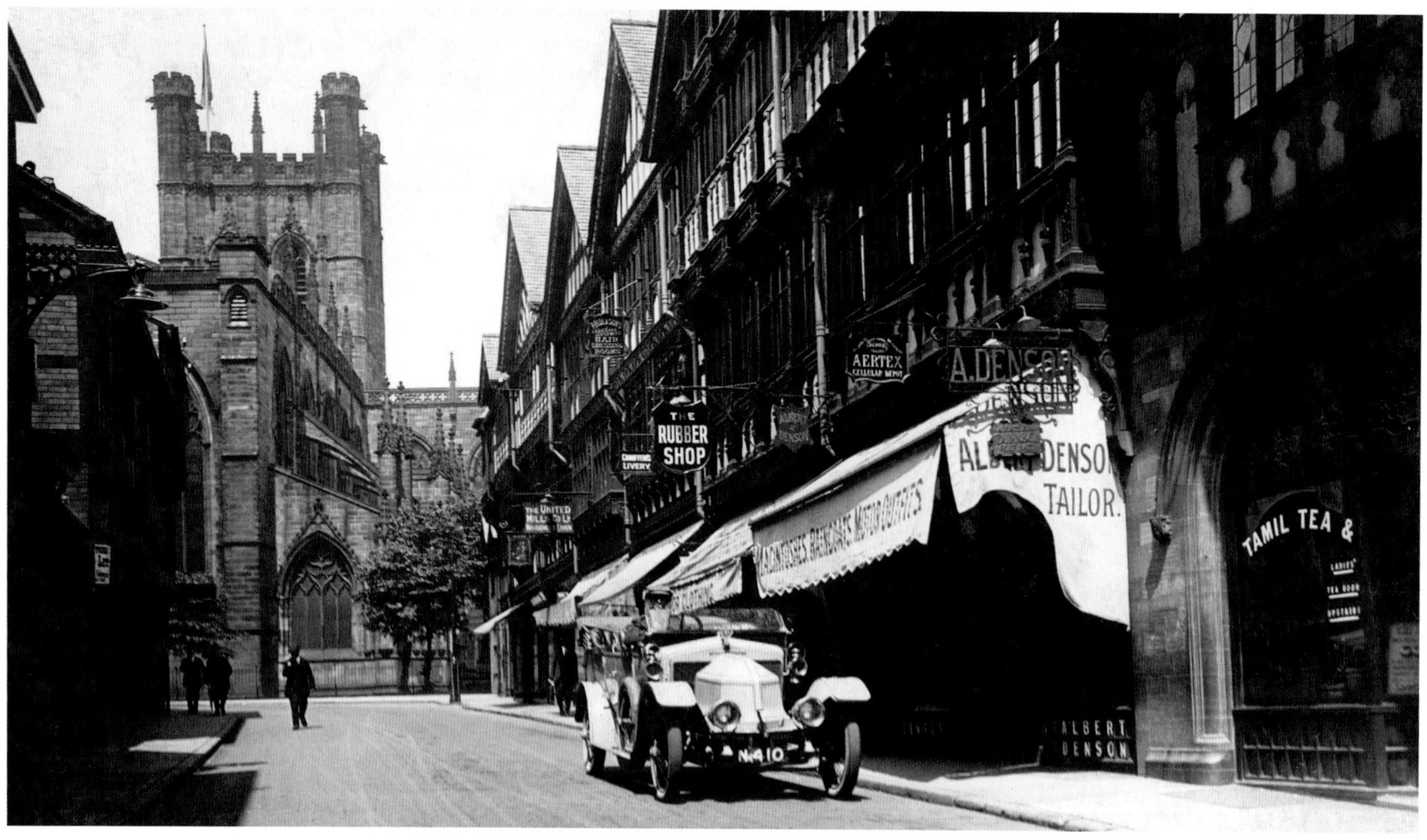

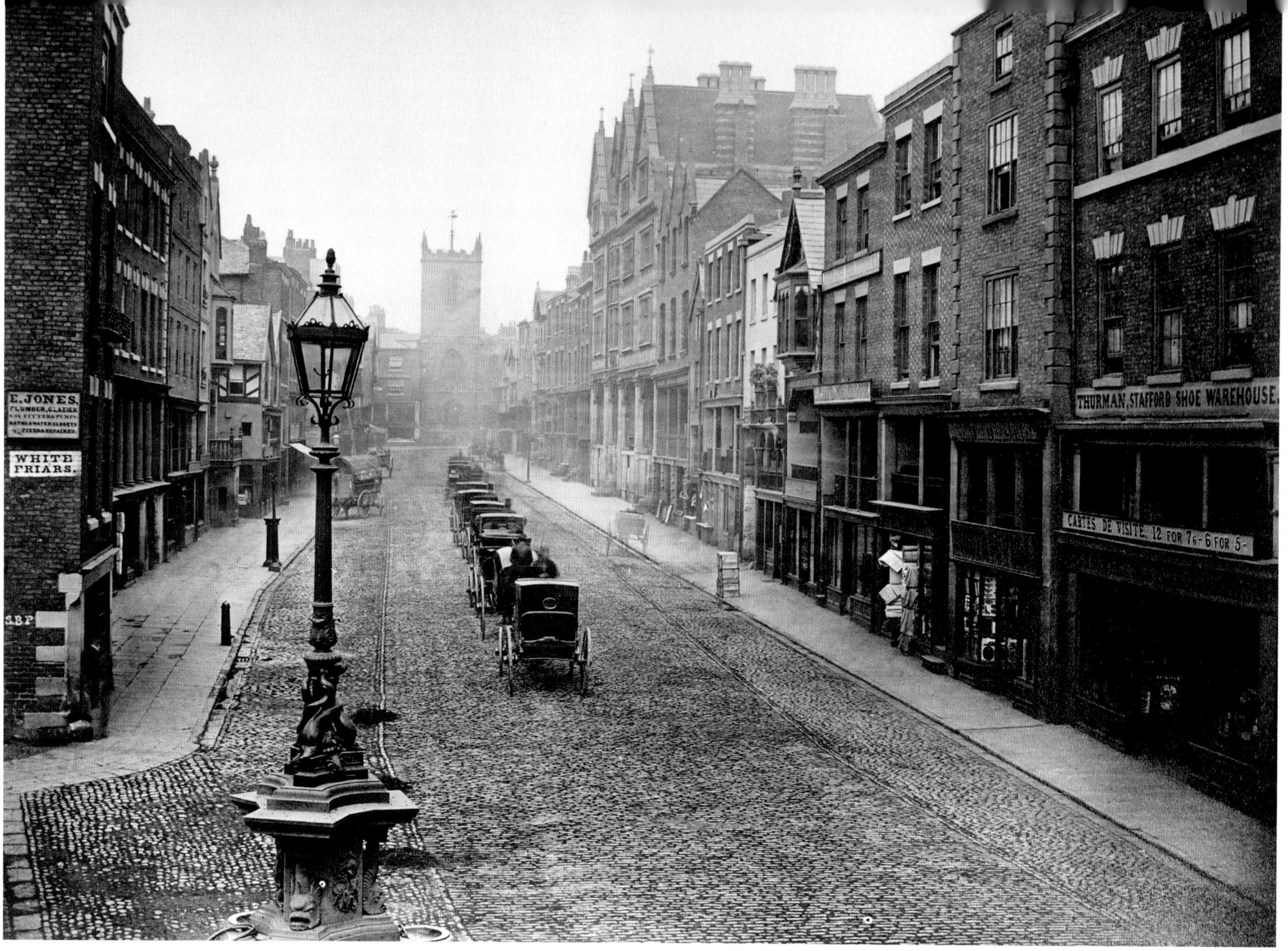
E. JONES,
WHITE FRIARS.
THURMAN, STAFFORD SHOE WAREHOUSE.
CARTES DE VISITE

THE RUBBER SHOP
AERTEX CELLULAR DEPOT
A. DENSON
ALBERT DENSON TAILOR.
TAMIL TEA &
ALBERT DENSON

BRIDGE STREET, CHESTER

Opposite above: Bridge Street, c1860
Atmospheric view north towards St Peter's Church at the junction with Eastgate and Watergate. Hansom cabs line up in the street. To the left is a fluted Doric pillar box cast by Smith and Hawkes. In the foreground is a splendid cast iron lamp column enriched with dolphins and grotesque fish around the base, which incorporates drinking bowls for animals. A variety of businesses offer their wares from furniture to shoes, and one sharp seller advertises Cartes de Visite – 12 for 7s 6d or 6 for 5/-!

Opposite below: St Werburgh Street, c1912
Looking north-west towards the gable of the unusually large south transept of Chester Cathedral. St Werburgh, an Anglo-Saxon princess and a nun for most of her life, is the patron saint of Chester. A shrine containing her remains was created in the Cathedral in the 10th century and attracted pilgrims from afar. In this picture the man in the Siddeley Deasy Torpedo parked in front of Albert Denson Tailors is almost certainly not a pilgrim – his state-of-the-art automobile is a product of the Coventry company that would become Armstrong Siddeley.

Above: The Falcon Inn Lower Bridge Street, 1900

Right: 10-12 Bridge Street, 1887
The timbered building carrying the legend 'Ye Olde Crypt' is known as Cowper House, after Thomas Cowper who built it in 1664. In 1839 excavations for a warehouse revealed a large mediaeval vaulted crypt which was unknown to the owners of Cowper House. The remarkable discovery caused a great stir in the city.

WIDNES

Top left: West Bank Viaduct, Widnes, c1920
The bridge over the Mersey between Widnes and Runcorn cut nine miles off the journey between Liverpool and London. The approach to this was a 59-arch viaduct that cut through Widnes and is the town's most prominent industrial landmark.

Above: Concrete Seacraft Company, Fiddler's Ferry, Penketh, 1918
View over the shipyard towards the River Mersey. Improvements in the technology of reinforced concrete led to its use in marine construction. Concrete Seacraft was founded in January 1918, with the first vessel rolling off the slipway in 1919.

Top right: Widnes's first motor bus, Farnworth Street, c1911

Opposite: Crewe Locomotive Works, Forge Street, Crewe, 1910
Fitting the buffers to a steam locomotive engine on the production line. The Grand Junction Railway set up its works at Crewe in the 1830s, which led to a large influx of railway industry workers and made the town a nexus for the rail network from London through the Midlands and the north-west. By 1870 the population had swollen to 40,000.

Merseyside

Liverpool

Pierhead, Liverpool, c1900

The Birkenhead Woodside Passenger Ferry awaits its next sailing in late afternoon. By the 19th century, the ferries were well-established as part of the everyday life of the city and its workers. Until the railway tunnel was opened in 1886, it was also the only way of crossing the river; despite the tunnel, the ferries continued to thrive and by the 1890s were carrying over 40,000 passengers a day. It was only after the road tunnel was constructed in 1934 that the numbers started to decline. Today, the ferries still run a commuter service, but there is also a focus on the tourist and visitor trade.

ELECTRIC RAILWA
FREQUENT SERVICE OF FAST TRAINS
TO SEAFORTH WATERLO
CROSBY
TO DINGLE AIGBURTH
HE PARKS.

WHITE STAR LINE

Right: White Star Line Offices, 30 James Street, Liverpool, 1898
The shipping company Ismay, Imrie & Company (clients for this photograph, and later owners of the ill-fated *Titanic*) commissioned Richard Norman Shaw, in collaboration with the Liverpool architect J Francis Doyle, to design their office block in James Street. The building is based on Shaw's earlier design for Scotland Yard in London.

Opposite: Pierhead, Liverpool, c1900
Two views looking towards Our Lady and St Nicholas Church to the left, and the Tower Buildings to the right. The top photograph shows a view across George's Dock. In both pictures the overhead railway runs alongside the quay. This was the world's first electric elevated urban railway and ran 13 miles from Dingle in the south to Seaforth in the north. In the bottom picture horse-drawn carriages and electric trams offer two other transport options for travellers using the liner and ferry terminal. The church tower was built between 1811 and 1815 by Thomas Harrison of Chester. The Tower Buildings also have a long history: the structure seen here, designed by architect James Picton in 1856, replaced a number of earlier buildings, which in turn had served as a fortifed residence, port buildings and a jail. The Tower also housed the semaphore signalling apparatus that received details of ships on their way past Holyhead to Liverpool. Picton's building was demolished early in the 20th century for the widening of Water Street and to make way for striking new riverside buildings.

Right: Water Street, Liverpool, 1895
Looking east towards the Town Hall in the murky distance. The Goree warehouses, named after a slave embarkation island off the coast of Senegal, are to the right at the crossing, and Prison Weint is to the left. Offices for the shipping and insurance companies predominate.

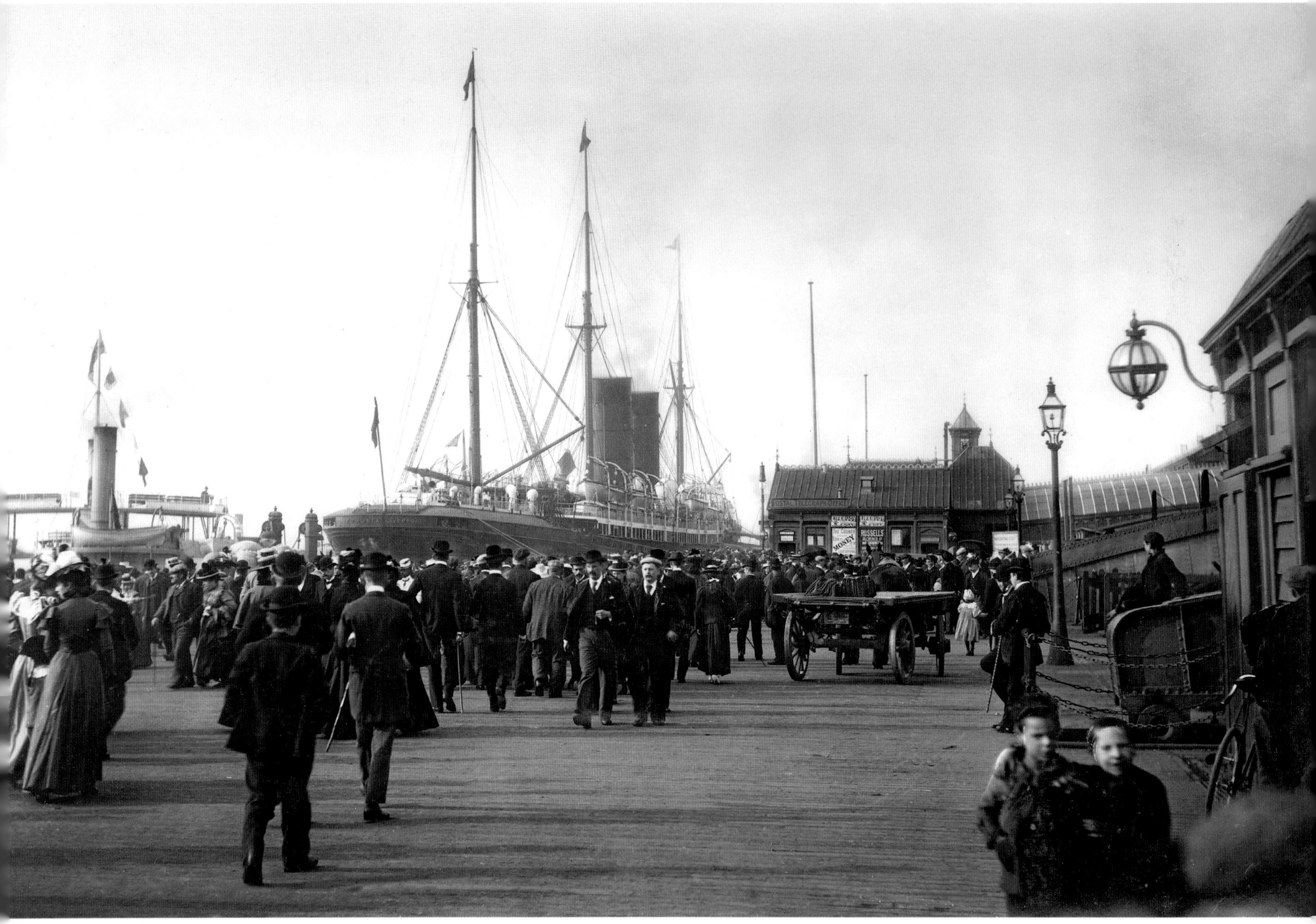

PIERHEAD, LIVERPOOL

Opposite above: Pierhead, c1900
Looking north towards the berthed SS *Etruria*. The quayside is crowded with afternoon promenaders. This vessel was the pride of Cunard when launched in 1885 to take passengers between Liverpool and New York. It was also equipped with sails, which explains the large steel masts. The young Winston Churchill sailed across the Atlantic in her in 1895.

Opposite below left: Pierhead looking south, c1900
The paddle steamer *Sapphire* is steamed up and taking on passengers from the floating landing stage, which overcame the problem of the shallow depth of the shoreline for larger steamships and liners. Temporary barriers separate the day trippers from the crowds visiting the larger ship alongside. The PS *Sapphire* was one of a trio of boats operated by New Liverpool Eastham Ferry & Hotel Co Ltd, commissioned around 1900 to take visitors to the pleasure gardens at Eastham.

Opposite below right: Duke's Grain Warehouse, Duke's Dock, 1956
Duke's Dock was built in 1773 by the Duke of Bridgewater for the trans-shipment of cargo carried on the Bridgewater Canal. Two barge holes in the base of the warehouse, one now partly blocked by a mezzanine, provided covered wharfage.

Above: London & North Western Hotel, c1900
View across Lime Street from St George's Hall. The hotel dates from 1871 and was designed by Alfred Waterhouse for the London North Western Railway in a French Renaissance style. The hotel is now a student hall of residence.

ROYAL LIVER BUILDING

Above: George's Pierhead, 1920
This aerial view shows 'The Three Graces' – the Royal Liver Building, the Cunard Building and the Port of Liverpool Building – which combine to create the city's distinctive waterfront. Built on the site of the former Tower Buildings and the George's Dock, which was closed in 1900 and filled in, the landmark edifices were completed in 1911, 1916 and 1907 respectively. This photograph also shows a floating landing stage connected to the main quay that includes covered gangways for passengers as well as a roadway for vehicles.

Opposite: The Royal Liver Building, 1912
Designed by architect Walter Aubrey Thomas and one of the first buildings to be constructed using reinforced concrete, the Liver Building is crowned by two clock towers, the nearest to the Pierhead with three faces, enabling passing vessels to synchronise their chronometers. Each tower is topped with the sculpture of a liver bird, the cormorant-like creature that is a symbol of the city. Built to house the offices of the Royal Liver Assurance Company, which employed 6,000 staff, it is an internationally recognised icon for the city.

Left: The elegant semi-circular portico at the main entrance to the Royal Liver Building, photographed in 1912.

CASTLE STREET

Above: St George's Crescent and Castle Street, Liverpool, c1900
View from Derby Square looking towards the Town Hall. Castle Street was widened in 1786, opening up the vista to the Town Hall. St George's Crescent was built around 1830. Penlington & Batty, located at No. 23, were high-quality watch and clockmakers and one of the select few suppliers of chronometers to the Admiralty. The frontage claims that they were established in 1819, and Batty continued under his own name after Penlington died. Virtually everything in this photograph except the Town Hall was obliterated in the Blitz of May 1941.

Left: Church Street, Liverpool, c1900
View looking east to the corner with Whitechapel. On the left is Bunney's General Store, advertising Oriental Goods and Novelties and with a fine display of household items in its large windows.

PARR'S BANK

Above left: Parr's Bank, Great Charlotte Street, Liverpool, 1904
Parr's was one of the north-west's leading banks, with head offices in Castle Street, Liverpool. The building shown here, designed by Liverpool-based architects Woolfall and Eccles, was demolished and part of the Clayton Square shopping centre now occupies the site.

Right: Parr's Bank, 20–26 Castle Street, Liverpool, 1901
An interior view of the banking hall at the headquarters of Parr's Bank, showing the glazed dome.

Above right: Adelphi Bank, 38 Castle Street, Liverpool, 1893
The banking hall, with the counter and its intricately worked metal screen. The walls are panelled with highly patterned marble. The architect, William Douglas Caröe (1857–1938), designed it to impress outside and in. Thomas Stirling Lee's ornate bronze doors, depicting icons of male friendship, would have looked at home on a Florentine church or palazzo.

LORD STREET, LIVERPOOL

Above: Lord Street, c1900

View west taken from Church Street at the junction with Whitechapel. To the left is the Don Men's Clothing Store, with its competitor Hope Brothers, which established its business in this location in 1887, to the right. A few buildings down is the triple-arched frontage of the Arcade.

Lord Street was a busy thoroughfare for trams – initially horse-drawn, but by 1901 the city ran all its trams on electricity. The obvious consequences were increased numbers of people coming into the city from the outskirts and a reduction in horse-drawn traffic, reducing the need for livery businesses and street cleaning.

THE ARCADE

Above and left: The Arcade, 81–89 Lord Street, Liverpool, 1901
The Arcade was designed by the Liverpool-born architect Walter Aubrey Thomas, who was also responsible for the Royal Liver Building. The Arcade opened in 1901, with a frontage of polychrome terracotta. Although Lord Street suffered damage in the Blitz, the worst occurred on the opposite side of the road and the Arcade has survived to the present day.

The interior (left) showing ground-floor shops viewed from the gallery, with the Lord Street entrance in the distance.

Above: Lord Street, Liverpool, c1890
Looking east from Derby Square to the crossroads at Whitechapel, visible in the far distance. Horse-drawn omnibuses ply the street; the lack of overhead power lines indicates that this is the transitional period, when horse-drawn buses and trams operated side by side. In the centre of the street cabs wait for fares. Interestingly, an aerial ladder on wheels is in the foreground; very tall ladders were used for window cleaning at the time, but this is more likely to be a static fire-fighting apparatus.

Left: David Lewis Northern Hospital, Great Howard Street, Liverpool, 1901
The entrance gates, courtyard and entrance block, as seen from Great Howard Street to its west. Designed by Edward Welch, who in an earlier partnership with Joseph Hansom designed Birmingham Town Hall, the hospital was built on the old Pig Market, replacing an earlier hospital that was swamped as mass immigration swelled the city's population – many fleeing the poverty and famine in Ireland. David Lewis, whose department store became the biggest in Liverpool, died in 1885, but a generous bequest meant that his philanthropic work continued into the new century.

Opposite: Corner of Richmond Row and Byram Street, Liverpool, c1895
A group of street urchins working as shoe-blackers. The street drinking fountain is strategically sited opposite the Morning Star public house to offer an alternative to alcohol. Two of the boys have no shoes, a sign of abject poverty.

Above: 53–63 Church Street, Liverpool, 1891
View of the Bon Marché shop that took its name from the grand Parisian store. With no frontage at street level other than the arcade entrance, Richardsons Clothing Store, Avondale Cafe Restaurant and the renowned tobacconist Henry Durandu occupy the ground floor. The architect of the building was Henry Shelmerdine. This photograph was one of many taken for the Leeds terracotta and faience manufacturer Burmantofts Company, whose work was liberally used in the exterior.

Left: Waterloo Hotel, Clayton Square, Liverpool, 1888
View across the Square to show the hotel frontage bearing the landlord's name, Robert Rimmer, who is listed in the May 1890 *Gazette* as being in receivership. The adjacent Prince of Wales Theatre looks redundant, so it appears that Clayton Square was going through difficult times. The whole area was demolished to make way for a modern shopping mall bearing the same name that opened in 1989.

LIME STREET, LIVERPOOL

Above: The Picture House, 65–67 Lime Street, 1912

Passers-by look at the billboards advertising silent films, including *The Relief of Lucknow*, made by the Edison company in 1912 to mark the 55th anniversary of the Indian Uprising. E A Owen's shopfront next door displays its wares, including books, stationery and leather goods.

EDGE HILL CUTTINGS

Above: Widening a tunnel at Edge Hill, Liverpool, c1882

The picture shows workers rebuilding the tunnel through the Edge Hill cuttings on the approach to the London and North Western Railway's (LNWR) Liverpool Lime Street station. Bricklayers and masons construct the tunnel arch supported on timber scaffolding, and hand-cranked cranes are being used to lift mortar and heavy blocks. The original tunnel can be seen to the left with an engine operating. The tunnel was widened and new track laid in 1884-85, to cope with increasing traffic. Two supervising engineers in suits stand on the rock dividing the previous twin-bore tunnel.

LIME STREET STATION

Above: Lime Street, Liverpool, c1890
Looking north up Lime Street towards the Wellington Monument and Walker Art Gallery on William Brown Street. St George's Hall is on the left of the picture, facing the the elegant elevations of the London and North West Railway Hotel. Horse-drawn trams and a hansom cab wait for passengers.

Right: A slightly different viewpoint showing more clearly the curved roofs of the north and south engine sheds. The southern vault, completed in 1874, was constructed in tandem with the LNWR Hotel to meet increased passenger traffic. The scale of the 1870s developments shows both the pride of the Victorian station builders and their confidence that large numbers of people would arrive by train and require first-class accommodation.

ADELPHI HOTEL, LIVERPOOL

Left: Ranelagh Street, 1911

Looking towards Copperas Hill and the Adelphi Hotel at the end of the street. The original Lewis's Department store shown here was destroyed by enemy bombs during the Second World War and was subsequently rebuilt on the same site but in a different style. David Lewis, the founder of the store, created a retail chain with large branches in Manchester, Birmingham and Sheffield. Central Station (entrance to the right), which opened in 1874 and was originally a large rail terminus at the end of the Cheshire Lines Committee (CLC) line to Manchester Central, was demolished in 1973.

Below: Second Adelphi Hotel, 1896

Liverpool's first Adelphi Hotel was built in 1826 on the site of Ranelagh Gardens. The second Adelphi, pictured here, was constructed in 1876, a short distance from Central Station. The hotel, with its French chateau-influenced exterior, was an imposing sight beckoning travellers into its sumptuous accommodation. It was renowned for its turtle soup!

Top left: Adelphi Hotel, 1911
The Midland Railway employed local Liverpool architect Robert Frank Atkinson to design the third Adelphi Hotel on the site in 1911. Atkinson used the latest building technology, and the picture shows the complex steel frame that supported the facing of Portland stone.

Above left: The opulent Hypostyle Hall in the Midland Adelphi Hotel, 1912

Top right: Midland Adelphi Hotel, Ranelagh Place, 1912
The east entrance of the Hotel on what is now Brownlow Hill, before the construction of the main front building.

Above right: The much plainer stripped classical frontage of the new hotel in 1914. The exterior of the building is little changed today.

NELSON MONUMENT

Above: Nelson Monument, Exchange Flags, Liverpool, c1900
View of the heroic 25-foot-high monument to Lord Nelson sited behind the Town Hall. The four figures around the base of the column, which was erected in 1813, represent his victories at St Vincent, the Nile, Copenhagen and Trafalgar. Nelson is shown with Victory and Death. In the background is the facade of the Exchange Buildings, designed by Thomas Henry Wyatt and completed in 1867. Built in French Renaissance style, they contained 250 public and private offices as well as a newsroom and stock exchange, all most lavishly embellished. As many as 4,000 merchants frequented the rooms and facilities daily. Wyatt's Exchange buildings were demolished in the 1930s, but their replacement was not completed until well after the Second World War.

COTTON EXCHANGE, LIVERPOOL

Opposite below right: Cotton Exchange, Old Hall Street, 1907
View of the original south-west facade of the building which was constructed by the Waring-White Building Company in 1906 to the designs of the architectural firm Matear and Simon. This impressive facade, predominently classical in design with Baroque corner towers, was demolished in 1967 and a new frontage added.

Opposite below left: Lyceum Club, Bold Street, c1920
Built in 1802 to house a subscription library which reportedly had a collection of over 10,000 titles in 1807, the grandly designed members' club also had a newsroom where daily London papers could be perused and reference maps consulted.

LIVERPOOL TOWN HALL

Right: Town Hall, Water Street, c1920
Situated at the junction of Water Street, Dale Street and Castle Street, the Town Hall was constructed around 1750 and designed by architect John Wood the Elder, renowned for his elegant work in Bath. When first built the ground-floor courtyard was intended as an exchange, but the gloomy surroundings drove the merchants outside to the square. The Town Hall remains one of the city's great landmarks.

WILLIAM BROWN
STREET
GRAND CONCERT

PICTON READING ROOM

Picton Reading Room, William Brown Street, Liverpool, 1895
William Brown Street gained its name from the MP and civic benefactor who granted the land and the funds to build Liverpool's first public library. The town council was the driving force, but it was individuals that funded these great public institutions. The Picton Reading Room was built adjacent to the William Brown Library and Museum, becoming part of Liverpool's Public Library, Museum and Art Gallery. Sir James Picton, Chairman of the William Brown Library, laid the foundation stone in 1875 and the building was opened in 1879. Architect Cornelius Sherlock emulated the Reading Room of the British Museum and added electric light for good measure: it was the first library in Great Britain to be lit by electricity.

LIVERPOOL BLUE COAT SCHOOL

Top left and right: The Blue Coat School, Church Road, 1906
The original Liverpool Blue Coat Hospital and School was founded in 1708 as a place where poor children could be accommodated and tutored. In 1899 the trustees took the decision to commission a new school building in Wavertree, which was then in the countryside. The designs were the work of the architectural practice of Frank Gatley Briggs, Harry Vernon Wolstenholme, Frederick Brice Hobbs and (Sir) Arnold Thornely. The pictures show (left) the Alfred Road frontage and (right) the girls' wing.

Middle left: The Blue Coat School dining room

Above right: William Brown Street, c1900
View west, with the Picton Reading Room of Liverpool Central Library far right and behind it (centre) the William Brown Library and Museum (now the World Museum).

Left: London City & Midland Bank, 23 Allerton Road, Mossley Hill, 1911
This early 20th-century bank was designed by architects Woolfall & Eccles in the Neoclassical style. The bank later became a branch of Midland Bank and, later still, HSBC.

CARRS' WAREHOUSE

Above left & right: Carrs' Warehouse, Midland Railway Goods Depot, Liverpool, 1927
Jonathan Carr began his bakery business in Carlisle in the 1830s, vertically integrating flour mills and the bread and biscuit lines. The business grew rapidly, achieving a Royal Warrant in 1841. Although his biscuit range was wide, as the photograph (above left) shows, the company was originally built on selling water biscuits that, like ship's biscuits, used water rather than fat to blend the ingredients, ensuring a long shelf life on distant voyages. Packing in tins as well as airtight cartons also helped. Carrs showed good brand management in their decorative packaging.
The LMS Goods Depot pictured was built at what is now the junction of Victoria Street and Crosshall Street for the storage and distribution of rail freight; it allowed railway wagons to be loaded and unloaded to and from road vehicles. These two photographs show how the road distribution side operated, with the stock in the warehouse (left) and the delivery vans being loaded through the bay (right). The building still exists as the National Conservation Centre.

GOREE PIAZZA

Top left: Goree Piazza, Liverpool, 1919
View northwards, with the White Star Line building to the right and the Royal Liver Building to the left. At the centre of the picture is Bent's Depot, the Liverpool brewers founded in 1821, which acquired the Thomas Montgomery Brewery of Stone in Staffordshire in 1889. The roadway is a hive of activity, with mainly horse-drawn traffic, but a few motorised vehicles are also on their way to and from the wharves. The warehouse complex, built at the end of the 18th century, took the name 'Goree' from the island off the coast of Senegal, today part of Dakar. Goree was an embarkation point for the Atlantic slave trade – a major contributor to the growth of Liverpool's maritime wealth.

Top right: Cunard Engine Works, Derby Road, Kirkdale, 1917
The exterior of the Cunard Engine Works, with a steam-powered traction engine pulling gun carriages along the cobbled road. Cunard had a number of engineering sites around Merseyside engaged in making engines, armaments and munitions for the First World War.

LOAD NOT TO
EXCEED 3 TONS
C.642.

BIRKENHEAD

Cammell Laird, Birkenhead, 1913
Cammell Laird, one of the most famous names in the history of British shipbuilding, was formed by the merger of Scottish entrepreneur William Laird's company – Laird, Son & Company of Birkenhead – and Cammell & Company of Sheffield at the turn of the 20th century. It supported the Allies' war effort by producing almost 200 commercial and military vessels during the Second World War, as well as playing a key role in the First World War.

Left: The battleship HMS *Audacious* being fitted out in a graving dock. The ship was a King George V-class battleship of the Royal Navy; her service was cut short when she was sunk by a German naval mine off the County Donegal coast in October 1914.

Opposite: A bay in the engine shop.

Above: Cunard Shell Works, Rimrose Road, Bootle, 1917
The interior of one of the shell workshops, showing women finishing heavy shell casings on large belt-driven lathes. During the First World War many factories were converted to making munitions and equipment for the war effort. In 1915 Cunard's store and engineering works in Bootle was adapted in this way. Four-and-a-half-, six- and eight-inch shells were brought to the works to be finished, checked and varnished before being taken to another factory in the area to be filled with explosive.

BOOTLE

Above: Derby Park, Oxford Road, Bootle, c1900
View across Derby Park, with the houses on Earl Road in the distance. Set out on land donated to Bootle Council by Lord Derby in 1891, it covered an area of nine hectares and was designed by the borough surveyor in 1893. It opened to the public in 1895 and remains an important amenity today.

Left: Pilkington Special Hospital, Borough Road, St Helens, 1918
Men in the carpentry workshop. The Pilkington Special Hospital was set up by James R Kerr and Pilkington Brothers, glass manufacturers, whose plant was in St Helens. The hospital was established in 1916 for the treatment and rehabilitation of servicemen wounded or disabled during the First World War.

BEBINGTON

Above: Eastham Ferry Hotel, Ferry Road, Eastham Ferry, Bebington, 1897
View of the celebration arch built at the pleasure gardens of the Eastham Ferry Hotel to commemorate the Diamond Jubilee of Queen Victoria. The gardens were a popular destination for day trippers from Liverpool.

Above right: Town Hall, Oriel Road, Bootle, 1902
The imposing Town Hall was built in 1882 to the designs of architect J Johnson.

Right: Bidston Court, Vyner Road, Bidston, Birkenhead, 1894
A horse-drawn coach stands outside the entrance to Bidston Court. The house was built in 1891 to the designs of architect E L Ould for Robert William Hudson, soap manufacturer. It was subsequently dismantled and moved to Royden Park, near Frankby, where in 1931 it was rebuilt and renamed Hill Bark. It is now a hotel.

WIRRAL

Top: Egremont Promenade, Wallasey, c1900
Children are intrigued by the photographer, while promenaders stroll along the front towards the resort of New Brighton. The New Brighton Tower is in the background.

Above: Children's Boating Lake, New Brighton, 1933
The boating lake was just one of the attractions in the 1930s. New Brighton also boasted a newly refurbished pier and an outdoor swimming pool that could accommodate 2,000 bathers.

NEW BRIGHTON

Above: Perch Rock Lighthouse, c1885
View from the pier, looking across the Mersey towards Bootle. The lighthouse sits next to the Perch Rock fort. The first light was fixed to a simple wooden 'perch', or large post, put up in 1683, but the foundation stone of the new lighthouse was not laid until 1827. Designed on the lines of Eddystone, the lighthouse was built of marble rock from Anglesey. Work was only possible at low tide, and the lighthouse was not completed until 1830. It was decommissioned in 1973.

Opposite below right: New Brighton Tower, c1900
The Tower was designed by the company that devised the Blackpool Tower and Southport Winter Gardens; it outdid Blackpool in height with its summit at 621 feet above sea level, making it the tallest building in the land. Open for business from 1898, it stood within the Tower Buildings complex which included many tourist facilities. Losing popularity during World War I it was dismantled and scrapped by the end of 1921. Many of the buildings were demolished but the Ballroom remained an important entertainment venue until fire destroyed it in 1969.

PORT SUNLIGHT

As the Industrial Revolution took hold, so did the growth in the factory system and the population needed to provide the labour. Living conditions for these workers were unhealthy and wretched and left a deepening impression on William Lever whose expanding soap manufacturing business gave him the opportunity to not only build his own factory, but also decent housing for his workers. He founded the model village of Port Sunlight on the Wirral in the late 1880s. In return for decent living conditions, reasonable rents and a share in the profits of his business, as well as schools and libraries, Lever's workers were expected to contribute as hard-working, committed workers.

Top: 8-14 Bridge Street, Port Sunlight, 1896
These Arts and Crafts homes were designed by Grayson and Ould for Lever Brothers as part of the model village of Port Sunlight to house the workers in their soap factory. The terrace was rebuilt following World War II bomb damage.

Above: Village Shop, 88–88A Greendale Road, Port Sunlight, 1896

Top: Sunlight Soap Works, 1897
Barrels of tallow and other soap ingredients stand stacked by a tramline with a large factory building in the background.

Above left: Sunlight Soap Works, 1897
Barrels of oil, used in the soap-making process, are delivered by barge.

Above right: Lever House, Wood Street, 1896
Dozens of clerks seated at rows of wooden desks in an office within the soap factory. Lever House was designed by architects William and Segar Owen for William Hesketh Lever and James Darcy Lever.

Left: The Lyceum, Bridge Street, 1896
A classroom at the former Port Sunlight Schools' Hall, now the Lyceum social centre.

A MODEL VILLAGE

Top left: Gladstone Hall, Greendale Road, Port Sunlight, 1896
Villagers gather for a group photograph outside the Hall, designed by William Owen.

Middle left: Shakespeare Cottages, Poets Corner, 1896
Semi-detached cottages, designed by Edmund Kirby for William Hesketh Lever in 1896, were modelled on Shakespeare's birthplace and demolished in 1938.

Bottom left: Bridge Street, Port Sunlight, 1896
The former schools and church building was designed by Douglas and Fordham for the model village and is now the Lyceum social centre.

Top right: Sunlight Soap Works, 1896
Women form the majority of the workforce in this photograph although a young man can be seen in the foreground packing Sunlight Soap into a wooden crate.

Above right: Hulme Hall, Port Sunlight, 1896
Built to provide dining facilities for female employees of the Port Sunlight Factory, the hall was designed by William and Segar Owen for William Hesketh Lever in 1901. It was later used as an art gallery when canteen facilities were provided at the factory. Later still it became a community centre.

WITHINGTON

Manchester

Piccadilly, c1880

View looking east from the Royal Hotel. In the foreground is the monument to Sir Robert Peel by the sculptor William Calder Marshall, erected in 1853 after Peel's death in office as Prime Minister in 1850. Born locally in Bury, his untimely death shocked the nation and prompted great generosity when public subscriptions were sought for the memorial. Located in front of the Manchester Royal Infirmary, which is just visible to the right, it was the first great commemorative statue to appear in Piccadilly Square. The central figure of Peel is flanked on each side by allegorical sculpture.

KING STREET

Left: Bank of England, 82 King Street, Manchester, 1898
Charles Robert Cockerell was asked to produce designs for branches of the Bank of England in Manchester, Liverpool and Bristol, of which the Manchester branch is the earliest (1845–46).

Below: Piccadilly, Manchester, c1900
View west towards the Royal Hotel, visible in the left middle distance. In the foreground is a memorial to the Duke of Wellington by Matthew Noble, installed in 1856 and unveiled by the mayor before a crowd of around 100,000. Figures depicting Victory, Mars and Minerva surround the granite plinth.

MANCHESTER TOWN HALL

Right: Town Hall, c1895

View south from Cross Street, looking across Albert Square towards the west front of Manchester Town Hall, built between 1867 and 1877 to the designs of Alfred Waterhouse. Faced in pale grey Spinkwell sandstone and deftly planned on a triangular site, the Town Hall is a masterpiece of High Victorian Gothic that incorporated the latest technological innovations, including fireproof construction, gas lighting and hot water heating. Its spectacular 280-foot-tall clock tower still dominates Albert Square.

Above: The Palace Theatre of Varieties, Oxford Street, c1910

Viewed from the junction of Oxford Street and Whitworth Street, the Palace Theatre was built as the Manchester Palace of Varieties by Alfred Darbyshire and F B Smith in 1891 with a seating capacity of over 3,500. It was substantially altered in the 1890s and in 1913, and refaced in 1953. In this picture the current show is *A Year in an Hour.* The opulent tobacconists on the corner carries the name of A Drapkin, a Russian emigré from Rostov. Drapkin arrived in England with his parents in 1897 and opened various emporia around the city. The Muratti cigarette brand advertised on the shopfront added a dash of the exotic Levant to the cosmopolitan character of the theatre.

RYLANDS LIBRARY, MANCHESTER

Opposite above left: John Rylands Library, Deansgate, 1900
When John Rylands died in 1888, his wife commissioned the architect Basil Champneys to design a library to house Rylands's collection of theological books. The library, built in the Gothic style between 1890 and 1899, later became part of the University of Manchester.

Opposite above right: Municipal School of Technology, Sackville Street, c1902
View of the south and west facades as seen from the corner of Granby Row and Sackville Street. Designed by Spalding and Cross, the building was begun in 1895 and completed in 1902. It subsequently became part of the University of Manchester and was renamed the Institute of Science and Technology (UMIST).

Opposite below: Piccadilly, 1895
View looking north-west towards the Wellington Memorial in the foreground.

Above: Piccadilly, c1914
A No. 34 tram speeds across an intersection in Piccadilly while a policeman controls cross traffic. Manchester had a large horse-drawn tram network from around 1875. By 1901, when electric trams started to be phased in, Manchester and Salford Tramways, the leading franchise, had a fleet of over 500 trams with more than 5,000 horses stabled to draw them over the 140 miles of tramways around the city. The Corporation of Manchester saw the modernisation of the tramways as a priority. It involved upgrading the tramlines and then adding overhead electric cables, so they took over the infrastructure from private owners and then leased back the tramline network, gradually replacing all the horse-drawn trams with new electric-powered ones.

STAR LIF
BUILDINGS
COPPOCK & BRATBY
BUILDINGS
SHERRATT & HUGH
The UNIVERSITY PRESS
34 BOOKSELLERS 34
BOOKSELLERS
H. LOWNDES
PATENTS

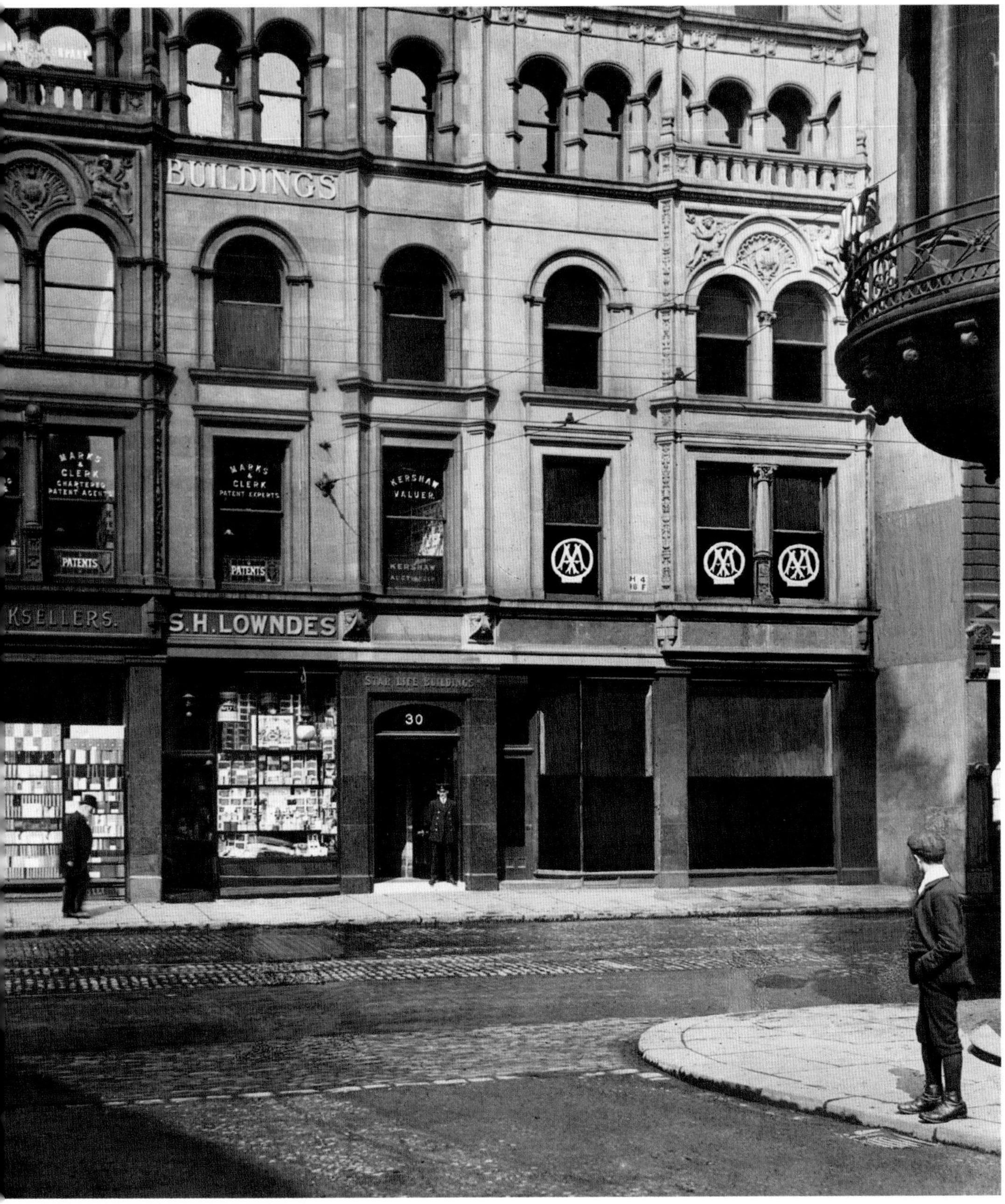

STAR LIFE BUILDING

Opposite: Star Life Building, 30 Cross Street, Manchester, 1907
Sited at the junction of Cross Street and St Ann Street, Manchester's renowned Sherratt and Hughes Booksellers occupied the ground floor from 1905, before being taken over by W H Smith in 1946. It retained its name until 1992 when it was bought by Waterstones, who closed the store in 1996. The offices are now known as Alliance House.

Left: The Cross Street facade of the Star Life Building, Manchester, 1907
The logo of the recently founded Automobile Association, whose offices were housed in the building, is visible in the first-floor windows.

Above left: Refuge Assurance Company, Oxford Street, Manchester, 1912
View of the courtyard to the rear of the building, which was designed by Alfred Waterhouse and opened for business in 1895. This photograph was taken soon after the building was extended by Paul Waterhouse, Alfred's son, between 1909 and 1912.

Above right: Triang Toy Shop, Oldham Road, 1927
A charming display of doll's houses, trains, pedal-cars and other toys in the basement showroom. A sign, styled like that of a railway station, points to Lines Brothers Ltd office. Three brothers, descendants of the Lines toy company family, formed their own business and invented the Triang brand. In 1927 they acquired a children's bicycle company in Birmingham and established new businesses across the country.

THE AMERICAN SHOE Cº
DEANSGATE ARCADE
SHEFFIELD MANUFACTURERS
WALKER & HALL
WHOLESALE

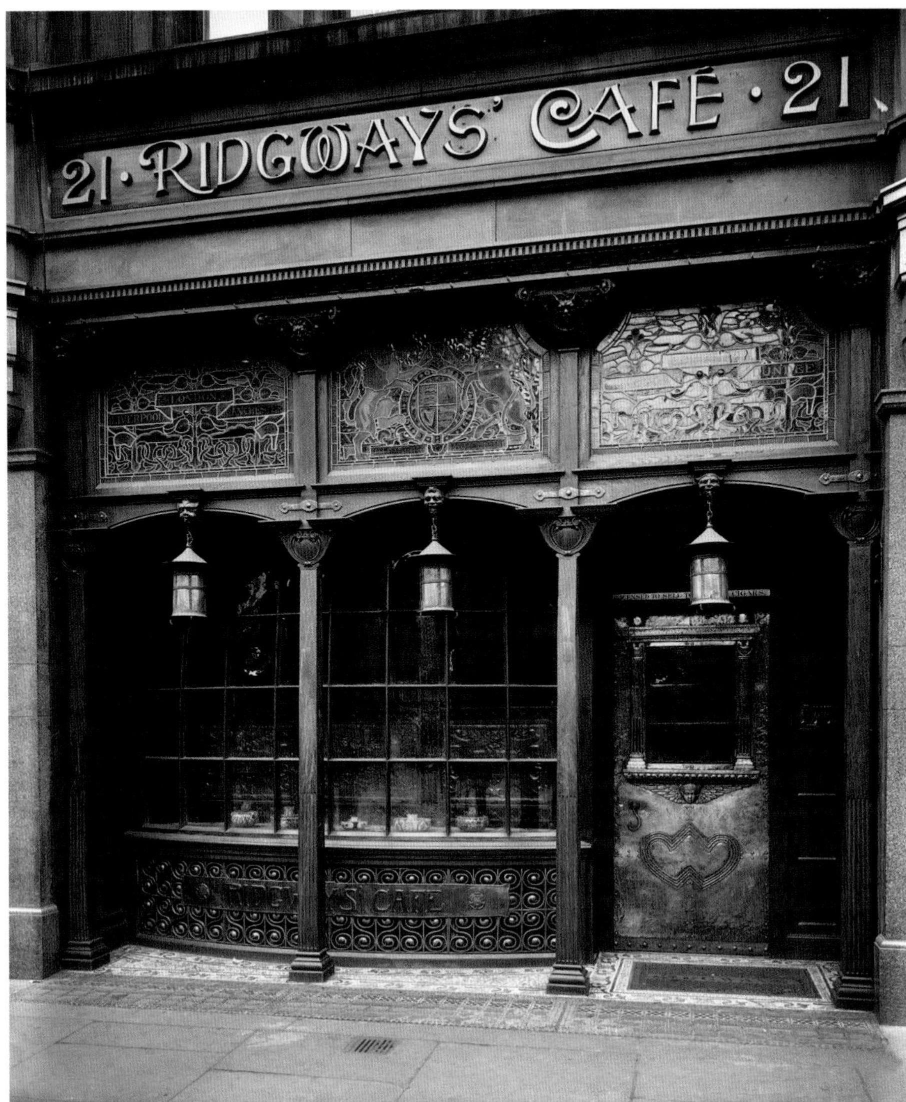

DEANSGATE ARCADE

Deansgate Arcade, 84 Deansgate, Manchester, 1900
Opposite: The Deansgate Arcade was designed by John Brooke and housed, among other shops and organisations, the offices of the North of England Society for Women's Suffrage, previously established in 1865 as Manchester National Society for Women's Suffrage, before changing its name in 1897.
Above: Interior of the Arcade from a first-floor balcony. Burmantofts commissioned both photographs to promote their ornate terracotta and faience work on the frontage. The arcade was demolished in 1955.

Above right and right: Ridgways' Café, 21 St Ann Street, 1901
The ornate shopfront (above right), designed by architect T Arnold Ashworth, and the interior (right) looking towards the Ladies' Dining Room, with beautiful painted murals on the coved ceiling, and Art Nouveau chairs.

56 OXFORD STREET MANCHESTER

This page and opposite: Tootal Broadhurst and Lee Warehouse, 56 Oxford Street, 1900
The firm of Tootal Broadhurst and Lee was one of the largest textile companies in Lancashire, with three of its own mills as well as the manufacturing and warehouse premises shown here. Unusually, its production included every element of the textile process from weaving through to clothing manufacture. In 1887 some 5,000 workers were employed by the company.

Above: The box room in the warehouse, showing women making boxes.
Right: Men in the packing room make goods ready for dispatch. In the foreground sits a package marked for the 'Officer Commanding 14th Hussars, Cape Town, South Africa'. The regiment was presumably engaged in the Second Anglo-Boer War (1899–1902).
Opposite above: Employees print and cut textiles in the Pattern Room.
Opposite below left: The Oxford Street and Great Bridgewater Street elevations of the warehouse.
Opposite below right: Girls and young women at work processing velveteen, a cotton fabric designed to imitate velvet.

MARKET STREET, MANCHESTER

Above: Market Street corner with Cross Street, c1914
Gridlock. An air of drama hangs in this street scene, crowded with several hundred pedestrians, horse-drawn vehicles, trams and a single motor wagon – the express parcel delivery truck of the L&NWR – all jostling for space.

Left Market Street, 1886
Looking west along Market Street from Piccadilly. Lewis's department store is visible to the left and Rylands to the right. Both establishments flourished as Manchester's commercial success generated wealth that could be spent in the local shops. The Rylands site is occupied today by Debenhams.

Below: Market Street, c1885
View east towards Piccadilly, with horse-drawn trams.

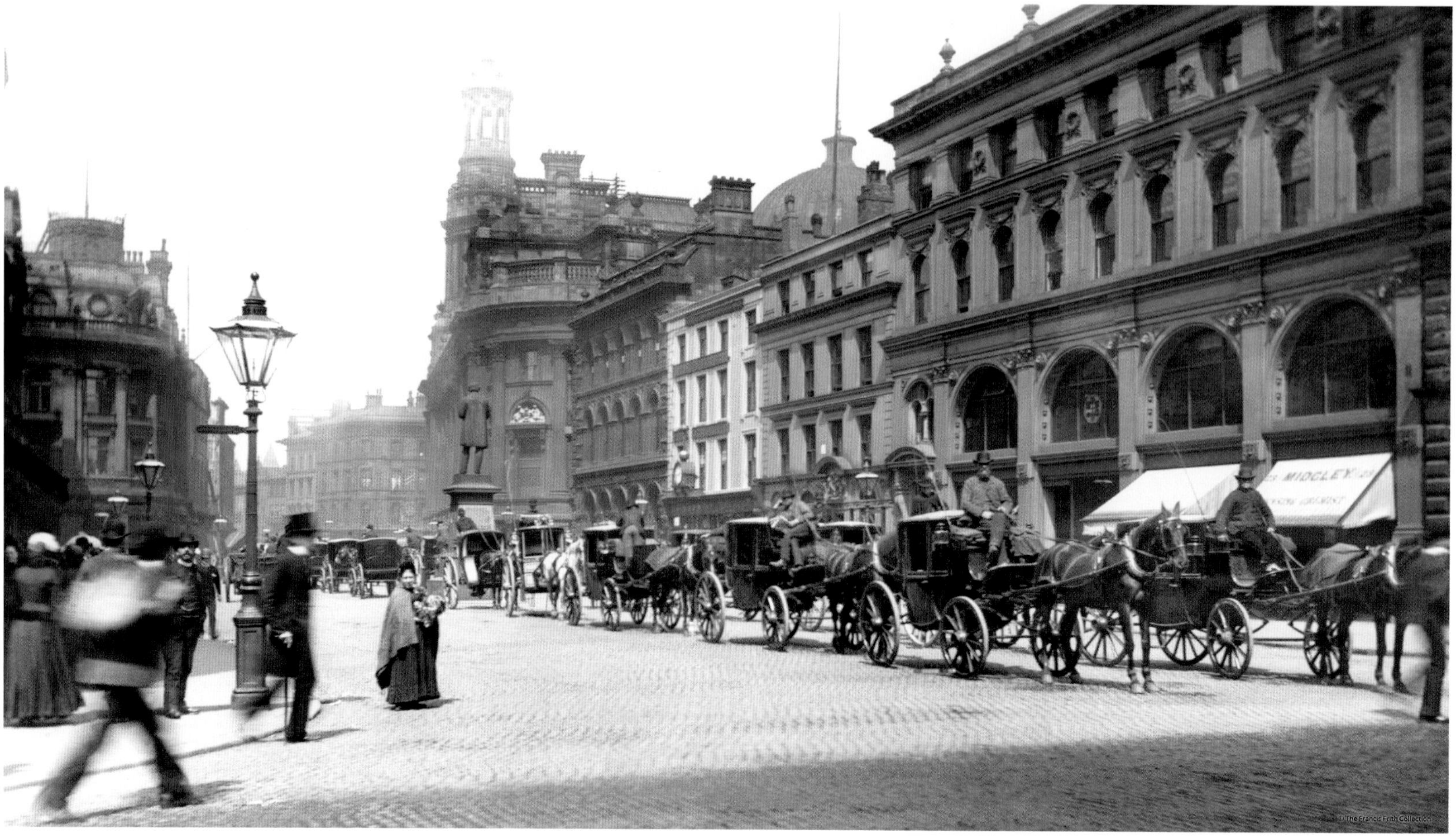
MIDGLEY

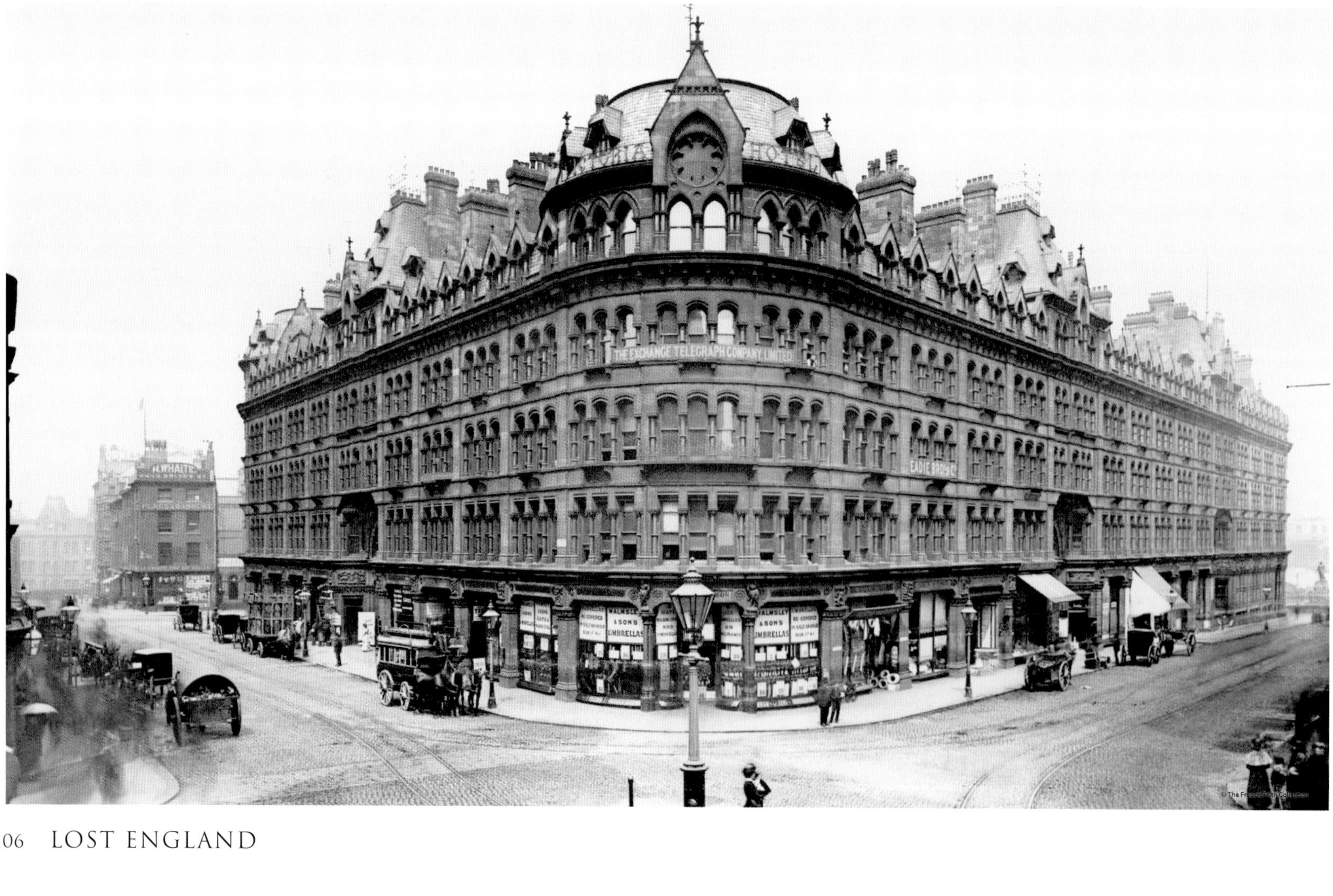
THE EXCHANGE TELEGRAPH COMPANY LIMITED
EADIE BROS & C°
UMBRELLAS
UMBRELLAS

ALBERT SQUARE

Above: Albert Square, Manchester, c1900
An open-top electric tram departs from the Albert Memorial. Sculpted in marble by Matthew Noble, the memorial commemorates the Prince Consort. It is enclosed in a large mediaeval-style ciborium designed by the architect Thomas Worthington. Noble was commissioned by the Lord Mayor, Thomas Goadsby, and the designs were personally approved by Queen Victoria. The Town Hall facade is in the background.

ST ANN'S SQUARE

Opposite above: St Ann's Square, Manchester, 1885
View north from St Ann's Church towards a rank of hansom cabs waiting for fares. This was a wealthy central business area with a brisk trade for cabs at all hours of the day, which started early and finished late. In the centre background is a memorial statue of Richard Cobden.

Opposite below: Victoria Building, Manchester, 1889
View south towards the corner of Victoria Street (left) and Deansgate (right), showing the ornate frontage of the Victoria Building. Elegantly turning the corner, it has shops at street level, offices above and the Victoria Hotel occupying the top five floors. The building was designed to be worthy of its position opposite the Cathedral. Its days of grandeur ended abruptly in December 1940, when bombing left it a burned-out shell that was demolished soon after. The site is now occupied by Number One Deansgate.

BACK-TO-BACKS

Left: Davies Street, Ancoats
The Manchester working classes lived in poor housing, had poor diets and low life expectancy, and endured long hours for low wages.

Left below: 71 and 73 Pottery Lane, Ardwick, 1909
By the mid 19th century Ardwick had grown from a village into a pleasant and wealthy suburb of Manchester, but by the turn of the century it had become heavily industrialised. As its industries fell into decline, so did Ardwick itself, deteriorating into one of the city's most deprived areas.

Opposite above: Ogden Street, Harpurhey, 1910
Photograph taken before development for a proposed new road to Crumpsall.

Opposite below left: 2–14 Violet Street and 93–105 Chester Street, Hulme, 1914
View from 62 Stott Street down the cramped back alley and tiny backyards. The number of people living in Hulme multiplied 50-fold during the first half of the 19th century as thousands of people flocked to work in the city's expanding textile mills. Houses were built rapidly and space was limited, creating slum neighbourhoods choked with smoke and toxic fumes from the railway and hundreds of factories and mills.

Opposite below right: Passage behind 46–82 Gunson Street
View from Barratt Street, showing typical homes before slum clearance.

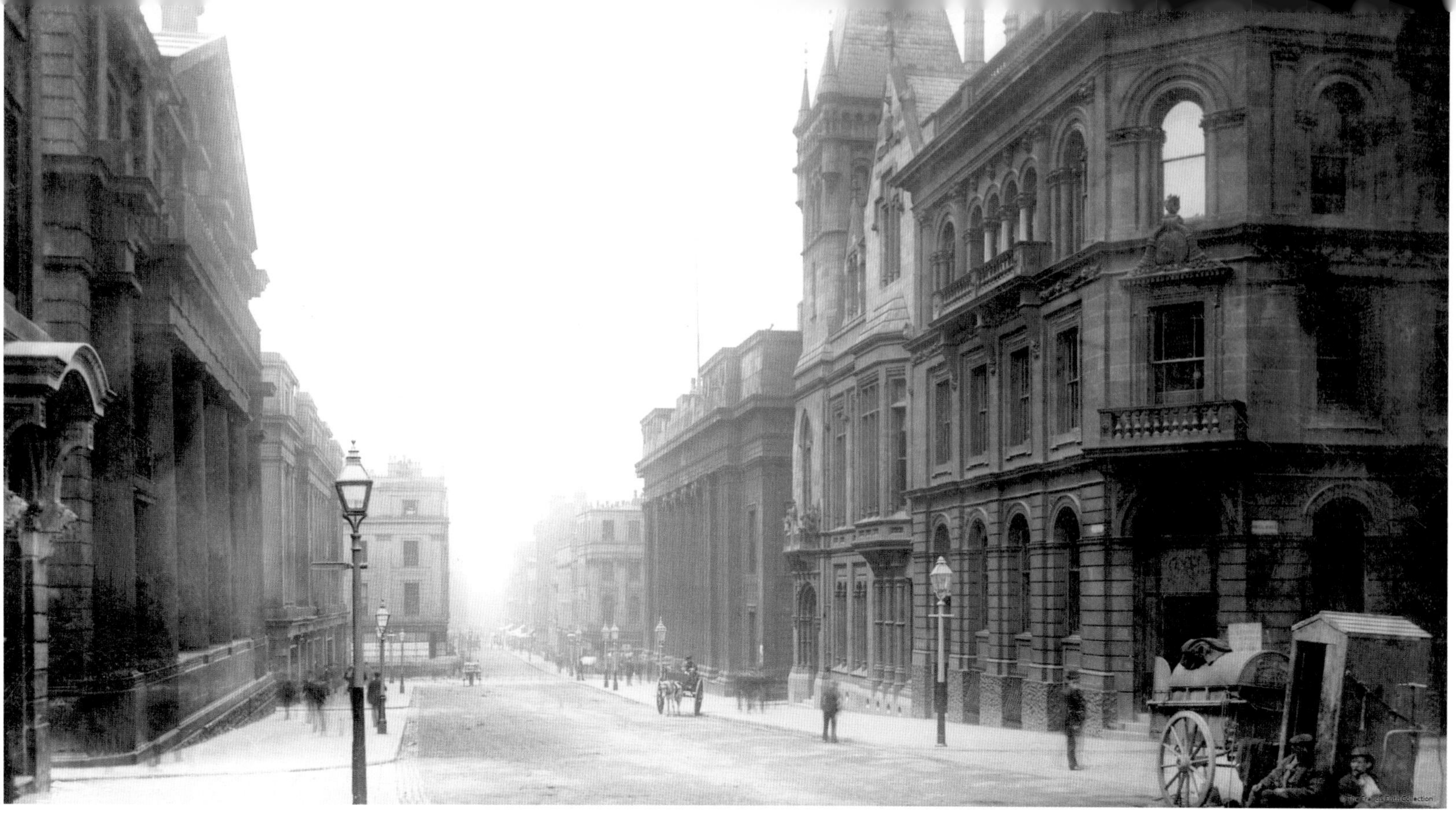

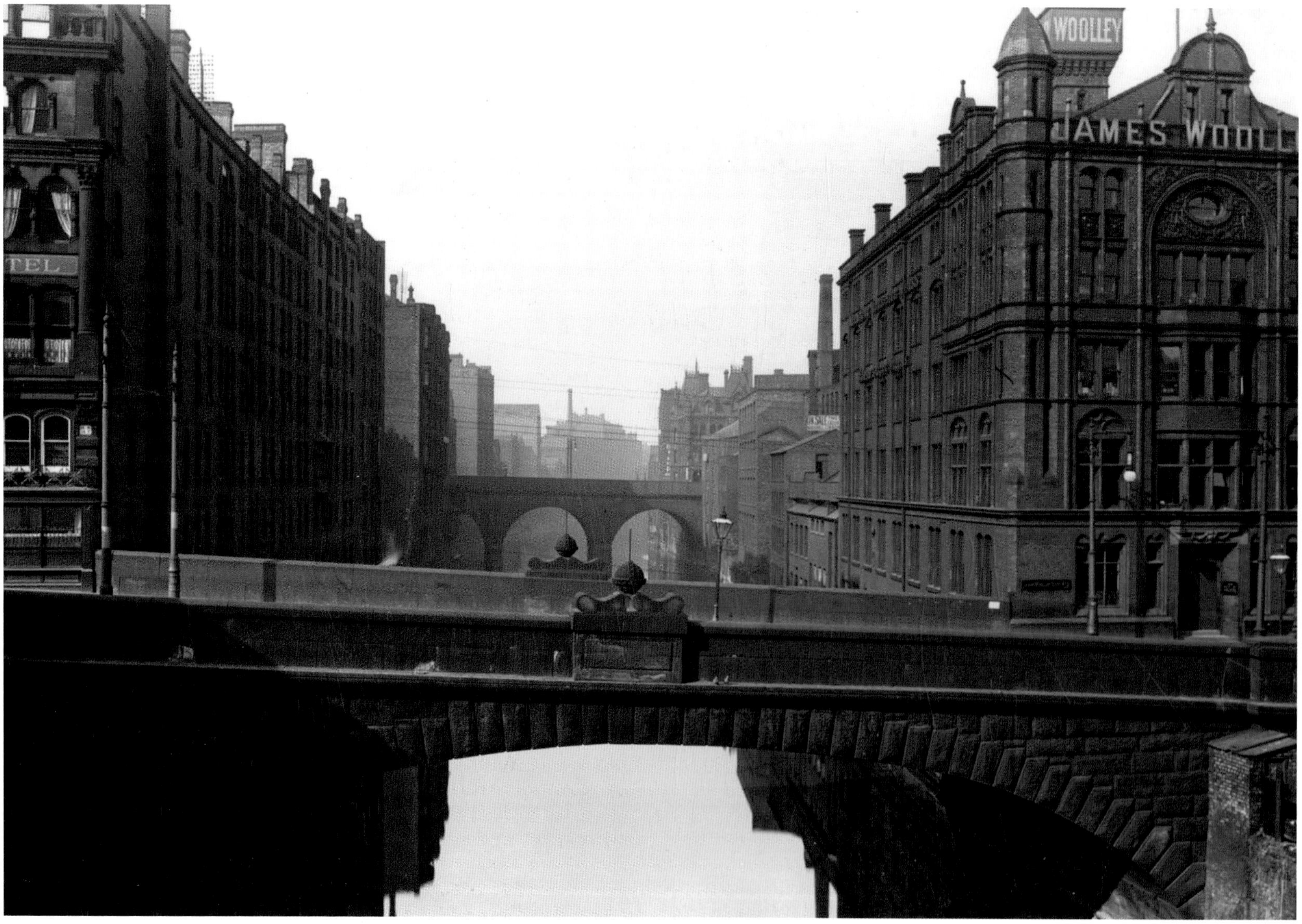

VICTORIA BRIDGE

Opposite below: Victoria Bridge, River Irwell, Manchester, c1900
View south-west along the River Irwell between factories and warehouses. The bridge in the foreground carries Victoria Bridge Street to its junction opposite the Cathedral. The distant bridge is Blackfriars. James Woolley and Sons Company Ltd was a pharmaceutical suppliers that boomed from simple retail premises in King Street in 1833 into the giant business that moved to the premises shown here on Victoria Bridge Street in 1892.

Opposite above: King Street, Manchester, 1885
View from the top of King Street west towards Cross Street. The third building from the right was Manchester's original Town Hall from 1825. It remained the centre of city administration until the new town hall opened in 1877, after which it became the Central Library. To its right is the Gothic frontage of the District Bank. In the foreground on the left stands the Manchester branch of the Bank of England.

Above: Manchester Ship Canal, Manchester Docks, 1900
Despite being 40 miles inland, the newly created Port of Manchester was enabled by the Manchester Ship Canal to become Britain's third busiest docks. Since its opening in 1894 the canal has handled a wide range of ships and cargoes, from coastal vessels to intra-European shipping and inter-continental cargo liners.

Greater Manchester

MANCHESTER SHIP CANAL

Right: Manchester Ship Canal, Acton Grange, Warrington, c1889
A staggering feat of Victorian engineering that transformed Manchester's fortunes. Navvies at work during the construction of the Manchester Ship Canal, showing the extracted soil being removed by train.

Above: Manchester Ship Canal, c1890
Looking south-west towards the Latchford Railway Viaduct from the excavation channel of the Manchester Ship Canal. The camera is positioned in the vicinity of the Latchford Locks some 21 miles from the entrance locks at Eastham, north of Ellesmere Port on the Mersey Estuary. Locks were needed both to preserve navigation and to allow vessels using the canal to ascend 60 feet to the terminus docks in Manchester's Salford Quays. One of the greatest examples of Victorian infrastructure ever created, the Canal, on which work began in August 1887, was first used in January 1894. The picture shows the formation profile and marker posts used for excavation levels. The pristine railway viaduct reveals the extensive rebuilding of bridges that had to be carried out by the railway companies prior to the Canal construction.

BOLTON

24 Deansgate, Bolton, 1895
Above right: The Deansgate frontage of the Bank of Bolton. This late Victorian bank building was designed in the style of an Italian palazzo by the architects Bradshaw and Gass and subsequently extended in 1907 to the size it is today. Most recently it has been a branch of the NatWest Bank.
Top left: The opulent banking hall seen from the entrance coruscated with shimmering glazed tile and faience.
Above left: The clerks' desks displaying customer ledgers, including one for Bolton Wanderers Football and Athletic Company.

DEANSGATE AND NELSON SQUARE

Opposite above: 46-48 Deansgate, Bolton, 1903
View east towards the corner of Market Street. The bank, most recently the premises of Royal Bank of Scotland, was designed by the architects Cunliffe and Freeman in a Renaissance Revival style. Although wider today, the course of Deansgate has changed little since mediaeval times. Although areas adjacent to the street have been cleared, some historic buildings remain. The two banks pictured are fine buildings, meeting the needs of a bustling and successful town that underwent 150 years of continuous growth based on textile production. Bolton resisted the effect of Manchester's massive growth for longer than some other towns in the City's shadow because, in addition to cotton mills, it specialised in bleaching processes and the manufacture of textile machinery. Its leadership in textiles was established when local man Samuel Crompton invented the spinning mule in 1779, revolutionising the production of yarn.

Opposite below: Nelson Square, Bolton, 1893
View east across the gardens, which were laid out in the year this picture was taken. The central path leads to an ornamental streetlamp. Beyond stands the memorial statue of Samuel Crompton, funded by public subscription and installed in 1862. To the left is the Pack Horse Hotel, and the taller building beyond is the Post Office on Bradshawgate. Nelson House, to the right, still stands, but it has lost its spire.

STOCKPORT

Top: Billingham and Keely's Grocery Store, Merchants Court, 1903
This photograph of the loading bay of the grocery store is carefully composed by photographer Alfred Newton. It is a classic portrait, but also a still life showing the staples for Victorian living as supplied by the company: an old fashioned flitch of bacon, crated biscuits, flour and starch. The hierarchy here is revealed in the clothing: the white-aproned individuals are the staff; Messrs Billingham and Keely stand at the rear, suited and waistcoated.

Above left: Railway viaduct, 1903
The 27-arch viaduct, opened in 1842 by the Birmingham and Manchester Railway Company, marches above the smoky rooftops of terraced housing. It is the largest brick structure in the UK. Today it still carries the West Coast mainline railway across the valley of the River Mersey. Factory chimneys can be seen in the background. Versions of this scene can be enjoyed in some of L S Lowry's paintings, which feature the viaduct.

Above right: High Street, 1903
View north towards the junction with Lower Hillgate. Stockport's geography and river system assured its rise as an important textile town. Silk was an early specialism, but in the 19th century hat-making became the industry most closely associated with the town. Hydraulic power drove both manufacturing processes.

STOCKPORT TOWN HALL

Above left: Town Hall, Stockport, 1908
The west elevation seen from Wellington Road South. The town hall was built to the designs of Sir Alfred Brumwell Thomas between 1904 and 1906 to serve the recently created County Borough of Stockport.

Above right: George's Church, Heaviley, Stockport, c1900
A view of the east end of the church from Buxton Road shortly after its completion in 1897. The building was designed by the architects Austin and Paley and paid for by George Fearn, a local brewer.

LEIGH

Above: Junction of Market Street and Bradshawgate, Leigh, c1890
The Rope and Anchor had many incarnations but thrived because of its location at the junction of the toll gates with the Bolton to St Helens Turnpike Road from 1762. As was often the case, the Rope and Anchor served not just as an inn but also for other forms of commerce and auctions. The smart wine vaults on the corner were an extension to the hotel and replaced an ancient smithy that was demolished in 1863. The parcels office of the NS&L Railway had space in the new building. The Anchor was tenanted from 1809 by the Greenhough family, whose name appears on the door. In 1893 the buildings were demolished for road widening and replaced with a much grander hotel.

ALTRINCHAM

Above: Market Place, Altrincham, 1897
View north towards the Market Place from Market Street. This area is believed to be the site of the original settlement of what is now a much larger town. Altrincham grew up as a rural market town south-west of Manchester. Local agriculture produced fine vegetables for the busy market, but it was transport developments that fostered the town's growth – first with industry benefiting from the Bridgewater Canal that connected the town to Manchester and Liverpool, and then when improved rail connections brought Altrincham within commuting distance of Manchester in the 1850s and 1860s. Thereafter the migration of wealthy middle-class Mancunians set Altrincham on course to become an elegant and well-to-do satellite of Greater Manchester.

BURY MARKET

Opposite above: The Market, 1902
Bury has hosted an important market since the 15th century. The local landowner, the Earl of Derby, funded the building of an open market area in 1841. As trade increased, improvements were needed and an iron and glass roof was added. Further impressive additions were made in 1868 by the Earl's architect. The market was destroyed by fire in the 1960s.

TOWN HALL SQUARE, ROCHDALE

Opposite below: Town Hall Square, 1913
Rochdale stands out among the many textile towns for its ebullience and civic pride. As well as the magnificent Gothic-style town hall, its civic amenities included a well-appointed college of art and a technical school. Rochdale's canal, opened in 1804, became the main waterway linking Lancashire and Yorkshire. This photograph shows the grand open space in front of the Town Hall. The bronze statue, centre, is of John Bright, the liberal and radical statesman born in Rochdale. Erected in the Square in 1891 and paid for by donors including the Provident Cooperative Society, the statue was moved to Broadfield Park in 1933. The free-thinking tradition of Rochdale was an important contributor to the history of the cooperative movement.

WINTER GARDENS
WINTER GARDENS &
ENTRANCE
WINTERGARDENS
WINTER GARDENS.
"not a dull moment"
6D ADMISSION 6D
ALL DAY.
BLACKPOOL
WINTER
GARDENS
TWO GORGEOUS BALLETS
BAND OF 60
FINEST VARIETY SHOW IN THE WORLD
6D ADMISSION 6D
THE ELLIOTTS
TWICE DAILY
WINT
"not a
6D

Lancashire

BLACKPOOL

Winter Gardens, Church Street, c1900

The main entrance to the Winter Gardens advertises the current attractions. The theatre and general entertainment centre was built in the 1870s and is still open to the public today.

BLACKPOOL BEACH

Left: The beach, c1900
A view looking north towards Blackpool Tower, with the Great Wheel in the distance. Holidaymakers throng the seafront and sailing boats awaiting day-trippers linger close to the shore. A slip road gives access from the promenade to the beach for the many horse-drawn vehicles using it – from bathing huts to tourist carriages. Children paddle in the shallows, no doubt in the hope of a donkey ride later when the tide is further out.

Below: Promenaders dressed in their finery at Blackpool, 1895

Opposite above: Blackpool Tower and Winter Gardens, c1900
The view south-east from the North Pier, with the Big Wheel visible in the background. The Tower was built in 1891–94 by Maxwell and Tuke, and was intended to rival the Eiffel Tower in Paris.

TALBOT SQUARE, BLACKPOOL

Above: Talbot Square, c1893

Centre left is an elaborate canopied drinking fountain from the Coalbrookdale iron foundry. It was erected in 1870, at the same time as the Promenade between Station Road and Cocker Square was completed. Public readings, athletic contests and brass-band performances were among the fundraising activities organised to pay for the fountain. The Theatre Royal, centre right, advertises the Talbot Dining Rooms, and the free use of a library and reading room in the days before plentiful public and subscription-free libraries.

Above: Talbot Square, Blackpool, c1900
View east from North Pier towards the Town Hall and its impressive clock tower, built in 1896. The drinking fountain shown on the previous page can also be seen here but in a different location – adjacent to public toilets. In the foreground shoeshine boys drum up business from three ladies passing by.

Left: Imperial Hotel, North Promenade, c1900
The 180-bedroom hotel was built between 1867 and 1868 by Clegg and Jones at a cost of £50,000. Still in use today, it is an important conference venue.

GREAT WHEEL, BLACKPOOL

The Great Wheel, c1900

Left: The Wheel was erected in 1895 by Walter D Basset on the Winter Gardens site at the corner of Adelaide Street and Coronation Street. Basset, a marine engineer, licensed the Great Wheel from the Chicago inventors, first building the Earls Court London attraction with a 21-year lease, then making his mark in Blackpool. The Wheel had 30 carriages, accommodating 1,200 people on each cycle and able to complete two cycles per hour. It was dismantled in 1907.

Below: Tourist attractions draw attention to their presence by advertising on their roofs for the benefit of visitors to Blackpool Tower's viewing platform and the 200-foot-high wheel.

BLUE HUNGARIAN BAND
VICTORIA PIER
BLUE
HUNGARIAN
BAND

VICTORIA PIER BLACKPOOL

Victoria Pier, c1900

The last of Blackpool's three piers to be constructed, the Victoria Pier opened on Good Friday 1893 to provide a promenade and entertainment for the increasing number of holidaymakers visiting Blackpool. Oriental motifs appealed to the Victorian public, and at the seaside exotic architecture, featuring onion domes and filigree ironwork, became part of the razzmatazz of the traditional British pier. In 1930 its name was changed to the South Pier (the others being the North and Central piers).

MORECAMBE, CLEVELEYS, BLACKBURN, LANCASTER

Top: Marine Road, Morecambe, c1890
Looking west along Marine Road Central and the Promenade, with the twin domes of the former People's Palace in the distance. The shallow shelving beach with its extensive sands made Morecambe an attractive resort to which the railways brought hordes of holidaymakers from the mid 1800s. Although many came from the Lancashire mill towns, others travelled from Yorkshire and Scotland.

Above: Victoria Road, Cleveleys, c1900
View of Cleveleys, looking west towards the beach in the distance, with shops and a bank to the left in the photograph. This scene is in sharp contrast to the crowds and entertainments of the larger resorts nearby such as Blackpool and Morecambe.

Opposite above: Market House and Town Hall, Blackburn, 1894
The Town Hall, opened in 1856, was designed by James Paterson in an Italian Renaissance style. Opened six years earlier, the Market House boasted an ornate frontage of three gables and a 72-foot-high campanile crowned by an illuminated clock. Blackburn was at the height of its expansion as a cotton town, with money for municipal improvements. National railway timetables necessitated the adoption of universal time throughout England. In Blackburn a time ball was installed, to keep the city synchronised with national time. At 1 pm on 2 May 1878 the time ball, assembled on the clock tower, made its first descent, triggered by an electric signal from the Royal Observatory at Greenwich; simultaneously, a cannon was discharged so that those not in sight of the tower would be able to set their clocks to official time at the meridian. Sadly, the clock tower was demolished in 1964 to make way for a new shopping arcade.

Opposite below: Town Hall, Lancaster, 1886
The elegant and imposing Tuscan-style portico of the Town Hall, built by Thomas Jarrett between 1781 and 1783 and surmounted with a fine cupola by Thomas Harrison, was an accomplished addition to the thriving market town and inland port that gave the county its name. The building is now the City Museum at the heart of the relatively well-conserved Georgian city centre.

© The Francis Frith Collection

© The Francis Frith Collection

WARING AND GILLOW FACTORY, LANCASTER

Waring and Gillow Factory, St Leonard's Gate, 1917

Above: The yard of Waring and Gillow's Lancaster factory, showing workers unloading sawn planks of wood from a horse-drawn cart. Waring and Gillow established a reputation for supplying high-quality furniture to some of the wealthiest families in the country. During the First World War their factories in Lancaster and London were used for the war effort, producing aircraft components and ammunition cases.

Right and opposite: Workers, including young girls, are involved in the various stages of production of ammunition cases.

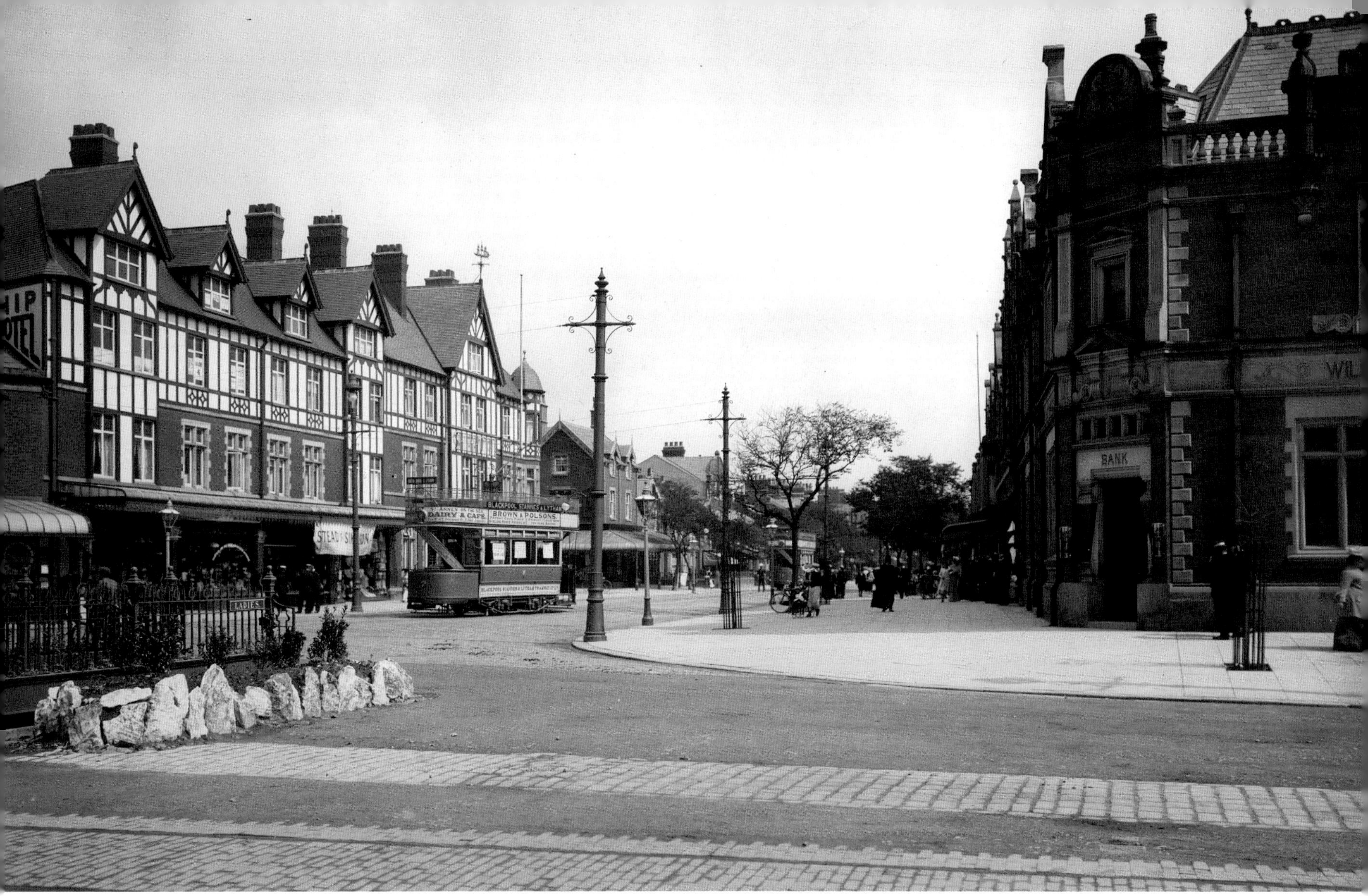

ICE CREAM

LYTHAM, LYTHAM ST ANNES

Opposite above: Clifton Street, Lytham, c1900
Clifton Street was on a major tram route, and the tramlines in the foreground connected to the sea front just 50 or so yards away. The view is still recognisable today and is now called Market Square.

Opposite below: Lytham St Annes, c1900
The north promenade and beach, where a kiosk has been set up to sell ice cream, and donkeys are ready to take children up and down the sands. A large bandstand can be seen in the promenade gardens at the left of the photograph.

Top: Pier Approach, Lytham St Annes, c1900
This broad and leafy street gave on to St Anne's Pier, which opened for visitors in 1885. A daily steamer service using the Pier took travellers to and from Blackpool and Liverpool. The town of St Annes-on-Sea was a new town, planned from conception as a holiday haven to compete with existing nearby resorts. As the town developed and transport improved, it became home to wealthy commuters to Greater Manchester.

Above: District Council Offices, Central Beach, Lytham St Annes, c1900
Located in Central Beach, the council buildings housed the Assembly Rooms and the Public Baths. The Assembly Rooms opened in 1862 and the Baths the following year. Around the time this photograph was taken, the management advertised Sea Water Baths with Ladies and Gentlemen Swimming for 6d, and Private Baths with first- and second-class tickets and options for hot, tepid or cold water.

TO LITERATURE ARTS AND SCIENCES

1905
CANTRELL & COCHRANE LTD
CANTRELL COCHRANE
C & C GINGER ALE
TABLE WAT
CANTRELL COCHRANE
C & C GINGER ALE

PRESTON

Opposite above: The Harris Art Gallery and Museum, Fishergate, c1920
View looking east from Cheapside, with the old Town Hall to the left. Raised high on a podium, this powerful gallery and museum building was designed by James Hibbert. It was opened in 1880 and named after its benefactor, Edmund Robert Harris, a local lawyer whose bequest of £300,000 made its construction possible

Opposite below: Goods Shed, West Lancs Station, Fishergate Hill, 1927
Two vans parked outside the Cantrell and Cochrane depot, photographed for the London, Midland and Scottish Railway. The station was also known as Fishergate Hill Station. Closed to passengers in 1900, it remained open for goods traffic until 1965. Cantrell and Cochrane was an Irish soft drinks manufacturer with large plants in Dublin and Belfast.

Above: Preston Public Hall, c1920
Built to house the Corn Exchange in the 1820s, the Hall functioned as a public meeting place long into the 20th century when the bulk of it was demolished to make way for a section of the ringway.

Left: Fishergate, c1920
The view east shows George Gilbert Scott's Town Hall to the left. Its clock tower was the second tallest in the land after that of the Houses of Parliament. The Town Hall, dating from 1866, was severely damaged in a fire in 1947, after which the council decided that repairing the building was not viable despite the wishes of the local population. Tragically, it was razed and the rubble scattered along the banks of the River Ribble. Further along Fishergate, next to the Town Hall, is one of the cupolas of the Miller Arcade and the spire of the Parish Church, now the Minster of St John the Evangelist.

SOUTHPORT

Top: Sea Front Promenade, c1900
Southport was one of the earliest coastal resorts in the north-west, but the opening of the railway line connecting the town with Liverpool in 1848, followed soon after by a rail link with Manchester, fuelled its popularity in the second half of the 19th century.

Above: Marine Lake, c1900
The area between the Promenade and the sea was developed into a large complex of water-based attractions. An early open cable car takes passengers from a small tower across the lake. Rowing boats could be hired, and a salt-water lido was built in 1914. For those who preferred to stay dry, donkey rides were available.

WINTER GARDENS

Above: Royal Hotel and Winter Gardens, Southport, c1900
The hotel is to the left, and the extensive indoor Gardens in the glazed building on the right of the picture. Evening promenaders stroll, while families gather in expectation around the Punch and Judy theatre in the foreground.

Right: Southport Pier, c1900
The entrance to the Pier and the Marine Bridge. Holidaymakers take a leisurely walk down the promenade or ride in style in a tourist carriage. The Pier, which opened in 1860, is the second longest in Britain after Southend and carried a tramway to the pierhead for travellers catching the coastal steamers.

LACE
W.J. WORDEN
SOLICITOR
W.J. WORDEN
SOLICITOR
COMMISSIONER FOR OATHS.
THE BANK OF BOLTON LIMITED

PICTUREDROME
THE WORLD IN MOTION

SOUTHPORT

Opposite above: The Opera House, c1900
The Opera House opened in1891, with a seating capacity of 2,000. This view shows horse-drawn carriages waiting outside for the wealthy and sophisticated clientele that the theatre was built to attract to the resort. The magnificent structure was destroyed by fire in 1921.

Opposite below left: Bank of Bolton, Chapel Street, 1895

Opposite below right: Picturedrome, Lord Street, c1920
This early purpose-built cinema, designed by Campbell and Fairhurst, was a local venture pre-dating the large cinema chains and was owned by Southport Picturedrome Ltd. The tariff of admission charges is displayed outside, with three performances given daily.

Right: Lord Street, c1900
View of Lord Street looking north, showing (from right to left): the Manchester and Liverpool Banking Co, the Atkinson Library and Art Gallery (built by Waddington and Sons in 1876–78), and Cambridge Hall (built by Maxwell and Tuke in 1873–74). The modern-day Atkinson Library includes the Bank, which was annexed in the 1920s.

Below: Lord Street, c1900
Lord Street was laid out from 1825 and speaks clearly of the town's aspirations to be a stylish resort. The future Napoleon III lived on the street for a short time, and it has been suggested that it was one of the models for the wide Parisian boulevards created by the Emperor's Prefect, Baron Haussmann, during the city's extensive reconstruction between 1853 and 1870.

CITY SHIRT AND FENT STORES.

CARLISLE
No 5 PLATFORM
MAIN LINE

Cumbria

CARLISLE

Opposite above right: Carlisle Railway Station, 1898

Carlisle's location made it a railway nexus; because the railways developed as separate private companies, there were several stations serving north–south and east–west routes. This station, also known as Carlisle Citadel, was built in 1847–48 for a Joint Station Committee and steadily outgrew the others. It was one of the busiest, used by seven different companies and serving eight routes.

Opposite above left: Market Cross, Market Place, Carlisle, 1898

View north towards the Market Cross, with the old Town Hall in the background. An Ionic column with a square base and a sundial on the top, the Cross was installed in 1682 on the site of an earlier cross. The Market Place in this strategic border city has layers of history, and this picture also tells other stories. Part of the frontage of the old Town Hall with its clock tower is emblazoned 'The City Shirt and Fent Stores': Carlisle grew as a textile and mill town, but that didn't bring wealth to all – 'fent' is offcuts, selvedge or remnants of fabric, suitable for the poor who could not afford better.

Opposite below: Courthouse, Court Square, Carlisle, 1898

The Courthouse was built in 1810 by Robert Smirke, the architect of many notable buildings of the early Victorian period, including the British Museum and Lancaster House in London. The Courthouse stood on the site of Henry VIII's citadel, and the round towers housed the court rooms.

Above: The Shipbuilding Yard and Naval Construction Works, Barrow-in-Furness, 1920

The discovery of rich iron ore deposits around the Furness Peninsula led to the rapid growth of Barrow. Its relatively remote location, combined with nearby coal in Cumberland, supported steel manufacturing, and also shipbuilding and munitions – particularly during the First and Second World Wars. Barrow specialised in building submarines – Vickers in Barrow was a world leader. Today the yard builds nuclear submarines.

THE LAKE DISTRICT

Opposite above: Allhallows Lane, Kendal, c1930
View north-west at the junction with Beast Banks. Allhallows Lane led from the Town Hall and was the starting point for the packhorse route to the west coast ports. Pru Shaw's Toffee Shop has two hopeful children outside. A. Hutton fruiterer next door offers a well-stocked display. On the site of this viewpoint stood the mediaeval Church of the Holy Cross and All Hallows, which survived until the 17th century and gave the lane its name.

Opposite below: Main Street, Cockermouth, 1898
A view east along the tree-lined street. The statue in the middle is of Richard Bourke, sixth Earl of Mayo, MP for the town from 1857 to 1868 and Viceroy of India from 1869 to 1872, when he was assassinated in the Andaman Islands. The commemorative statue was funded by public subscription and installed in 1875.

Right: Park Temperance Family and Commercial Hotel, Keswick, 1898
View of the hotel across the weir on the River Greta. The Temperance Movement launched the first Temperance hotel in 1833 and gained momentum with the formation of the Band of Hope in 1847. Temperance hotels sprang up around the country, Keswick becoming a notable spiritual retreat for abstemious evangelical Christians. The first Keswick Convention was held in 1875.

Below: Market Place, Ambleside, c1910
View north from the corner of Church Street towards the Royal Oak Hotel and the White Lion Hotel. The market town's location, just north of the tip of Windermere, was the terminus of horse-drawn transport until the turnpike was built in 1770. Prior to that, the only way north to Grasmere and the Lake District's sublime landscape was by horse or donkey; all commerce was conducted by packhorse. Ambleside was an early visitor attraction, leading to the building of accommodation for tourists brought by carriages such as the stagecoach waiting outside the White Lion seen here.

WINDERMERE

Above: LNWR Station, 1909

Railways brought many tourists to the Lake District; a charabanc (early motor coach) is shown leaving the station on the way to Grasmere. The ghostly figure of a boy can be seen standing to the right of the cyclist, partially removed from the glass plate with retouching ink.

Opposite below: Platform in Windermere Station c1930

A party of three people look as if they are waiting to greet travellers in the spotless station interior; the man in plus fours is dressed as the archetypal English country gentleman. Posters on the wall to the right advertise local attractions, while signs direct passengers to the pick-up locations for their onward journey by car to places such as Ambleside.

THE BOWDER STONE

Left: The Bowder Stone, Borrowdale, 1898

Celebrated for its size and precarious appearance, the Bowder Stone was, and still is, one of the Lake District's most famous natural attractions. This photograph shows a group of tourists at the foot of steps that provided an easy route to the top of the stone. Local landowner and eccentric Joseph Pocklington had begun to encourage visitors to the Bowder Stone in the late 18th century, adding a mock hermitage, a druidical stone and a cottage to house a guide who could show people round. Not surprisingly, Pocklington was criticised for spoiling the landscape.

PENRITH

Above: Middlegate, c1890

A view north-west along Middlegate, the main north–south thoroughfare of the town, which followed the route of the old Roman road to Carlisle. The west coast road to Scotland took travellers over the treacherous Shap Fell before descending to Penrith. The town has a ruined castle, built in the 15th century to protect the town from border reivers and Scottish incursions.

Opposite above: Market Square, c1890

View north-west towards the Clock Tower, which was erected in 1861 to commemorate Sir Philip Musgrave of Edenhall. The Musgraves' baronetcy dated back to 1611. Their seat in the Lake District at Hartley Castle was demolished in the early 18th century and its stone used for Edenhall, the new family residence close to the River Eden just outside Penrith. Sir Philip was only 33 when he died.

SEDBERGH

Opposite below: Main Street, c1900

View from the Market Place looking east, with the shop on the left selling farming tools, and the Sedbergh Café and Bakery further down the street. Sedbergh (pronounced Sedber or Sebber), a small market town populated by farming folk, was historically a part of the West Riding of Yorkshire. Wool sheared from its many sheep was taken to local mills, where it was turned into yarn that supplied a lively domestic knitting industry.

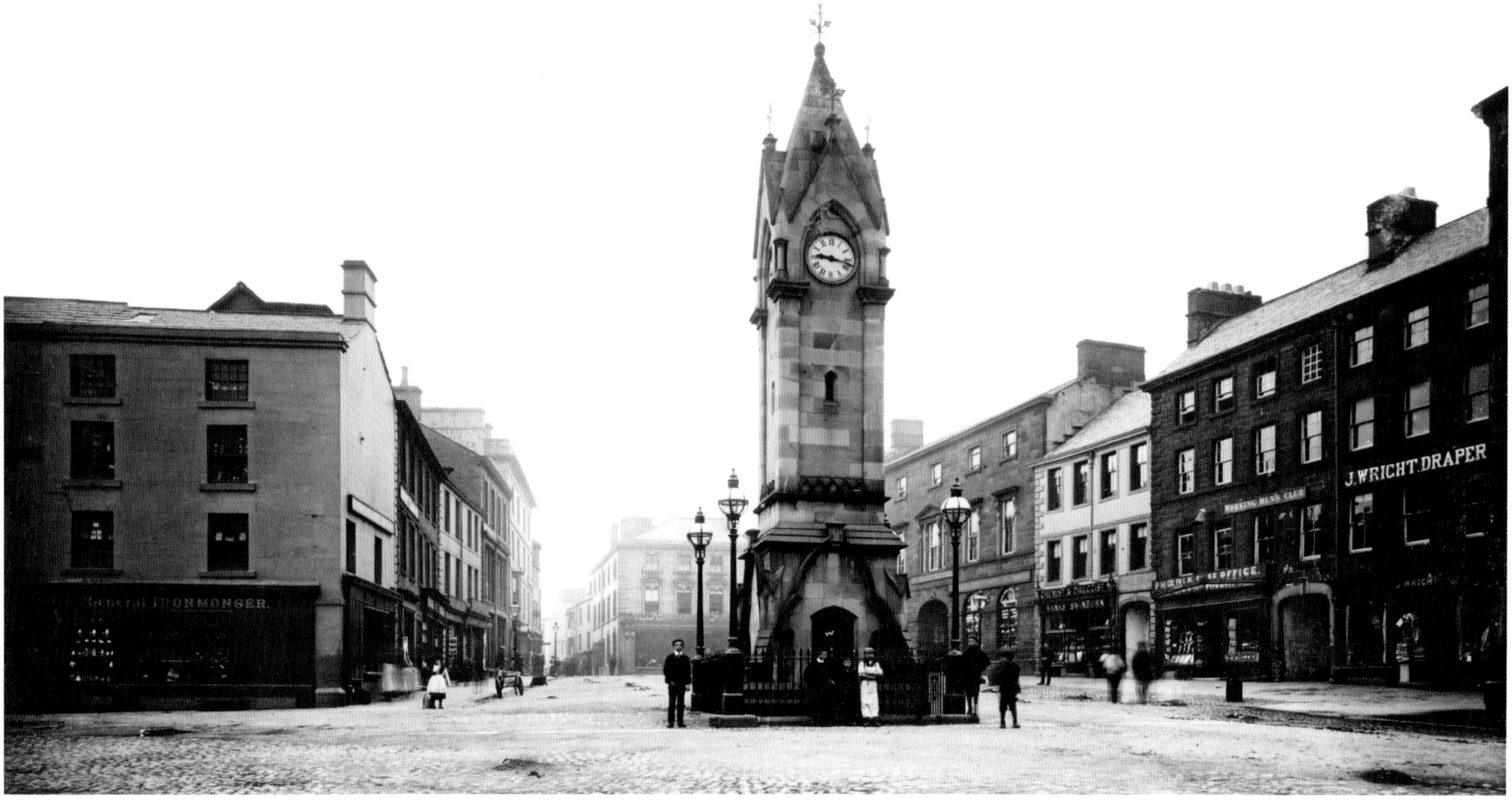
IRONMONGER.
J. WRIGHT DRAPER

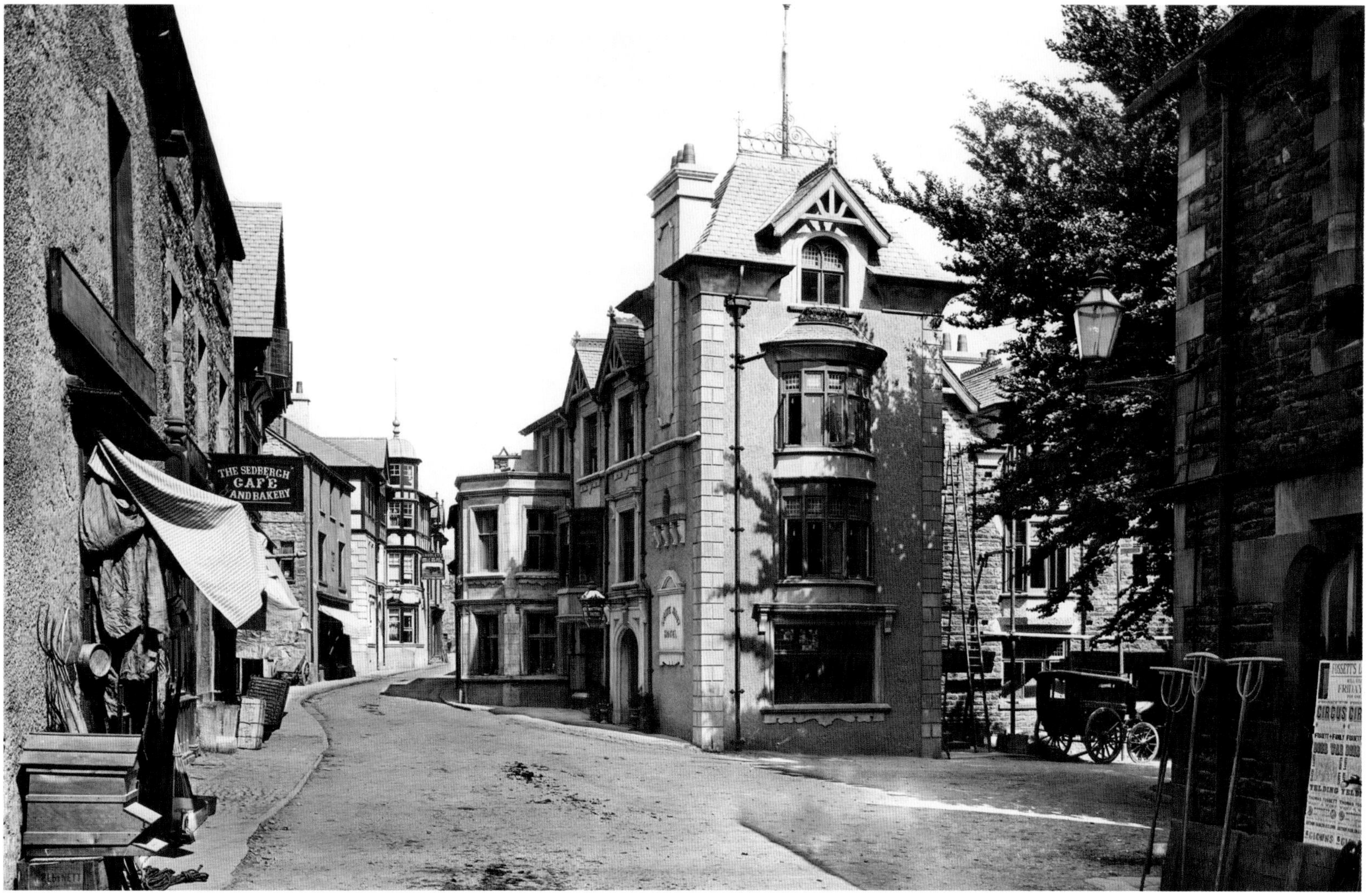
THE SEDBERGH
CAFE
AND BAKERY

ROYAL

North East

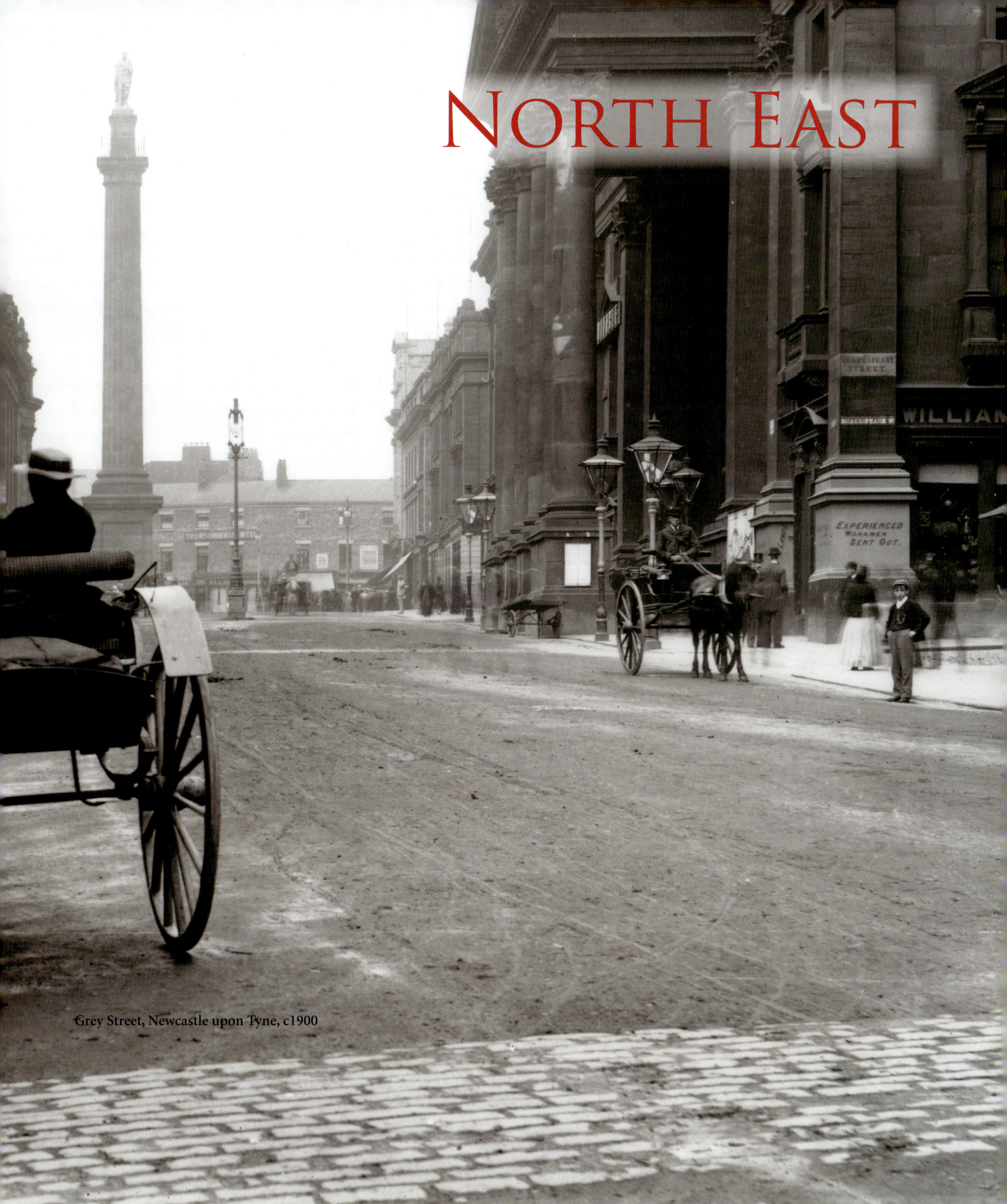

Grey Street, Newcastle upon Tyne, c1900

Northumberland

LINDISFARNE

Above: Lindisfarne Castle, Holy Island, c1890
Looking east at one of England's most romantic views. Holy Island derived its name from the ancient priory founded by St Aidan around 634. The scriptorium of the Priory produced the exquisite Lindisfarne Gospels. The 16th-century castle, built using masonry from the dissolved priory, sits on a volcanic extrusion accessible from the mainland only by a causeway at low tide. The original castle was restored by Sir Edwin Lutyens for the publishing magnate Edward Hudson from 1903.

Left: Woods Restaurant, Berwick-upon-Tweed, 1902
Although of no historical significance, this cafe reflects an increasingly important pastime of the age when affordable travel required the accompanying pleasure of lunch or afternoon tea, ushering in the institution of the English tea room.

Opposite top left: Moot Hall, Market Place, Hexham, 1902
Looking east across the Market Place towards the Moot Hall, with the Shambles to the right. An important market town, established on a terrace above the floodplain south of the River Tyne, its Abbey made Hexham a powerhouse of the region in mediaeval times. The Moot Hall was a fortified town gateway dating from the 15th century and was used as the bailiff's office and a courthouse. A modern version of the Shambles, or meat market, still stands in the Market Place today.

BERWICK

Top right: Royal Border Bridge, 1902
Built by Robert Stephenson, the son of George, between 1847 and 1850, the viaduct still carries the mainline railway across the River Tweed; a locomotive can be seen travelling south. In front of the bridge is the White Wall, built in 1296, which extended from Berwick Castle to the riverbank. It terminates in a gun tower dating from c1540.

HEXHAM

Above: Fore Street, 1902
View south near the junction with the Market Place. The elegant rusticated stone doorway to the right, crowned by a segmental pediment, is the entrance to the livery stables of the White Hart Inn, landlord W Haugh.

ALNWICK

Left: Market Place, c1890
The market cross on the left, and the Town Hall with its clock tower in the background. The livestock market is in progress. The town of Alnwick shared the strategic importance of the adjacent castle, the seat of the Percy family, earls and later dukes of Northumberland. Constant border skirmishes with the Scots meant that the town was defended with walls. The adjacent Great North Road and the town's proximity to the coast increased its importance for trade, guaranteeing a busy market.

Left: St Michael's Pant, Market Street, c1890
View east along Clayport Street at the junction with Fenkle Street. The Pant was a drinking fountain located opposite one of the entrances to the Market Place, to the right just out of shot, with a large trough for animals. Erected in 1755 and restored at the end of the 19th century, it depicts the figure of St Michael slaying the Dragon. Public fountains were the main source of free, fresh drinking water – not only for local residents, who did not have piped supplies, but also for the many draught animals passing through the town.

Left: Pottergate, Alnwick, c1890
View west towards Pottergate Tower, from the junction with Narrowgate. The fortified gateway was part of the town's walled defences, which were established in the 15th century. Rebuilt at the expense of the town in 1768 in the Gothick style, it included an ornate spire reminiscent of St Nicholas Church in Newcastle. It was irreparably damaged during a great storm in 1812 and the spire taken down. The Low Pant in the foreground is a Victorian structure over the site of the first fountain in the town that dated from 1611.

Below: Berwick-upon-Tweed, c1910
Fishermen with their nets on the banks of the Tweed. Fishing – and salmon fishing in particular – had been an important industry for the town for centuries. The development of ice houses during the 18th and 19th centuries allowed the industry to expand its trade in fresh – rather than just smoked, cured or salted – salmon further afield to the important London markets.

County Durham

DURHAM

Above: South Street, c1910
Looking south along the steep cobbled street running parallel with the River Wear in the centre of Durham. The sign on the left is for Melvin Bone, a smoke curer or chimney sweep; to the right is a general provisions shop. The backs of the buildings to the left look out over the river to Durham Castle.

Left: North Road, c1910
View north-east towards the railway viaduct. The dome-topped building is the Miners' Hall, built in 1875. Despite its impressive architectural features, it was not large enough to accommodate the several hundred delegates making up the assembly and was superseded by a larger Miners' Hall in 1915.

DARLINGTON

Above: High Row, 1893
A view towards the junction of High Row, Houndgate, Blackwellgate and Skinnergate. During the early 19th century, Darlington remained a small market town. As the century progressed, powerful Quaker families, such as the Pease and Backhouse families, were prominent employers and philanthropists in the area. Darlington's most famous landmark, the Clock Tower – designed by Alfred Waterhouse, who was responsible for London's Natural History Museum and Manchester Town Hall – was a gift to the town by the industrialist Joseph Pease in 1864.

Right: Tubwell Row, 1903
On the left, bedecked in flowers, are the premises of the seed merchants and nurserymen Kent & Brydon.

HARTLEPOOL

Left: Church Street, c1900

Looking south-west towards Christ Church. A double-decker electric tram can be clearly seen making its way down Church Street. Although the electric tram network opened in 1896, using the tramway from a former steam-powered tram system, horse-drawn carriages were still in use. The trams ran until they were replaced with trolley buses in the early 1920s. Christ Church dates from 1854 and is today the town's art gallery.

Above: Market Place, Middlesbrough1912

View looking north-west; the Old Town Hall is on the left behind the clock tower, with its main frontage opposite St Hilda's Church. The original Town Hall, designed by WL Moffat, was built in 1846. As the population of Middlesbrough mushroomed, it was supplanted by a much grander Gothic building by G G Hoskins in 1889. The town was little more than a homestead at the beginning of the 19th century, but the discovery of ironstone nearby and the development of docks fuelled its phenomenal growth in the second half of the century. St Hilda's, the town's parish church, was built in 1840 and demolished in 1969. Although most of the buildings seen here have been razed, the area is a stone's throw from one of the town's best-known sites – the gigantic transporter bridge over the nearby River Tees, built in 1911.

TEESSIDE

MIDDLESBROUGH

Above: Albert Park, 1896

Looking east through the main gates of Albert Park. The town's first mayor, Henry Bolckow, was conscious of the damaging effects of pollution and effluent from the rapid rise of industry, and the cramped living conditions in the town's densely packed terraces. He bought a plot of land, which he gave to the Council to build a green lung – a people's park – for Middlesbrough. Opened in August 1868 by Prince Arthur of Connaught, it was named after his father, Albert.

Left: Corporation Road, 1901

The iron and steel industry propelled Middlesbrough's rapid expansion throughout the second half of the 19th century. By 1900 the population had reached 90,000. The large building on the right is the Wesleyan Chapel. In the background is the tower of Hoskins's Gothic Town Hall.

HENRY A. MURTON
ENTRANCE 8 & 10 GRAINGER STREET
WATERPROOFER
HOUSE FURNISHING
28 BAINBRIDGE & CO. 26
22 BAINBRIDGE & CO. 22
50/- NO EXTRAS
RISI'S
M. TONEY

Tyne and Wear

NEWCASTLE UPON TYNE

Left: Bigg Market, c1920
Looking east along Bigg Market towards the Town Hall, which was completed in 1865 and demolished in 1973. To the left of the Town Hall is Cloth Market and to the right, Groat Market. Bigg Market's history dates back to mediaeval times, when a particular type of barley – Bigg –was traded. The market's importance was increased by its being sited on the Great North Road, the main highway between London and Scotland. To the left is Bainbridge's, one of the the world's first department stores. In 1838 Emerson Muschamp Bainbridge was a founder of a shop that included 23 different sections under one roof. The business snowballed and in 1865 occupied a 500-foot stretch of Market Street with entrances on Grainger Street and here in Bigg Market. Bainbridge's was acquired by the John Lewis Partnership in 1953, moving to the site of its current premises in Eldon Square in 1976.

SANDHILL

Left: Bessie Surtees House, 41–44 Sandhill, Newcastle upon Tyne, c1880
The main façade, with a horse-drawn cart and a hand cart in the street. At the time the photograph was taken, these were the premises of James D Hedley, shopkeeper, J & E S Edminson, wine and spirit merchants, and G Edminson, corn dealers. Originally two separate houses, Milbank House (44) started life as a 16th-century timber-framed building; the actual Surtees House (41) is mainly 17th century. The two were joined together in the 1930s by Lord Gort. The house is famous as the house from which Bessie Surtees, a merchant's daughter, eloped in 1772 with John Scott, who became Lord Eldon, Lord Chancellor. Now in the care of English Heritage, part of the building is open to the public.

Below: Sandhill, Newcastle upon Tyne, c1920
A later photograph of showing the railway viaduct in the background.

Opposite above: Grainger Market, Grainger Street, Newcastle upon Tyne, c1910
The covered market was commissioned by local builder and developer Richard Grainger to the designs of John Dobson. The Central Arcade housed the fruit and vegetable market. The original timber roof was replaced in 1904 in steel and glass, depicted here.

Above left: High Street Gosforth, c1900
A packed horse-drawn brake and horse-powered trams travel along the road. The new council offices are under construction in the background.

Above right: St George's Terrace, Jesmond, c1910
Suburban Newcastle. A typical row of local shops, with flats above, including newsagents A H Robinson.

COLLINGWOOD BUILDINGS

Collingwood Buildings, Collingwood Street, Newcastle upon Tyne, 1903
Above right: Originally designed as a hotel, Collingwood Buildings was taken over during construction by Barclays Bank.
Above left: The elaborately carved stone portico of Barclays Bank.
Left: The sumptuous interior of the bank, looking along a corridor lined with mahogany screens.

THE SIDE

Above: The Side, Newcastle upon Tyne, c1910
Looking west towards the arch of the railway viaduct high above the street. The photograph shows how the railway cut through existing streets and buildings with breathtaking bravura. Two railway companies originally came into the town: the York, Newcastle and Berwick Railway (YN&BR), and the Newcastle and Carlisle Railway (N&CR). The YN&BR merged with other companies in 1854 to form the North Eastern Railway (NER), which absorbed the N&CR in 1862.

EMPIRE VARIETY THEATRE

Top: Empire Variety Theatre, Newgate Street, Newcastle upon Tyne, 1891

Looking across the orchestra pit towards the proscenium (left) and the main auditorium seating (right). The Theatre was built by Pringle of Gateshead for the theatre's proprietor, Farquhar M Laing, and designed by the architects Oliver and Leeson. Accommodating up to 2,000 people, the auditorium's outstanding features included electric lighting that illuminated both the interior lights and the footlights. From the central dome hung a gilded chandelier – or 'electrolier' – holding twenty-one 32-candlepower lamps. The audiences, accustomed to the flicker and fumes of gas lighting, must have been dazzled by the brilliance of the new theatre's decor and the light thrown onto its stage.

LEAZES PARK

Above: Leazes Park, Newcastle upon Tyne, 1894

A unique feature of Newcastle is the Town Moor – 1,000 acres of common land within the city boundaries. Leazes Park came about when 3,000 working men petitioned for a recreational area in the city. It was created by landscaping an uncultivated area of moor south of the main Town Moor. The first public park on Tyneside, opened in 1873, it boasted extensive planting, an ornamental lake, a bandstand and the terrace pictured.

ROYAL STATION HOTEL

Top left: Royal Station Hotel, Neville Street, Newcastle upon Tyne, 1893
Built adjacent to the Central Station, the 1892 extension of this railway hotel was designed by the architect William Bell, then the principal architect for the North Eastern Railway.
Top right: The first-class Refreshment Room in the Royal (North Eastern) Station Hotel. Burmantofts Company commissioned the interior photographs to show how their decorative architectural terracotta tiles and fittings were used in the building.
Above left: The bar in the first-class Refreshment Room.

NEW BRIDGE STREET

Above right: New Bridge Street Goods Station, Newcastle upon Tyne, c1910
Again the work of NER architect William Bell, this goods station was built in 1906 using new techniques of reinforced concrete, making it a cutting-edge, purpose-built bulk storage and handling terminus. It could accommodate six goods trains and transfer bulk or packaged goods such as flour in a highly efficient way. Among the well-known companies that used Bridge Street as their permanent northern depot were Cadbury and Fry's – both of whom have their names emblazoned on the outside of the building.

CENTRAL STATION

Left: Newcastle Central Station, 1894
Built between 1845 and 1855 by John Dobson and extended in the early 1890s by William Bell, Newcastle Central is one of the finest station buildings of the Victorian age.

Below: Forth Banks Goods Station, Pottery Lane, 1893
Inside the goods shed at Forth Bank, designed by the North Eastern Railway Company architect Thomas Prosser in 1874, with two hydraulic Armstrong cranes in the foreground. The spectacular growth of Newcastle and its insatiable demand for goods capacity kept the NER in a state of continuous expansion. A very large transhipment facility with a sizeable undercroft ideal for storing ale, it was used by numerous breweries from as far afield as Burton-on-Trent as their local depot.

LAING ART GALLERY

Left: Laing Art Gallery, Higham Place, Newcastle upon Tyne, 1906
View of the south-eastern corner and tower seen from New Bridge Street, with Higham Place to the right. Built between1903 and 1904 to the designs of the architectural firm Cackett and Burns Dick, the Gallery was funded by the eponymous benefactor, Alexander Laing, whose fortune had been made from his wine and spirits business. It was donated to the municipality without any art for the interior, but Laing was confident of the generosity of his peers to provide suitable hangings and other artefacts. Fortunately, he was correct. The current collection, which specialises in British artists, comprises many important paintings as well as applied art and sculpture.

Below: Newcastle Central Station, Neville Street, c1920
Looking east towards the station's main entrance, with a taxi rank in the foreground, trams to the left and St Nicholas Cathedral in the background. John Dobson's station was opened by Queen Victoria in 1850. Its development was complicated by the geography of the city and the need to bridge the steep Tyne gorge. Robert Stephenson's magnificent double-decker High Level Bridge enabled trains to travel directly across the Tyne and into the newly built Central Station. The new bridge was formally inaugurated in 1849 by Queen Victoria in the royal train, her progress witnessed by many thousands of spectators on the bridge and on boats in the Tyne below.

MELBOURNE STREET

Above left: Addison Potter and Son, Melbourne Street, 1894
View of the long-demolished malthouse, the premises of Addison Potter and Sons, maltsters, which were acquired during a massive expansion by Newcastle Breweries.

Above right: Hodgkin, Barnett, Pease, Spence & Co Bank, 9–17 Collingwood Street, 1891
The bank, built between 1890 and 1891 to designs by the architect R Johnson, is a short distance along Collingwood Street from the future Collingwood Buildings.

QUAYSIDE

Opposite above: Quayside, Newcastle upon Tyne, 1928
View west from the north bank of the Tyne towards the Tyne Bridge, with the Swing Bridge and High Level Bridge beyond. The Quayside is in its heyday. Pedestrians navigate their way through the bustling riverside lined with ships loading and unloading their cargoes.

Opposite below: Grainger Street, Newcastle upon Tyne, 1900
Richard Grainger developed some of Newcastle's finest buildings and streets between 1824 and 1841, and many parts of the city, including Grainger Street, are named after him. The young boy on the right of the picture has no shoes in this busy street scene photographed at the beginning of the 20th century.

TWO BRIDGES

Above: Two Bridges, River Tyne, c1900
View from the south bank of the River Tyne towards the Swing Bridge and High Level Bridge. The low-level Swing bridge linking Newcastle and Gateshead is on the site of a Roman bridge built by the order of the Emperor Hadrian in AD 122. The Swing bridge was designed by Sir W G Armstrong and Company under the supervision of the Tyne Improvement Commission. Building work began in 1868 and the bridge was completed eight years later. It had to swing open to allow ships to pass into the docks. The High Level bridge, providing a crossing for both railway and road transport, was designed by Robert Stephenson, son of the local steam engine pioneer George Stephenson.

E.W. YOUNGER & Co. Ltd
TRANSPORT SPECIALISTS.
JOHN BAXTER & Co. Ltd
HAULAGE CONTRACTORS
XN-5270

E. HARKER 40
MAKERS
FIXERS
ALL KINDS
BLINDS

DOG LEAP STAIRS

CASTLE GARTH

Opposite: Castle Garth, Newcastle upon Tyne, 1894
View north at the junction with the Black Gate, where it rises steeply towards Side and St Nicholas Cathedral beyond. The quaintly named Dog Leap Stairs descend from here to Side. According to legend, Bessie Surtees was swept away up the stairs on horseback by her lover, Lord Eldon, in 1772. He was to become Lord Chancellor and one of the city's most celebrated sons.

Top left: Lemington c1900
Lemington developed in the 19th century because of its proximity to coal deposits as well as the nearby water transport.

Above left: Back Maling Street, Newcastle upon Tyne,
Flights of worn stairs lead from the street to the front doors of the dilapidated houses of Nos. 6–9 Back Maling Street.

PADDY'S MARKET

Top right: Paddy's Market, Quayside, Newcastle upon Tyne, c1900
Customers and vendors stand beside second-hand clothes for sale that are displayed on the ground in front of M Ripley's general store.

Above right: Arthur's Cooperage, The Close, Newcastle upon Tyne, 1884
The business house of J Arthur, known as Arthur's Cooperage, on The Close, photographed in 1884. Today the building has been converted from one manufacturing barrels and casks to a pub and restaurant, but it retains the name.

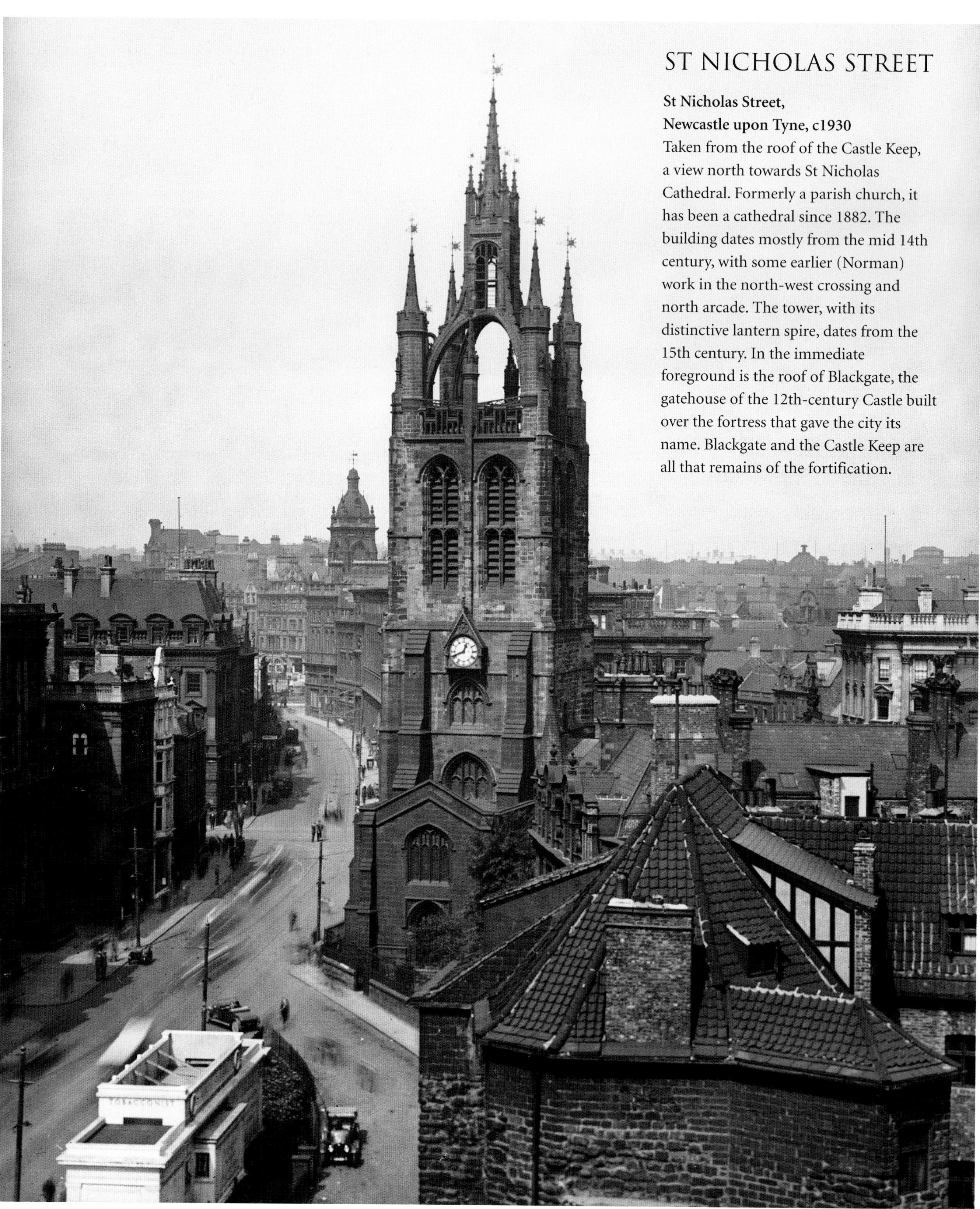

ST NICHOLAS STREET

St Nicholas Street, Newcastle upon Tyne, c1930

Taken from the roof of the Castle Keep, a view north towards St Nicholas Cathedral. Formerly a parish church, it has been a cathedral since 1882. The building dates mostly from the mid 14th century, with some earlier (Norman) work in the north-west crossing and north arcade. The tower, with its distinctive lantern spire, dates from the 15th century. In the immediate foreground is the roof of Blackgate, the gatehouse of the 12th-century Castle built over the fortress that gave the city its name. Blackgate and the Castle Keep are all that remains of the fortification.

BYKER

Above: Gordon Road, Byker, 1910
A group of children watch street sweepers in slouch hats at work on a cobbled road between a row of terrace houses and a school. The man on the right is clearing out a gulley.

GATESHEAD

Left: Pelaw Bank, Heworth, Gateshead, 1900
A view towards Pelaw Bank, with St Mary's churchyard wall to the right and the old vicarage to the left.

TYNEMOUTH

Above: Long Sands, c1890
The beach, crowded with people, has several groups of bathing machines on the shoreline. The Tynemouth Aquarium and Winter Garden on top of the cliff opened in 1878. It was later named the Tynemouth Palace, and later still, The Plaza.

Right: 50 King Street, South Shields, 1886
Crossling and Company and Henry Potts at 50 King Street.

Opposite above: Laygate Lane, South Shields, 1900
Laygate Lane is one of a number of sturdy Victorian terraces in South Shields; many of them were built speculatively by developers as the town expanded thanks to the coal and alkali industries. In 1850 South Shields (including Westoe) became a municipal borough; Harton was added in 1901, and Cleadon Bank and Harton Village in 1921.

Opposite below: The Low Lights, Mouth of the Tyne, North Shields, c1890
A paddle steamer is moored in the foreground, with the sails of Dutch sailing vessels and other craft beyond. Viewed from the sea, the alignment of the lights from the two white towers on the quay ensured safe navigation of the mouth of the Tyne. Auty Ltd, the photographer, was based in Tynemouth.

SUNDERLAND

Above: Sunderland, 1889
A group of poor women and children sitting around the steps to a shop in a slum area of Sunderland.

Left: Mowbray Park, 1900
The park was created in the 1850s out of Bildon Hill and the old quarries on its north face. This picture shows the glass and cast iron Winter Gardens built on the back of the Library and Museum. The ornate structure was destroyed by bombing during the Second World War.

SUNDERLAND TOWN HALL

Town Hall, Fawcett Street, 1891

Top left: By the 1880s Sunderland Corporation had realised there was an urgent need for a new building from which to run its affairs. When plans to build a Town Hall in Mowbray Park were abandoned, the Shrubbery in Fawcett Street was identified as an ideal location and purchased by Sunderland Corporation. Ipswich architect Brightwen Binyon provided the desired classical design, and Mayor Edward Richardson laid the foundation stone in September 1887. Three years later the building was completed at a cost of £50,000. It was demolished in February 1971 amid much local controversy.

Top right: Reception Room

Above left: The Council Chamber

MONKWEARMOUTH

Above right: Primitive Methodist Chapel, Charles Street, Monkwearmouth, 1891

In 1932 several of the larger Methodist denominations, including the Primitive Methodists and Wesleyans joined to form the Methodist Union.

RAVINE FOOTBRIDGE

Right: Roker Park, Sunderland, c1890
Looking east from the beach towards the Ravine footbridge in Roker Park. The land for the park was given to the town by Sir Hedworth Williamson and the Church Commissioners as a space for public recreation by all classes, and also to mark the centenary of the Sunday School movement. Opened in 1880, it is adjacent to the coastal cliffs; the beach is only accessible via the ravine.

Below: High Street West, Sunderland, 1900
A view of the prosperous-looking town centre. The street is crowded with men, which probably means that it is either a Sunday or a public holiday.

FAWCETT STREET, SUNDERLAND

Above: Fawcett Street, c1900

Built on the coast straddling the River Wear, which brought maritime commerce and shipbuilding to the town from early in its history, Sunderland flourished from the mid 19th century. Coal production and its port facilities made it one of Britain's most important towns, and one of the world's largest centres of shipbuilding.

This photograph, looking towards the Town Hall, shows the recently electrified tram system. Trams were largely horse-drawn until the Corporation decided that electrification was the way forward and bought out the private companies to consolidate the tram network. The first electric tram route, from Fawcett Street to Roker, was opened with great ceremony on 15 August 1900.

North Yorkshire

BEDALE

Top left: Market Place, 1907
Looking north towards St Gregory's Church. In the foreground is the 14th-century Market Cross, which stands at the meeting of the main mediaeval roads of Wynd, Emgate and Market Place. Fine three-storey Georgian houses illustrate the growing wealth in the 18th century from the local fulling and tanning industries. The cobbled area on the left of the picture is the old Market Place.

HARROGATE

Middle left: Cold Bath Road, c1900
View from the north end of Cold Bath Road, looking east across The Stray towards buildings in Prospect Place. The steady growth of the town as a spa began in the 17th century with the discovery of mineral wells but accelerated with the arrival of the railways. To meet the needs and social standing of visitors taking the waters, a host of elegant buildings sprang up to house both the facilities and their users. The Stray was established, in the wake of the enclosure of common lands, as 200 acres of public space linking the various spas and wells so that visitors could promenade between them.

STAITHES

Bottom left: Staithes, c1890
The tide is relatively high in this photograph, hence the local fishing boats, called cobles, drawn up above the tideline. At low tide the true nature of the shore is clearer, and the design of the coble, with its flat bottom and shallow draft, makes more sense, enabling it to pass over hidden rock formations.

Above: Robin Hood's Bay Dock, c1900
View looking north-west towards New Road from the dockside at Robin Hood's Bay. The main occupation of this picturesque coastal town was ostensibly fishing, but smuggling was rife as the isolation of the village and its remote waters helped evade customs and excise on illicit cargo shipped in from the Continent.

Right: St Michael's Church, Malton
This splendid Norman building, viewed from the south, has undergone restoration at various different times since its construction, including the addition of a tower in the 15th century. However, much of the original fabric remains, including the pillars and the capitals of the north aisle, the capitals in the south aisle and probably the font.

SCARBOROUGH

Top left: The Spa, c1900
View from the Esplanade showing the Spa in the foreground and the beach and harbour in the background. Mineral streams were first discovered in the 16th century, but it was not until the development of the railways that Scarborough blossomed as one of the earliest seaside and spa resorts in the country.

Middle left: Scarborough, c1900
View north over the bay towards the Grand Hotel in the foreground (left) and the Castle in the background (right). Bathing huts clustered on the beach and cobles, with their masts raised, are moored in the shallows. The Grand Hotel opened in 1867. One of the first purpose-built hotels in Europe, it was claimed to be one of the largest in the world with 365 rooms – one for every day of the year.

RICHMOND

Left: Market Place
Looking towards Holy Trinity Church and the stone obelisk, erected in 1771 on the site of an earlier market cross. One of the shops advertises itself as a '6d & 1d' Bazaar'.

STAITHES

Left: Staithes, c1900

A bare-foot boy leans in the doorway of a narrow street looking at the camera. One of a series taken by Thomas Watson, this photograph was used by the Victoria County History to illustrate the *History of the County of York North Riding*, published in 1923.

WHITBY

Below right: Whitby Abbey, c1910

View from the east of the ruined Benedictine Abbey. Dating from the 7th century, the Abbey was destroyed in 1540 during Henry VIII's dissolution of the monasteries.

Below left: Church Street, c1910

Looking north towards the town hall, whose clock tower can be seen in the distance. To the modern eye Whitby is quaint and picturesque, but this street scene bears witness to its commercial prosperity, with its sturdy buildings and numerous shops. Not just a pretty harbour town, Whitby had a boat-building industry and a lively tourist trade. It also produced alum in addition to its fishing and maritime activities, which included large-scale whaling.

YORK

Above: Low Petergate, c1896

View north-west at the junction with Goodramgate towards York Minster in the distance. The timber-framed jettied building (right) is a late 17th-century survivor. Others with gables can be seen beyond on the left beneath the twin towers of the Minster, one of the glories of mediaeval ecclesiastical architecture. Built in phases over 200 years on the site of a 7th-century timber church, its Great East Window completed in 1403 has the largest expanse of mediaeval stained glass in the world. Strategic views of the Minster are now protected to avoid the visual harm caused to the setting of so many other historic buildings across England by tall buildings and misguided new development.

Left: Shambles, c1900

York's narrow streets – the archetypal image of England's mediaeval urban townscape – with jettied storeys almost meeting overhead. Shambles is the name given to the meat market where animals were slaughtered before the institution of large-scale abattoirs. Most of the buildings pictured here, some of which date from the 14th century, would have housed butchers. The group to the right are standing at the opening of Little Shambles; although the street level has risen over time, the scene is still very recognisable today.

Opposite: Trinity Lane, 1902

The arrival of the photographer was a notable event. Residents emerge from their homes to be captured at a fleeting moment in time. The varied architectural styles of the buildings reflect their diverse ages from 1500 to 1850. Note the horizontal sliding sash windows known as Yorkshire casements.

NEWS
OF THE
WORLD

JUBBERGATE

Top and above left: Jubbergate, York, c1900
Jubbergate is an old thoroughfare connecting Newgate, the Shambles and Parliament Street. The name has a Jewish connection and most likely refers to the return of a Jewish population to this area of the city in the 13th century after the massacre of 1190, which wiped out the entire Jewish community.
Everything needed by the household of the day could be bought at Websters (top) – note the wash tub and dolly, as well as the trunks and household wares. Forrington and its unnamed neighbour (above left) offer Cycle Storage and Perambulators for hire from the ground floor of the 16th-century corner building. Note the clay pantile roofs, first introduced from Holland in the 17th century and commonly used in York and across eastern England.

Above right: Black Bull Hotel, Finkle Street, York, c1900
Landlord W E Goodall and his family or staff pose for the camera outside their 16th-century premises. The bracketed lantern advertises the pub and music hall.

ALL SAINTS' CHURCH, YORK

Above: All Saints' Church, Pavement, c1910
View south-west towards the junction of High Ousegate, Coppergate and Piccadilly. The church dates from the 14th century, and the landmark lantern tower is a distinctive rarity. As the Guild church of the city, it is the last resting place of 34 Lord Mayors. In front of the east end, farm machinery and implements are set out for sale – an overspill from the market taking place on Parliament Street, where the stalls are just visible in front of the Gothic-style Barclays Bank built in 1901. Numerous carts, including a North Eastern Railway parcels van, service the busy market.

Left: St Martin le Grand, Coney Street, c1900
View of the east end of the church showing the large cantilevered clock, which remains one of York's landmarks. A clock has hung over Coney Street since 1668, but the version depicted was part of an installation in 1856 that incorporated the metal figure of a naval officer mounted on top, known affectionately as the Little Admiral. The figure, dating from 1778, revolved as part of the chiming mechanism. The 11th-century church was virtually destroyed during one of the notorious Baedecker raids in April 1942, which also left the Guildhall in ruins. St Martin was partially rebuilt, with the south aisle turned into the nave; happily, its exceptional stained glass had been removed to safety as a precaution and was undamaged in the bombing.

HOLY TRINITY, YORK

Above left: Holy Trinity, Goodramgate, c1905
View east towards the churchyard gate. Holy Trinity sits in the shadow of the Minster. This dilapidated gate remains in place today and in slightly better condition; the sign on the gate asks 'earnestly' for 'offerings towards repairs', with the inference that the church is out of use. The large poster to the left of the gate advertises an amateur dramatic production of the hit comic opera Dorothy at the Theatre Royal, with dates in April 1904.

Above right: Gas works, York, c1910
The chimney belongs to the York United Gas Company in Monkgate, established in 1826. York was one of the earliest cities to have a coal gas network, although until 1850 this was mainly enjoyed by the wealthy and by businesses.

Right: Newspaper seller, York, c1910
The street vendor was captured by local photographer William Hayes, whose prolific images appeared on many local postcards of the period. Hayes had a particular interest in the social realities of the time. This man's stall is a canvas satchel as he sells the latest editions of popular newspapers in what might be the Minster Close.

LADY PECKETT'S YARD, YORK

Above: Ebor Dairy, Lady Peckett's Yard, 1910

Located between Pavement and Fossgate, the yard is named after Alice Peckett, the wife of John Peckett, Lord Mayor of York in 1701. Founded by the grocer, confectioner and philanthropist Joseph Rowntree in 1866, the dairy churned fresh butter each day. The Rowntree family were members of the Society of Friends – or Quakers – and champions of social reform. The Sunday or Sabbath School Movement set out to improve the moral and educational welfare of the poor. Influenced by Joseph Sturge's work in Birmingham, the first adult school opened in Peckett's Yard in 1857 to deliver basic education to illiterate adults, as well as ministering to their mortal souls. In 1899 Seebohm Rowntree conducted a pioneering survey of York. He found that over a quarter of the population were living in poverty.

West Yorkshire

BRADFORD

The wealth of the great industrial cities of England, such as Bradford, posed a moral dilemma for many who were conscious of the environmental and human cost of the Industrial Revolution. They strived to use their new-found wealth to improve society for themselves and their fellow men. This spirit of philanthropy surfaced in public buildings, institutions and amenities, and often in more radical measures such as Titus Salt's visionary decision to move his mills and workforce from Bradford's toxic environs to form a new purpose-built model community at Saltaire.

Above left: Bradford Town Hall, Town Hall Square, 1875
View from the north, with the canopied Gothic monument to Titus Salt in the foreground. Lockwood and Mawson were chosen to design the building after an architectural competition. Designed in a 13th-century Gothic style, with a tower modelled on the Palazzo Vecchio in Florence, it is one of the most accomplished Victorian public buildings and was intended to outdo its rivals in Leeds and Halifax.
Top right: The east elevation of the Town Hall extension on what would later be Norfolk Gardens. Norman Shaw's design added another council chamber, more committee rooms and a banqueting hall in 1909.
Right: The council chamber in the Bradford Town Hall extension.

Opposite below right: Cartwright Memorial Hall, Lister Park, Bradford, 1905
The south front viewed from the south-east. Designed by Sir John Simpson and E J Milner Allen in an Edwardian Baroque style, the Hall was built over three years between 1900 to 1903 as an art gallery and museum funded by equal contributions from Lord Masham (who had once owned the estate and house on which the hall was built) and Bradford Corporation. The name commemorates Dr Edmund Cartwright, inventor of the power loom and wool combing machine to which Bradford owed much of its prosperity.

Opposite below left: Cartwright Memorial Hall, Bradford
Interior showing the colonnade and exhibition cases in the room known as the 'Loggia'. In addition to the permanent displays, masterpieces were loaned from all over the country when the Hall was the centrepiece of a great exhibition in Lister Park in 1904.

Opposite above: The Wool Exchange, Market Street, Bradford, c1900
Bradford's superb Victorian townscape. The grand Gothic Revival architecture of the Wool Exchange, with its tall clock tower, is a potent symbol of the importance of wool to the wealth of Bradford and a counterpoint to the Town Hall, which can be seen soaring skywards in the distance. The city was built on wool, first as a cottage industry and then propelled by the latest technology, making Bradford into a pulsating centre of steam-powered mills. The Exchange, designed by Lockwood and Mawson, took three years to build, its foundation stone having been laid in 1864 by the then Prime Minister, Lord Palmerston.

YORKSHIRE COLLEGE

Above: Yorkshire College, University Road, Leeds, 1895
The Yorkshire College of Science buildings were originally designed by Alfred Waterhouse, with later additions by his son Paul. Founded in 1874, the college formed the nucleus of the future Leeds University.

Top left & right: Yorkshire Penny Bank, 2 Infirmary Street, Leeds, 1894
Interior views of the bank showing its lavish decor: the service counter (left) from the customer's side, and the view from the manager's booth, overlooking the service side of the counter (right).

LEEDS SCHOOL OF MEDICINE

The School of Medicine admitted its first students in 1831, one of 10 provincial medical schools founded between 1824 and 1834. The first year's intake was 13 students, but admissions rose steadily and various premises were used by the growing School. By the 1880s the roll had swollen to 80 students per year, and overcrowding meant that premises in Thoresby Place, adjacent to the Infirmary, were purchased in 1889.

Opposite top left: Leeds School Of Medicine, Thoresby Place, 1895
The south facade of the New Medical School, now called the Old Medical School, built between 1891 and 1894 to the designs of William Henry Thorp. This photograph was commissioned by Dr R N Hartley, a member of the Ophthalmology section of the British Medical Association at the time and likely to have been a Professor at the School of Medicine.
Opposite top right: The hexagonal lobby of the main entrance on St George's Street.
Opposite middle left: The Histological Laboratory, with microscopes and gas burners on top of the long wooden benches.
Opposite middle right: Rows of tables in the Dissecting Room.
Opposite bottom left: The School's Pathological Museum
Opposite bottom right: The Bone Room within the Anatomical Museum, Leeds School of Medicine.

LEEDS GENERAL INFIRMARY

Leeds General Infirmary, Great George Street, 1895

Top left: View from the south-east. The main block of Leeds General Infirmary was built between 1863 and 1868 to the designs of Sir George Gilbert Scott, with extensions in 1891–92 by George Corson. Gilbert Scott and the Infirmary's Chief Physician, Dr Charles Chadwick, opted to use a pavilion system for the new Infirmary, providing accommodation for almost 300 patients in separate wings linked to the central block by arcaded corridors. The pavilion plan, intended to promote better ventilation to prevent the spread of infection, was pioneered by Florence Nightingale. The building cost £100,000 to complete and was officially opened on 19 May 1869 by HRH The Prince of Wales (later King Edward VII).
Top right: The Post Mortem Room.
Middle left: Interior view of Ward No. 6, with nurses and patients seated by the beds.
Left: The Central Hall in Leeds General Infirmary, looking along the length of the hall and its cast iron roof. A tennis net has been set up in the centre of the room.

CORN EXCHANGE

Above: Corn Exchange, Call Lane, Leeds, c1910
View looking east towards the main entrance. The exchange, designed by Cuthbert Brodrick and completed in 1862, has a strong French influence – especially the dome. Brodrick had studied in Paris and was inspired by the Bourse de Commerce.

Left: St Anne's Cathedral, Cookridge Street, Leeds, 1905
View looking south from Great George Street. St Anne's Roman Catholic Cathedral and Presbytery were designed by John Henry Eastwood and S K Greenslade, and built between 1902 and 1904 in an Arts & Crafts Gothic Revival style. Eastwood was a founder member of the Guild of St Gregory and St Luke, devoted to the improvement of church craftsmanship.

STENNING
OLD GOLD & SILVER BOUGHT
CURIOSITIE SHOPPE

COUNTY ARCADE

Opposite: County Arcade, Briggate, Leeds, 1904
Leeds is renowned for its sophisticated arcades, which bear comparison with the best in Europe. With a decorative wrought iron gate at one end, the County Arcade is a fine example. Designed by the architect Frank Matcham, it is part of the Victoria Quarter shopping area in the centre of Leeds. The photograph was taken for Burmantofts Co, whose decorative faience and terracotta was used in its construction.

LEEDS TOWN HALL

Above: Leeds Town Hall, Park Lane, c1910
View looking north-east across Victoria Square from what is now The Headrow. The Town Hall was one of the seminal public buildings of the Victorian age and a powerful symbol of the city's ambition. Designed by Cuthbert Brodrick in an exuberant French Neoclassical style and built between 1852 and 1858, it was designed as a multi-purpose civic complex to accommodate a mayoral suite, Council chamber, courtrooms, offices and a vast concert hall for 8,000 people. It is dressed in local Darley Dale stone; the grand Corinthian order marching round the building is repeated around the stunning clock tower above. Inside, the great organ by Henry Smart and William Spark is one of the finest in Europe. At the Town Hall's official opening by Queen Victoria in September 1858, some half a million people thronged the streets to witness the proceedings.

WAKEFIELD

Top left: Town Hall, Bond Street, 1900

The tall octagonal corner tower of Wakefield County Hall, as seen from Wood Street to the east. The Town Hall was built in 1898 as the headquarters of West Riding County Council; the Gothic design was the work of James Gibson, while the interior, laden with symbolism, was designed by the gifted Art Nouveau sculptor Henry Charles Fehr.

Top right: View from Bond Street

Above left: The Council Chamber, with its richly decorated ceiling

Above right: Free Art Nouveau decoration within an octagonal vestibule, with a view through a doorway to the staircase.

CORN EXCHANGE, WAKEFIELD

Left: Corn Exchange, Westgate, 1885

The Wakefield Exchange Company was set up in 1836, and the foundation stone of the building was laid in May 1837. Sited at the top of Westgate to meet the significant amount of commerce passing through the town and its markets, the Exchange opened for business in 1838. As well as corn, the trade included wool and other commodities. Wakefield's location on the River Calder made it an inland port, but the changing fortunes of the town led to the Exchange becoming a billiards hall and cinema. A small fire was used as an excuse for demolition in 1962.

HALIFAX

Below: Crown Street, 1896

The town's 19th-century wealth came from the cotton, wool and carpet industries and, like most other Yorkshire towns, it had a large number of weaving mills, many of which have been lost or converted to alternate use.

South Yorkshire

DONCASTER

Above: Millns & Company, Sepulchre Gate, c1925
As well as advertising Rudge Whitworth motorcycles and bicycles, the business offers gramophones for sale. Although new consumer products began to appear on the market, dealer networks were not immediately established, leading to some odd pairings as retailers embraced the latest craze that might not fit with their current product lines. The advertisements offer easy purchase plans – was this a sign of current financial constraint, or of confidence in the healthy finances of the clientele?

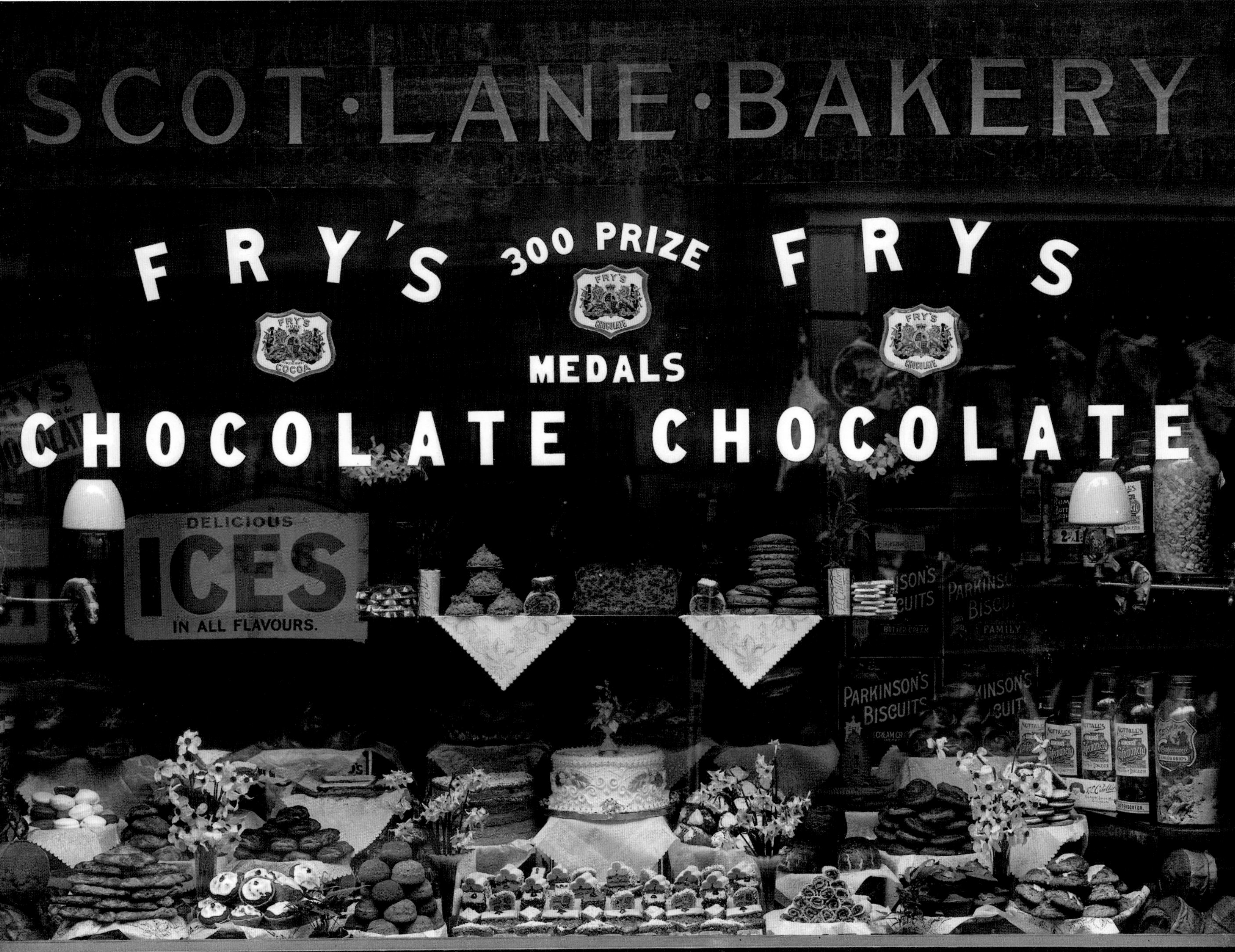

SCOT LANE, DONCASTER

Above: Scot Lane, c1920
This picture from the collection of Doncaster area photographer Luke Bagshaw shows a cornucopia of treats on display in the bakery window, including a jar of Nuttalls Rum and Butter drops at two ounces for one penny!

Opposite below: High Street, Doncaster, c1880
View north looking along the snow-covered street, which is part of the Great North Road, one of the most important routes in the country. The imposing building middle left is Mansion House, the seat of the Mayor and one of only three Mansion Houses in the country at that time. Completed in 1748, it reflected the city's wealth, which was further increased during the Industrial Revolution. Doncaster's coal reserves and the Don Navigation made it a major railway centre and a focus of steel production. In the background Clock Corner can just be made out – a large early 19th-century clock cantilevered over the street to allow it to be seen along the length of the High Street.

DONCASTER HIGH STREET

Opposite above: High Street, c1910
A view towards the north of Clock Corner offers a closer look at the grandeur of the city centre. The building on which the large cantilevered clock was mounted was remodelled, the clock relocated and a new one erected as a more conventional clock tower in 1894. The domed classical corner building, built in 1897, now houses the HSBC bank. Wrights Umbrellas occupies a much older 17th-century building.

Above: Market Place, Doncaster, c1910
View looking down Scot Lane from the Market Place.

ROTHERHAM BRIDGE

Opposite below: Chapel of our Lady, 1895
Dating from 1483, the chapel was built for the benefit of travellers and funded by donations. Added to the existing bridge over the River Don, it was small but richly decorated. After the Dissolution the chapel was turned into an almshouse before falling into ruin. Following repairs in the 18th century, the chapel was used as a jail until 1826 and thereafter as a rented dwelling until it became a tobacconist and newsagent from 1888 – as in this picture. The chapel was finally returned to its original purpose after renovation in 1924.

SHEFFIELD

Left: The Corn Exchange, Broad Street, c1900
Built for the Duke of Norfolk in 1881, the Central Hall of the Corn Exchange was gutted by fire in 1947; the offices surrounding it were demolished in 1964. The area around Broad Street – Castle Folds – was a market hub, with the Corn Exchange housing a regular auction and the wholesale fruit and vegetable market opposite. The ale house in the foreground advertises 'Gilmour's Windsor Ales and Stouts'.

Below: Christ Church, Attercliffe, c1900
The foundation stone was laid by the Duke of Norfolk in October 1822 and the church consecrated in July 1826. Damaged by bombing in 1940, it was eventually demolished.

MAPPIN ART GALLERY, SHEFFIELD

Above: Mappin Art Gallery, Weston Park, c1910
Formerly a private house, Weston Park was converted between 1886 and 1888 by Flockton and Gibbs to form a gallery to house the collection of work bequeathed to the city by the Rotherham businessman John Newton Mappin. It now forms part of the Weston Park Museum.

Left: Brunswick Wesleyan Chapel, South Street Moor, Sheffield, 1904
The imposing chapel, another victim of Second World War bombing, was not demolished until the 1950s. A local landowner 'saved' the columns and deposited them in open ground near Boots Folly in nearby Bradfield. Tramlines can be seen in the foreground, with electric power lines overhead. Sheffield's tram system was fully electrified by 1902.

SHEFFIELD TOWN HALL

Town Hall, Pinstone Street, 1897
Far left: A view of the Town Hall, designed by E W Mountford, soon after completion, looking towards the corner of Surrey Street. The ornate carvings embellishing the building were the work of F W Pomeroy, an eminent sculptor who specialised in monumental and architectural work. His friezes depict Sheffield's industries. A statue of Vulcan crowns the clock tower.
Left: The entrance hall and grand staircase decorated in preparation for the grand opening by Queen Victoria.
Above: Queen Victoria arrives in her carriage outside the main west entrance during the official opening on 21 May 1897.

CAMMELL LAIRD & CO

Above: Cyclops Works, Carlisle Street East, Grimesthorpe, 1913
Two men operate the armour plate-rolling machine at the works, part of the shipbuilding firm Cammell Laird and Company. Charles Cammell and Company's Grimesthorpe Works were built in 1865. The merger with Laird, Son & Company took place in 1903.

Left: 1 High Street, Sheffield, 1897
Pawson and Brailsford's building at the junction of High Street and East Parade. In the later 19th century a number of specialist printing firms appeared, Pawson and Brailsford being the largest and best known of those in Sheffield because of the trade catalogues they printed for the city's manufacturing businesses. They transformed the relatively humble premises of their stationery business by investing in a new building that was erected in stages on their existing site at the top of the High Street. The extra storeys above the retail premises generated rent from solicitors and insurance companies.

MIDLAND RAILWAY STATION

Above: The Midland Railway Station, Sheffield, c1910

The station, designed by Charles Trubshaw, opened in 1870 at the same time as changes were made to the routing of the Midland Railway's main London line. Its refurbishment and expansion in 1905 included the addition of the stone arches seen in the photograph.

NORFOLK PARK, SHEFFIELD

Top: Norfolk Park, c1910

Built by the 13th Duke of Norfolk on land set aside by the 12th Duke in 1841, the Park opened free to the public in 1848. The handsome gateway on Granville Road was erected in 1876 by Henry Fitzalan Howard, the 15th Duke, who, like his predecessors, was hugely influential in the development of 19th-century Sheffield, both as a landowner and an investor. In 1897, as Lord Mayor of the city, he welcomed Queen Victoria to the Park where 50,000 children assembled to entertain her. Henry donated the Park to Sheffield in 1910.

SHEFFIELD CATHEDRAL

Above: Sheffield Cathedral, c1910

View from the south-east. The church building dates from the 1460s, but the north and south walls of the nave were rebuilt in 1790–93. Later, in 1880, it was restored and extended by Flockton and Gibbs. The church was granted cathedral status in 1914.

Right: Sheffield Botanical Gardens, Clarkehouse Road, c1900

The three glass pavilions at Sheffield Botanical Gardens. The gardens were laid out between 1834 and 1836 by Robert Marnock, with the pavilions completed by 1838. Designed in the style of, and named after, Sir Joseph Paxton, they were originally linked by the open colonnades that can be seen in the picture; these were altered in the mid 20th century.

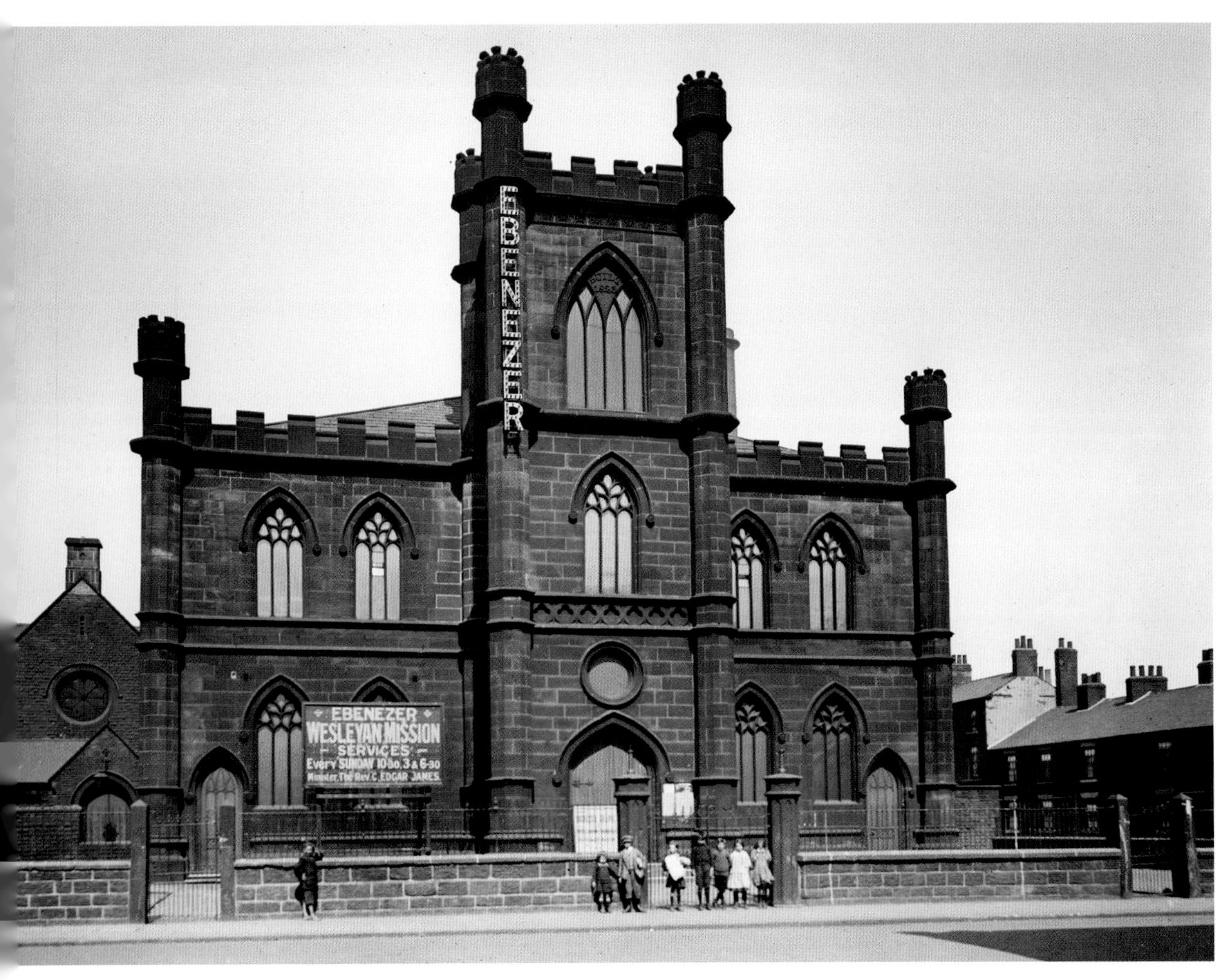

FITZALAN SQUARE SHEFFIELD

Above: Fitzalan Square, c1900
View across the Square towards Haymarket. Hansom cabs and electric trams mingle in the busy Square, laid out in 1881 on the site of the old market quarter, which was moved from the city centre to where the cattle would be less intrusive. The large cab shelter and clock tower seen centre left were demolished in 1913 to make way for a bronze statue of Edward VII.

Left: Ebenezer Wesleyan Mission Church, South Parade, Shalesmoor, c1910
View looking north-east. This capacious church accommodated over 1,500 people when it was consecrated in 1823.

TOWN HALL SQUARE, SHEFFIELD

Top right: Town Hall Square, c1910
On the left in the foreground is a statue of Queen Victoria by Alfred Turner (1904), with flanking figures depicting maternity and labour. The Albany Hotel stands to the right, with the Yorkshire Penny Bank on its ground floor. The spire of St Marie Cathedral Church is just visible behind the hotel.

Middle right: Fitzalan Square, Sheffield, c1900
Looking east towards the old Post Office (left) and the Birmingham District and Counties Bank (right). The Head Post Office moved into new premises in 1910 on the other side of the Square. Two trams stand in the foreground: the number 40 has recently arrived in the Square, while passengers board the number 22 for Newhall Road.

Bottom right: Fargate, Sheffield, c1900
View towards Fargate, looking north from the direction of Town Hall Square, with Fields Oriental Cafe at No. 34 on the left. Most of the rest of the block is occupied by Proctors, a large draper's store.

Humberside

KINGSTON-UPON-HULL

Left: Central Picture Theatre, 47 Prospect Street, 1915
The classical building also housed the Central Cafe and the Central Chocolate Shop. The cinema was destroyed during the Blitz in 1941, one of six obliterated in air raids on the city that year. Local architect Peter Gaskell, who designed this and several other picture palaces in Hull, was made the city's Lord Mayor in 1918.

Below left: Market Place, c1900
The gilded statue of William III on a horse, designed by the Flemish sculptor Pieter Scheemaeckers the Younger in 1734, stands on a stone pedestal with an inscription calling the King 'our great deliverer'. Hull's loyalty to the monarch is reflected in its full name, but was subject to conditions. When James II made clear his intentions to restore Catholicism as the state religion, the strongly protestant citizens of Hull fiercely supported the deposition of James in favour of William of Orange, who was subsequently crowned King William III in 1689. The city already had very strong trading links with Holland. The statue and its four lamps were removed to safety during the Blitz, but the buildings surrounding it were all demolished after the Second World War. The statue remains in the same location today, amid modern buildings. However, King Billy still looks out over one of the most lavishly appointed sets of Victorian underground public conveniences in the country.

HOLY TRINITY CHURCH KINGSTON-UPON-HULL

Above: Holy Trinity Church, Market Place, 1880
A view of the west end of the Church, built between 1300 and 1425. Restored on several occasions, most notably by Sir George Gilbert Scott between 1859 and 1872, it is alleged to be the largest parish church in England by floor area. When the transepts were added in the early 14th century, this was the first record of bricks being substantially used in church architecture. In this picture an ice cream street vendor tempts the faithful and passers-by.

Right: Alexandra Hotel, 69 Hessle Road, Kingston-upon-Hull, 1896
View south-east at the corner of Ropery Street. The photograph was commissioned by Leeds-based Burmantofts and Company, who supplied the ornate terracotta and ceramic finishes on the building facade, including the Hotel's name panels, which remain in place today.

VICTORIA SQUARE

Opposite above: Victoria Square, Kingston-upon-Hull, c1915

View looking west to City Hall, constructed in Baroque Revival style in 1903. Intended as a civic amenity, the building included a 3,000-seat auditorium and an organ, and also the Victoria Art Gallery until it moved to the Ferens Gallery across the Square in 1927. Today City Hall's ashlar facade is pristine, but like so many other buildings in the city it was blackened by industrial pollution soon after it was built. On the right is one of Hull's pre-Second World War landmark buildings, the Prudential, designed, like the company's London Head Office in Holborn, by Alfred Waterhouse. In May 1941 the building was destroyed by German bombs, leaving only the Tower standing; deemed unsafe it was pulled down the following day. Victoria Square was also a terminus of the tram system.

GUILDHALL

Right above: The Guildhall, Alfred Gelder Street, Kingston-upon-Hull, c1915

View of the monumental facade from the south-west, with pedestrians and a tram in the street. Close to the Queen's Dock, the Guildhall, designed by Sir Edwin Cooper and completed between 1906 and 1914, was the seat of the City Council.

DOCK OFFICES

Opposite below: Hull Dock Offices, Queen's Dock Avenue, Kingston-upon-Hull, 1903

Built in 1871 by C G Wray in an Italianate style and decorated with dolphins and other maritime symbols, the offices were the home of the Hull Dock Company, which ran the local dock system. The building was acquired by the City Council in 1968 and converted for use by Hull Maritime Museum, which moved there in 1975. The fluted Doric column in the foreground is the Wilberforce Monument. William Wilberforce was born in Hull and the column, designed by W H Clark in 1834, commemorates his work in the abolition of slavery. The statue on top, an afterthought, was sculpted by a local man, Mr Feort. The entire monument was relocated in 1935. The Queen's Dock was later infilled and is now Queen's Gardens.

QUEEN'S DOCK, KINGSTON-UPON-HULL

Above: Queen's Dock, c1915

View from the south-west area of the Dock, looking east. The statue and cupola at opposite ends of the Guildhall rise above the rooftops in the distance on the right. When built in 1775 by the Hull Dock Company, Queen's Dock was the largest in the country. Originally known just as the Dock, it was given the name Queen's after Victoria visited in 1854. It was the base for the country's biggest whaling fleet, comprising 60 whalers.

LONG MAY VICTORIA REIGN
S.HARDY
BAKER&PROVISION M HANT
BLUNT&EVANS
S.HARDY

East Midlands

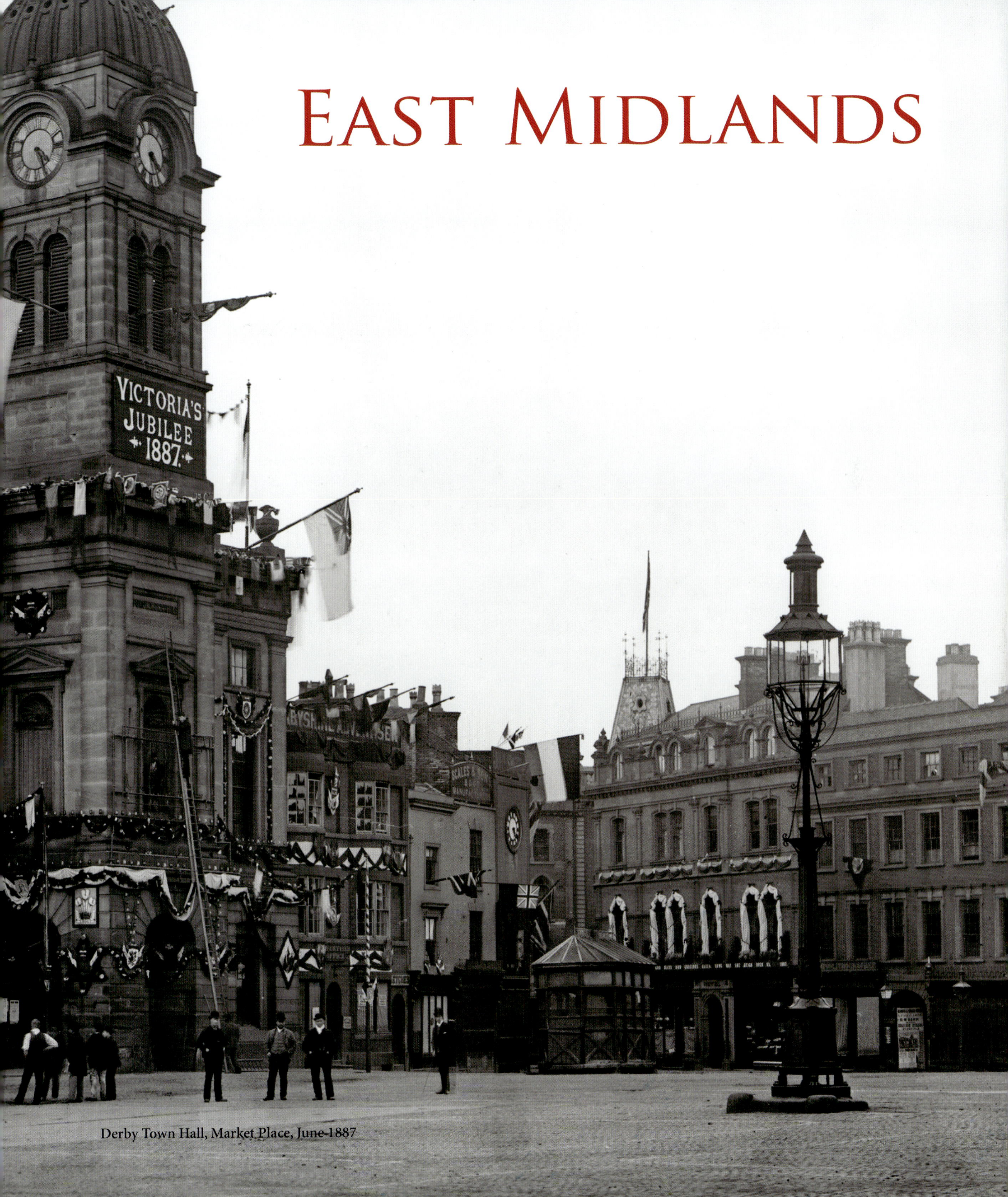

Derby Town Hall, Market Place, June 1887

Derbyshire

DERBY

One of the five boroughs of the Danelaw, Derby was established on the banks of the River Derwent and emerged as a leading city of the Industrial Revolution, with first its textile mills and then its railway engineering works.

Opposite: Queen Street, 1924
View south down Queen Street towards the Cathedral of All Saints, which boasts the oldest peal of bells in the world and is the last resting place of Bess of Hardwick and Georgiana, Duchess of Devonshire. The half-timbered building, left, still survives as Ye Old Dolphin Inne. Dating from 1530, it is the city's oldest pub.

Below: London Road, 1896
View north with the Wesleyan Chapel, built in 1861, to the right on the corner of Canal Street. Opposite, out of sight, are the grounds of the Royal Derbyshire Infirmary, opened by Queen Victoria in 1891.

Right: Midland Railway offices, Derby, 1923

WALKER LANE
Cadbury's
CHOCOLATE
CIGARETTES

Above: Buxton Crescent, Buxton, 1899
A view taken from the Town Hall shows The Slopes, an area of walks leading to Buxton Crescent. The Crescent was built for the fifth Duke of Devonshire between 1780 and 1784 by John Carr. It was later turned into three hotels: St Anns, The Central and The Great.

ASHBOURNE

Above: Church Street, c1900
View east, with the White Hart public house to the right of the photograph. Further along the street is the gibbet-style sign for the Green Man and Black's Head Inn that stretches right across the street – where it remains to this day. The footway is surfaced with a ribbon of stone slabs flanked by river cobbles.

Opposite above: Market Place, c1900
Looking east towards Woodisse & Desborough ironmongers and engineers, with a fine Victorian Gothic drinking fountain outside. An early 19th-century water hand pump stands outside the Local Board Offices, which were designed by Benjamin Wilson in 1861.

Opposite below: Hardwick Old Hall, c1900
The birthplace of Bess of Hardwick, the second richest woman in England after Elizabeth I. Bess used her wealth to extend the Old Hall to accommodate a household of 200 while building the new hall. Her descendants favoured Chatsworth, another of her stately homes, and the Old Hall fell into ruin and was quarried for building material.

IRONMONGERS
& DESBOROUGH
IRONMONGERS
WOODDISSE & DESBOROUGH
KENN

CHESTERFIELD & MATLOCK BATH

Above: St Mary And All Saints Church, Chesterfield, c1910
Looking north along St Mary's Gate from Spa Lane. The church spire was added to the tower in about 1362. It is twisted 45 degrees and leans 2.9 metres from its true centre.

Opposite below right: Stephenson Memorial Hall, Corporation Street, Chesterfield, c1910
Built in 1879 by public subscription as a memorial to George Stephenson, the railway pioneer, who lived at Tapton Hall, Derbyshire.

Opposite below left: Matlock Bath, 1890
The Matlocks – Matlock Bath, Matlock Bridge and Matlock Bank – grew to be popular health and leisure resorts after hot springs were discovered in the late 17th century. The Midland Railway hoped that striking images like this publicity photograph would encourage more visitors to travel to the area, known as a 'miniature Switzerland'. In the mid 19th century around 20 hydros offered spa treatments in the picturesque surroundings of the Derwent Valley.

Opposite above: North Parade, Matlock Bath, 1921

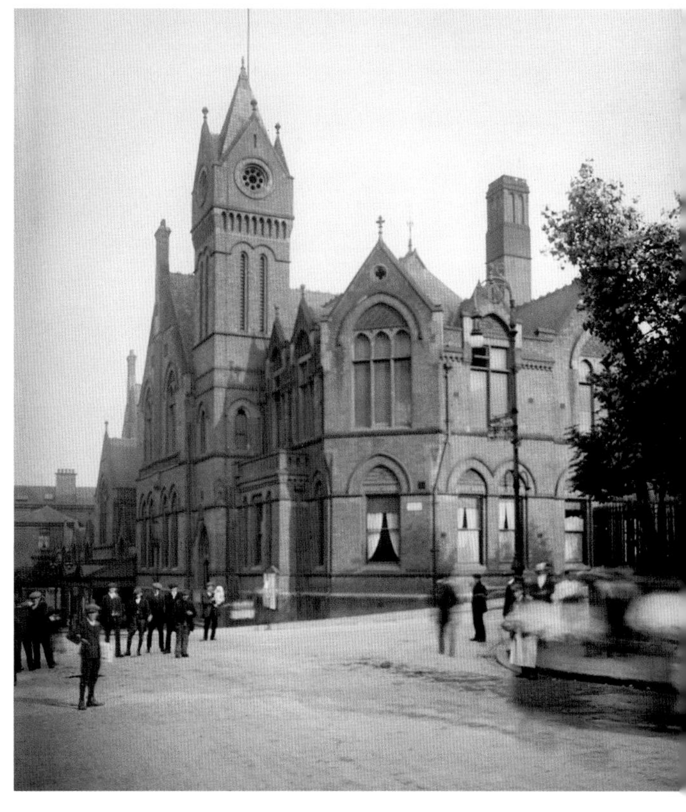

Nottinghamshire

NOTTINGHAM

Above: Market Square

Looking north across the square to Market Street towards the Corinthian portico of the Theatre Royal, which closes the vista beyond. Funded by lace manufacturers John and William Lambert, the theatre was completed in 1865 at a cost of £15,000 and later remodelled by Frank Matcham in 1897. Handmade lace and hosiery had flourished in the town since the Middle Ages, but from the early 19th century it developed into a world centre of mechanised lace production in a complex of handsome red-brick industrial buildings in the eponymous Lace Market.

Left: Queen Street, c1905

View looking south-east towards the Market Square. Two beautifully dressed girls are in the foreground, with a younger child trailing behind. The handsome buildings around them are quite new, built on a cleared slum area in the 1890s. In the middle distance to the left, a granite obelisk at the junction with King Street commemorates the fallen of the First Boer War.

GOOSE FAIR, NOTTINGHAM

Above: Goose Fair, Market Square, c1914

The view north-west from South Parade towards Long Row Central and Griffin & Spalding's store. Originally held in Nottingham's Market Place for eight days in October, the fair possibly got its name from the hundreds of geese that were driven from Lincolnshire and Norfolk to be sold in Nottingham. Goose Fair was first mentioned in the Nottingham Borough Records of 1541, although it was probably in existence much earlier than this. It gradually became so large that, following complaints about congestion and disruption in the city, the Fair was eventually moved to Forest Recreation Ground, about a mile north of the Old Market Square.

NOTTINGHAM PRISON

Right: HMP Nottingham, Perry Road, Sherwood, c1895

Group portrait of staff and warders at Nottingham Prison, which opened in 1891, with the administration block, chapel and clock tower in the background.

NARROW MARSH NOTTINGHAM

Opposite: Kirk's Yard, Narrow Marsh, 1919

Narrow Marsh lay in the shadow of the sandstone cliff on which High Pavement and the Lace Market stand, beyond the buildings seen here in the background. The area took its name from the swampy banks of the river Leen and was crammed with slum dwellings with no sanitation, leading to endemic cholera and other diseases, made worse by the influx of visitors to the city seeking cheap accommodation and the services of prostitutes that frequented the area.

Marsh Farm, the dilapidated timber-frame house (centre) probably dates from Tudor times and shows a marvellous patchwork of repairs. The circular plaque on the wall advertises Gallahers Irish Roll, a popular tobacco of the day, indicating that the premises had been used as a shop.

The whole neighbourhood, also known as Red Lion Street, was demolished in the late 1920s–early 1930s.

Above left: Caunts Yard, Ruston's Place, Bellar Gate, 1919

One of a series of photographs taken by the City Council Health and Engineers Departments to record poor housing conditions, prior to the slum demolition accompanying the post war housing programmes of the 1920s. Back-to-back housing was common, with no internal plumbing, no through ventilation, open drains in the communal yard with a solitary water tap at the end of the drain. The people living here shared toilet closets and a wash house at the end of the yard. The women pictured are 'rag picking': sorting through old clothes, repairing and salvaging some, removing buttons and lace, before selling the remainder for rags.

BOUGHTON

Left: Junction of Ollerton and Walesby Roads, Boughton, c1905

A man draws water from the hydrant to fill the washtub on his wheelbarrow. During the 19th century, supplying clean water to houses in towns and cities was a priority for municipal authorities to counter diseases such as cholera. Rural areas had to wait longer for direct supplies to individual homes. However, a pumping station in Boughton opened in 1905 which distributed mains water to access points like this until the infrastructure could be expanded.

W. TAYLO
SPIRIT MERCHANTS.

MANSFIELD

Raised to importance by King John as a hunting retreat in the middle of Sherwood Forest, Mansfield later became a bustling industrial satellite of Nottingham.

Opposite: Market Place, Mansfield, 1903
The view looking west. The market square was created after much demolition following the Improvement Act of 1823. In the centre stands the elaborate Victorian Gothic Cavendish Monument, designed by T C Hine and completed in 1849, to commemorate the life of Lord George Bentinck, son of William Bentinck, fourth Duke of Portland, a major local landowner.

Top right: Church Street, Mansfield, 1910
Built by the Midland Railway in 1875, the spectacular railway viaduct bisects the town centre.

Middle right: Market Place, Mansfield, 1900
Entrance to the Market Place, viewed from beneath the viaduct, with the Bentinck Memorial in the distance.

Bottom right: Market Place, Mansfield, 1900
View south-west across the market, with the Town Hall visible to the right of the monument. In the distance are the signals of the Midland Railway viaduct.

Above: Nottingham and Nottinghamshire Bank, 43 Kirkgate, Newark, 1897
This landmark building was designed by Watson Fothergill, whose extravagant Gothic Revival style was also adopted by this bank for its head office in Nottingham. An apartment for the manager and his family was included as standard.

Leicestershire

LEICESTER

Left: Thomas Cook Building, 5 Gallowtree Gate,1896
Designed by Joseph Goddard as a memorial to Cook, who died in 1892. At first-floor level is a frieze of four panels illustrating important milestones in Cook's career as a travel agent. The dates 1841 and 1894 carved into the second-floor frieze commemorate the date of the first trip he organised and the date of the building. Burmantofts Company commissioned the photograph, and it is likely that they manufactured the ornate terracotta facade.

Below right: London Road Railway Station, c1895
The station was first used on 4 May 1840, when a train of four first-class and six second-class carriages, pulled by the 'Leopard' steam engine, arrived from Nottingham. All that remains of the first building are a pair of Egyptian-style gateposts in Campbell Street. The new station frontage on London Road remains as a well-preserved late Victorian building, although the interior of the booking hall and the platform structures were reconstructed by British Rail in the 1970s. The station clock is the only hand-wound example in the UK. The original Campbell Street station was the starting point of the first excursions arranged by travel agency magnate Thomas Cook.

Below left: Town Hall, Town Hall Square, 1885
Looking east towards the tower from what is now Horsefair Street. The town hall was built between 1874 and 1876 in free Renaissance style by the architect F J Hames.

Opposite: Queens Hotel, 14 Rutland Street, 1889
Standing at the junction with Charles Street, the hotel was designed by the architect Arthur Wakerley.

Top: Liberal Club, Bishop Street, Leicester, 1889
Leicester was a bastion of nonconformist radicalism. The Liberal Club lay at its heart. Designed by the architect Edward Burgess, the club house was built between 1885 and 1888.

Above and right: Silver Arcade, Silver Street, Leicester, 1901
Interior view (above) between Silver Street and Cank Street; the arcade continued south from Cank Street, this section being completed in 1891. Exterior view southwards (right) to Silver Street entrance at the junction with High Street.

LEICESTER

Opposite top right: Alexandra House, 47 Rutland Street, 1909
Faire Brothers & Company's bootlace warehouse at the junction of Rutland Street and Southampton Street. Faced in terracotta, the warehouse was built for Sir Samuel Faire between 1895 and 1898 to the designs of Edward Burgess.

Above: London Road, 1890
View of shops, designed by the architect Arthur Wakerley, on the corner of London Road and Highfield Street. A local man, Wakerley designed various Leicester landmarks including a synagogue, a police station and a number of council houses.

Right: Parr's Bank, 2 St Martins, 1904
The bank, founded by Sir Thomas Pares in the late 18th century, was acquired by the Parr's Banking Company and rebuilt in its current form between 1900 and 1902. The St Martins area of Leicester was built over the Greyfriars Priory, razed by Henry VIII. The mortal remains of Richard III, interred in the Priory and recently discovered under a car park, have now been laid to rest in Leicester Cathedral.

MELTON MOWBRAY & LEICESTER

Opposite: The Market Place, Melton Mowbray, 1889
The Central Refreshment Rooms in the foreground, with the tower of St Mary's Church beyond to the right. Note the finely laid road surface of granite setts.

Top left: Granby Street, Leicester, 1904
A tram makes its way down the street; electric trams replaced the horse-drawn variety in the city in 1904 after extensive construction works. The Turkey Cafe, in the right foreground, an Art Nouveau building designed by the versatile local architect Arthur Wakerley, opened in the city centre in 1901.

Above left: The Free Library on Braunstone Gate, Leicester, 1904

Right: Water Works, Swithland Reservoir, Quorndon, Leicestershire, 1896
Victorian infrastructure. Fresh piped drinking water transformed public health and life expectancy. Exterior view of the main range of the Pumping House and Well House, with a long lower range to the rear (top right). The six polygonal filter beds, looking towards the central hexagonal draw-off tank, with Renaissance-style gazebo and balustrade (middle right). Construction work on the bridge at the north-east end of the waterworks' dam causeway, with the draw-off tower, reservoir and dam visible beyond it (bottom right).

CENTRAL REFRESHMENT ROOMS
COFFEE TAVERN
CADBURY'S
CHOCOLATE
SINGER'S SEWING MACHINES

Northamptonshire

BOUGHTON & BYFIELD

Above: The Carpenters Arms, Boughton, c1900
People gather outside the inn, which advertises accommodation for cyclists. The horse and cart appears to be loaded with household items.

Left: Golding & Adams, High Street, Byfield, c1910
Staff and customers pose outside the local grocery shop. The shop boys are wearing long white aprons. Behind them, the windows are piled high with goods for sale, including Cerebos salt and Hudson's dry soap.

Above: Haycock & Russell, Banbury Lane, Byfield, c1900
The picture illustrates the wide range of delivery methods used at the time: pony and trap, horse and cart, basket on wheels and a wheeled handcart. The shop, which has a promotion of Cambridge lemonade, could supply most household items – all part of its claim to be 'The Central Stores'.

Right: Byfield Post Office, c1900
A team of posties in their uniforms pose outside the office with bikes and the post office dog. Urgent messages could be sent electronically by telegraph, the subsequent printed telegram delivered by hand to the receiver's door; this job was probably performed by the boy to the right in the picture. Today both these premises are private residences.

CHARWELTON

Charwelton Station, Charwelton, Northamptonshire
Opened in 1899, Charwelton Station was on the Great Central Line from London to Rugby and the north. It was closed in 1963 as part of the Beeching cuts when the Great Central Railway was seen as duplicating other lines.

Top left: 1901. A porter moves a crate of 'Tabs' cigarettes on a trolley.

Top right: 1904. A station employee puts up a poster outside the waiting room advertising the county show. Another poster gives the improved rail timetable to London.

Above left: 1900. A large steam engine for power and a small makeshift hut for shelter at the ironstone quarry near the village.

Above right: c1857. Labourers involved in the construction of the Great Central Railway near Charwelton. The steam-powered crane lifts bricks onto railway wagons.

Opposite above: A welcoming party, at 10.25 am on 18 May 1905, awaiting the arrival of HRH The Duchess of Albany.

Opposite below: c1900. Byfield Station. View over the platforms from the footbridge.

BOOKING OFFICE
CHARWEL
GREAT CENTRAL
GREAT CENTRAL RAILWAY
MAIN LINE
EASTERN SECTION

M R

R. HAYCOCK,

Opposite top left: Eydon, 1903
Abbotts shop can be seen on the left, while residents of the village stand on the pavement on the right. The smallest boy is holding the hoop he has been bowling. The road surface is made of rammed earth.

Opposite top right: Cox's Lane, Hellidon, c1897
Haycock's Grocers' Store. Local village shops sold a wide variety of goods and were a key focus of village life. As transport and distribution links improved, shops became more specialised, leading to the gradual demise of the village general store over the following 100 years.

Opposite middle left: Near Hellidon, 1902
Mechanised farming. Farm workers harvesting with a horse-drawn Hornsby Reaper.

Opposite middle right: Weston and Weedon, 1907
Agricultural workers use a horse-powered elevator to build haystacks. The horse in the foreground is harnessed to a portable horse engine.

Opposite bottom left: Cox's Lane, Hellidon, c1904

Opposite bottom right: St Osyth's Lane, Oundle, c1890
Looking north towards the spire of St Peter's Church. Workmen are unloading barrels from a horse-drawn cart outside the 16th-century Angel Inn.

Top left: The Pomfret Arms Hotel, High Street, Towcester, 1904

Top right: George Row, Northampton, c1900
Looking towards the Court House with Edward Godwin's Guildhall beyond, completed in High Victorian Gothic style in 1860.

Middle right: School Street, Sulgrave, c1900
People outside the General Supply Stores. The large house on the right of the shop was known as St Baldreds and dates from the early 18th century.

Bottom right: High Street, Weston, c1900
A mother with a child in her arms and several other children in the street. All are well dressed and wear stout shoes or boots. A teenage boy is driving the trap and the young woman at his side, holding a young baby, appears to be a maid.

Lincolnshire

Above: Barges at Brigg, 1901

The Ancholme River, connecting several small waterways via Brigg to the Humber at South Ferriby, was first canalised in 1635, but it was from 1767 that the Ancholme Navigation flourished. Agricultural products and coal were the main cargoes carried on this route. These barges are moored at the wharves on the old river. The County Bridge, built in 1828, is visible in the background (left). The canalised new river bypassed the bend in the old river on which Brigg was built.

Left: Market Place, Brigg, 1901

Looking east towards the Town Hall from Bridge Street; the building in the centre of the photograph, known as Buttercross, now houses the visitor information centre. The peaceful scene belies this strategic thoroughfare which was to become the A18 trunk road until eventually it was diverted around the town.

GRIMSBY

Above: No. 2 Fish Dock, 1907
Despite its relative proximity to the larger Kingston-upon-Hull docks across the Humber, Grimsby flourished in the mid 19th century because of its more direct connection south to London. Its fishing fleet was once the largest in the world. In this picture, steam-powered trawlers moored against the wharves and the empty boxes and barrels await the prolific catches of cod, haddock and herring being brought to shore by the fleet. In the background stands the Hydraulic Tower, built to an Italianate design similar to the Torre del Mangia in Siena's Piazza del Campo. Its head of water drove the machinery of the lock gates.

Left: Waterfront, 1899
The archetypal salty dog. A crewmaster leans over the bow of his trawler in the fish docks. The trawlermen were originally local, but as the success of the Grimsby fleet grew it attracted crew from the south-west and London in sizeable numbers.

CLEETHORPES

Top left: Cleethorpes Pier, 1898
The length of the pier, like that of its nearby counterpart at Skegness, accommodated the low tide mark, stretching not into the sea but into the Humber Estuary. Built by Head Wrightson, the pier opened on the August bank holiday 1873, its cost being met by the Manchester, Sheffield and Lincolnshire Railway, which became the Great Central Railway in 1897.

Above: Cleethorpes Central Promenade, 1899
The view south along the front with the Pier Gardens to the right. The top of the 'Keep' of Ross Castle – a mock ruined fort built by the railway company and opened as a visitor attraction in the same year as the station – can be seen in the distance.

Top right: The railway station, Cleethorpes, 1898
The photograph shows how close the station was to the water. Passengers arriving would have stepped out of the train and almost immediately onto North Parade, with the Pier just 100 metres away, in all its pristine splendour. As Cleethorpes grew as a visitor attraction, the station was enlarged to meet the increased traffic from all over the north of England and further afield.

SKEGNESS

Top: Skegness Pier, c1900
When first built in 1881 to the designs of Clarke and Pickwell, the pier was one of the longest in Britain. Its length was necessary because of the shallow shelving beach. Pleasure boat day trips were a key entertainment of the era, and the length of the pier ensured that steamers could operate irrespective of the tide. Barely visible to the left and beyond the pier is a line of bathing huts, showing how far the tide went out.

Above left: The Parade, c1900
Skegness's popularity increased owing to the efforts of Thomas Cook, who encouraged holiday makers from the Midlands to visit. This led to the first Butlins holiday camp being sited in the town in 1934.

Above right: The beach, c1900
Looking north-east towards the pier, where a pleasure boat is moored. In the foreground is a bathing machine. A man in a top hat reclines on the sand (far right).

Left: Skegness Railway Station, 1898
The entrance viewed from Lumley Square.

GRANTHAM & BOSTON

Above and left: Angel Hotel, High Street, Grantham, 1904 (above), 1899 (left)
The mediaeval hostelry dates from the 14th century and is alleged to be the oldest surviving English inn. Richard III is said to have signed the death warrant for the Duke of Buckingham here.

Bottom left: Market Place, Grantham, 1899
View across the Market Place. The spire of St Wulfram's Church can be seen in the distance.

Opposite above: Market Place, Boston, 1899
Looking north from the Assembly Rooms. The Market Place is thought to be one of the earliest areas of settlement in Boston, which at one time was at the head of tidal navigation on the River Haven. In the Middle Ages the fens had not been drained and the landscape was fluid. Markets are recorded in the town from as early as 1130, and the annual Boston Fair was one of Europe's great trade events. Boston's fortune was established by the growth of the English woollen trade. Its inland docks made it an important trading centre for the fenlands and, at its height, it was one of England's busiest ports.

Opposite below: Tower Street, Boston, 1893
View facing east across the River Witham towards St Botolph's Church, one of England's largest parish churches and tallest parish church towers. From the time it was built in the early 1500s, the tower has been affectionately known as the Boston Stump. In the days before lighthouses, lamps were suspended in its lantern to aid night-time navigation. Even in daylight the tower is a landmark across the fens, visible for many miles around.

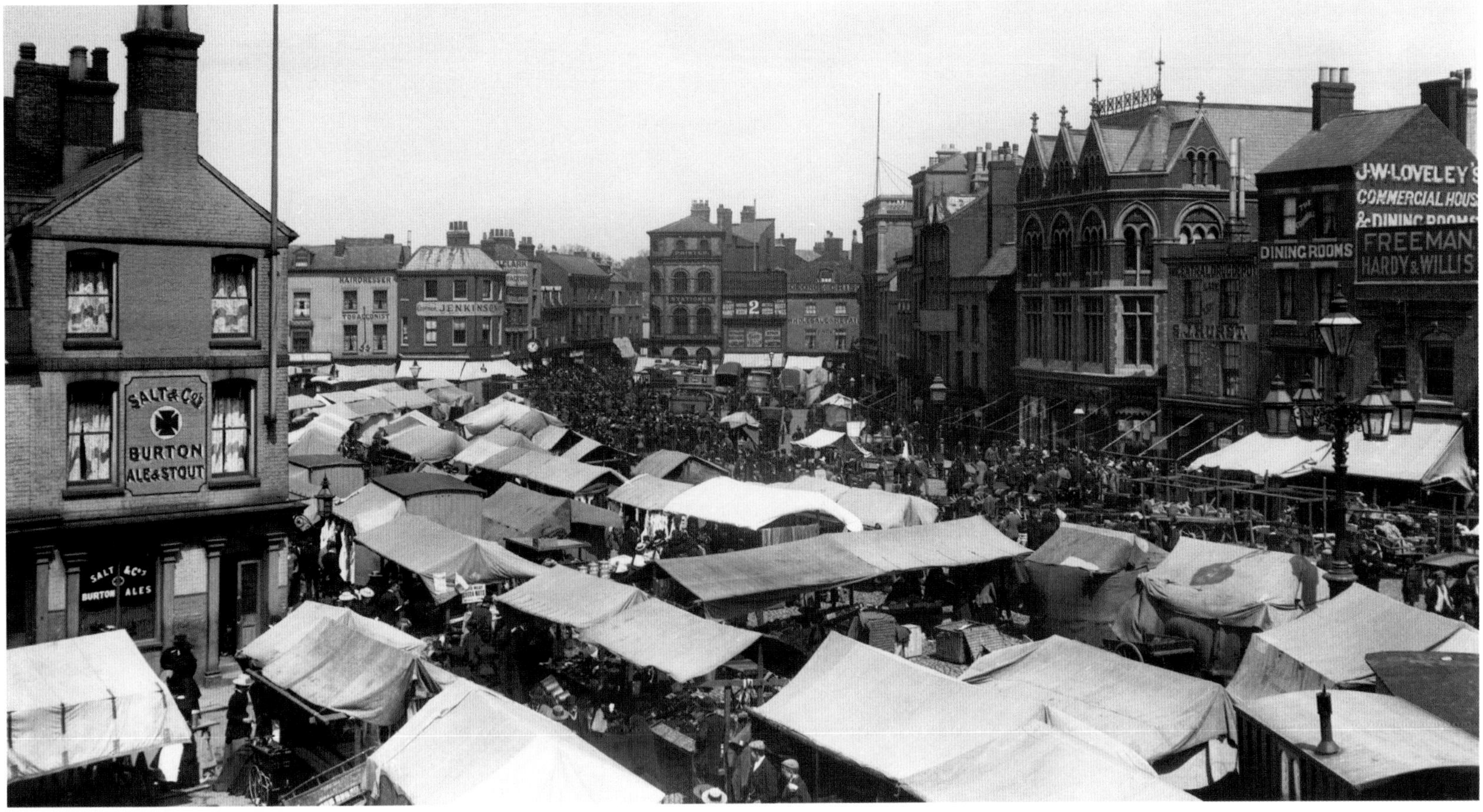
J·W·LOVELEY'S
COMMERCIAL HOUS
DINING ROOMS
FREEMAN,
HARDY & WILLIS
DINING ROOMS
SALT & Co's
BURTON
ALE & STOUT
BURTON ALES
JENKINS

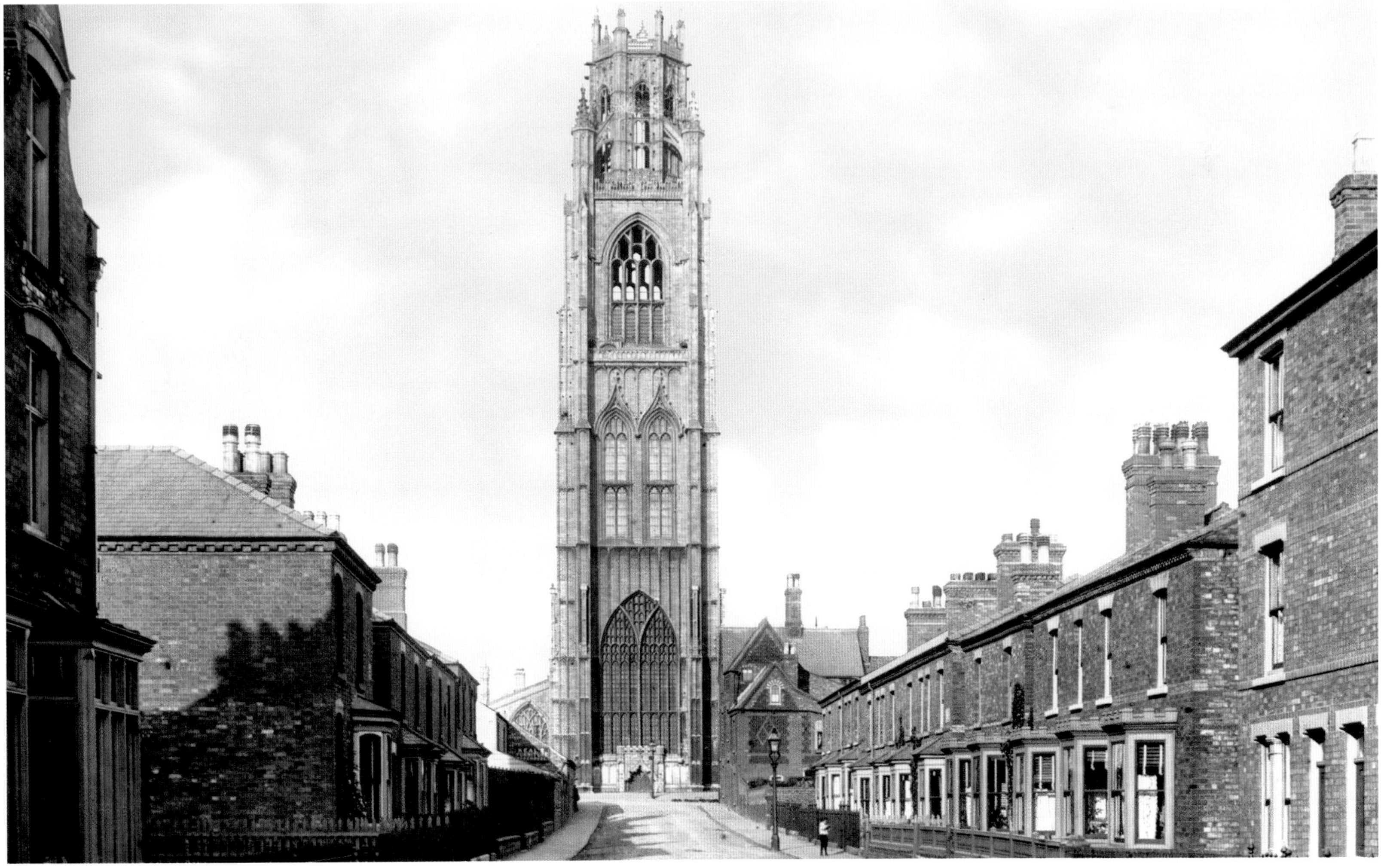

LINCOLN

Left: Lincoln Cathedral, c1920
One of Britain's most spectacular ecclesiastical buildings, Lincoln Cathedral towers over the mediaeval city. Building work was completed in 1092, its creator, Bishop Remigius, dying two days before its consecration. The Cathedral is built of stone hewn from the rock on which it stands. One of the four remaining original copies of the Magna Carta is held in the cathedral – although at present it is on loan to Lincoln Castle.

Below: Guildhall and Stonebow, 1901
View from the south along High Street, leading uphill to the cathedral. This remarkable picture shows one of the main gateways to the city centre. Built from local limestone in the 1520s, the chamber above was the seat of the city council. The carved arms directly above the arch (the Stonebow) are those of King James I.

SCUNTHORPE

Above: St John the Evangelist, Church Square, Scunthorpe, 1902
The church was built of ironstone, the raison d'etre of Scunthorpe and its modern-day steel industry. Completed in 1891, it is now an arts centre. The surrounding shops and houses are long gone.

Right above: Market Place, Market Rasen, 1900
Market Place, with the church of St Thomas in the distance.

Right bottom: Holy Trinity Bridge, Crowland, c1900
The bridge was built between 1360 and 1390 by Benedictine monks to cross the River Welland, but it now stands high and dry near the market place in Crowland. Until the early 17th century the river flowed through the village and divided into two channels beneath the bridge. Water was directed to the nearby monastery through a water gate. Unique in Britain, it is formed from three pointed half-arches in the form of a triangle and was originally crowned with a tall canopied cross. The stone statue on the right side of the bridge, erected in 1720, is believed to have come from Crowland Abbey.

Birmingham Town Hall, Victoria Square, 1913

West Midlands

CRANE & SONS
New & Second hand
Pianos
PIANOS
10/
ORGANS
5/
BRANCH
GREAT PIANO
WAREHOUSE
PRINCIPAL SHOW

Birmingham

Opposite: Mason University College, Paradise Street, 1897
View from the square, with the Chamberlain Memorial and curved end of the Central Free Library in the foreground. The University of Birmingham grew out of Mason College. The Memorial, erected in 1880, was designed by J A Chamberlain (no relation), enriched with mosaics by the Venetian company Salviati Burke and Co and a fine portrait medallion by the sculptor Thomas Woolner.

Above right: Stephenson Place, c1890
The statue of local businessman Thomas Attwood presides over the busy junction of Corporation Street and New Street. Unveiled in 1859, it stood here until 1925, when it was moved to Calthorpe Park and then to Larches Green.

Bottom right: New Street, c1890
On the left in the middle distance is the famous King Edward VI Grammar School, founded in 1552 and rebuilt by Charles Barry in Tudor Gothic style in 1837. It was during the erection of this building, which was demolished in 1936, that Barry first met Augustus Pugin, who helped to design the interior. In the far distance is the distinctive spire of Christ Church.

BIRMINGHAM CITY CENTRE

Top left: Paradise Street, c1890
Beyond the shops and tea houses, the south-west corner of the Town Hall can be seen centre with the frontage of Christ Church to its right.

Middle left: Corporation Street, c1910
Looking north-east with the sumptuous Victoria Law Courts to the left, completed by Sir Aston Webb and Ingress Bell in 1891. Opposite is the soaring tower of the Methodist Central Hall of 1904 by E & J A Harper. Both used red brick and blood-red terracotta from Gibbs and Canning of Tamworth, the local manufacturer, who also supplied material for the Natural History Museum in London.

Below: Snow Hill Station, c1900
Established in 1852, Snow Hill was the Birmingham station for the Great Western Railway, but from its earliest days it struggled to compete with its grander rival at New Street. The boundary wall boasts a fine display of posters and enamel advertisements.

Opposite above: New Street junction with Corporation Street, c1900
New Street underwent substantial development during the 19th century to become the city's principal thoroughfare and shopping street, linking Victoria Square with the Bull Ring. Handsome Italianate and classical buildings can be seen lining the street. In this photograph, barriers are being erected in preparation for a procession.

Opposite below: Corporation Street, 1920
Horse-drawn and motorised vehicles compete for space, with people thronging the pavements beneath the richly modelled facades of the offices above. The banner across the street announces a Midland Music Competition Festival in May.

QUEENS CORNER
BAGS
SHAW'S BROW IRON Co
WATSON DENTIST
CORNISH
GREAVES 36
619

VES. 36
PATTISON
DERBY RESULT

NEW STREET

Above: New Street, Birmingham, c1895

View south-east from the Town Hall. This bustling scene shows a variety of transport, with a cyclist adjusting his gaiters in the foreground and delivery vehicles mingling with private pony and traps, horse-drawn omnibuses and hand carts. The building on the right is the New Birmingham Post Office, which opened for business in 1891. On the left is Christ Church, sited at the end of Colmore Row, founded in 1805 and demolished in 1898–99. The statue of Sir Robert Peel is flanked by elegant cast iron lamp columns with globe lanterns.

Left: Council House, Victoria Square, Birmingham, c1910

View looking north-east across the square from Paradise Street. The Council House, designed by H R Yeoville Thomason and completed in 1874, is crowned by a pediment with sculpture showing Britannia receiving the manufactures of Birmingham. It was extended almost immediately to create a new Art Gallery and Museum and Gas Corporation offices, marked by the slender tower (far left). The marble statue of Queen Victoria, by Thomas Brock, was erected in 1901.

VICTORIA SQUARE

Above: Victoria Square, Birmingham, c1880
A similar view to opposite above, but more southerly and 15 years earlier, showing the buildings cleared to make way for the new General Post Office between Hill Street (to right) and New Street (to left), with the statue of Sir Robert Peel to the extreme left. The city stood in the vanguard for public house reform. Corbett's Temperance Hotel carries a large rooftop placard for Montserrat Lime Juice Cordial.

Right: Town Hall, Birmingham, c1920
View down New Street from the south-east corner of the Town Hall colonnade. Charles Edge took over the completion of the Town Hall in 1834, when the original architects Hansom (the designer of the hansom cab) and Welch were declared bankrupt. Having undergone various changes during the late 19th and early 20th centuries, it has now been restored to its former glory. The magnificent organ in the Georgian assembly room formed a centrepiece for the Town Hall's recent re-opening.

BROAD STREET, BIRMINGHAM

Below: Broad Street, c1895

View across Broad Street towards Bellamy & Wakefield at the junction of Paradise Street. The Council House is only a short walk away, and the chimney of the Atlas Works rises in the background. The picture was taken from the entrance to Old Wharf, where the Midland Canal terminated in the city centre. A superb brachiated lamp column carrying globe lanterns marks the junction.

Opposite top left: Bull Ring, 1905

The area surrounding St Martin Church, originally residential, was gradually overtaken by trade – first cloth, then foodstuffs. At the end of the 18th century the houses were cleared, along with the market cross, to make way for a market place; a covered market was built in 1835, although the street market continued, as the picture shows.

Opposite top right: The Church of St Martin, c1885

Rebuilt by Julius Alfred Chatwin in 1873–75 in a spiky Victorian Gothic style, St Martin's is the original parish church of Birmingham, now known as St Martin in the Bull Ring. The building immediately behind and to the right is St Martin's Hotel.

Opposite below: Birmingham Town Hall, c1910

In the view looking north-west across Victoria Street, a Mitchells & Butlers Brewery dray makes late afternoon deliveries, while to the right a motor taxi waits for fares. In the background (right) the former Liberal Club building can be seen.

Left: St Peter and St Paul's Church, Witton Lane, Aston, 1902

View from the south-west towards the chancel at the east end. This Anglican parish church was founded before 1086, although nothing visible of the original structure remains. The 15th-century spire was renewed in 1776–77 by John Cheshire, and substantial alterations were made to the building between 1879 and 1890 by Julius Alfred Chatwin.

MOAT LANE

Moat Lane, Birmingham, c1905
Above: View north-west towards St Martin Church. Smithfield Market buildings are to the left, apparently in need of repairs. Opened at the Whitsun Fair in 1817, Smithfield Market originally traded in cattle and horses. By 1883 this activity had broadened to include a wholesale vegetable market, but before the turn of the century livestock had been moved away from Smithfield. Today, the market has been expanded and subsumed into the Bull Ring Indoor Market, and the site of the original cattle market is now Moat Lane Car Park.
Opposite: Earlier view (1901) up Moat Lane from a slightly different angle.

Left: The Queen's Hotel, Birmingham
Built in 1854 in a grand Italianate style to the designs of J V Livock, the hotel served the needs of the rail passengers arriving at New Street Station. The ornate open-work iron lift doors show the luxurious detail of the building. Widely regarded as the best hotel in the city, it was demolished shortly after this record photograph was taken.

SUMNE
GARDEN
SEEDS
AGRI
SE
HAY, STRA
THORLEY'S FOOD
LATE
EDWARD FREE
HOP, SEED & C
WAREHOU
WALTER

THE BULL RING MARKET

Left and opposite top right: The Bull Ring Market
During the Victorian era the market expanded to include a large number of shops and businesses set up by immigrants. The Lord Nelson statue was a focus for preaching and political protests.

Opposite top left: The Market Hall
Designed by Charles Edge in Greek Revival style, the huge market hall was completed in 1835 at a cost of almost £45,000. Over 600 market stalls were accommodated beneath its vast iron roof.

Below: The corner of Easy Row and Edmund Street
One of a series of roads on the old Colmore Estate, Edmund Street originally stretched from Temple Row in the city centre past St Philip's Cathedral to the northern end of Newhall Street. These 18th-century merchants' houses were demolished during the 1960s for the new Central Library, which was opened in 1974. A fascinating array of posters can be seen on the return frontage.

Opposite below: A steam tram in Moat Row
The first steam trams appeared in Birmingham in 1882. This one has Sparkbrook, a district of Birmingham, on its sign.

THE COMET
THE COMET
T.F. PETT & Co
WATERPROOFERS

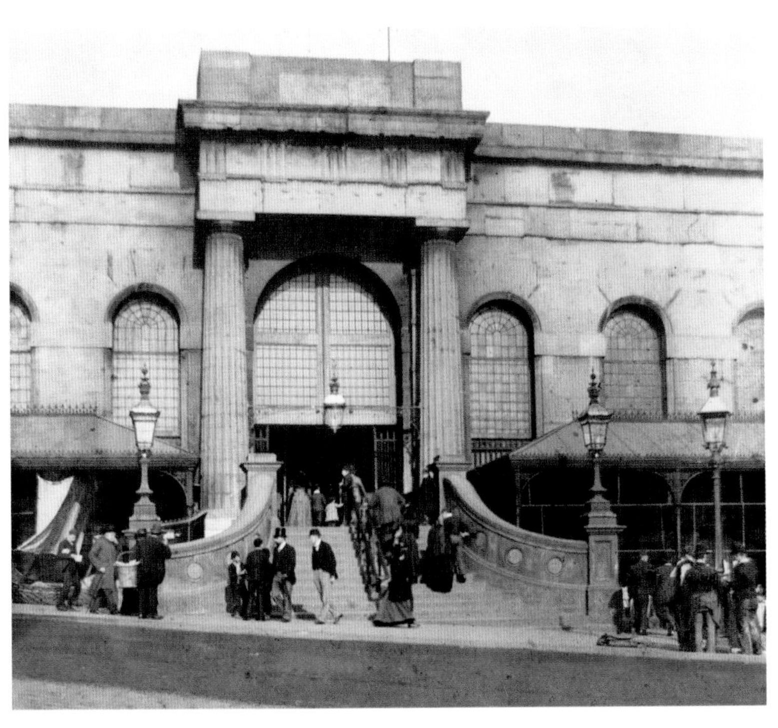

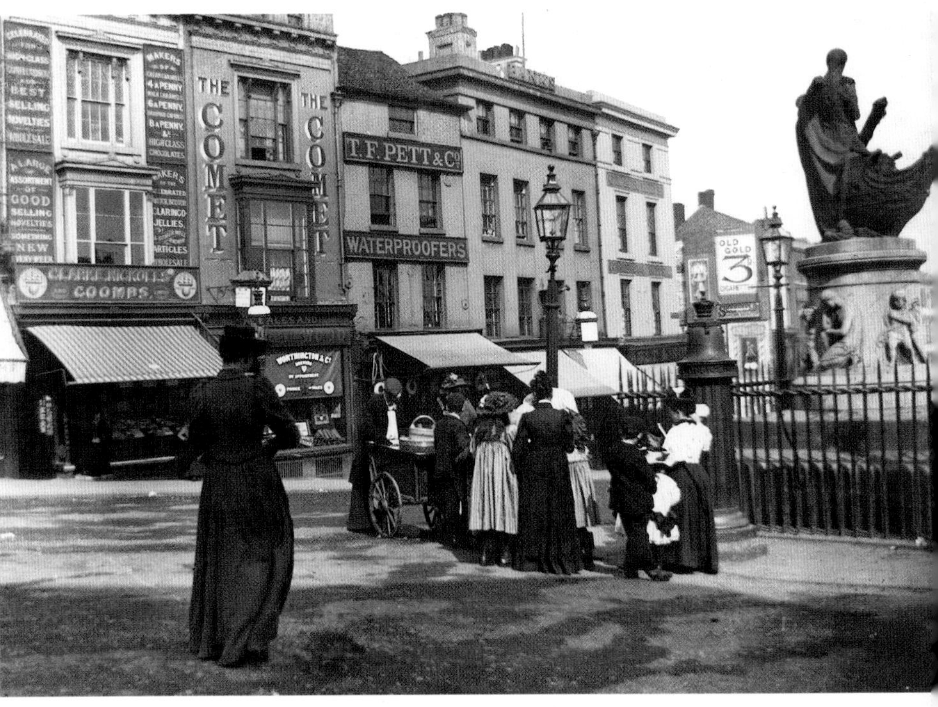

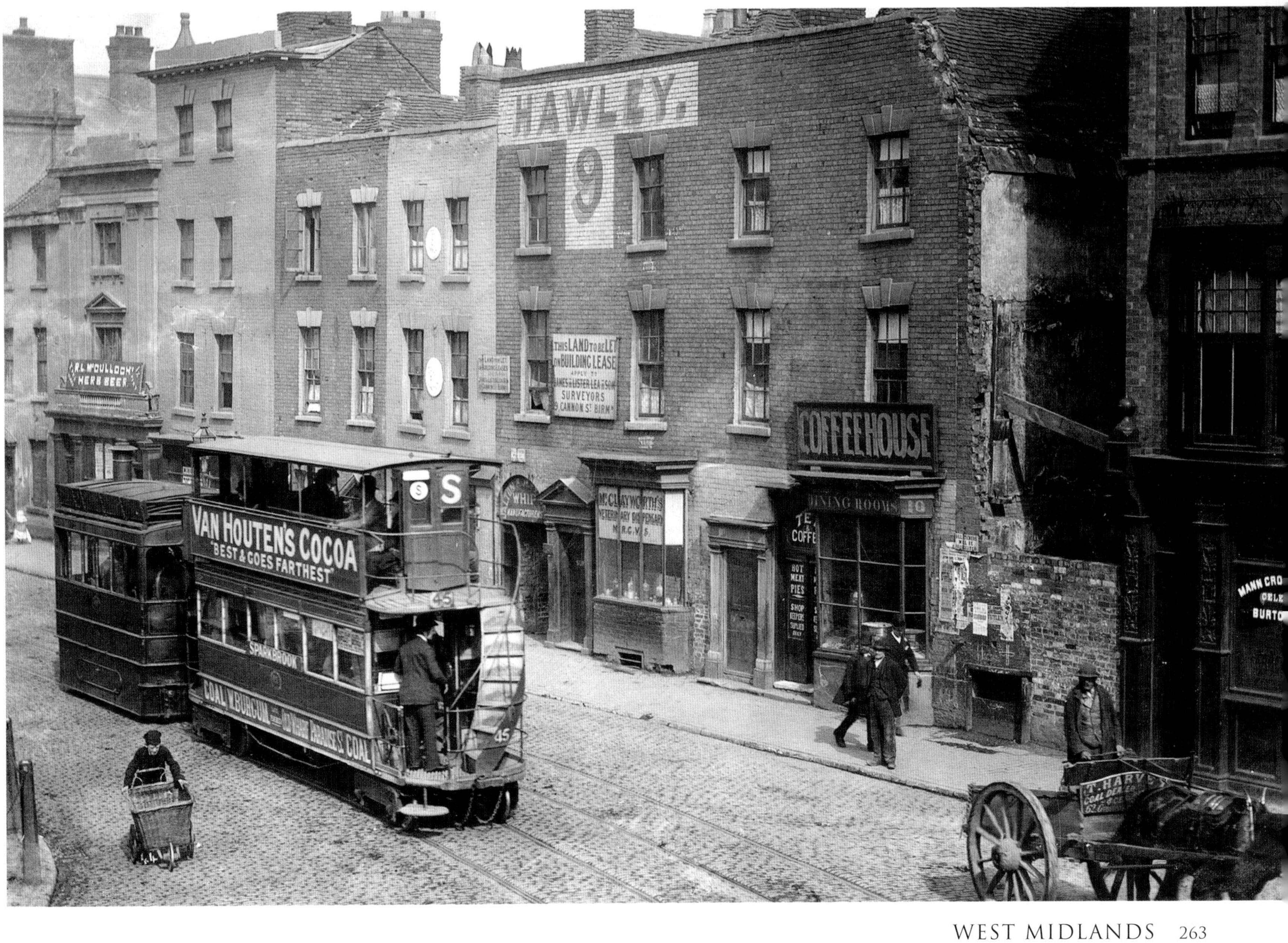
HAWLEY.
9
THIS LAND TO BE LET
ON BUILDING LEASE
SURVEYORS
5 CANNON ST BIRM
COFFEEHOUSE
DINING ROOMS 10
VAN HOUTEN'S COCOA
"BEST & GOES FARTHEST"
S
SPARKBROOK

THE LIBERAL CLUB, BIRMINGHAM

Opposite: The Liberal Club, Edmund Street, 1886
On the corner of Edmund Street and Congreve Street, the Liberal Club was opened in the presence of Joseph Chamberlain, then mayor, and 2,000 of Birmingham's notables in January 1880. The architect, J A Cossins, also designed Mason College next door. The building had numerous incarnations before being demolished in 1964, when the area was redeveloped to include the municipal offices and public library. Congreve Street was replaced by Congreve Passage, and Edmund Street shortened to make way for Chamberlain Square.

Above left: The Colonnade Hotel, New Street, 1883
The architect W H Ward was regarded as a master of Renaissance-style architecture and the Colonnade, built in 1882, as his finest work, but this was not enough to stop it being demolished in 1961.

Above right: Council House, Victoria Square, 1886
View from Colmore Row, looking towards the east corner of the Council House. The design of the building was the subject of a national competition that was won by architect H R Yeoville Thomason. It took five years to build, after Joseph Chamberlain laid the foundation stone in 1874.

Right: Cobden Coffee Palace, Corporation Street, 1883
View north-west to the junction of Cherry Street. Built by the Birmingham Coffee House Co, whose directors were supporters of the temperance movement, the building was named after Richard Cobden, a colleague of John Bright and a leader of the fight for free trade and the abolition of the Corn Laws in the 1840s. John Bright, a strong supporter of the temperance movement, officially opened the building in 1883. The hotel remained in this location until 1959, after which it was demolished and the site redeveloped for Rackhams department store. It was subsequently bought by House of Fraser, the current occupant.

VICTORIA LAW COURTS

Opposite: Victoria Law Courts, Corporation Street, Birmingham, 1891
The Law Courts were designed by Sir Aston Webb and Ingress Bell, after a national competition overseen by the architect Alfred Waterhouse in 1886. The building, opened by the Prince and Princess of Wales in July 1891, is faced in blood-red terracotta. Opposite is the cleared site for the Methodist Central Hall.
Opposite bottom left: The Great Hall in the Law Courts, seen from the gallery.
Opposite bottom right: The criminal court, looking towards the bench.

Above: Richard Lunt & Co Ltd, Old Square, Birmingham, 1897
View of the textile wholesalers premises. This photograph was commissioned by Burmantofts Co to promote its terracotta or faience products. Burmantofts was a trading name of Wilcox & Co and named after the area of Leeds where the company was based. Their products were used widely across Britain, including for the lustrous interior of the National Liberal Club in London.

Above: Norton and Company, Corporation Street, Birmingham, 1891
This block of shops and offices were the premises of Norton and Company, furniture and carpet store, as well as the Capital and Counties Bank.

MASON COLLEGE BIRMINGHAM

Mason University College, Paradise Street, 1897
Established as a college of science by Josiah Mason in 1880, the college was intended to train graduates in mathematics, physics, chemistry, natural sciences, physiology and engineering to serve local industry. Many consider its demolition in the 1960s for the new public library to have been an act of civic vandalism at a time when little thought was given to conserving the city's superb heritage.

Above: The polychrome Victorian Gothic frontage seen from beside the Chamberlain Memorial.

Left: The chemical laboratory

Opposite (clockwise from top left): The library, the medical theatre and the natural history museum.

BIRMINGHAM UNIVERSITY

Right: Victoria Square, 1909
King Edward VII in his carriage during the royal visit to Birmingham for the official opening of the new buildings of the University of Birmingham, designed by Aston Webb and Ingress Bell. The grant of its charter in 1900 was a milestone in England's education system and recognition of the success of Mason University College. Joseph Chamberlain's sustained drive to improve the city's amenities led to the raising of £250,000, including donations from Andrew Carnegie, the Scottish-American industrialist. Birmingham, the first independent English university, set the standard for all major provincial cities. Fittingly, Joseph Chamberlain was the university's first Chancellor.

Above: Temple Row, 1909
The visit by King Edward VII and Queen Alexandra on 7 July 1909 prompted the erection of decorated archways by local artisan groups; here the Metallic Bedstead Manufacturers greet the royal visitors with an array of metal bedsteads. Other arches were raised by the School of Art, the Water Department and the Cycle Manufacturers.

Opposite: Mason College
(Clockwise from top left): The anatomical theatre, the physics laboratory and the botanical laboratory.

ROYAL SOCIETY OF ARTISTS

Left and below left: The Royal Birmingham Society of Artists building, New Street, 1912
The RBSA was a highly influential body in the later Victorian period, particularly within the Pre-Raphaelite and Arts & Crafts movements. Increasing financial pressure in the early years of the 20th century led to the landmark New Street building being demolished and rebuilt as part of a commercial redevelopment. The entrance hall, with attendants, is shown below.

Above: Bristol Road leading to the city centre.

Opposite top right: Bournville, July 1909
The Girls' Baths, a swimming pool complex in the Birmingham suburbs. Bournville Village was a model village founded by chocolate manufacturer and social reformer George Cadbury.

Opposite bottom right: Scottish Provident Institution, Colmore Row, 1886
In the Victorian era Colmore Row was one of Birmingham's most prestigious business addresses. As well as being the location of the Grand Hotel, it housed many insurance companies, including Scottish Provident. The architects of this impressive Venetian Gothic building were Osborne and Reading.

Opposite left: White Horse Hotel, Congreve Street, 1908
Interiors of the hotel following refurbishment by local architects Wood & Kendrick. Top to bottom: the public bars, the grill room looking towards the buffet, and the kitchen.

THE DON
ASSOCIATION OF
WOOLLEN MANUFACTURERS
GENTLEMENS CLOTHING
FIRST COST
WARWICK HOUSE
WARWICK CHAMBERS

WARWICK HOUSE.
SELLING OFF
MUCH BELOW COST!
PREMISES COMING DOWN.

WARWICK HOUSE

Above: Warwick House, New Street, Birmingham, 1890
Completed in 1839, Warwick House was Birmingham's first department store. The shop was commissioned by the draper William Holliday and sold a variety of household fabrics and furniture. Its classical frontage with fluted Corinthian columns and pilasters was extended and refurbished in the 1850s. Holliday, Son & Co had two other premises, on Corporation Street (previous pages) and Union Passage.

Left: Corporation Street, Birmingham, 1886
Designed by the architect William Hale for Liberty's in the 1880s, this fine Tudor Revival building with carved timbers and intricate Gothic stonework is another of the city's lost jewels. Liberty's was an important patron of the city's Arts & Crafts artisan workshops. The construction work was undertaken by John Bowen & Sons, who were responsible for many of the major building projects in Victorian Birmingham, including the Victoria Law Courts and the Mosley and Balsall Heath Institute.

Right: A R Dean and Company, Corporation Street, Birmingham, 1897
This double-fronted building housed A R Dean, a house furnishing company, and Pitman's Birmingham Vegetarian Hotel and Restaurant. The terracotta ornamental frieze was the work of Benjamin Creswick, a sculptor who was mentored by John Ruskin. Creswick started his working life as a knife grinder in Sheffield, but his gift for sculpture was noticed by a number of people, including a friend of Ruskin's, who made the introduction. In 1889 Creswick was hired by the new Birmingham Municipal School of Art.

Bottom: James Lloyd and Co, Hurst Street, 1893
The elegant James Lloyd & Co perambulator factory designed by T W F Newton and A E Cheatle.

GENERAL HOSPITAL

Birmingham General Hospital, Steelhouse Lane, 1897
Above: Princess Christian of Schleswig-Holstein arrives by carriage at Birmingham General Hospital for the opening ceremony. The hospital was designed by William Hensman in rich red brick and terracotta in a similar style to the Victoria Law Courts. Note the superb figurative sculpture on the carriage porch and central memorial.

Left: One of a series of photographs showing preparations for the opening ceremony of the hospital, with the centrepiece flanked by two stunning towers.

Opposite bottom right: Exterior of the Nurses' Home in a simplified red brick and terracotta design.

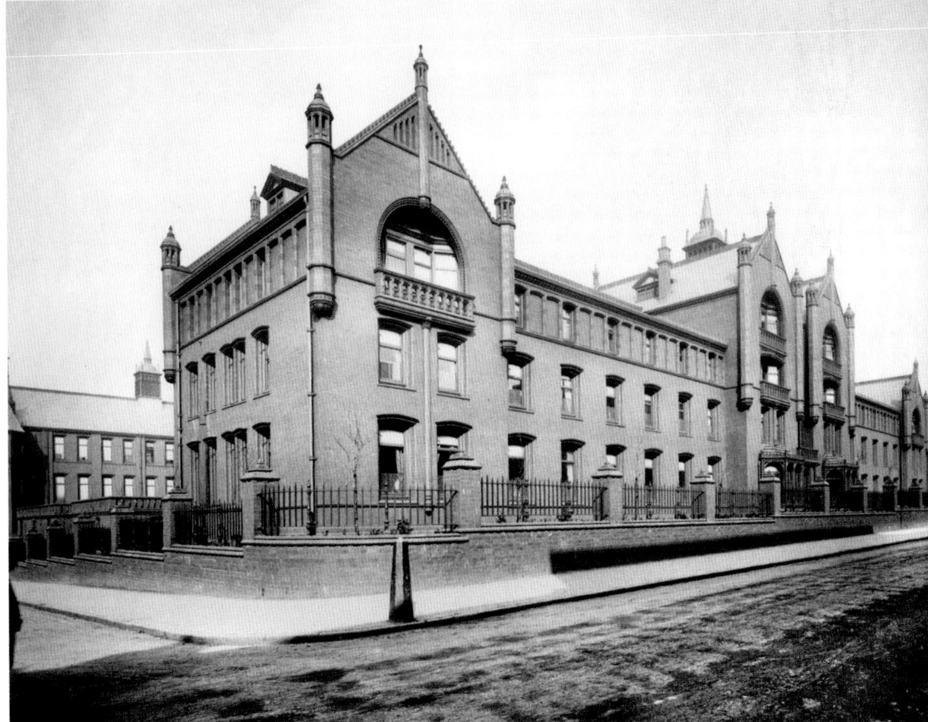

COLMORE ROW

Top right: Colmore Row, Birmingham, c1890
A view looking north-east along Colmore Row, with the Council House in the foreground and the railings of Christ Church churchyard visible to the right. Before this area of Birmingham was developed in the 18th century, Colmore Row was a country lane called New Hall Lane, connecting the roads from Birmingham to Dudley and West Bromwich in the Black Country.

Above left: Grand Hotel, Colmore Row, c1894
Interior of the restaurant, looking towards the entrance. The Grand Hotel was remodelled internally in 1890–91 by John Henry Chamberlain and William Martin.

Top left: Lionel Street, Birmingham, 1897
The premises of H W Ward and Company, tool makers. The company specialised in lathes, but in 1914 it equipped an entire automobile production line for a single customer.

OTH WAREHOUSE.
Silks
Serges
THS & DRESS GOODS.
Costumes
Suitings
84
83 INNES·SMITH & Co. 83
BOOTH DENTIST
83
HAYDON CHAMBERS
T. HAYDONS COAL OFFICES 83
SUMMER MANTLE SALE
HALF PRICE
THE LOU

HIGH STREET

Opposite: Innes Smith and Company, High Street, Birmingham, 1898

The premises of a wine merchants, this building was designed by the architects Newton and Cheatle. Unfortunately, this part of the High Street was redeveloped in the latter half of the 20th century.

Above: The Open Air Market Smithfield, Birmingham, c1890

The Drovers Arms, on the right rear of the photograph, stands on the corner of Bradford Street and Moat Row. A steam-driven tram passes by to the right of the market.

Top: Old Cattle Market, Moat Lane, 1901

SMETHWICK

Left: Chance's Glassworks, Spon Lane South, Smethwick, c1920
Workers at various types of machinery used in the glassmaking and finishing processes. Chance's was established in the early 19th century and produced window, optical and specialist glass of all kinds, including window glass for the Houses of Parliament in London and over one million square feet for the Crystal Palace. This photograph was taken for the Sturtevant Engineering Company Limited, which created fans and air conditioning systems, and whose heating and ventilation units were installed in the Chance Brothers' factory.

Above: Birmingham Small Arms Company, Armoury Road, Small Heath, 1917
Women working in Machine Shop One of the factory, which was founded in 1861 and produced rifles, Lewis guns, shells and vehicles.

HAMSTEAD

Above: Hamstead Colliery, near Birmingham, 1908
Families at the pithead await news of victims of a mining disaster. The deep veins of coal were mined with some risk, as was proven when a fire broke out underground and 26 men died from inhaling poisonous fumes.

Left: Hartley's Jams Depot, Lawley Street, 1927
Hartley's Jams were made in factories in Liverpool and Bermondsey, then transported by train around the country to dispersal points. Here, two delivery vans await loading and unloading at the Lawley Street Goods Station.

WARSTONE LANE

Left: Warstone Lane Cemetery, Birmingham, c1900

A notable feature of the Warstone Lane Cemetery is the two tiers of catacombs, whose unhealthy vapours led to the Birmingham Cemeteries Act requiring that non-interred coffins should be sealed with lead or pitch.

The remains of John Baskerville, famed for his typography and printing, were moved here from the crypt at Christ Church when it was demolished in 1898 to make way for developments in Council House (later Victoria) Square. His exhumed body was in such a good state of preservation that it was exhibited in a warehouse for some time before locals complained of the smell and he was re-interred.

NEW STREET STATION

New Street Station, Stephenson Street, Birmingham
Top: c1901. Queen's Hotel sits behind the cramped entrance to the station where horse-drawn cabs wait in the street for hire.
Above left: c1920. By the 1920s the setting of the Queen's Hotel and the entrance to New Street station were transformed and expanded.
Above right: c1900. Built by the London and North Western Railway Company in the 1850s, the station boasted what was then the largest arched single-span iron and glass roof in the world, spanning a width of 212 feet (65 m) and being 840 feet (256 m) long.

Opposite: Edmund Street, Birmingham, 1897
Eveson Coal and Coke Company premises on Edmund Street. The building, with its handsome terracotta facade, was designed by Newton and Cheatle for George J Eveson.

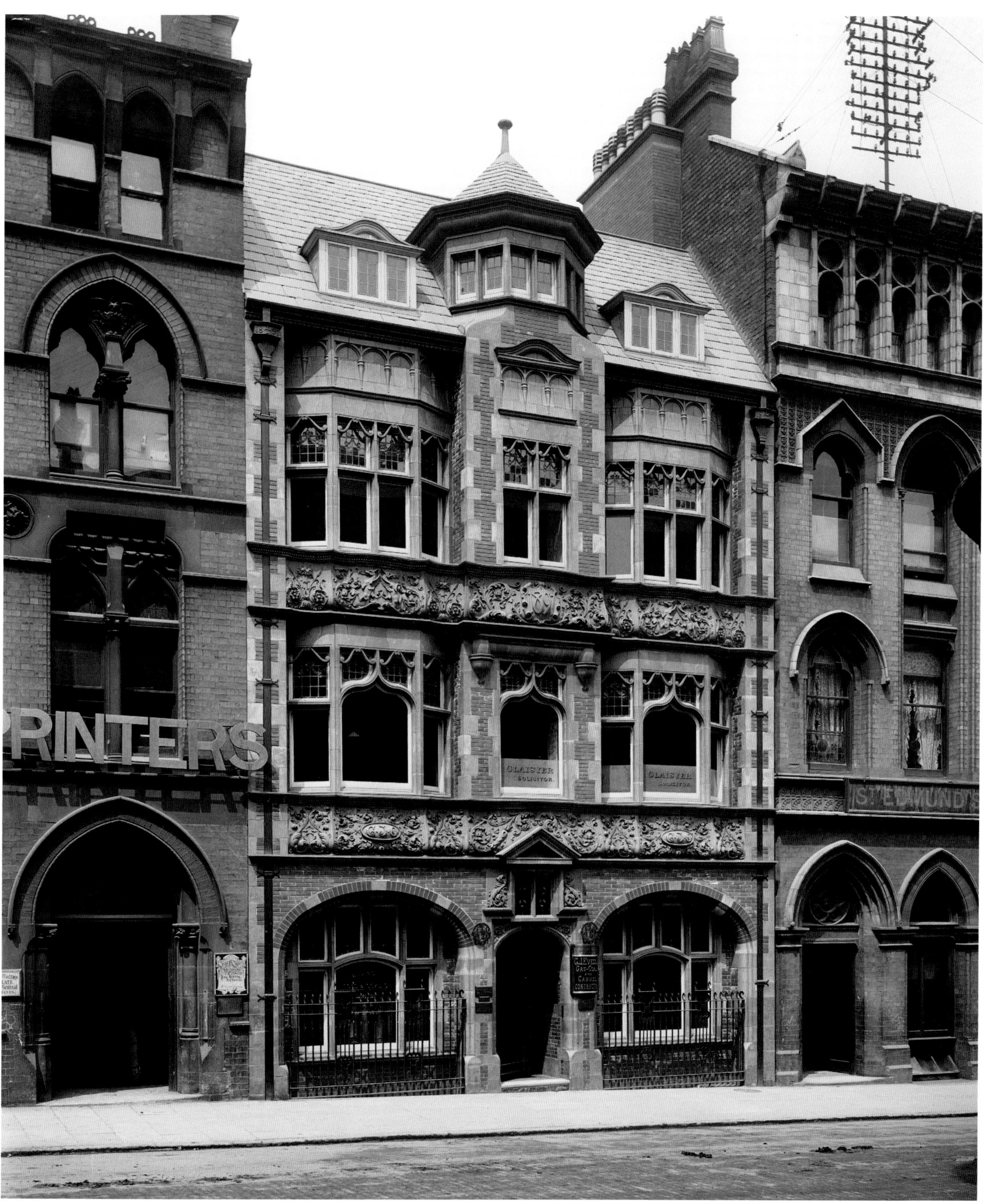
PRINTERS
GLAISYER
SOLICITOR
GLAISYER
SOLICITOR

SLUM PROPERTIES

Birmingham Corporation made a survey of all 'slum properties' at the beginning of the 20th century. Some of the extraordinary photographs can be seen here. Most people in Victorian industrial cities lived in back-to-backs built in courts or rows.

Above: 4, 5 and 6 in Number 2 Court, St James's Place. The cramped, insanitary interiors and foetid air encouraged the tenants to spend as much time as possible outside their oppressive homes.

Left: 6–14 in Number 10 Court, Cheapside

Opposite above: 33–35 Cheapside
Early 19th-century court houses. The narrow arched entry leads beyond to Court Number 7, Pettifers Buildings, where a child squats in the rubble.

Opposite below: 102–104 Bagot Street
A group of poor children, some with no shoes, sit outside their squalid homes. Court Number 6 can be glimpsed behind.

McDOUGALL'S
SAMES
CORPORATION
Fry's Chocolate
R. WHITES
LEMONADE
GINGER BEER
SODA WATER
AMERICAN
CREAM SODA
HUDSON'S
SOAP

W. CANNING &
CHEMICAL MANUFACT

INFANT MORTALITY

There were more than half a million back-to-backs in cities across Victorian Britain. As late as 1945 Birmingham still had more than 30,000 of these slum dwellings. At the time these photographs were taken more than 3,000 children died in Birmingham every year before their first birthday.

The last surviving court of back-to-back houses in Birmingham – Numbers 50–54 Inge Street and 55–63 Hurst Street – is now operated as a museum by the National Trust.

Below: 11–13 Chapel Terrace, Saltley Road
The gas works can be seen in the background. Prized gardens were rarely appropriate for growing food.

Left: 244 Farm Street
In spite of the beguiling advertisements for Football Oats, Colman's Mustard, Fry's Chocolate and Bo-Peep Soap, this finely detailed early 19th-century shopfront next to the entry to Court Number 57 has only a meagre display of goods available in the window.

Opposite above: Watery Lane
Families congregate around one house and the arched entrance to the court beyond; windows were left open to ventilate the cramped accommodation.

Opposite below: Reconditioned slum housing at 18 Court, Clarkson Street.

COVENTRY

Coventry's status as an important industrial centre grew with the building of the Coventry Canal in the late 18th century and the arrival of the London to Birmingham Railway in 1838. Renowned for its silk weaving in the early 19th century, by the 1890s it was an industrial centre producing bicycles, machine tools and cars. The Daimler car factory – the first in Britain – opened in 1896. Triumph, Armstrong Siddeley and Singer all followed, supported by myriad engineering and electrical workshops. The beautiful old town, with its mediaeval buildings, was already threatened by the expansion of new industries before its catastrophic damage in the Blitz.

Top left & right: Dunlop Pneumatic Tyre Company Limited, Alma Street, 1897
Street view (left) and interior of the carriage tyre shop (right), showing employees at work.

Above: Greyfriars Green, c1900
Looking across to the three spires of Coventry Cathedral, Holy Trinity Church and Christ Church. 'Greyfriars' refers to the Franciscan Friary, which had been founded here by 1234; it was dissolved by Henry VIII in 1538.

PEPPER LANE

Above: Pepper Lane, Coventry, c1930

The Cathedral viewed from the west. The original Cathedral church was named for St Michael and was one of the biggest churches in the country when it became a cathedral in 1918. Like most of the surrounding mediaeval streets in the old city, it was destroyed during the Blitz on 14 November 1940 along with over 60,000 houses.

COVENTRY

Above: Church of St John The Baptist, Spon Street, c1884
Built in 1344 in local red sandstone with a grant from Edward II's consort, Queen Isabella, the church was remodelled by George Gilbert Scott in 1877.

Right: Butcher Row, c1889
Looking north towards a range of timber-framed buildings. Established around the 12th century, picturesque Butcher Row was demolished in 1936 to make way for Trinity Street, part of a destructive wave of pre-war civic clearances by the city authorities.

Opposite top: Priory Row, c1910
The church of the Benedictine Priory of St Mary was Coventry's first cathedral, almost completely destroyed by Henry VIII in 1539. The ivy-covered foundations running down the centre of Priory Row may be those of the south wall of the nave. To the left is a 17th-century timber-framed building, and to the right, parts of the Bluecoat School built in 1856–57.

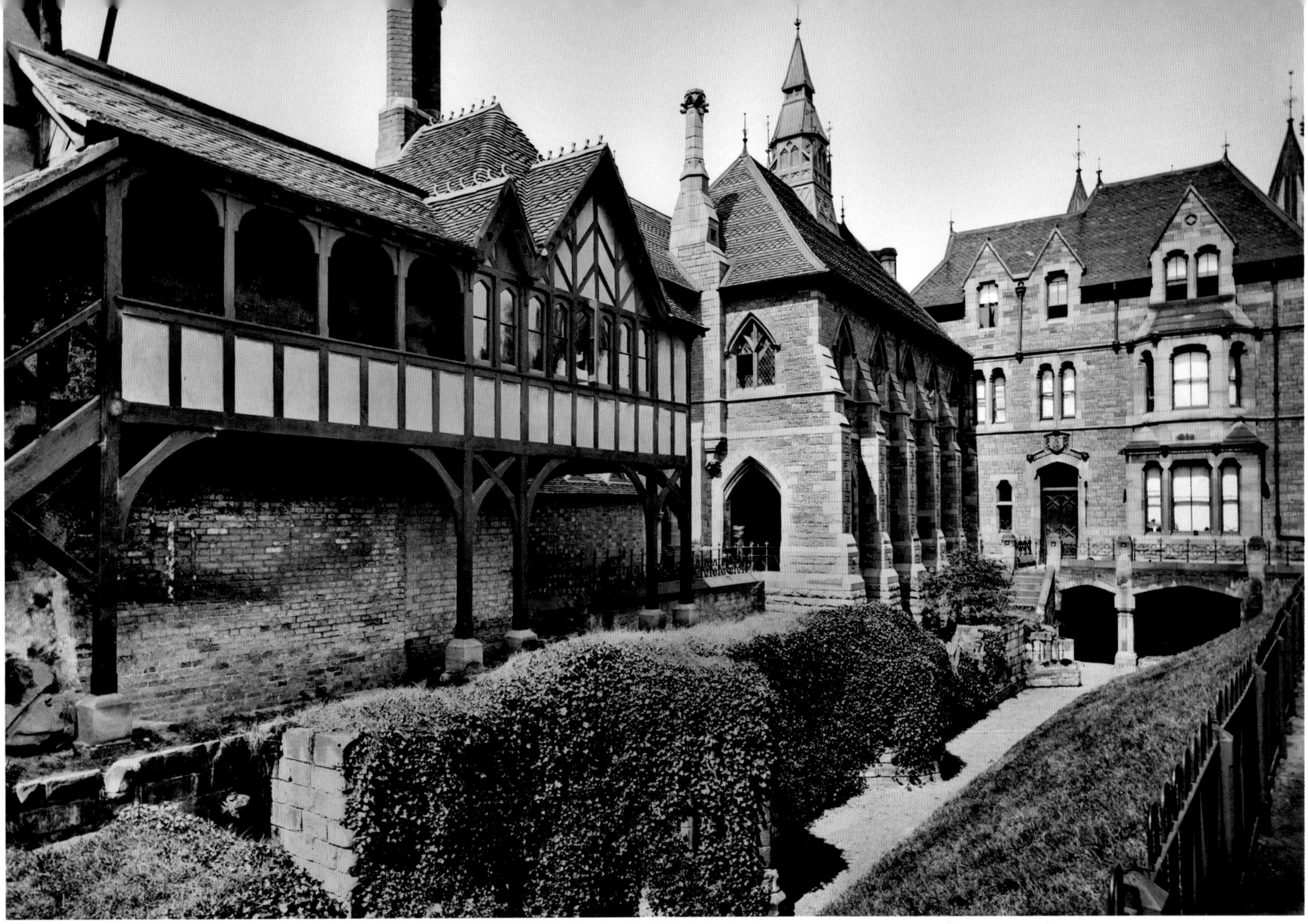

FORD'S HOSPITAL

Right and far right: Ford's Hospital, Greyfriars Lane, Coventry, c1890
Also known as Greyfriars Hospital, the institution was founded in 1509 by William Ford, a local merchant, who endowed an almshouse for five men and a woman. By 1800 the charity was confined to women only. The north side of the hospital was directly hit by a bomb in 1940 that killed eight women. One of the most famous timber buildings in the country, the hospital narrowly escaped demolition by the relentless modernist City Architect Donald Gibson. The building was restored in 1951–53, using the original timbers. Today the fine timbered courtyard remains much as it appears in this photograph (far right).

DUDLEY

Above: Market Place, c1930
In the foreground is the ebullient Dudley Fountain – one of the grandest drinking fountains to be erected outside London, a monumental sculpture nearly 30 feet high designed by James Forsyth in 1867. Presented to the town by the Earl of Dudley, it was inaugurated by his wife. At the other end of the Market Place stands the church of St Thomas. Crowning the skyline is the Norman castle, whose grounds house Dudley's renowned zoo.

Right: Dudley Zoo, 1930
The Bear Pit and its viewing terrace. The pioneering modernist design of Dudley Zoo was the work of Berthold Lubetkin and the Tecton architectural practice. All 12 buildings were innovative, using reinforced concrete and exploited the complex topography of ravines and unmapped limestone workings surrounding the castle. The enclosure pictured was for polar bears, with other bears and big cats roaming the ravine beyond.

Left and below: A Harper, Sons & Bean, Dudley, c1915

In 1907 George Bean became chairman of the company, which had been founded by Absolom Harper in 1822. Originally a supplier of car parts, during the Great War the company manufactured aero engines, shrapnel and shell cases for the government. By 1916 Bean was producing around 21,000 shells a week. The photograph (left) was taken in the die shop, some of the workers looking very young. In the picture below shells for 12-, 14- and 18-pounder guns are lined up on tables. Many of the machines are operated by women. After the war the company manufactured the Bean Motor Car.

WOLVERHAMPTON

Far left: Queen Square, c1920
View north-west towards an equestrian statue of Prince Albert by Thomas Thorneycroft, erected by the town in 1866. Following Prince Albert's death, Queen Victoria made her first public appearance here for the unveiling of the statue, which gave her so much pleasure that she knighted the mayor, John Morris. The tower of St Peter's Collegiate Church can be seen beyond the market stalls.

DUDLEY STREET

Above: Dudley Street, Wolverhampton, c1900
The bustling street scene portrays a prosperous town with shops offering factory-produced consumer items. Freeman Hardy & Willis, to the right in the photograph, was opening its chain of shoe shops across the Midlands at this time.

Opposite top right: Star & Garter Royal Hotel, Victoria Street, Wolverhampton, c1880
This 16th-century hotel was built as a three-storey timber residence on what was then Cock Street. Charles I allegedly took shelter here on the march to Edge Hill, hence the 'Royal' reference. Rebuilt in the 19th century, the historic inn was sold and demolished in 1904.

Opposite below: Town Hall, Lichfield Street, Bilston, c1880
View looking west to the junction with Church Street. The Italianate building, dating from 1872, reflects the growth in status of the town from a village on the outskirts of Wolverhampton to a burgeoning coal mining area and later a centre for steel production. Note the unsealed road surface and the Post Office lantern to the right of the picture.

Above: Market Hall, under construction, Wolverhampton, c1902
Built to designs by the borough engineer J W Bradley, the elegant market hall, which housed the wholesale market, was largely constructed in brick and masonry with the roof carried on cast iron pillars. It was demolished in 1973 to make way for the new Civic Centre.

Shropshire

LUDLOW

Left: Broad Street, Ludlow, c1900
Looking north towards the Butter Cross, with the tower of St Laurence's Church, established in the 11th century, visible beyond. The street is eerily devoid of both people and traffic.

Below: High Street, Ludlow, 1923
View east towards the junction with Broad Street. The dome and columned portico of the Buttercross can be seen in the middle of the picture. Built in 1746 to the designs of William Baker of Audlem, it occupies the official centre of the town.

Opposite top: High Street, Market Drayton, c1915
A gleaming motor car is parked outside Gouldbourn Ironmongers, which has an impressive array of pails and pitchforks in the window.

IRONBRIDGE

Above: Ironbridge, 1892

The birthplace of the Industrial Revolution; the world's first iron bridge spans the gorge of the River Severn. Completed in 1781 to the designs of Abraham Darby III, the cast iron structure was a technological marvel of its age. Ironbridge is now a World Heritage Site.

SHREWSBURY

Above: Abbey Church of the Holy Cross, c1890
Originally part of the Benedictine Abbey of St Peter and St Paul, founded between 1083 and 1090 and dissolved in 1540, the present Holy Cross Church contains much original fabric. Damaged in the siege of Shrewsbury in 1645 during the Civil War, it was only restored in 1860.

Top right: Abbot's House, Butcher Row, c1890
A remarkably complete and significant surviving example of a late mediaeval town house. It was built by the Abbot of Lilleshall as an investment for his abbey. The trees used for the wooden frame were cut down in 1457–58, the town bailiffs and the abbot's carpenter being mentioned in records as attending a frame-raising ceremony in 1459. The ground floor comprised shops with tenement flats above.

Middle right: Raven Hotel, Castle Street, 1912
Elegant gentlefolk and their large expensive car are pictured outside the Raven Hotel, the best in the town. It closed in December 1959 to make way for a new Woolworths, when the old hotel was demolished and replaced with a bland new frontage, much to the dismay of the townspeople.

Opposite top: Looking north along Castle Street, 1911
To the left is the unusual brick Gothic frontage of the Raven Hotel

Bottom right: Wyle Cop, c1890
Looking south towards numbers 71–73, which date back to c1460. Although still used as retail premises, the three-storey jettied building is now called Henry Tudor House as he is said to have stayed there while marching with his army to Bosworth Field to defeat and supplant Richard III.

Opposite bottom: High Street, 1911
Looking north towards the junction with Pride Hill; the large timber-framed town house built in 1596 for wool merchant Robert Ireland is on the left. The black and white frontage to the right was built by the merchant Richard Owen in 1592. Adjacent is the ornate frontage of the Alliance Insurance building dating from 1892.

Staffordshire

LICHFIELD

Above: Lichfield Cathedral, 1880
View from the north-west. One of the country's most impressive cathedrals, Lichfield suffered during the Civil War when it was used by both sides as a fortified stronghold. Cannonballs shattered the roof and the central spire; parts of the building never recovered. George Gilbert Scott oversaw its extensive restoration between 1855 and 1878.

Left: Hanley, c1900
The small rural villages of Staffordshire were overrun by the pottery industry in the 19th century. By the 1870s there were over 4,000 bottle kilns disgorging a permanent haze of atmospheric pollution that blocked out the sun and caused a high death rate in the small towns of the area, such as Hanley and Burslem.

BIDDULPH

Above: Bradley Green, 1902

The small village of Bradley Green, known since 1930 as Biddulph, developed into a larger town with the building of the pit and iron works in 1857. Goods were transported from the town along the new canal system and the toll road and railway line through Biddulph. With the closure of the industries, Bradley Green, together with the other villages and hamlets along the Biddulph valley, merged under one name – Biddulph.

STONE

Top: High Street, Stone, 1900

View north-west, with the Crown Hotel in the foreground on the left. Historically a well-known coaching inn in an important staging town, the Crown dates from 1778. The town was important as a transport hub for canal, river, road and rail routes

Warwickshire

WARWICK

Left: East Gate, c1900
View east along Jury Street. St Peter's Chapel, with a clock tower built over the archway, is of 15th-century origin. The archway was largely rebuilt in 1788 by Francis Hiorn and is now a part of King's High School for Girls. The lower part of the building incorporates the mediaeval masonry of the original town walls.

Below: Market Place, c1910
Looking east towards the Shakespeare Restaurant on the corner of New Street. Leath's, central right, offered the latest technology in bicycles and sewing machines.

ROYAL LEAMINGTON SPA

Top: Christ Church and the Clarendon Hotel, The Parade, Royal Leamington Spa, 1922

This simple church was built in the 1840s and demolished in 1959, returning the land to open space in Beauchamp Park. That apart, this elegant scene remains largely unchanged, with the terrace housing the Clarendon Hotel and elements of the terrace opposite still in existence.

Above: The Parade, Royal Leamington Spa, c1900

Looking north, the Town Hall clock tower is to the right of the picture. The Leamington & Warwick Tramways & Omnibus Company operated a tramway service between Warwick and Leamington Spa between 1881 and 1930. The trams were pulled by horses until 1905, which explains the lack of overhead electric cables.

Right: Village pump, Grandborough, 1901

A young servant girl has been sent to fetch water from the village pump. Two urchins are on the same errand. Before houses had running water, fetching water from the local pump was a heavy but essential daily chore.

MORETON MORRELL

Left: Moreton Morrell, 1902
The Public Elementary School was built in 1869 on land presented by E Greaves Esq. Today it is the village hall. Beyond lies a 16th-century timber-framed cottage.

Below: Post Office, Moreton Morrell, 1906
With the introduction of public telephones, the Post Office became one of the hubs of village life. The untreated wooden pillar to the right of the postmistress is probably an early telegraph pole.

Opposite top left: Coventry Road, Dunchurch, 1905
View looking south-east towards the distant Market Cross. This sleepy scene would have been very different in the coaching era, when Dunchurch was an important staging post on the main London to Holyhead and Leicester to Oxford routes. A cluster of substantial coaching inns brought business to the town. Later the road was designated the A45. Today the M45 bypasses the town to the south.

Opposite top right: Old Gaydon Inn, Gaydon, 1905
The Lighthorne Cricketers put on a show in front of the public house for the photographer and a small crowd of supporters.

KINETON

Above left: St Peters Church, Bridge Street, 1906

Above right: Central Stores, Southam Street, c1910
Chandler's Stores proudly shows off its motorised delivery van. Mr Chandler can be seen standing outside the shop with its elaborate display of Cadbury's chocolate and cocoa.

Left: Kineton School, c1910
Built in 1892 for boys and girls, the school could accommodate up to 180 children.

RUGBY

Left: Market Place, 1910
Looking south-east across the Market Place towards the Clock Tower and the castellated tower of St Andrew's Church on the left, one of the oldest parts of the church dating from the mid 13th century. It is 4.45 pm. The Clock Tower, with gas lamps attached, was built in 1897 to mark Queen Victoria's Diamond Jubilee. Market stalls can be seen selling china, bric-a-brac and braces of rabbits, and to the left horse-drawn cabs wait for fares. A cabmen's shelter was erected here in 1877, its roof visible on the right of the picture.

Above: The same scene a decade later shows motor taxis, the cab shelter in a different location and gas lamps now in the street. The imposing north-east tower with its spire which can be seen in this picture were added to the church by the architect William Butterfield during its extensive reconstruction in 1899.

STRATFORD-UPON-AVON

Above: Chapel Street, c1890
View north-east towards the Shakespeare Hostelrie and jettied timber-framed shops. To the left of the hotel is the Town Hall. The original building, constructed in the reign of Charles I, was destroyed in a gunpowder explosion in 1643; the structure seen here is largely the result of rebuilding in 1644 and further renovations in 1863.

Left: The American Fountain, Market Place, Rother Street, c1900
Erected in 1887 to celebrate Queen Victoria's Golden Jubilee, the fountain-cum-clock tower was donated to the town by the American newspaper publisher and wealthy philanthropist George Childs. Designed by Jethro Cossins of Birmingham in muscular Victorian Gothic style, the monument was unveiled by the actor Henry Irving in October 1887 to reveal a wealth of literary quotations celebrating the bard and the merits of pure water.

STRATFORD-UPON-AVON

Above: Church Street, 1878
Looking north-east towards the Guild Chapel; to the south of it is the old Grammar School, which Shakespeare is thought to have attended, with a row of almshouses in the right foreground. The school was built in 1428 as the home of a religious guild founded in the 11th century.

Left: Shakespeare Hotel, Chapel Street c1900
Looking south-west towards the Guild Chapel; the Shakespeare Hotel is to the left.

ANNE HATHAWAY'S COTTAGE

Top right: Anne Hathaway's Cottage, Cottage Lane, Shottery, Stratford-upon-Avon, c1900
Known in Shakespeare's day as Hewlands Farm, this thatched timber-framed building, constructed in the 15th century, was the home of Shakespeare's wife.

Middle right: Shakespeare Memorial Theatre, 1879
The theatre, still under construction in this picture, was built on a riverside site donated by Charles Edward Flower, owner of one of the town's biggest breweries. Designed as an Elizabethan fantasy by the architects Dodgshun and Unsworth, it opened in 1879. In 1926 a fire destroyed much of the theatre and it had to be rebuilt. Elisabeth Scott's design was chosen, making her the first woman to win a major architectural competition in Britain.

Below: Bridge Street, 1892
Looking west from the junction with Waterside towards Market Place and the Market House in the distance. In the coaching era, Bridge Street was the main thoroughfare into the town and a natural location for a number of inns, including the Golden Lion and the adjacent Red Horse seen to the right of this picture.

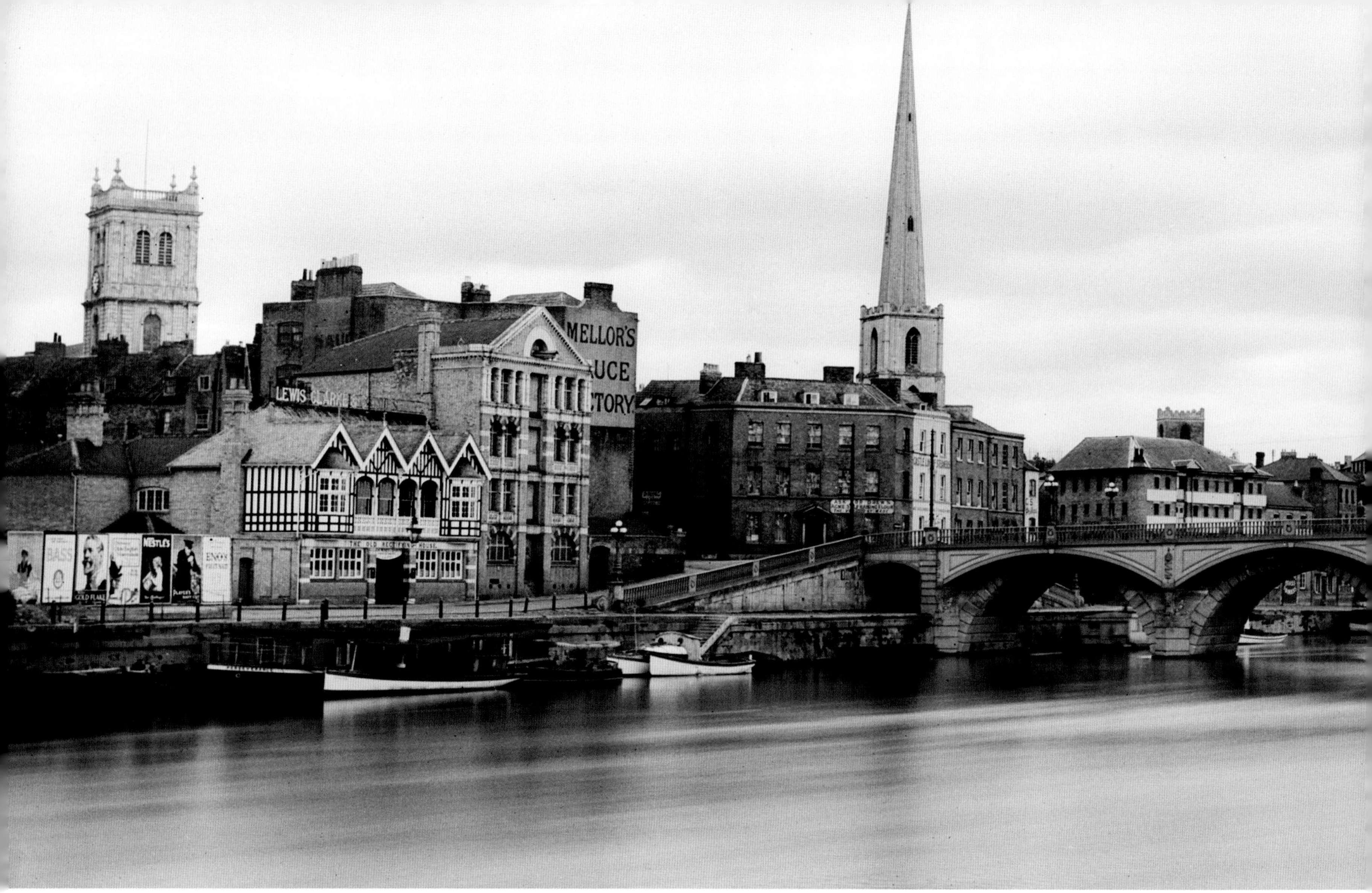
MELLOR'S
BASS
NESTLE'S
ENO'S
GOLD FLAKE

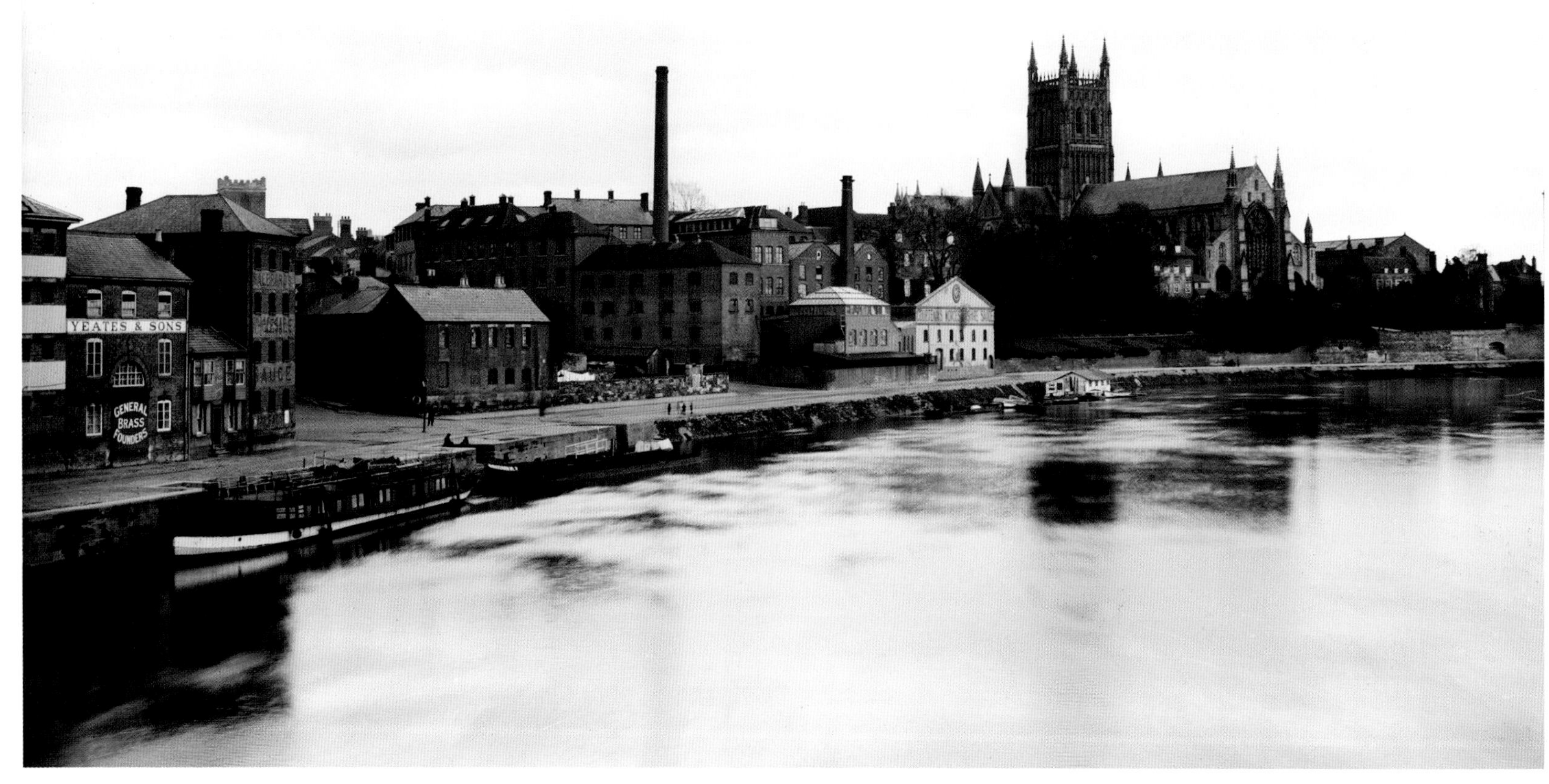

YEATES & SONS
GENERAL
BRASS
FOUNDERS

Worcestershire

WORCESTER

Above: Worcester Bridge, 1926
View south-east, with Worcester Cathedral in the background. In the early 14th century Worcester was the only crossing point between Bridgnorth and Gloucester, stimulating the growth of the city. The current bridge was built in 1781.
Opposite below: South of the bridge are wharves and warehouses, with the Norman cathedral beyond. The main building dates from the 11th century, above an earlier crypt. The Severn Waterway increased the industrial output of Worcester when the Birmingham and Worcester Canal connected the city to Birmingham in 1815.

Right: Edgar Tower, Cathedral Precinct, 1892
Looking east from within the Cathedral Close through the gateway towards Edgar Street. The tower was rebuilt in the early 14th century, when it was the gatehouse to the bailey of Worcester Castle. It is now the entrance to College Green. Extensive restoration of the Cathedral and its surrounding buildings took place in the mid to late 19th century, including renovations by George Gilbert Scott in the 1860s.

BROADWAY

Left: Lygon Arms Hotel, High Street, 1900

In the 16th century the hotel was known as the White Hart, having previously been an Elizabethan manor house occupied by wealthy wool merchants. The Cotswold estate on which the inn was built was bought in 1820 by General William Lygon, a veteran of Waterloo, and its name changed soon after. Its importance as a coaching inn on the London to Wales route continued. Around the time of this picture the hotel changed hands again and Sir Aston Webb was appointed to refurbish the property, creating the luxury hotel it is today.

BROADWAY

Above: High Street, c1900

Looking east towards the New Inn on the left and the Tudor House on the right. A former coaching inn dating from the 17th century, since 2013 Tudor House has been a branch of the Ashmolean Museum. The adjacent building with the large clock and spire is Trinity House.

HAGLEY

Opposite top left: Hagley Station, c1900

The station opened in 1852 on the Oxford, Worcester and Wolverhampton line, which connected with the GWR. The station footbridge, dating from 1884, still exists.

DROITWICH SPA

Top right: Salters Hall, Victoria Square, 1892
Droitwich Spa owed its prosperity to the massive salt reserves lying beneath the town. These had been exploited since Roman times, hence the numerous Roman roads radiating from the town. Salt was mined in rock form, but also rose naturally as brine in pits that facilitated easy extraction. John Corbett, a local salt entrepreneur, expanded the salt industry in the 18th century and developed Droitwich as a spa town, the brine baths being thought to offer relief for many ailments. Salters Hall, which could accommodate up to 1,500 people, was built by Corbett in 1881as an amenity hall for salt workers. In 1933 it was demolished for a cinema by a new owner.

Above left: The Worcestershire Hotel, Worcester Road,1892
Photographed soon after it opened in 1891, this handsome corner building was constructed for John Corbett and opened as the Worcestershire Brine Baths Hotel, an important part of the 'Salt King's' spa development. By the 1980s it was vacant and decaying, and the hotel was demolished to make way for luxury apartments.

Above right: Raven Hotel, St Andrew's Street, 1892
View from the south-west of the timbered Elizabethan building alleged to have hosted Charles I on his way to subdue the city of Leicester.

EVESHAM

Above: Jubilee Tower, High Street, c1900
Built in 1887 by G H Hunt to mark Queen Victoria's Golden Jubilee, the tower forms part of the much older Town Hall complex dating from 1586. The arcade beneath was originally open with market stalls and the town stocks, which were later moved to the Almonry.

Left: Abbot Reginald's Gate, Old Rectory, c1900
View from the market place, showing the Norman gateway that links the town and the Abbey cemetery. The timber-framed rectory in the foreground probably dates from the 15th century.

Opposite top: High Street, 1890
View looking south, with the Abbey tower in the middle distance. The Benedictine Abbey can trace its origins to St Egwin in the early 700s. It grew to become one of the wealthiest and most powerful, making it an early target for dissolution. In 1540 the main building was demolished and plundered for stone, leaving only the bell tower standing.

EVESHAM ABBEY

Above: Evesham Abbey, 1890

Pedestrians and horse-drawn traffic on Bridge Street leading into the town, with the Abbey tower to the left. Water played a key part in the siting of mediaeval abbey communities. Nestled in a broad meander of the River Avon, the Abbey once formed the nucleus of the town. The wide floodplain of the Vale of Evesham, with the perennial risk of heavy flooding, has always made the siting of bridges here challenging.

PERSHORE

Left: High Street, Pershore, 1900
The Pershore Supply Stores stands on the corner of Broad Street; the building still exists, although it is no longer a grocery store. The tower of the Anglo-Saxon Abbey can be seen in the background. It became the Parish Church after dissolution in 1539, with renovations by George Gilbert Scott in the 1860s.
Above: Bridge Street, Pershore, 1900

Opposite top left: Pershore Old Bridge, 1900
View across the bridge, which spans the River Avon just outside the town. The original bridge was constructed in the 15th century. It still stands but is used solely as a footbridge.

MALVERN

Top right: Promenade Gardens, c1890
Looking north, with the Mount Pleasant Hotel on the left in the foreground. The purity of the mineral springs and wells of the Malvern Hills, combined with their scenic beauty, led to the development of Malvern as a spa town from the 17th century. Its narrow roads and out-of-the-way location have kept much of the historic beauty of the area intact.

Above: Belle View Terrace, c1910
Overlooking the historic priory church and beyond, the Terrace was a hub of the town. Here, in the 1840s, a chemist by the name of Lea originated a formula that was taken up by a successful local businessman, Mr Perrins, who went on to market it as the internationally renowned Worcestershire Sauce.

HEREFORD

Above: The Old House, High Street, 1907
View north towards the junction with Corporation Street in the area known as High Town. The spire of St Peter's church rises beyond. The timbered and jettied Jacobean building, erected in 1621, is all that remains of Butchers' Row; it has been open to the public since 1929 as a museum.

Right: Wye Bridge, c1910
The iconic bridge occupies a site that dates back to a mediaeval wooden structure. The present-day bridge with its six arches has been repaired frequently, but nonetheless has stood the test of time. The tower of the Cathedral can be seen in the background. Boatmen with boats for hire linger looking for trade.

Herefordshire

Above: Fawley Station, Kings Caple, 1908
Opened on the Hereford, Ross and Gloucester Railway in 1855, Fawley Station closed in 1964. The station staff and railway crew, the latter repairing the line, pose for the camera.

Right: Red Lion Hotel, Weobley, c1900
View from Broad Street towards the Red Lion Hotel, with the tower of St Peter and St Paul's Church beyond. The steeple is believed to be the second tallest on a parish church in England.

SATURDAY
CHINA
GLASS
PARR

LEDBURY

Opposite: Market House, c1890
View across the High Street towards the Market House, where a billboard advertises 'Waif-Saturday', a street collection for destitute children. The timber-framed Market House was begun c1617 and completed after 1655, probably by John Abel, the King's Carpenter.

Right: High Street, c1900
Looking north towards the Market House, with the clock tower of the Barrett-Browning Institute in the background. The latter was built as a community centre on the site of a former tannery and named after the poet Elizabeth Barrett Browning, who had a local connection. A national competition to design the building received 45 entries. Brightwen Binyon's design, in Tudor Revival style, was the winner and the centre was opened by the writer Sir Henry Rider Haggard in 1896.

Below: High Street, c1910
View north-west from New Street.

CANADA
THE CAPITAL and COUNTIES BANK Ltd
PRINTING WORKS
SWAN
PENS

EAST ENGLAND

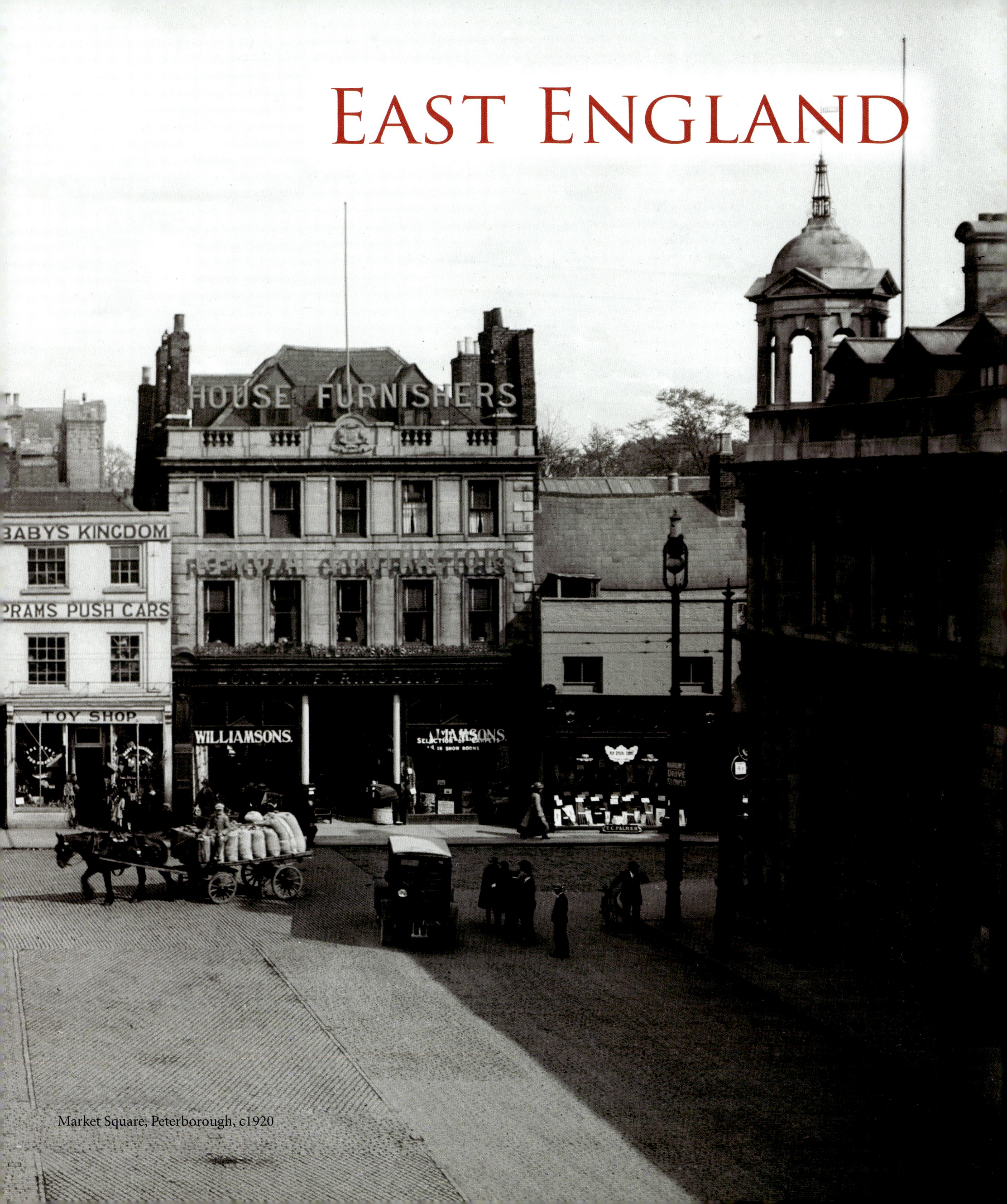

Market Square, Peterborough, c1920

Cambridgeshire

CAMBRIDGE

Opposite top: Magdalene Bridge, c1896
View looking north-east to the bridge over the River Cam and Magdalene College on the other bank. Built in 1823 to Arthur Browne's design in Gothic Revival style, the bridge is close to the historic site of a Roman ford and a later 8th-century bridge. Magdalene College was founded in 1428 as a hostel of the Benedictine order, and later known as Buckingham College, before its re-foundation in 1542 as the College of St Mary Magdalene. Its modest beginnings are reflected in the brick construction of the majority of its buildings. Samuel Pepys is perhaps its most famous alumnus.

Opposite below: Senate House and Gonville & Caius College, c1896
View looking north from King's Parade and on into Trinity Street. The College was founded by Edmund Gonville in 1348 in a different location; the current site has been occupied since the 1350s, when the College was moved here by William Bateman. Saved from ruin in 1557 by John Caius, who greatly expanded the College buildings, it was given its current name by a Royal Charter. Many notable architects have contributed over the years, including John Soane in the 1790s and Alfred Waterhouse in 1870, whose eponymous building is pictured.

Top right: King's Parade, c1890
A different perspective with a similar viewpoint further south in King's Parade. The Senate House to the left of the frame was designed by James Gibbs in Neoclassical style and opened in 1730. Its original purpose was to house the University's Council of the Senate, but it is now mainly used for degree ceremonies.

Middle right: Market Square, c1890
The ornate structure in the middle is a public drinking fountain in Gothic style, dating from 1850.

Bottom right: River Nene, Wisbech, 1899
Wisbech was, and remains today, Cambridgeshire's link to the North Sea, enabling trade with the lowland ports of Europe, and in particular the Baltic ports – as shown by the *Graf Bismarck*, registered in Rostock and moored at the wharf. A similar vessel, a type of ketch known as a Baltic Trader, is moored further along next to a more modern steamship. Two different worlds meet here, but at this point in time both are important to the culture and economy of Britain's coastal trade.

Norfolk

CROMER

Top left: Church Street, Cromer, c1890
View looking eastwards to St Peter and St Paul's Church, with the Bower Bakery in the foreground on the left. Dating from the 14th century, the church was substantially refurbished in the 19th century. At this time the windows were enlarged and impressive stained glass added, including work from Morris & Co, designed by Burne-Jones. The tower, with its far-reaching views, is open to the public and remains a popular visitor attraction in the resort.

Above right: High Street, Cromer, c1890
St Peter and St Paul's Church can be seen in the background. The hostelry sign on the right beyond the parked carriage belongs to the Kings Head Inn, dating from the 17th century and still in business today; it provided stabling for the carriage which ran between Cromer and North Walsham.

Middle left: Gorleston-on-Sea, 1904
View along the promenade towards the Cliff Hotel, one of Norfolk's grandest until gutted by fire in 1915.

Bottom left: Hall Quay, Great Yarmouth, 1904
Sea trips on passenger steamers left from the Quay at least twice a day during the main tourist season.

GREAT YARMOUTH

Above: Wellington Gardens, 1904
The Winter Gardens are on the left in the background, with the entrance to Wellington Pier to its right.

Middle left: Britannia Pier, Marine Parade, 1904
Constructed in 1858, the original pier was demolished in 1899 after a ship collided with it during a storm. The present steel and timber structure dates from 1900–02.

Below left: The Winter Gardens, 1904
Purchased from Torquay Council in 1903 by the Great Yarmouth Council for £1,300, the Gardens became a popular visitor attraction. Council Surveyor J W Cockrill thought it would be desirable 'to lengthen the season with better class visitors, and on wet days to provide for 2,000 persons under cover'. Flowerbeds run around the inside of the building, and in front of the rows of seats is a small stage where musicians would perform to entertain visitors.

GREAT YARMOUTH

Opposite top left: Great Yarmouth, 1897
View across the River Yare, looking north-east towards the Town Hall on Hall Quay, with South Quay to its right. The Town Hall was a relatively new building, having been opened in June 1883. A variety of boats are moored along the quays; on the west bank (left) a sailing barge is so heavily laden that the water is almost at deck level. Across the water on Hall Quay, another barge is similarly laden alongside two North Sea ketches.

Opposite middle left: Town Hall, Hall Quay, 1897
With Hall Quay in the foreground, every available wharf space is occupied by sailing boats stretching as far as the eye can see.

Opposite top right: Great Yarmouth, 1904
The open-air beach theatre, photographed from the revolving observation tower on North Drive.

Opposite middle right: South Beach Gardens, 1896
Looking south over the seafront at Great Yarmouth, with the Wellington Pier in the distance. The Winter Gardens were yet to be installed. In the far distance, beyond the pier, the outline of the harbour buildings is visible and also the 144-foot column of the Norfolk Naval Monument raised to honour Nelson and completed in 1819.

Opposite bottom left: Marine Parade,1896
Ranks of carriages wait for passengers to take the tour along the extensive promenade. More curious is the row of miniature carriages on the beach just behind the benched carriages: they are drawn by long-horned goats, clearly a novelty for children. On the left of the picture is Lockhart's cafe selling cocoa and tea, with the Foulsham Hotel next door; to its right is Maritime House, which still exists today at 25 Marine Parade, housing the Tourist Information Centre.

Above: Market Place, 1904
View across the market place towards Great Yarmouth Minster, which dates from the 12th century and is the country's largest parish church. The market place is also one of the largest in England.

Opposite bottom right: Southtown Tower Mill, c1895
Often known as High Mill or Press's Mill and built in 1813, the tower reached 122 feet to the tip of the 20-foot lantern, making it the tallest windmill ever built in Europe. The mill was wide enough to allow carts to drive through and unload inside the tower. Around 1850 another three stones were added, driven by steam and enabling the mill to run without stopping, day and night. It ceased working in 1898. Sold at auction in 1904, the mill was demolished soon after and its bricks used to build local housing.

REGENT STREET

Above: Regent Street, Great Yarmouth, 1904
Banks and shops line the street as an electric tram approaches the Town Hall. Horse-drawn trams first ran in Great Yarmouth in 1902 and were converted to run on electricity two years later.

MARINE PARADE

Top left: Revolving Tower, Marine Parade, Great Yarmouth, 1904
The Revolving Tower was invented by Thomas Warwick, an engineer from London. Erected in North Beach Gardens in 1897, it was in use until 1939. It was one of only five such structures in England. The mechanism propelled customers upwards in the ring-shaped carriage, which rotated as it rose up the 150-feet-high tower, giving panoramic views over the coast and the town.

Below: Marine Parade, Great Yarmouth, 1904
The Revolving Tower is visible in the distance. Marine Parade, running behind the beach, is crowded with tourists wearing formal clothing for their afternoon promenade. The first building on the left was the town's sea baths, built in 1759: small, individual baths were filled with water pumped from the sea. The trams ran between Britannia and Wellington piers and into the town.

Left: Wellington Pier, Great Yarmouth, 1904
The pier dates from 1853 and was designed by Peter Ashcroft, an engineer for the Eastern Counties Railway. It was extensively rebuilt when J S Cockrill added the new entrance pavilion seen here in 1903.

Opposite below: South Beach Gardens, Great Yarmouth, 1896
Looking north towards Britannia Pier, the large building on the left is the Royal Marine Hotel. Women and children enjoy a stroll along the promenade; two young boys nearest the edge are fashionably dressed in sailor suits.

NORWICH CATHEDRAL

Above left: Tombland Alley, 1947
View through the archway under 14 Tombland, a mid-16th-century house built for Augustine Steward, a former mayor of Norwich. The view continues through the 15th-century Erpingham Gate and into the Cathedral precinct, with the west front of Norwich Cathedral in the distance ahead.

Top right: Norwich Cathedral through Erpingham Gate, c1900
The Norman cathedral was completed in 1145. Its stonework of Caen limestone was shipped across the English Channel from France, along the River Wensum and finally by canal to the construction site. Originally it had a lead-covered timber spire, but following a disastrous fire in 1463, it was replaced in stone in 1480. In 1830 the west front was remodelled by Anthony Salvin.

Above: Prince of Wales Road, Norwich, c1904
View east from Castle Meadow. The Royal Hotel, which had a grand opening in 1897, sits on the left. It took its name from a historic coaching inn half a mile away that was demolished in developments around the Market Place. Edward Boardman, a local architect of note, designed the luxurious new hotel with an exterior featuring ornate brickwork and terracotta known locally as Costesseyware, a speciality of George Gunton in Costessey. The hotel immediately became a business and social hub for the city, complementing the Agricultural Hall, opposite, which opened in 1882 for the use of the farming community, but which also hosted public lectures and other entertainments. Anglia Television made the Agricultural Hall its home in 1959, renaming the building Anglia House.

NORWICH MARKET PLACE

Above: Market Place, c1890
View south across the market, which has been a thriving centre of the city's commerce for over 900 years. The church of St Peter Mancroft, financed by the city's merchants and built in 1430–55, is in the background. To the right are the smart shops on Gentleman's Walk.

Left: Norwich Castle, c1900
Looking north across the sheep market to the 12th-century castle keep. Built in Caen stone with distinctive blank arcading, it is part of the motte and bailey castle commenced around 1075 to subjugate East Anglia. In 1887 the City bought the castle for use as a museum and art gallery, which it remains today.

WYMONDHAM

Left: Market Cross, Wymondham, Norfolk, 1924
Built between 1617 and 1618 to replace the mediaeval market cross lost in a fire in 1616, the upper floor of this charming octagonal structure is carried on decorated arched braces above an open ground floor.

Below left: Market Place, North Walsham, Norfolk, 1890
North Walsham was given the right to hold a weekly market in the mid 13th century. The market cross was originally built by Bishop Thirlby during the reign of Edward VI to shelter traders and their goods. The first cross was destroyed by fire and rebuilt in its unusual current form in 1602.

Below right: Lady Street, Lavenham, Suffolk
A milk cart makes its way down the street early one morning. The building on the right is the old wool hall, dating from the 1400s. Lavenham is one of England's finest mediaeval towns, with a profusion of superb timber-framed houses – many of them originally the homes of prosperous wool merchants.

Suffolk

Above: St Andrew's Church, Covehithe, c1900
The mediaeval church from the south-west as seen from the road. A new church with a thatched roof was built within the ruins of the nave in 1672 and can clearly be seen in this photograph.

Left: Windmill, Earl Soham
Originally built with a two-storey roundhouse containing two pairs of stones, the mill ceased work in 1917 and the upper part was demolished in 1947. The brick roundhouse was later reduced in height and converted into a dwelling.

Far left: Brandon, c1930
A flint knapper at work making gun flints.

LOWESTOFT

Left: South Pier, 1896

Promenaders in their finery stroll alongside the new Pavilion constructed in 1891 to replace the old Reading Room which burned down in 1885. The lighthouse at the end of the Pier, visible in the distance, was built in 1847 to mark the entrance to the harbour.

BURY ST EDMUNDS

Below: Cornhill, 1898

Bury St Edmunds was laid out in a grid pattern devised by Abbot Baldwin in the 11th century. Cornhill was the site of an extensive market place which, over time, was filled in by buildings including the Corn Exchange and the Traverse, which housed a full-time Fire Station. Of the buildings in the picture, only the Post Office remains today.

IPSWICH

Left: Wolsey's Gate, College Street, 1893
Cardinal Wolsey, who was born in Ipswich, planned to build a college there.The gateway was erected first but when Wolsey fell out of favour with Henry VIII over the annulment of his marriage to Catherine of Aragon, the rest of his plans fell into disarray and the college itself was never completed.

Below: Fore Street, 1893
The epitome of harmonious organic growth over time. The picture shows buildings spanning 400 years. Ipswich is one of the oldest continuously inhabited towns in England. Under the Romans, the area around Ipswich formed an important route inland to rural towns and settlements. Thomas Gainsborough lived and worked here, and in 1835 Charles Dickens stayed in the town and used it as a setting for scenes in *The Pickwick Papers*.

S. WALDEN
THAXTED.
DUNMOW.
TAKELEY
HATFIELD B'OAK

Essex

Opposite top left: White Hart Hotel, High Street, Brentwood, c1910
Two parked cars mark the end of the coaching era. The White Hart Hotel provided accommodation and livery services for travellers, including coaching stables as seen here. It also ran its own coach into London. In the second half of the 19th century, at least 40 coaches a day would stop here.

Opposite top right: Mill Green, Broxted, c1930
A rural idyll. A cyclist rests his tandem against the finger post to consult his map. Broxted Windmill stands in the background. Built in 1815, it ground its last corn at the outbreak of the First World War and then fell into disrepair before being demolished in 1953.

Opposite middle left and right: T T Nethercoat & Co, The Quay, Burnham-on-Crouch, 1915
The Splicing Room (left), with seated men making rope handles. Although Nethercoat & Co were chandlers and sailmakers by trade, the employees turned their skills to the war effort in 1914. Here they are making handles for ammunition carriers. In the Inspection Room (right) men check hundreds of rope and canvas ammunition buckets manufactured on site. First World War munitions were hazardous and had to be handled with great care to avoid sparks. These baskets ensured that ammunition could be moved with a modicum of safety.

Opposite below left: Gross, Sherwood and Heald, Jenkins Lane, Barking, 1910
Women working at the paint works labelling empty tins and cans ready for filling.

Opposite below right: Church Street, Saffron Walden, 1913
Workmen appear to be laying concrete paving. The absence of utilities in most small towns and villages at this time meant that ordinary households were not supplied with water, gas or electricity.

Left: 9-15 King Street, Saffron Walden, 1913
Frank Hardwick's Fish, Game and Poultry merchants is on the corner of Market Passage, with a horse-drawn cart in the foreground.

Above: High Street, Colchester, c1921
The shop frontages of Nos 21 and 22 High Street. Note the beautifully detailed early 19th-century shallow bay window above the gilt and glass fascia of Heasman's.

OMPSON
URNINGHAM. & PERFUM
SHAVING
SALOONS
AIR CUTTING & SHAVING
SALOONS

SAFFRON WALDEN

Opposite: Town Hall, Market Place, Saffron Walden, 1913
A group of young boys stand in front of the red-brick Town Hall, which was built between 1761 and 1762. It was subsequently given its impressive, if rather incongruous, half-timbered gable in 1879.

Right: Mills at Walton-on-the-Naze, c1910
This atmospheric picture shows a tide mill and a post windmill on what is now Walton Mere. Both were probably used for processing cereal crops. The tide mill was in continuous use by one John Archer from 1832 until 1892, when he died. Unused thereafter, it was demolished in 1921; that same year the post windmill fell down as a result of decay, making room for the local sailing clubhouse that occupies the site today.

CLACTON-ON-SEA

Below: Town Hall, Clacton-on-Sea, 1904
Built in the 1880s, the Town Hall housed a bank on its ground floor, with the upper floors occupied by the Council and the Operetta House Theatre. The landmark clock tower, along with the angled frontage, was destroyed by bombing in 1941.

COLCHESTER

Above: High Street, 1904

The Baroque Town Hall, designed by John Belcher, exudes late Victorian confidence and civic pride. Faced in red brick and Portland stone, it was completed in 1898. The landmark 162-foot Victoria clock tower is decorated with four statues representing the principal activities of the town: fishing, engineering, military defence and agriculture. The two impressive buildings to the right of the picture are (left to right) the Grand Theatre and the Shoulder of Mutton Public House, both extant, although now converted to other uses. In the distance stands the Jumbo Water Tower at Balkerne Gate, constructed in 1882 but no longer part of the water system.

Above: The Shire Hall, New Street, Chelmsford, 1897

Built in 1789–91 by John Johnson, the County Surveyor, to accommodate the County Council and Courts, the Hall is one of Chelmsford's most imposing public buildings. Frederick Spalding, a well-known photographer, established his premises on the far left of the picture; the top storey is a glazed pavilion to maximise light into the studio.

CHELMSFORD

Above: Tindal Street, 1920

Named after the locally born judge and Chief Justice of the Common Pleas, Sir Nicholas Tindal, the street housed local businesses such as the Spotted Dog – the building with three first-floor bay windows seen here. The Spotted Dog and other buildings on the west side of the street were demolished as part of the development of the High Chelmer shopping precinct, which opened in 1972.

Left: The Conduit, High Street, 1898

The Conduit, carrying a later elaborate wrought-iron overthrow and lantern, was built in 1814. It was funded by the parish and a local merchant, Robert Greenwood, to provide drinking water for visitors to the town. Deemed to be a danger and an obstruction to traffic, it was relocated to its present site in Tower Gardens in 1940.

WALTHAM ABBEY

Above: Highbridge Street, c1900
Looking east towards the tower of Waltham Abbey Church, which underwent two renovations: in the mid 1800s and later in 1904. It was fortunately not severely damaged when a V2 rocket wiped out a number of buildings in the street during the Second World War.

SOUTHEND-ON-SEA

Left: Southend-on-Sea, 1898
Bathing and boating at the waterfront, with landing stages and the Pier in the background.

Opposite top: Southend-on-Sea, 1910
A view from Britain's longest pier, looking towards the five-star Hotel Metropole built in 1901.

THAXTED

Above: Guildhall, Town Street, 1927

The Guildhall, built between 1450 and 1475 as a market hall and council chamber, appears little changed today, although it has in fact seen much alteration over time. The two-span roof was constructed and the external walls pargetted in the early 18th century. The decorative plasterwork was removed around 1911 to expose the timber frame, which was then blackened; the windows were re-ordered and renewed, and arches were inserted between the vertical timbers of the first floor. Finally, the timbers were lime-washed in the mid 1970s and today are closer to their original appearance.

ROCERY WRIGHT & BROWN'S WAREHOUSE
COBB & Co's ENTIRE
SHIP HOTEL
CIGAR STORES
CIGAR STORES

SOUTH AND SOUTH EAST

The Parade, Margate, c1900

Bedfordshire

BEDFORD

Opposite below: High Street, c1900
Looking north towards the junction with St Peter's Street, where the trees begin on the right. Traditional canvas apron blinds protect merchandise from the sun in the shop windows. Blott's Drapers to the right has a cast iron framed first-floor display window of the kind that became popular after the advent of double-decker buses.

Opposite top left and right: Great Ouse Embankment, 1923
View over the placid waters of the Great Ouse with its stone embankment balustrade (left), where rowing boats are ready for hire (right).

Above: Silver Street, c1900
Looking towards the High Street from Silver Street. The railway reached Bedford in 1846, fuelling its growth from a small market town with an ancient lace-making industry into an important engineering centre.

LUTON

Above: Diamond Foundry, Dallow Road, 1913
The interior of the grinding shop at Diamond Foundry, the Luton factory of the Davis Gas Stove Company Limited.

Right: The Connor Hat Factory, Bute Street, 1928
To the rear can be seen the straw goods factory at 40 Guildford Street. Both enterprises were engaged in the production of straw goods and hats, an industry that had become well-established in Bedfordshire and Hertfordshire by the end of the 17th century. By the early 20th century most hat manufacturing in Luton was concentrated in factories in the Bute Street area, close to the railway station with its direct links to London.

Opposite above: George Street, 1897
The view east from Market Hill towards the old Town Hall, designed in 1846, in the distance. In the foreground is a memorial to Lieutenant Colonel Lionel Ames, local landowner and magistrate. 'The Pepperpot', as it was known to locals, was an ornamental fountain supplying drinking water to patrons of the Corn Exchange, from where this photograph was taken.

LUTON TOWN HALL

Above left: Town Hall, Upper George Street, 1936
The 'new' Town Hall, designed by Bradshaw, Gass and Hope, was completed in 1936 to replace the 1847 building that was burned down in the notorious 'Peace Riots' of July 1919, when a mob, incensed by the elitist behaviour of the mayor during the Peace Celebrations, first wrecked the apartments and then set the entire building ablaze.

CHICKSANDS PRIORY

Above right: Chicksands Priory, 1893
A phaeton carriage arrives at the front entrance of the Priory. It is driven by Lady Osborn, the recent widow of the sixth Baronet, George Robert Osborn, who had died the year before. Chicksands, originally a Gilbertine Monastery dating from the 12th century, was the home of the Osborn family for around 400 years, until it was sold to the Crown Commissioners and used for military purposes in the 1930s.

Hertfordshire

HERTFORD

Above: Fore Street, 1922

View north-east towards the Corn Exchange on the left and the old Post Office opposite on the right. Both buildings are extant. The Corn Exchange, built on the site of the old Butcher's Market, opened in 1859. To the immediate left, Nos. 15–23 were businesses owned at the time by Alfred Elms Neale; his father Samuel, from whom he inherited the business, had run furniture and drapers shops in the street. The family seem to have been important traders in the town. Alfred later owned a motor car dealership on Church Street.

ALDBURY

Top: Village pond, c1930

Forever England. View north-east across the village pond of this archetypal Hertfordshire village. The Greyhound Public House is centre left, with a single car outside. The photograph is taken from approximately the position of the village stocks, which still remain.

ST ALBANS

Left: St Albans Town Hall, c1930
Looking south across the Market Place towards the Ionic portico of the Town Hall, built in 1831 to the designs of George Smith. Its Palladian facade remains a landmark of the town centre. To the right in the distance, the ancient tower of St Albans Cathedral is visible. The mainly Romanesque Benedictine Abbey, dating from the 12th century, acted as the parish church and continued to do so after it was given cathedral status in 1877. On 22 May 1455 a Yorkist army under Richard, Duke of York, routed a Lancastrian force after intense fighting around the Market Place that resulted in the capture of King Henry VI.

CHEQUER STREET, ST ALBANS

Above: Chequer Street, 1921
View looking south from what is today the HSBC bank, its colonnade visible to the right. The gently curving street leads downhill towards the valley of the River Ver, which gave St Albans its Roman name of Verulamium. Today the scene remains much the same, except that the road is narrowed with wider pavements. A motorcycle and side-car (foreground right) and several cars and vans can be seen.

WATFORD

Above: Market Place, c1890
Looking north-west down the street, with carts and wagons outside the Spread Eagle public house to the left. The Essex Arms and SPQR Stores stand opposite. Between them is the entrance to the Corn Exchange, occupying the rear of the hotel built in 1855 on the site of the old Market Hall, which burned down in 1853.

Opposite above: 18–28 High Street, c1890
The Coachmakers Arms public house to the left, with its sign advertising Sedgwick's Watford Ales, shows it was tied to the brewery, which traced its roots back to the 17th century and was acquired by William Sedgwick in 1862. The company's premises in Watford High Street adjoined those of another brewery, Benskins. The latter bought Sedgwicks in 1923 after swallowing up most of the other local breweries and before in turn being acquired by the brewing giant Ind Coope in 1957. The presence of two substantial breweries in Watford gave it a reputation as a brewing town, but other trades thrived, especially after the Grand Union Canal, and then the railway, improved the town's transport links.

WATFORD GRAMMAR SCHOOL

Opposite below left: Watford Grammar School, c1900
Founded by Elizabeth Fuller in 1704, Watford Grammar School moved from its original site next to the parish church in 1881 to new premises in Derby Road, where it remained until the early 1900s. In 1907 the girls moved to Lady's Close and in 1912 the boys' school relocated to a site on Rickmansworth Road, where it remains today.

Opposite below right: Red Lion Yard, 81 High Street, c1890
Watford had two main intersections for coaching traffic, one at either end of the High Street, so there was great demand for accommodation. The Red Lion's frontage was on the High Street, with its carriage entrance giving onto Red Lion Court and the Yard. Close to the Essex Arms, it appears to have had another two inns opposite, and there were numerous others along the High Street.

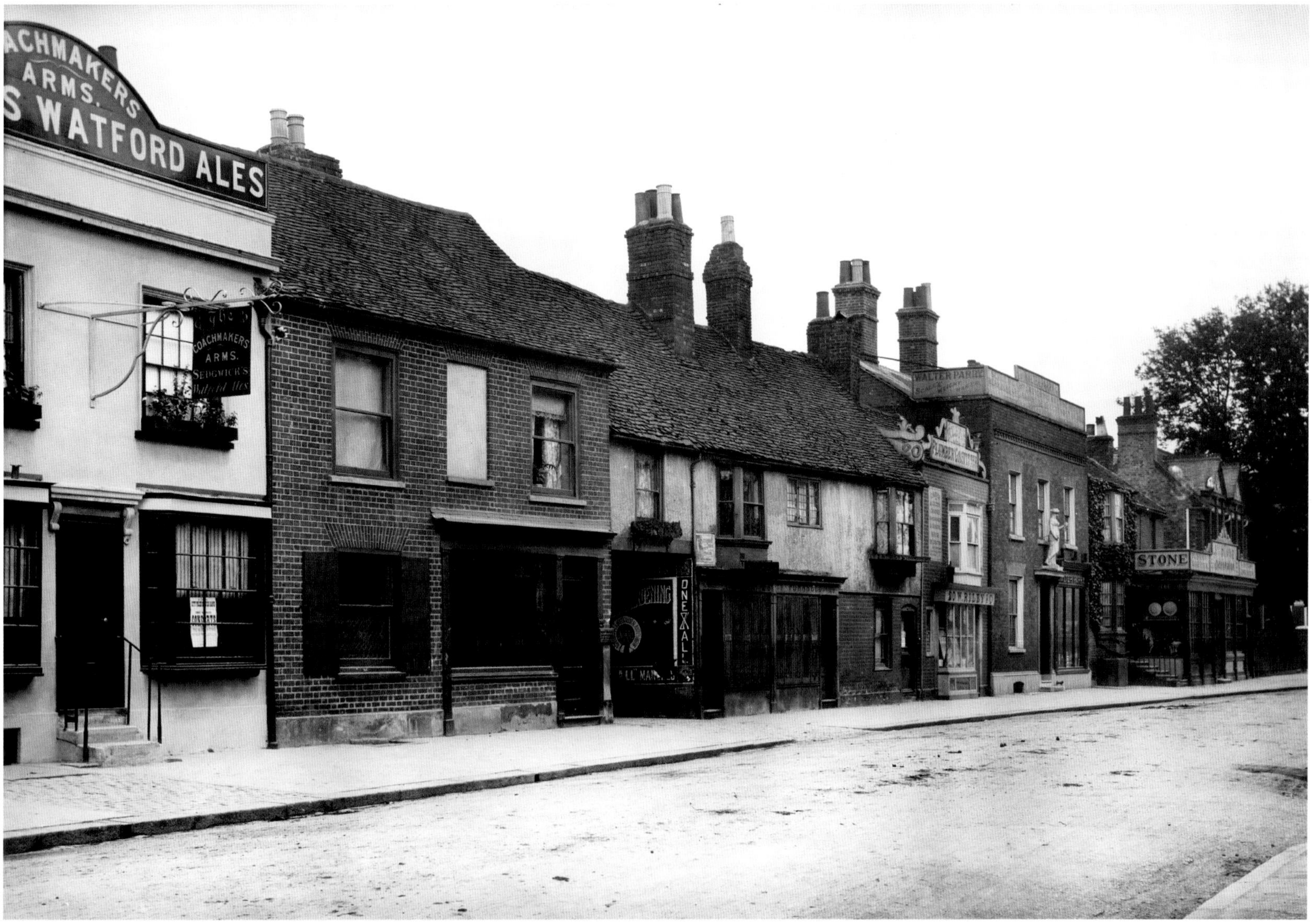

RED LION
RED LION
BENSKIN'S
ALES & STOUT

HIGH STREET

Above: The Compasses public house, 68 High Street, Watford, c1900
Another Sedgwick public house, the Compasses, on the corner of High Street and Market Street. The butchers to the left of the pub had been demolished to make way for the new side street. The window shown top left above the street sign has been incorporated into the building, which remains on the corner of Market Street today and includes a plaque relating its history. The advertising on the gable of the Green Man Inn beyond is for Freeman Hardy & Willis, announcing their 'Famous Boots and Shoes'.

CASSIOBURY PARK

Cassiobury Park, Watford, c1900
Opposite below: Cassiobury House was an Elizabethan mansion, the seat of the Earls of Essex. The Tudor building, dating from 1546, was substantially altered in the Gothic style by James Wyatt in the early 19th century. Watford Council bought the estate, Cassiobury Park, in 1909 to be used as a public park, with some land taken for housing. The house remained unsold, so the contents were auctioned and the building demolished for salvage in 1927. The staircase, an ornately carved wooden piece by Grinling Gibbons, is now held by the Metropolitan Museum of Art in New York.
Opposite above: Built in 1802, the lodge gates to Rickmansworth Road were a landmark until they were demolished in the 1970s for road widening. When the Park grounds were privately owned by the Earl, the public were allowed access by ticket. The Grand Union Canal, routed through the Park in the late 18th century, remains a picturesque feature today.

MOOR PARK

Left: Moor Park, Rickmansworth, c1900
This refined Palladian-style mansion is an extensive remodelling from the 1720s, by the Venetian architect Giacomo Leoni, of an earlier country house originally built for the Duke of Monmouth in 1678–79. The grandiloquent interior is decorated with murals by Sir James Thornhill and the Venetian artists Francesco Sleter and Jacopo Amigoni, with an exquisite ceiling depicting Aurora and the Dawn by Antonio Verrio.

Below: High Street, Rickmansworth, 1897
Looking east towards the junction with Church Street. The site of the building to the immediate left is now occupied by W H Smith; those on the right with the first-storey bay windows are extant and are occupied by the Nationwide Building Society.

RICKMANSWORTH

Left: Plough Public House, Mill End, c1900
A number of mills operated in Rickmansworth, processing silk, cotton and paper as well as cereals; the chimney of one can be seen on the right of the photograph. Mill End ran south–west from the High Street, generally following the course of the River Colne. The Plough was a Benskins-tied pub.

Above: Mill End, c1900
View in the opposite direction. The Rose and Crown, bought by local brewer Samuel Salter in 1767, came to be referred to as The Tree because of the large tree in the courtyard.

HIGH BARNET

Opposite: St John the Baptist, High Barnet, c1900
View north-west, showing the chequered chancel end at the junction of High Street and Wood Street. The church dates from the mid 15th century.

Top left: High Street, c1895
St John the Baptist church is in the distance. The view is from an elevated position, possibly from the building at the corner of the High Street and St Albans Road. In the foreground on the right is The Wellington public house, with the twin steeples of the High Barnet Methodist Church beyond. The Wellington no longer survives, and the main part of the church has also gone, but the steeples provide a dramatic entrance to The Spires shopping centre, opened in 1989.

Above: Hadley Common, c1910
Local residents pose by one of the gates of Hadley Common, once part of Enfield Chase, a royal deer park. When the Chase was enclosed in 1777, an area of some 240 acres was given to the villagers of Monken Hadley in compensation for their loss of grazing and other rights. The gates remain and have recently been restored.

SAYER
DRAPERY, CARPET
BERRILL'S
BAZAAR
BAZAAR
PRINTING OFFICE.
THE OLD
BULL INN
BOOKS

Buckinghamshire

AYLESBURY

Left: The Kingsbury, 1887

The triangular open space to the north of the Market Square is busy with local people shopping. The buildings are decorated with flags and bunting to celebrate Queen Victoria's Golden Jubilee.

Below: Market Square, 1888

The view north across the square shows the clock tower of 1876, designed by David Brandon. The cast iron lion resting on a stone base was part of a monument to Lord Chesham brought from the grounds of nearby Waddesdon Manor in 1888; it comprised two lions and a bronze statue of the Baronet. The piles of splintered wood in the square and the date of the picture mark the installation of the memorial to Lord Chesham, the wood being protective packaging for its carriage from Waddesdon.

BEACONSFIELD

Top left: High Street, 1902
Miss and Mrs Clark pose for the camera outside their chinaware shop.

Above left: The Police Station, Dinton, 1902
The charming former gate lodge to Dinton Hall, a 17th-century manor house now in private ownership, here used as the village police station. The woman and child at the gate are most probably the policeman's family.

Top right: Water Pump, Barton Hartshorn, 1901
A woman and a young girl, possibly her daughter, collect water from the village pump, a scene repeated throughout England until fresh water was piped to people's homes.

AKEMAN STREET STATION

Above: Constructing Akeman Street Station, Woodham, 1905
The somewhat ill-fated Great Central line between Grendon Underwood and Princes Risborough was authorised in 1899 and opened in 1906. This picture shows work in progress on the station, one of two small halts on the line between Ashendon and Grendon Underwood, the other being Wotton. The station was closed in 1930.

BUCKINGHAM

Left: 34–36, High Street, Buckingham, 1912
View south-east from Market Hill, with the King's Head public house centre of the picture. The Old Gaol, now the town museum, is just out of frame to the left. The scene today has changed: the old King's Head, third building from the left, has disappeared to make way for Moreton Road; the building on the far right is the new King's Head, though half of the premises have been demolished to make way for a parade of shops.

Below: Woottons Store, Dinton, 1904
Frozen in time. A group outside the Woottons Store in Dinton. One sports a solar topee. Another, perhaps from the local militia, wears a slouch hat, uniform and a sabre or cane. All are well dressed, suggesting an outing or occasion of some kind.

HADDENHAM

Top right: J Plater's Cart, Van & Carriage Works, Haddenham, 1903
Staff at Plater's pose for a group photograph; the suited gentleman is probably J Plater, standing behind nine of his staff working across three different crafts: carpenter, wheelwright and blacksmith. Two of the four apprentices look particularly young, barely 12 years old – the school leaving age at this time. As well as the traditional skills of the coachbuilder and wheelwright, working mainly with wood, the rising motor trade and use of iron and steel affected other small village enterprises around the country. In some, the cartwright and the blacksmith had separate premises, and cartwheels were rolled along to the smithy to be shod. Plater's had an integrated workshop so the blacksmith might also make carriage bodies, as seen in the centre of this picture, with the metal body of a trap in progress. One of the blacksmiths, in a leather apron, holds a club hammer and a piece of wrought metal.
The carriage wheel behind the boy with the mallet is not only finely spoked and shod with iron, but has a solid rubber tyre added to the rim: a sign of changing times.

Middle right: Grendon Underwood, c1906
Signalmen outside a signal box on a branch line built jointly by the Great Central Railway and the Great Western Railway linking the village with Ashendon.

Bottom right: Country lane, Dinton, 1904
A group of children pose for the camera, with the youngest just fitting into a rather basic perambulator. During the second half of the 19th century baby carriages in various styles grew in popularity. The idea that fresh air was good for an infant had taken hold, and the news that the Queen had purchased a pram from Hitching's Baby Stores, which had a branch at Hyde Park Corner, boosted sales.

TAPLOW

Left: Rectory Road, Taplow, 1885
In the centre of the village, two travelling punchinellos or performers, one with a monkey companion and the other a 'one-man band', make their pitch between St Nicolas' Church, just out of shot to the right, and the Oak and Saw pub, converted from terraced timber-framed cottages. Constructed in the mid 1750s using materials from salvaged wooden ships that were towed a distance of over 40 miles upstream on the Thames to Taplow, the cottages were adapted to form a public house in 1852.

Above: Crown Inn, Crown Square, Haddenham, 1904
The landlord Alfred Smith, is probably in this mixed group – perhaps the jovial man in his shirt sleeves to the right of the front door, with his wife holding the family pet terrier, and two children leaning against the picket fence. A poster advertising the annual Tring Agricultural Show at Tring Park in August 1904 leans against the wall on the left.

HIGH WYCOMBE

Top left: Great Western & Great Central Railway Office, Frogmore Gardens, 1902
The two collaborating railway companies shared upper-floor offices, while W V Baines, a removals and furniture storage company, occupied the ground floor.

Top right: Church Street, c1900
John R Dring, a draper and clothier, occupied a Tudor building on the corner of White Hart Street, selling fabric and sewing materials, linen tableware and fine underwear, as well as outerwear.

Above left: High Street, c1900
The slightly sleepy High Street, with elegant, mainly Georgian frontages on the northern side. In the distance on the right-hand side of the road is the Red Lion Hotel, from whose portico a young Benjamin Disraeli made his first political speech.

Above right: Market Place, 1902
Looking north-west towards the Guildhall, designed by Henry Keen and built for the Earl of Shelburne in 1757. The Market Place itself dates from 1604 and was remodelled by Robert Adam in 1761, at which time he also rebuilt the nearby Cornmarket.

REGATTA

Top left: Regatta, Marlow, 1885
Looking east along the Thames, which is crowded with small rowing boats and steamers; All Saints Church and the suspension bridge are seen beyond. The Marlow Town Festival and Regatta, which has been held annually since at least 1855, takes place in June, just before the more famous Henley Regatta further upstream.

MARLOW BRIDGE

Top right: Marlow Bridge, c1900
Workmen load large logs onto a river barge using a form of jack. The suspension bridge over the Thames, designed by William Tierney Clark and constructed between 1829 and 1832, remains a well-loved landmark close to the fashionable Compleat Angler hotel. Clark also designed the world-famous chain suspension bridge across the Danube that linked Buda with Pest in 1839.

HIGH STREET, MARLOW

Above: High Street, 1896
Georgian town houses lie on both sides of the street. At the end, in Market Square, is the former Town Hall, presented to Marlow by Sir Thomas Williams (the 'Copper King') in 1807. Comprising a covered market, fire station and assembly room, it later became the Crown Hotel, an important coaching inn. The obelisk in the middle of the square was erected in 1822 by the Trustees of the Hatfield to Bath Turnpike, which passed through Marlow and had a toll gate near this point.

BORLASE SCHOOL, WEST STREET

Above: Borlase School, West Street, 1896
The school was founded on its present site in 1624 by Sir William Borlase in memory of his son Henry, MP for Marlow, who died that year.

Right: Monks Risborough, 1904
A family group poses for the photographer. At the time of this photograph just 8 per cent of the population were employed in agriculture, compared with almost a quarter 60 years before. Many villagers, like this family, occupied tiny, time-worn cottages.

NEWPORT PAGNELL

Above: North Square, Newport Pagnell 1913
View south along High Street, looking towards the tower of St Peter and St Paul's Church. Once one of the largest towns in Buckinghamshire and an important market town, Newport Pagnell is situated close to the confluence of the Great Ouse and Ouzel rivers. Today, despite its continued expansion, the town has been overshadowed by its immediate neighbour, Milton Keynes.

Left: Red Lion Inn, Sandpit Hill, Tingewick, 1904
A group of children stand outside the Red Lion public house, whose landlord at the time was Edmund Grantham. Today the inn looks rather different: the lime-washed walls have been stripped to reveal the warm stone beneath, and a generous thatch replaces this worn-out roof.

WADDESDON

Above: Waddesdon Manor, 1905
This palatial country house was built between 1874 and 1883 for Baron Ferdinand de Rothschild in the style of a 16th-century French chateau to the designs of the French architect Gabriel-Hippolyte Destailleur. The gardeners, with their carefully arranged tools, pose for the camera. Behind them is the iron-framed aviary built in 1889. The extensive gardens were such a revelation that in 1890 Queen Victoria came to see them.

Right: Preston Bissett, 1904
A group of boys pose on the kissing gate at Preston Bissett with the school house behind them. Ten years later, they would more than likely be fighting on the Western Front.

Oxfordshire

ABINGDON

Above: Market Square, 1897
County Hall looks down across the market square of Abingdon, filled with people, floats, brass bands, banners, and horses and carts on the occasion of Queen Victoria's Diamond Jubilee. The excitement of the crowd is palpable, as people assemble after a procession through the street.

Left: County Hall, Market Square, 1888
The Baroque-style building was constructed around 1680 to house the assizes when Abingdon was the county town of Berkshire. The open arches of the ground floor accommodated market stalls. It is believed that the builder, Christopher Kempster, followed a design by Christopher Wren. The statue of Queen Victoria, whose regal gaze is focused on the business being conducted by her subjects in the chambers of County Hall, was erected in 1887 to celebrate her Golden Jubilee.

OCK STREET, ABINGDON

Above left: Independent Chapel, Ock Street, 1880
The Independent Chapel, to the right, was built in 1862 for a large Congregationalist group in the town. An expansion of an earlier chapel, it could seat 600 worshippers. The Neoclassical frontage, faced in ashlar, looks over an 18th-century public fountain fed by a conduit.

Above right: Abingdon Bridge, c1900
View south along Bridge Street, towards the Maud Hales section of the bridge; the Nag's Head, the white painted building on the left, stands on Nag's Island. The mediaeval bridge comprised a series of three separate spans with a total of 14 arches; further south, it formed a causeway over the Thames floodplain.

Right middle: Queen's Hotel, Market Square, c1900
Built in 1864 of red and yellow brick, the Hotel replaced the old Queen's Arms. The older building was located in the Town Square to attract traffic from the junction of two turnpikes on the road connecting Oxford and Southampton. From the 1790s a stagecoach, known as the Southampton Frigate, left the city at 6 am on Monday, Wednesday and Friday to arrive at Oxford's Angel Inn in the evening of the same day. In this photograph a coach and four, with passengers and footmen posing for the photographer, stands in front of the hotel ready to depart for Faringdon. The hotel was demolished in the 1960s to make way for new shops.

Right below: East St Helen Street, 1890
A view towards St Helen's Church from one of the earliest streets in the town. Many of the houses have mediaeval cellars.

ABINGDON

Above: Primitive Methodist Chapel, Ock Street, Abingdon, c1900
Looking east, with the twin spires of the chapel, built in 1845, on the right. Primitive Methodism sought a return to more simple, but firmly defined, fundamentals as an alternative to the well-established worship of the Wesleyan elders. By the time this photograph was taken, the differences were blurring. The two movements merged in 1932.

BANBURY

Opposite below: Town Hall, Banbury, 1878
Looking west down the High Street during the cattle market towards the Town Hall. Designed in the Gothic Revival style by Edward Bruton, it was built in 1854 with later additions in 1891, and still commands the centre of the town.

Above right: High Street, Banbury, c1878
Betts cake shop and Neale & Perkins Ironmongers occupied a fine mid-17th-century triple-gable house, embellished with carved bargeboards and three curved bay windows enriched with ornamental pargetting.

Above left: Banbury Cross, c1900
The Cross dominates the picture with the tower of the Parish Church of St Mary the Virgin behind. Designed by J Gibbs of Oxford and erected in 1858, the Cross was built to commemorate the marriage of Queen Victoria's daughter Victoria, the Princess Royal, to Frederick, Crown Prince of Prussia; they were to be the future parents of Kaiser Wilhelm II. The site was believed to have had a mediaeval cross, though this is contested.

Top right: The George Inn, Botley, 1892
View from Seacourt stream showing a group outside the Inn engaged in Beating the Bounds – a laborious traditional ceremony requiring parishioners to walk around the parish boundary and thrash the marker stones with willow sticks. As the picture reveals, this was thirsty work.

Top left: Church Army Press, Cowley, c1900
Interior view of the workshop with typesetters at work at their tables in the foreground while the letterpress sits behind them.

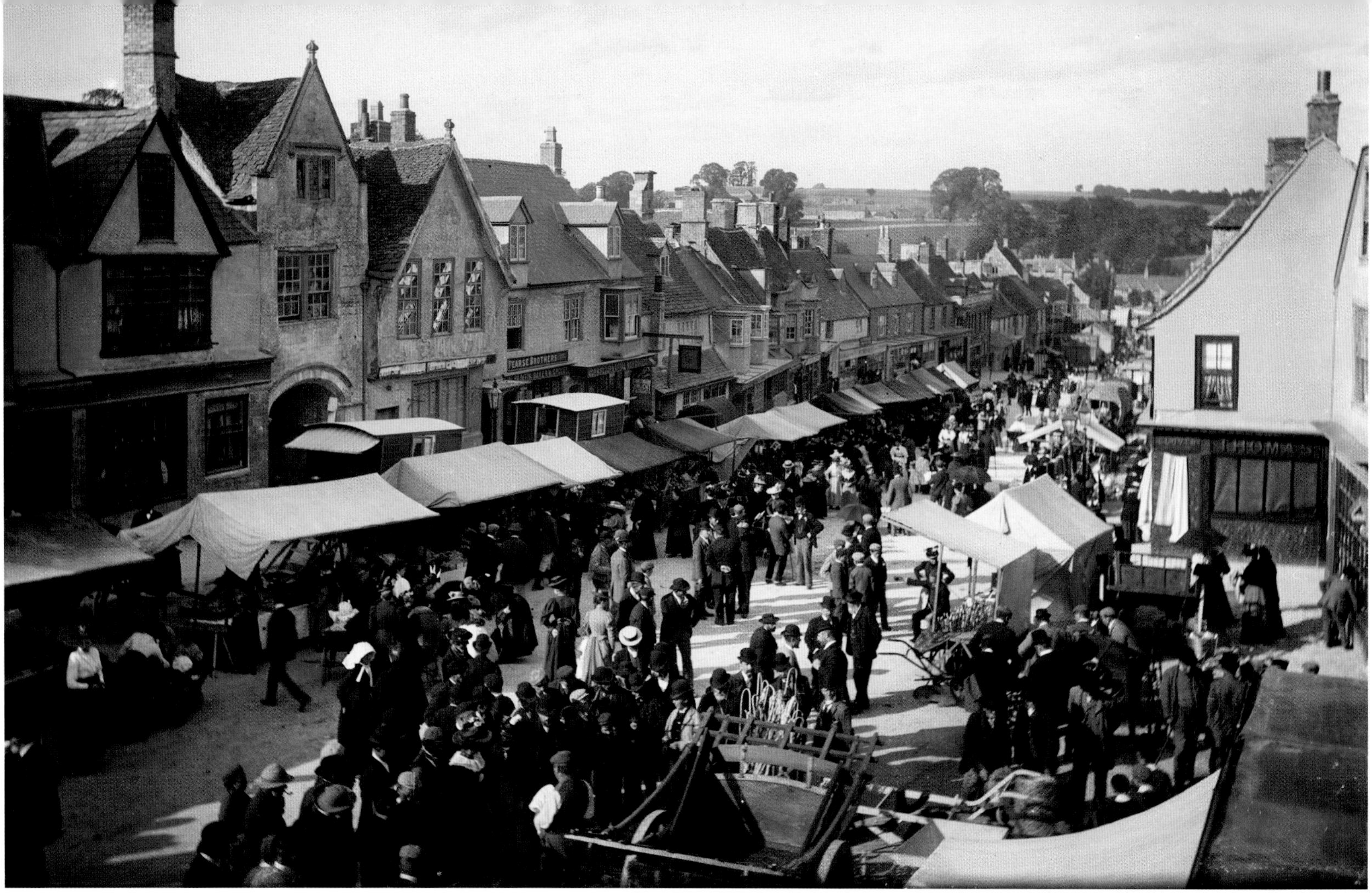
PEARSE BROTHERS

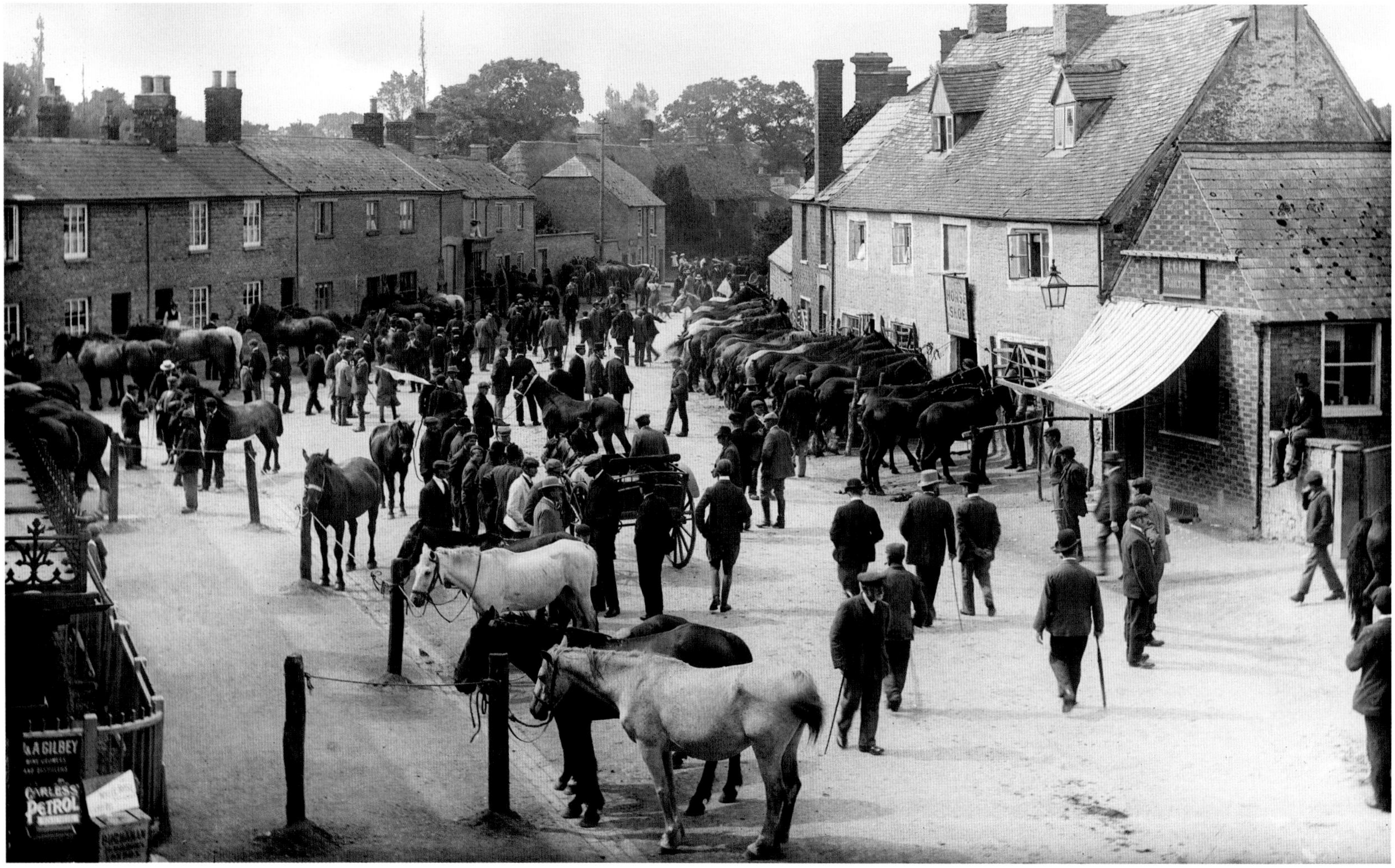
A GILBEY
PETROL

BURFORD

Opposite above: High Street, Burford, 1895
A view of the street looking north during the Hiring Fair showing market stalls set out in the main street. Fairs like this took place after harvest at Michaelmas, when new annual contracts between owners and farm workers were sealed with a shilling. Stalls and other attractions flocked to the fair towns to take advantage of agricultural labourers having money in their pockets,

Opposite below: Bampton Horse Fair, Bampton, 1904
The Horse Fair in Bridge Street with the appropriately named Horseshoe public house in the background. Held over the August Bank Holiday, the annual fair reached a peak of popularity during the first decade of the 20th century.

Above: Cherwell New Cut, Oxford, 1884
The New Cut was constructed to ease the flow of the River Cherwell at its confluence with the Thames, at the same time introducing a new northern boundary to the island of Aston's Eyot. The shored-up bank of the Cherwell can be seen towards the left rear of the picture; the field beyond is now occupied by the Oxford University sports complex.

Middle right: St Andrew's Church, East Hagbourne, 1904
Looking towards the 15th-century village cross with the church tower beyond. Around the cross are several well-constructed timber-framed cottages, one with herringbone brick panels.

Right: Days Lock, Little Wittenham, 1885
Workmen rebuild the lock, which dated back to the 1790s. The navvies manually operate the pile driver as the steam engine lies idle. While the canal system was still being extended at this time, much of it was decades old and required a lot of maintenance.

FARINGDON

Above: Oxford Street, 1895
The townspeople of Faringdon watch the photographer as he takes the picture looking up Oxford Street from the Market Place. The Bell Hotel is to the right. Because of its position on the London to Cirencester road and the route from the Cotswolds to the south-east, Faringdon became an important staging post for wool traders, with a large number of inns and taverns for travellers.

Left: The Market Place, 1904
Granted a Royal Charter by Henry III in 1218 to hold a weekly market, Faringdon became the main market centre for the area. Here, the cattle market is under way, with the Salutation Inn to one side and the churchyard to the other.

WOODSTOCK

Above middle: Market Street, Woodstock, c1900
Well placed for nearby Oxford to the south and with Blenheim Palace on its doorstep, by the end of the 19th century the historic market town of Woodstock was established as a visitor attraction and remains so today.

Above: Blenheim Palace, 1903
A fire brigade rally is held in the grounds of Blenheim Palace. Different brigades are represented by a team of firemen and a horse-drawn tender with the name of their town inscribed on the side.

FINMERE

Top right: Finmere Station, 1904
The station was built by the Great Central Railway Company between 1898 and 1899 on the line from Sheffield through Nottingham and Leicester to London with its new terminus at Marylebone. The station sign reads 'Finmere for Buckingham'. The county town was only five miles away, although it was already served directly by the London and North Western Railway. Behind the porters are posters advertising tickets for trips to London – a journey unthinkable for most people before the coming of the railways.

Top left: Stationmaster's House, 1904
The stationmaster poses with his family outside his house, from which a set of steps leads straight up to the platforms of Finmere Station in the background. The station closed to passenger traffic in 1963, and this stretch of the Grand Central line was closed as part of the Beeching cuts in 1966.

Above right: Finmere Post Office, 1904
The woman in the photograph is probably Rachel Paxton, sub-postmistress until 1915. After a fire in 1959 and several changes of location over the next 40 years, Finmere Post Office finally closed its doors in 1999.

HENLEY-ON-THAMES

Opposite above left: Hart Street, 1890
St Mary's Church, with its distinctive flint and stone chequer-patterned church tower with polygonal angle buttresses, dates from the 16th century.

Opposite below: Bell Street, 1890
Monk's clothing store on the corner of the junction between Bell Street, Hart Street and the Market Square in Henley-on-Thames. The handsome drinking fountain was designed by James Forsyth and erected in 1885; in porphyry and stone and topped with a short-crocketed spire, it has subsequently been relocated beside St Mary's Church. Higgins Library on the opposite corner has a diverse range of stock – from the photographs shown in the window to violin and banjo strings, essentials for the day trippers who entertained themselves by making their own music. The sign for Beningfield & Son, Auctioneers and Estate Agents, shows that they also have offices in Haymarket, London.

Opposite above right: River Thames, 1897
Well-to-do guests enjoy the best seats on the river to watch the Henley Royal Regatta from a hospitality barge. Many of the women have veils in place, while the men sport straw boaters, which were in fashion at the time.

RIVER THAMES

Above and top: River Thames near Oxford, c1900
Spectators crowd the footpath and the river during one of the numerous competition events held on the Thames. The college barges on the opposite bank indicate an Oxford University event, the most important of which remains the Summer Eights, held on the Isis stretch of the Thames in May.

ST GILES' FAIR

Top left: St Giles' Fair, Oxford, 1905
At this annual event held at the beginning of September, a large crowd has gathered in front of Thurstons Colormatography (top left) showcasing the fairground bioscope – a new name for a magic lantern and moving picture show.
Top right: The merry-go-round at the Fair in 1895 attracts both adults and children.

WITNEY

Above left: Church Green, 1900
Crowds mill around at the Witney Feast, a fair with mediaeval origins held in September. A day of piety was followed by trading, feasting and entertainment, provided by the merry-go-rounds and stalls.

Above right: Earley's Blanket Factory, c1900
The wealth of the market town of Witney, like that of many of its Cotswold neighbours, was built on wool. Witney was renowned for its blanket manufacturing with, at one point, five factories in the town. Earley's was the largest and the last to close, in 2002. Here, woollen fleece is fed into the processing plant at the first stage of blanket weaving.

THAME

Opposite above: Cornmarket, c1900
A busy market-day scene, with penned sheep in Cornmarket and the Upper High Street. Men look over the sheep, bargaining and chatting.

Opposite below: New Town Hall, 1887
The exterior of the New Town Hall, built in 1887 by H J Tollit in an eclectic freestyle to commemorate Queen Victoria's Golden Jubilee.

NAG'S HEAD INN
SOAP
THORLEY'S
FOOD FOR CATTLE
LACTIFER
NEWS
WORLD

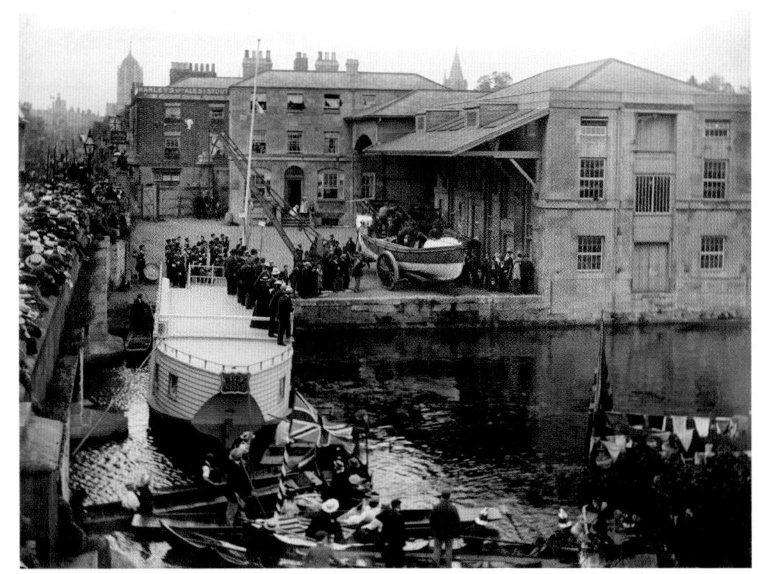

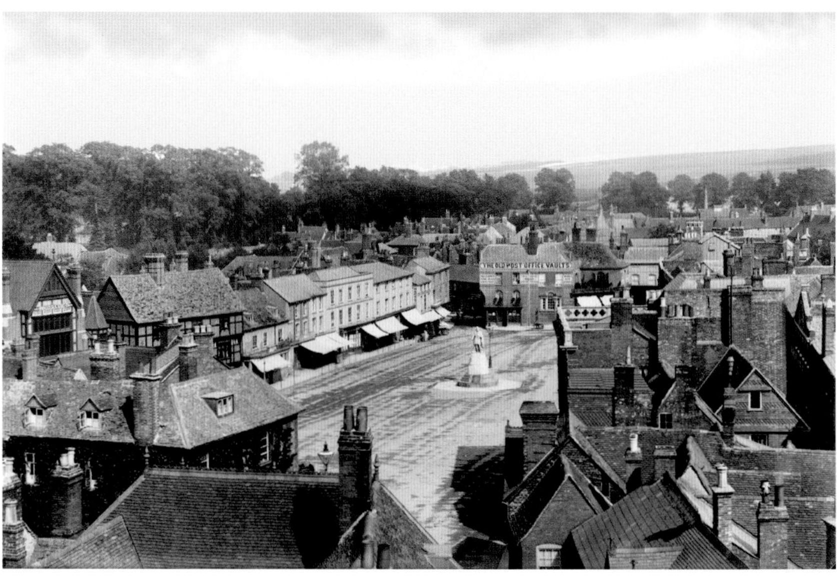

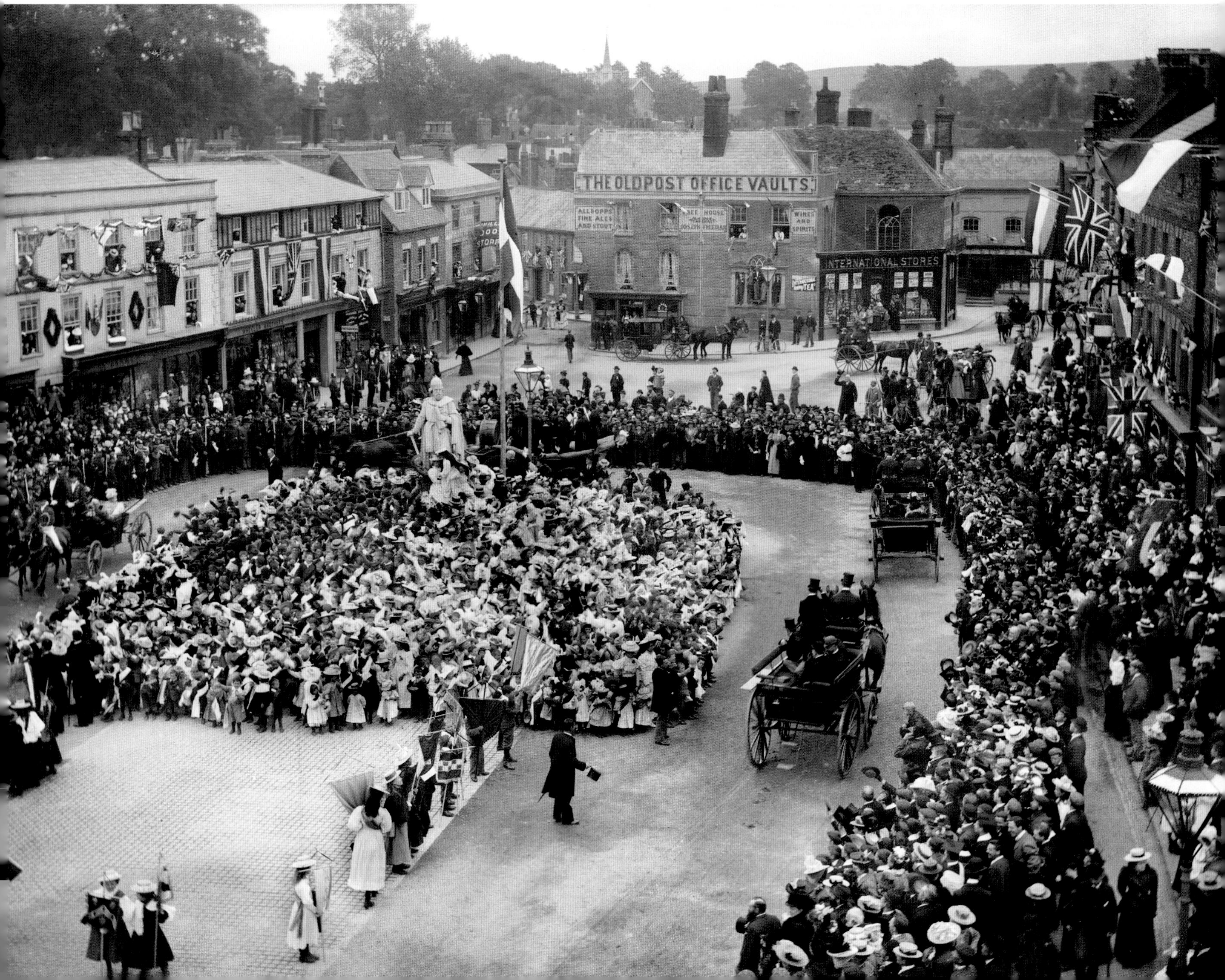
THE OLDPOST OFFICE VAULTS
ALLSOPPS FINE ALES AND STOUT
WINES AND SPIRITS
INTERNATIONAL STORES

WANTAGE

Opposite above right: Market Place, 1890
Looking west over the Market Place from the tower of St Peter and St Paul's Church. As well having a Market Charter, Wantage has held fairs since the 13th century, when the right was granted to the long-established local Fitzwarin family.

Opposite below: Market Place, 1898
The same viewpoint as above, but a very different scene, with crowds of people in Market Place welcoming Edward, Prince of Wales, to the town in 1898. The Prince's carriage leads on the far left of the picture behind the statue of Alfred the Great; other dignitaries follow, with a brass band playing in the second carriage. Police constables line the route, and the town's children, wearing ceremonial sashes, crowd around the statue with their teachers.

Above: The Market Square, 1890
The Baptist Chapel is centre with the Town Hall in the foreground.

SALTERS YARD

Opposite above left: Salter's Yard, Folly Bridge, Oxford, 1900
Salter Brothers boatyard was established in 1858 and specialised in building large college barges. An annual fundraiser for the RNLI is underway: it included the launch of a lifeboat into the river to demonstrate its buoyancy.

OXFORD

Top left: Bodleian Library, 1895
Founded in 1602 by Sir Thomas Bodley, the Bodleian Library is one of the oldest in Europe. This view shows its panelled wooden ceiling and bookcases dating from around 1600.

Top right: New College, 1901
College cooks prepare joints of meat. A spit of chickens is leaning against the wall ready to be roasted over the open fire on the rotating spits above.

Middle left: The Quad, Worcester College, 1885
Looking north through the open arcade, probably designed by Nicholas Hawksmoor, and built soon after 1720.

Above: Front Quad, The Queen's College, 1903
Looking west along the south arcade over the parked bicycles of members of the college. The fine Baroque quad, strongly influenced by Nicholas Hawksmoor, was built gradually during the first half of the 18th century.

Left: Manchester College, Mansfield Road, c1900
The college, founded originally in Manchester in 1786 as a theological training college chiefly for Unitarians and other non-conformists, moved to Oxford in 1889. The college library was built soon after, between 1891 and 1893, by Thomas Worthington.

MAGDALEN BRIDGE

Left: Magdalen Bridge, 1895
A large crowd gathers on the bridge on May Morning to hear the college choir sing from the top of the tower. This annual tradition celebrates the coming of spring; following the hymn, the bells of the college ring out over the city for 20 minutes.

THE HIGH

Below: The High, Oxford, 1909
View south-west to 94 High Street; the timber-fronted building was erected in 1902 in a 16th-century style. The entire row of houses to the right of it was demolished to make way for Oriel College's Rhodes Building designed by Basil Champneys and built between 1909 and 1911.

ST MARTIN'S CHURCH

Above: St Martin's Church, Carfax, Oxford, 1890
This view west at Carfax, the crossroads of the High Street and Queen Street, shows the east end of St Martin's from The High, as it is known locally. The first St Martin's was built in the 11th century and for generations acted as the town church. When the building was deemed unsafe in 1822, it was demolished – except for the tower – and rebuilt. The need to widen the crossroads and improve access into Cornmarket in 1896 led to the complete demolition of the later part of the church. Only the 13th-century tower, now known as the Carfax Tower, remains.

MARTYRS' MEMORIAL

Opposite above: Martyrs' Memorial, St Giles, Oxford, c1900
The memorial cross, designed by George Gilbert Scott and installed in 1843, commemorates the burning at the stake of the reforming prelates Thomas Cranmer, Hugh Latimer and Nicholas Ridley at a site close to the monument in Broad Street. Its erection was highly symbolic at the time, with the growing strength of the Oxford Movement, which aimed to revive Roman Catholic traditions in the Anglican Church. A group of Anglican clergy raised the money to pay for the monument. This view shows the statue of Cranmer, a Bible under his arm, by the sculptor Henry Weekes. In the background is the tower of St Mary Magdalen Church.

BISHOP KING'S PALACE

Right: Bishop King's Palace, St Aldates, 1920

Looking north along the west side of the street, the photograph shows the main range of buildings (the two buildings beyond the alleyway on the left) erected between 1622 and 1628 by Thomas Smith and probably incorporating an earlier structure. The better-known west range is an earlier house of the 16th or 17th century with five gables.

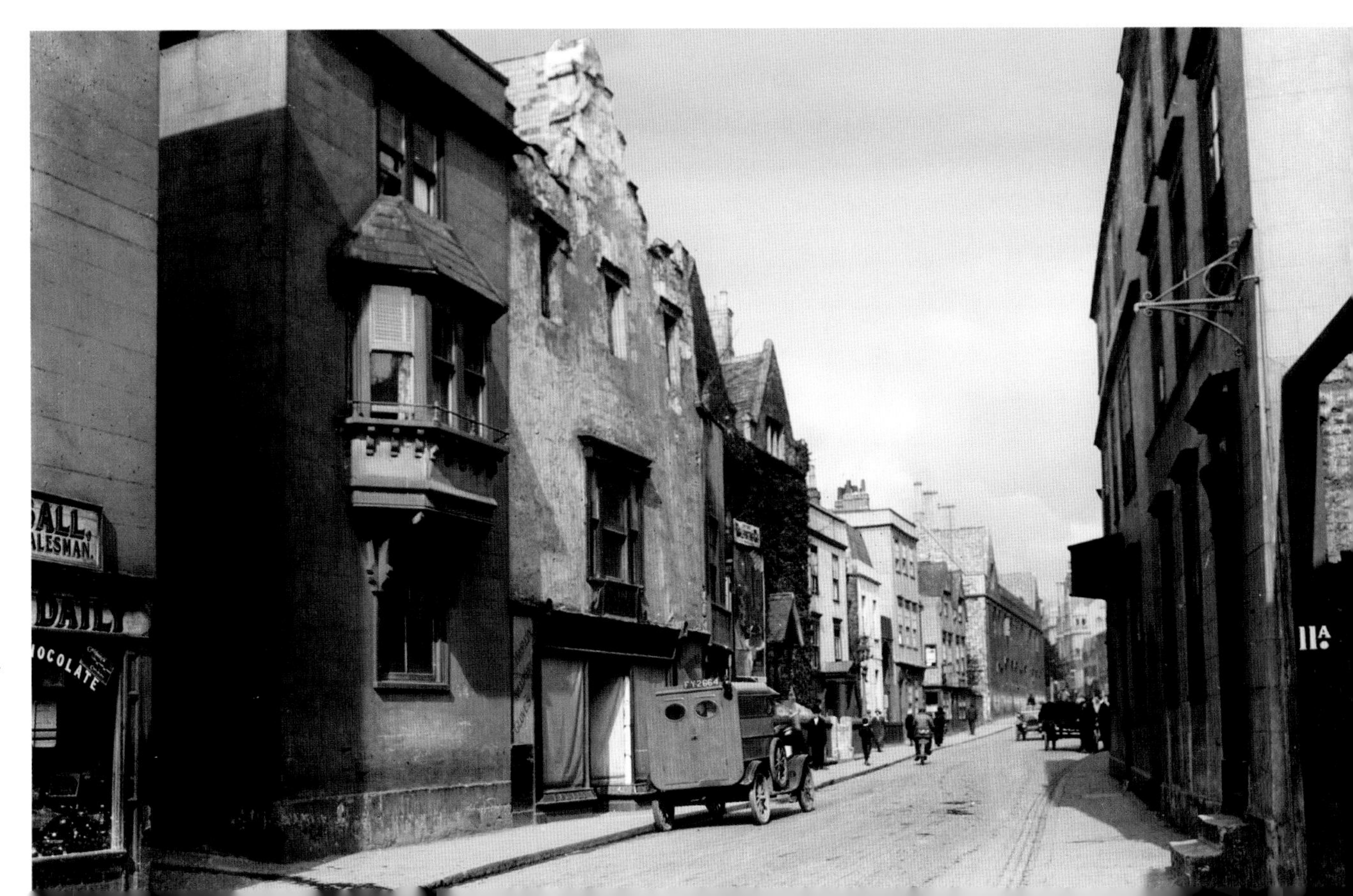

ST GILES, OXFORD

Right: Parker's Motor House, 68 St Giles, c1920
The Oxford Cycle Company opened its premises here in 1893 and by 1900 had added 'Motor Car' into its company name. From 1922 to 1925 it was simply Oxford Motors Ltd. The building, along with Nos 69–73, was demolished in 1937 to make way for an extension to the Taylor Institute library.

In 1912 another Oxford bicycle specialist turned to manufacturing motor cars. William Morris's Garage was established in 1909, and by 1913 his Cowley factory was producing the Bull-nosed Morris in large numbers. In 1925, the year Parker's ceased trading in St Giles, Morris Motors produced 56,000 vehicles.

PARKER
CO 68
67
MOTOR CARS
PETROL
AGENT FOR
MOTOR CARS
DUNLOP
DUNLOP SPECIAL
WARWICK
CAMBRIDGE
EDINBURGH
DUNLOP MOTOR TYRES IN STOCK
RESIDENCE.
TYRES
FC-803
MICHELIN ACCESSORIES
STOCK MICHELIN TYRES
MOTOR REPAIRS
PARKERS
OXFORD
PALMER
LC 1265

OXFORD TOWN HALL

Above: Town Hall, St Aldates, c1900
The grand organ in the main hall, with its lavishly decorated plaster ceiling. The site on St Aldates was originally occupied by the Guildhall, which was demolished to make way for the city's first Town Hall in 1752. This in turn was replaced by the current building in 1897. The compact concert organ was designed by John Stainer and built in 1897 by 'Father' Henry Willis, the leading organ builder of his day, whose instruments were installed in St Paul's Cathedral in London and St George's Hall, Liverpool.

TAUNT PHOTOGRAPHERS

Above and top right: Taunt's Shop, 9–10 Broad Street, Oxford, c1890
Henry Taunt leased these premises in 1874 after moving from the Cornmarket. In 1894 the property owner locked him out of the shop and demanded money, forcing Taunt into bankruptcy. Despite this setback, Taunt started up again in 1895 on The High.

Top left: Morrells Brewery, St Thomas Street, Oxford, c1900
Exterior view of the cast iron gateway with a cart laden with barrels in the entrance.

FRANK COOPER'S WORKS

Frank Cooper's Works, Victoria Buildings, Park End Street, Oxford, c1900
Above right: A laden cart stands outside the frontage of the Frank Cooper Marmalade Factory opened in 1900 to meet increasing demand for the product.

Above left: The interior of the factory showing women and girls shredding fruit. All wear aprons over their everyday clothes, and some have removable sleeves to protect their clothes. When he first started his business, Cooper sold his marmalade from his shop on The High, where it was made at the back of the premises.

Top left: The interior of the new buildings at Park End Street showing the mixers and vats. The marmalade was based upon the recipe of Frank Cooper's wife, Sarah.

RIVERSIDE

Above: Workers with osiers, Riverside, 1900
On the left, bark is stripped from osiers using a metal device clamped to a wooden beam. The willow wands were made into a range of objects, such as the eel traps next to the foreman on the right. Workers to the rear are in the process of basketry weaving. Everyone wears a hat, but the man in charge is wearing a jacket and a bowler hat – a sign of his higher status.

QUEEN STREET

Above: Queen Street, Oxford, 1897
Flags and bunting decorate the street during celebrations to mark Queen Victoria's visit for her Diamond Jubilee; Westgate can be seen in the distance. To the right the four-storey stone building is Thomas Hyde & Company's clothing warehouse, which occupied premises on Queen Street from 1839. Its success funded this elegant building, designed by Frederick Codd. Faced in bath stone, it was constructed in 1877; the balconies adorning the frontage were removed in the 1960s, but the building remains. This photograph was taken from the approximate location of the modern-day Marks & Spencer.

Opposite above: Cowley Road, Cowley, 1914
Two early motor buses manufactured by Daimler, one with an open upper deck carrying advertising by local companies. In the roadway the old horse-drawn tramlines can be seen in the block paving, flanked by macadamised surfaces.

Opposite below: The High, Oxford, c1905
Two horse-drawn trams pass in the street with advertising panels attached to their roofs. Magdalen Bridge, at the end of The High and a main thoroughfare into the centre of Oxford, was widened in 1899 by the Oxford Local Board to accommodate horse-drawn trams. By 1913 motor buses had made their appearance spelling the end for these trams.

COWLEY Rd & STATIONS
DEAL WITH US ONCE AND YOU WILL ALWAYS
HARRIS BROS
WARDROBE DEALERS
51, GEORGE St & 7 COWLEY Rd
STOP
OXFORD
Daimler
DU 4148
LITTLEMORE & COWLEY TERMINUS
via COWLEY VILLAGE.
OXFORD
Daimler
FC-1638

MARGETTS
For HATS
MARGETTS
For HATS
BOSWELLS CIRCUS
DAY PERFORMANCES
WATER CARNIVAL
"CLEANLINESS"
NIXEY'S
REFINED
BLACK LEAD.
2
VAN HOUTEN'S COCOA BEST & GOES FARTHEST
3

ST CLEMENTS, OXFORD

Above: St Clements, 1910
The annual toy fair held in St Clements on the Thursday before Michaelmas. The fair, originally for hiring servants, survived until the 1930s.

Left: The Cattle Market, Gloucester Green, c1900
The traditional focus for Oxford's market in mediaeval times was Carfax; tradesmen had their permanent premises in surrounding streets and had not far to go to set up their stalls for market day. The sale of livestock, poultry and fish was an important part of the market, but the driving of herds of cattle into the city centre brought chaos and filth, as it did in many towns of the period, so the markets were moved to the outskirts. Gloucester Green, an open space outside Gloucester College, hosted a fair during the 19th century, and in 1835 the cattle market moved there, with a covered area and permanent corrals. This photograph bears witness to its importance and popularity.

THE HIGH

Right: The High, Oxford, c1900

Labourers lay the substrate of a new macadam surface over the old granite setts with the aid of a steamroller to create a smoother surface. The steamroller has a brass plate – Oxford Corporation No.2 – and on the front is a prancing pony with Invicta underneath, the logo of the Rochester-based steam engineering company Aveling & Porter.

Below: Lake Street, New Hinksey, 1890

Looking north along the flooded street where most of the houses open directly onto the road; occupants with an enclosed frontage are assessing the damage. On the right is the Crown Inn. New Hinksey was part of suburban railway expansion and the need to house the many railway workers. Lake Street takes its name from the reservoir at the end of the road, a flooded gravel pit whose gravel had been used in railway construction. Being built on the low-lying fields in the Thames floodplain made New Hinksey prone to flooding (see following page).

NEW HINKSEY

Above left: Flooded railway line near New Hinksey, 1894
The tracks are under water on this stretch of the mainline running parallel with Abingdon Road, south of the city. The men on the bogey – a mix of managers and labourers – seem to be assessing the flood and any related damage with probes, using staffs to propel the cart. The entire area south of the Thames is badly flooded as far as the eye can see.

Top: 75-81 The High, Oxford, c1900
Road resurfacing continues outside the Examination Schools. Designed by T G Jackson, the building was constructed for the administration of the Oxford University exam system and completed in 1882.

Above right: Rewley Road Station, Oxford, 1914
Porters and station staff pause on the platform for the photographer. The station was built between 1851 and 1852 in prefabricated sections for the London and North Western Railway.

RIVER THAMES

Left: Frozen River Thames, c1891
The Thames froze over in 1891 and 1895; a common test of this novelty was with a coach and four that could weigh several tons. The picture shows a crowd of spectators, with barges moored against the bank in the background.

Below left: LNWR Railway Station, Rewley Road, 1914
Carriages wait outside the station while staff pose in front of the poster adverts. A panoramic scene of North Wales takes pride of place. Passenger traffic ceased in 1951; the station was dismantled in 1999 and rebuilt at the Buckinghamshire railway centre in Aylesbury. Rewley Road station was built on the site of old Rewley Abbey, now occupied by the Said Business School.

Above: Gasworks Bridge, St Ebbe's, c1886
View looking north-west towards the construction site of the new iron railway bridge over the River Thames following the Oxford Gas Light and Coke Company's south bank extension in 1882. This fascinating photograph shows the simple techniques of building in use at the time with the iron parapets erected section by section then filled in with beams to take a footpath and single-track railway.

WELLSTEEDS
COSTUMIERS
WELLSTEEDS
MILLINERS
DRAPERS
WELLSTEEDS
WELLSTEEDS
Wellsteeds

Berkshire

READING

Wellsteeds, 126–133 Broad Street, Reading, 1920
View from the north-east of Wellsteeds costumiers, milliners, drapers and outfitters shop. The company vans and drivers line the street. With the coming of the railway to Reading in 1840, Broad Street, nearer to the train station, took over from Minster Street as the main commercial road and shopping area for the town. In the second half of the 19th century the family-run department store Heelas moved into Broad Street along with Wellsteeds. The former was eventually bought by the John Lewis Partnership in 1947 and remains on the same site today. Wellsteeds survived a bombing raid in 1943. It was eventually acquired by Debenhams and moved to the Oracle Shopping Centre.

READING TOWN HALL

Above: Town Hall and St Laurence Church, Friar Street, 1875
View looking east to the exterior of the Town Council Chamber and Clock Tower, by Alfred Waterhouse, next to St Laurence Church, before the construction of the Jubilee statue to Queen Victoria in 1887.

Left: Central Cinema Playhouse and Cafe, Friar Street, 1921
The Central Cinema eventually became the ABC, although the site is now occupied by the Ibis Hotel.

Opposite above: Reading Market Place, 1890
Looking towards St Laurence Church; a cabmen's shelter is in the foreground. Also providing simple food, cabmen's shelters were introduced to keep thirsty cabmen away from public houses.

Left: Mill Lane, Reading, 1890
A view along Mill Lane towards St Giles Mill, showing the water tower and pumping station. The St Giles millstream was cut from the River Kennet. Baynes and Beard, the name on the bridge, were timber merchants. The watermill, on the site of one of six mills mentioned in the Domesday Book, was demolished in 1903. The waterway remains in part, but these buildings have been replaced by the city's inner ring road and the Oracle Shopping Centre.

Left: Broad Street, Reading, c1900
Looking east along the city's main shopping street; the tram lines can be seen in the centre of the road. Horse-drawn trams first arrived in Reading in 1879, but were being replaced by electric trams from 1903.

Below: Market Place, Newbury, 1890
View north over the Market with the Corn Exchange to the right. Traders sell from stalls and covered wagons, with one seller, in the foreground, attracting a large crowd with what appears to be chinaware. The pedimented Corn Exchange was built by J S Dodd between 1861 and 1862. The London & County Banking Company is at the back of the square, and to its right the Old Waggon and Horses and the White Hart Hotel.

NEWBURY

Above: The Jubilee Clock, Broadway, 1890
The clock, erected to commemorate the Golden Jubilee of Queen Victoria in 1887, lies at the three-way junction with the London and Bath roads. From 1828 a substantial obelisk supported a large gas lamp on this site, which aided the movement of coaching traffic through Newbury. The main route to Bath passed through the north of the town, setting down at Speenhamland, an important stop that provided handsomely for wealthy travellers with inns such as the Chequers, which can be seen in the background on Bath Road (now Oxford Street). The new clock fulfilled all the functions of the Speenhamland Lamp, with a drinking fountain and lighting provided by four branching gas lanterns. The cannon beneath the statue was captured from the Russians in the Crimean War. The clock stood here until 1929 when being considered a hazard to motorised traffic, it was replaced by the Clock House, which remains in the part-pedestrianised area.

MAIDENHEAD

Above: James Hews, Ironmongers, King Street, c1900
Foundrymen pose in the yard of their work premises holding some of the tools of their trade with various iron pipes in the background. Their jobs and status can be guessed at from the clothes they are wearing: the boss and office workers, or possibly shop assistants, wear a jacket, collar and tie, while the workers and apprentices have flat caps and leather aprons. The men wearing bowler hats would have been overmen (foremen).

KING STREET

Above: The Bell Hotel, King Street, c1900
The busy street is decorated with bunting and flags. The crowd awaits the arrival of an important visitor, no doubt a regular occurrence given its proximity to nearby Windsor Castle.

Left: Thames Hotel, Ray Mead Road, 1891
With the Thames a few yards to its right, the riverside hotel attracted much waterborne trade for its proprietor, Henry Woodhouse.

COOKHAM

Top: Cookham Lock, c1880
View north-west towards the River Thames and the footbridge, which gives pedestrian access to the lock from Cookham village.

Above: Cookham Lock, 1885
On a busy bank holiday the lock is full of various small boats, including punts and a larger classic Thames steamer.

BISHAM

Opposite above: The Bull Inn, Marlow Road, 1890
Drays are loaded with barrels of beer outside the inn, which enjoyed good passing trade on the way to Marlow Bridge just down the road.

BRAY

Above: Kimbers Lane, 1885

Timber-framed houses line the lane heading towards the tower of St Michael's Church in the distance. Those to the right have brick infill panels and dormer windows. This stretch of road is known today as High Street; Bray itself has been transformed from a sleepy Berkshire village into a gastronomic magnet for the fashionable. The building directly in front of the church is now the Michelin-starred pub The Hinds Head. Owned by celebrity chef Heston Blumenthal, the Fat Duck restaurant is housed in the building adjacent to the timber-framed cottage on the right.

SLOUGH

Top: White Hart Hotel, 45 High Street, 1883

The White Hart Hotel, dating from at least 1657, was one of many coaching inns that formerly lined the High Street and Bath Road. The Black Boy Inn can also be seen on the left. Today the centre of Slough is virtually unrecognisable as the town of 150 years ago; it was extensively demolished to improve through traffic along the A4 prior to the construction of the M4 in the 1960s.

Above: Slough Railway Station, 1883

Built in 1882, the station was finally opened in 1884. The current building was the fifth station on the site, designed by J E Danks in an eclectic Second Empire style.

Opposite below: High Street, 1875

A woman with an umbrella raised for shade waits in the cart outside the shops. There is little to suggest in this sleepy scene that the road is a major Victorian thoroughfare, the main road to Bath from London. Its quietness is perhaps a testament to the popularity of the railway.

WINDSOR CASTLE

Above: Windsor Castle, 1888
Looking east from the junction of Peascod Street and the High Street with the Golden Jubilee statue of Queen Victoria by Sir Joseph Edgar Boehm in the foreground. One of England's largest castles, and also a Royal Palace, Windsor Castle dates from the reign of William the Conqueror, although the first stone buildings were erected by Henry II between 1165 and 1179. The royal standard flies from the Round Tower, with the State Apartments to the rear. The Edward III Tower is further along to the right. Towards the rear left, just beyond the King Henry VIII Gate, a group of people watch a squad of Foot Guards parading in full uniform, including bearskins.

Opposite below right: Church Street, c1910
Looking north along Church Street towards the King Henry VIII Gate entrance into Windsor Castle.

Surrey

STAINES

Top left: Town Hall, 1883
A view across the River Thames towards the Victorian Town Hall, a blend of Italian and Flemish influences in white brick and stone. It was designed by John Johnson between 1879 and 1880. Situated in a small market square, the Town Hall was converted into an Arts Centre in the 1990s and later into a pub.

Above: High Street, Staines, 1895
Located on the main road to the West Country and a convenient distance from London, Staines was a major stopping point for stagecoaches. The linoleum factory, for which the town became well known, was established north of the High Street in 1864.

Top right: Walton-on-Thames, Surrey, 1884
View of a 17th-century cottage and its occupants. Mentioned in the Domesday Book, and now a wealthy suburb within London's commuter belt, Walton-on-Thames has much earlier Celtic, Roman and Anglo-Saxon origins.

WEST MOLESEY

Field's Candle Works, 1890

Left: Exterior view of the main building at Field's Candle Works in West Molesey. Now demolished, the works occupied a large house called The Priory and surrounding buildings. They were set up by J C and C Field Ltd in the mid 19th century and used for the bleaching of wax to make candles. With the arrival of gas and then electric lighting, the use of candles diminished, leading to the eventual demise of candlemakers like Field's. The factory closed its doors in the 1890s.

Above: Exterior view of the shop and court, with workers and a group of children gathered outside. Note the discreet street numbering on the gas lantern.

EPSOM DOWNS

Left: Epsom Racecourse, Epsom Downs, 1890
Epsom Races on Derby Day with a merry-go-round in the foreground and the grandstand beyond. Established by the 12th Earl of Derby (Edward Smith Stanley) in 1779, the race was originally run on a Thursday but in 1838 was moved to a Wednesday to fit in with the railways' timetables.

Above: Surrey Walking Club,1924
A crowd of locals turns out to watch as competitors on the Surrey Walking Club's annual London to Brighton pass through Crawley. To the right is the George Hotel, an important coaching inn on the London to Brighton route in the days of horse-drawn transport.

REDHILL

Top: Petrol service station, 1927
By the 1920s motor cars were beginning to replace horses as a method of transport. Initially, village blacksmiths stocked fuel at their forges, but the 1927 Roadside Petrol Pumps Act allowed local authorities to licence fuel pumps, and petrol stations began to appear in towns and villages. This newly opened petrol service station at Redhill, Surrey, had restrooms and smoking rooms.

GUILDFORD

Above: High Street, c1925
On the left is the Astolat Olde Tea Shoppe, and on the right, Jackson's garage. In the foreground a white-coated policeman controls the traffic.

Kent

CANTERBURY

Left: 44–45 High Street, c1930

The Queen Elizabeth's Guest Chamber – originally the Crown Inn – dates from the late 16th century. Elizabeth I entertained the Duc d'Alencon here in 1573, hence the date on the facade. These sumptuous premises were leased to local nobility with the provision that they would be available to the Queen when visiting Canterbury. The ornamental plasterwork, or pargetting, resembles blocks of cut stone, or ashlar, with heraldic devices set between the second-floor windows, which are later 18th-century sashes. Today the Guest Chamber hosts a cafe and tea rooms on the first floor, with shops below.

Below left: City Mills, c1920

Known as the Abbot's Mill and using the waters of the River Stour to feed its millstream, the Mill was built in 1792 and destroyed by fire in 1933. One of many historic mills in the city, the original building was made of wood and took its name from nearby St Augustine Abbey, which owned it. The Abbey was founded by Augustine in AD 598 and thrived for nearly a thousand years until the Dissolution.

Below right: Burgate, c1900

A view down Burgate Street with the surviving tower of the former St Mary Magdalen Church in Canterbury in the foreground. The tower was built in 1502, but the body of the church was demolished in 1871.

CANTERBURY CATHEDRAL

Above: Canterbury Cathedral, c1900
An atmospheric view eastwards across the rooftops towards the west end of the Cathedral. Founded by St Augustine in 597, the original Cathedral and its later Saxon replacements were subsumed into the Norman building commenced in 1070. By 1498 the Cathedral was largely complete in the form seen here, including an extension of the famous Bell Harry tower. Extensive remains of the former monastic buildings surrounding the Cathedral can still be seen today – an integral part of the outstanding universal value of the Canterbury World Heritage Site designated by UNESCO in 1988.

Above: Christchurch Gate, Canterbury Cathedral, 1903
A sublime view of one of the most important examples of mediaeval cathedral architecture in Britain: the towering west end of the Cathedral viewed through the main gate to the precincts, which dates from 1502.

Below: **Westgate, Canterbury, 1894**
View from St Dunstan's Street. Built of squared ragstone blocks and completed about 1380 by Archbishop Sudbury, the gate into the walled city was equipped with a drawbridge and served as a prison in the 19th century.

FAVERSHAM

Left: Maison Dieu, Ospringe Street, Ospringe, c1894

The Hospital of the Blessed Mary of Ospringe, commonly known as 'Maison Dieu' or God's House, was founded in 1230 to care for the sick and elderly and to shelter Canterbury pilgrims. Still known as Maison Dieu, it probably also accommodated secular chantry priests. The building incorporates remnants of the original 13th-century stone undercroft beneath an early 16th-century jettied timber-framed upper floor. Much of the undercroft was removed in 1894 when a shopfront and corner entrance were inserted. The shop flourished throughout the first half of the 20th century and survived air raids during the Second World War. In 1947 the Ministry of Works took over the building, reinstating the stone door arch, which had been preserved, and the undercroft's stone walls.

Below left: Faversham, c1915

Storefront and staff of Wale and Company, grocers. The notice in the shop window refers to ration cards registration. There was no compulsory scheme for rationing in Britain until 1918, when sugar was rationed, but cards were issued early in the conflict so that the government was prepared for all eventualities.

HERNE BAY

Below: The Downs, c1900

Looking out to sea with the pier in the distance, as people enjoy a band playing in the open bandstand. A shelter to the right offers protection from harsher weather. At this time a steamer service operated from London to Herne Bay, which was little more than a hamlet until it developed as a resort. The third pier, completed around the turn of the century, was the second longest in the country after Southend. It spanned the shallow shoreline to deeper waters beyond to allow access by steamers.

WHITSTABLE

Top: High Street, c1900
The Duke of Cumberland Hotel sits at the end of the street at the junction with Harbour Street and Horsebridge Street. Once called the Hart Inn, it dates from the early 17th century and was the location of the headquarters of the Oyster Dredgermen, who held court once a year in an upstairs room.

Above: Tankerton Beach, c1900
With the harbour and town beyond, the beach seems quiet. In the 18th century Whitstable was a fashionable resort for Londoners, who took the steam packet down the Thames to patronise some of the first bathing machines (see centre rear of picture) and partake of the town's famous oysters. Salt production was another key industry, exploiting the surrounding salt-water marshes and the breezes for evaporation.

CHEMIST

NOW OPEN
CAMERA
OBSCURA
BEAUTIFUL EFFECTS
CAUSED BY REFLECTION
CHARGE
TWO PENCE.
OBSCURA

MARGATE

Margate, c1900
Opposite above: An afternoon view looking west along the promenade towards Market Street with the White Hart Hotel to the left. At this hour the seafront is a hive of activity with horse-drawn omnibuses and carriages. Street vendors are at work: shoes are being blacked, and an ice cream seller stands by the kerb in the centre of the picture.

Above: A similar view taken from further west along the front. Peak afternoon crowds are milling on the promenade, most walking but many using horse-drawn vehicles; a miniature goat-drawn carriage is being led in the middle right of the picture.

Opposite below: The Iron Pier, c1900
In the foreground, at the start of the pier, which was designed by Eugenius Birch, a camera obscura is open for business. South of the pierhead, on either side, are two slipways with lifeboats ready to launch. These operated from the 1890s until the eastern slipway was finally damaged beyond repair in a huge storm in 1978.

Above: Newgate Gap, Margate, c1900
The Gap was originally cut as an access for farmers to allow them to gather seaweed to fertilise their fields. In the 19th century, with the growth of tourism, it became more important for access to the beach for leisure. The Gap split the promenade, so in 1861 a wealthy landowner, Captain Hodges, funded the building of a footbridge.

BROADSTAIRS

Top left: Viking Bay, c1900
Three Thames sailing barges are moored in Viking Bay, while two men in the foreground are loading carts with sand. Bathing huts can be seen in the background, standing on the shoreline. The barges, likely to be from the River Medway or the Thames, have probably delivered building materials for the growing seaside town. With their lee boards drawn up, the flat-bottomed barges could get close to the shore.

Top right: Bleak House, Fort Road, c1900
Standing on the cliffs and originally built as a fort in the 1790s, this imposing house became the seaside home of Charles Dickens in the early 19th century. As well as writing *David Copperfield* here, he was inspired to write *Bleak House* during one of his visits. Originally called Fort House, it was renamed Bleak House after Dickens's death in 1870.

VIKING BAY, BROADSTAIRS

Opposite below: Viking Bay, c1900
Ranks of bathing machines in the shallows line the shore, as holidaymakers bathe in the sea. The steep stairs on the right are for pedestrians to access the beach, avoiding the longer ramp through the harbour buildings used by carts. Another set of stairs that ascend from the beach, barely visible in the centre of the picture, are tunnelled into the cliff and emerge to the south of the bandstand. They are alleged to have been constructed to commemorate the arrival of captured French Colours and were named the Waterloo Stairs thereafter. More colourful stories refer to tunnels in the chalk being used by smugglers. The hidden tunnels and steps inspired John Buchan's novel The *Thirty-nine Steps,* which he wrote in 1915 while convalescing in the town.

Above right: Jubilee Clock, c1900
Built to commemorate Queen Victoria's Golden Jubilee in 1887, the Jubilee Clock also provided shelter from the weather to holidaymakers while offering a splendid view over the beach and the English Channel beyond.

Middle right: Viking Bay, c1900
The view towards the south end of the bay, with the Jubilee Clock on the cliff top.

SANDWICH

Bottom right: The Barbican, High Street, c1920
View from the bridge over the River Stour. The Admiral Owen's public house can be seen through the archway. Dating from the 14th century, the Barbican is one of two well-preserved gates to the fortified mediaeval town. As one of the Cinque Ports, wealthy Sandwich needed strong defences; these were achieved with a combination of walls, ditches and ramparts. None of these, however, proved adequate when the town was sacked by a French raiding force in 1457. This coastal area of East Kent is much changed from when Sandwich was founded – Thanet at that time was an island, separated from the mainland by the Wantsum Channel, and Sandwich was much closer to the sea.

DEAL

Top left: North Parade, c1900
Deal, like Hastings old town, retained its character as one of the Cinque Ports until well into the 20th century: a sedate but picturesque sea front, to which one could escape to draw on the healthy sea breeze. The complete absence of cars or transport adds to the air of quiet repose.

Middle left: Old Deal, c1900
Holidaymakers and tourists amble through Old Deal, where signs of its seafaring activities are evident. In the foreground, fishermen and sailors are grouped around a large windlass used to winch boats over the shingle above the tideline. The beach is just a few yards to the right, out of frame. The Royal Exchange Hotel, to the left, is now residential, but none of the buildings in the centre background of the picture have survived.

Bottom left: Fishermen on the shore at Deal, c1900
Fishermen wearing traditional sou'wester-type waterproofs, which differ little from those worn until recently.

Opposite above: Victoria Road, c1900
In the 19th century Deal attracted the wealthy and genteel, as conveyed in this view of gracious Victorian villas, enriched with timber fretwork valances, close to the seafront.

Opposite below left: Deal Pier, 1901
A view from the shore, as children in the foreground watch an entertainer perform in a miniature horse-drawn theatre. In 1838 the engineer John Rennie, who had designed Margate Pier, was commissioned to build one at Deal. Timber piles were sunk, but the full design was never completed and it was destroyed by a storm in 1857. The iron pier pictured, designed by Eugenius Birch, was its replacement in 1864.

Opposite below right: The Pier, c1900
A view looking inland along the Pier from the Pavilion with holidaymakers taking advantage of the long walk.

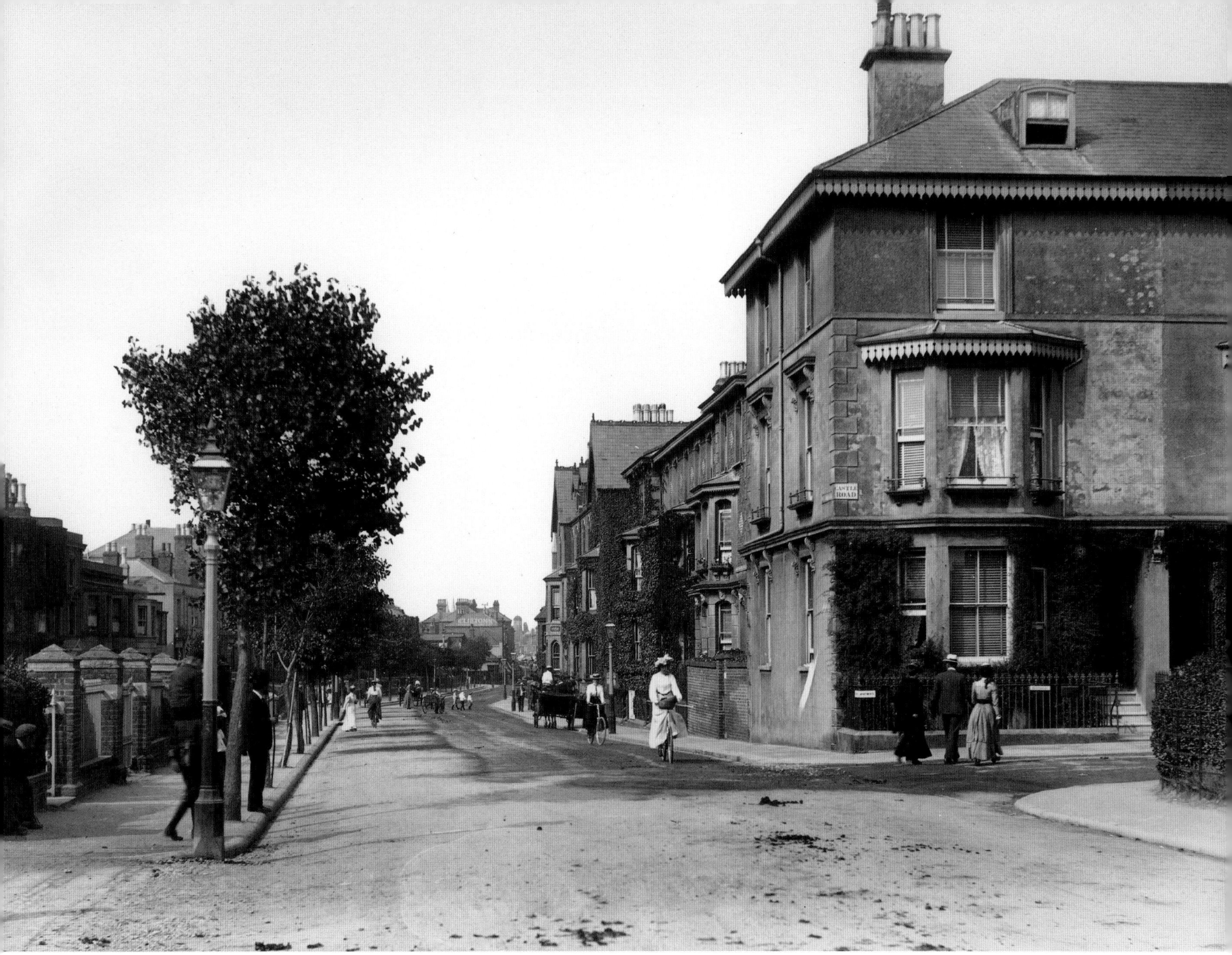
CASTLE
ROAD

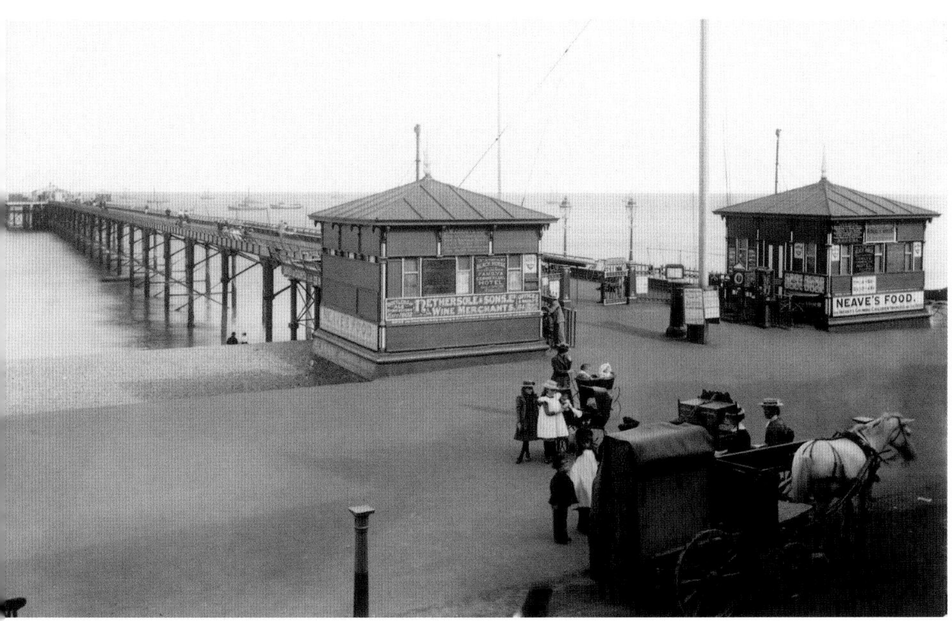

WINE MERCHANTS
NEAVE'S FOOD.

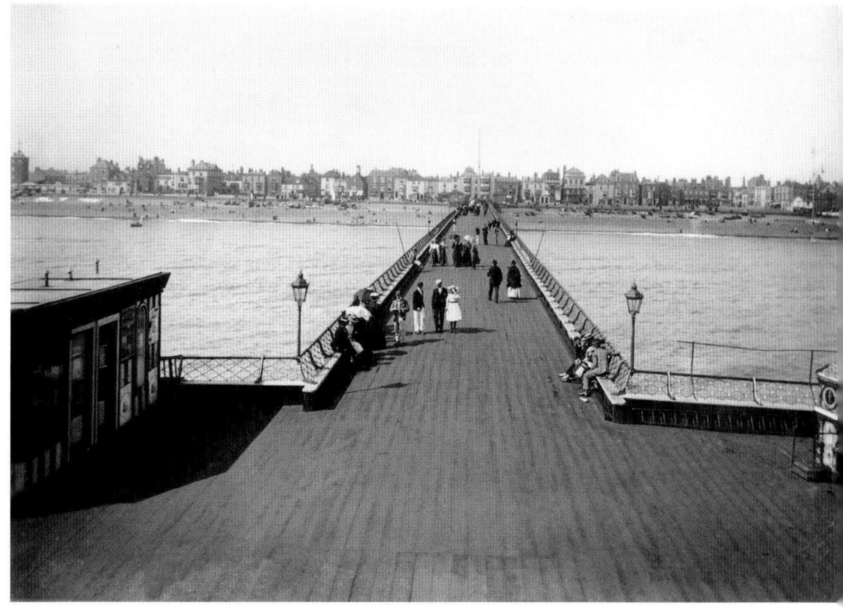

DOVER

Opposite top: The Parade, c1900
Looking across the town towards Dover Castle on the cliffs beyond. Dover is located between two areas of high ground – the natural defences of the white cliffs to the north-east, and the western heights to the south-west. The castle is a spectacular landmark of immense historical and strategic significance. Beneath is a warren of tunnels that were hewn from the chalk during the Napoleonic Wars and extended during the Second World War. The evacuation of British troops from Dunkirk was coordinated from here in May 1940. Today the port facilities are greatly changed from those seen in the photograph: the pier was dismantled, and the site is now part of Dover's huge harbour.

Opposite middle: The Parade, c1900
Granville Gardens had a bandstand, and a restaurant and bar occupied the Granville Pavilion, the low building between two terraces in the centre of the picture. It was closed for the duration of the Second World War, and a barrage balloon was tethered here. Dover was devastated in the war, and the Pavilion, along with all of the buildings to its right, was demolished and the area simply grassed over.

PRINCE OF WALES TERRACE, DEAL

Above: Prince of Wales Terrace, Deal, c1900
Looking north along the sea front at Deal with holidaymakers walking up and down the promenade and fishermen busy on the shore. Deal has never had a harbour, and so the local fishing boats, known as Deal cutters, were simply pulled up onto the beach.

FOLKESTONE

Below: The Leas, Sandgate, c1900
This gracious terrace remains one of the town's landmarks with its views over the English Channel from the cliff top. Folkestone's importance grew from humble fishing settlment to a hub of rail and ferry transport during the 19th century. Its harbour, built by Thomas Telford, predated Dover's by many years and the railway connection to the ferry port made this the principal crossing point for Boulogne.

HYTHE

Above left: High Street, c1900

The Smugglers Retreat, which was demolished in 1907, is believed to have held a light that was illuminated in the projecting upper-storey window to signal the all-clear to smugglers waiting offshore to land their contraband.

TUNBRIDGE WELLS

Above right: Royal Tunbridge Wells, 1925

In 1606 Dudley, 4th Baron North, took a holiday from his unhealthy London lifestyle and retired to the Kent countryside where he discovered a chalybeate spring. On taking the water he noticed an improvement in his health, and wells were dug to make the waters more accessible. This picture shows the original Georgian building that gave access to the well; steps down to the well are just inside the railings. The building was later to become a branch of Boots.

RAMSGATE

Above: Ramsgate Harbour, c1900

View south across Albion Park towards the Custom House and the outer harbour beyond. Ramsgate Harbour, dating back to 1749, was constructed as a safe haven for shipping after a catastrophic storm in 1703. The strong sea defences made it an important Channel port during the Napoleonic Wars; it had a substantial garrison, and large numbers of troops travelled through it on their way to the European battlefields. A fine legacy of elegant 18th- and 19th-century terraces survives in the town.

Opposite below: New Road, c1905

A number 47 tram winds up New Road to awaiting passengers. In 1901 an electric tram service was established across Thanet, connecting Ramsgate, Broadstairs and Margate, with the number 47 service connecting Ramsgate Harbour with Broadstairs. New Road, built in 1894, is today Madeira Walk, part of a scheme by the council to enhance the town by evoking the character of a subtropical island. The rocks in this picture were pinkish in colour, and entirely manmade from a material called Pulhamite.

THE ROYAL PARADE

Above: Royal Parade, Ramsgate, c1900
Royal Parade was part of New Road which ran along the harbour and up the East Cliff. Following the course of Military Road, it was widened into the harbour area by brick arches built to support the roadway. Royal Parade takes its name from George IV's conferral of the 'Royal' title on the harbour. The Royal Hotel took advantage of the elevated status of the port and was fortunate to remain in place, unlike the Royal Albion, which was demolished to make way for Madeira Walk. Royal Parade transformed the appearance of Ramsgate, screening the steep cliffs rising from sea level and modernising the harbour-side area.

ROCHESTER

Above: Packham's Furniture Removals, 41 High Street, 1894
This Jacobean timber building, with its jettied upper storey and grotesque carved mullions, stood at the corner of Pump Lane, which became Northgate. The store was demolished when Jackson's grocers next door expanded. The scene resembles a townscape from a Dickens novel, and Rochester, close to the author's home at Gad's Hill, provided the backdrop and inspiration for a number of his works, including *David Copperfield* and *Great Expectations*.

Opposite middle left and right: Old Parr's Head, Parr's Head Lane, c1885
On the sloping lane leading up to Eastgate from river level, the pub and its surrounding area of fine weather-boarded vernacular houses was demolished in 1890 to make way for the railway viaduct running to the east of the High Street.

Opposite above right: Rochester Cathedral, 1909
Rochester Cathedral, dedicated to Christ and the Blessed Virgin Mary, was consecrated in 1130 with further building work in the 13th century. The River Medway, with its docks and cranes, can be seen beyond, together with the railway line, which runs on a raised causeway above the river floodplain.

Opposite above left: Rochester Cathedral, 1934
This later picture shows the west end of the Cathedral. The clean architectural lines were achieved following substantial restoration by George Gilbert Scott and John Loughborough Pearson. The Cathedral tower, not completed until 1343, had to be taken down and rebuilt in the late 1820s; it was finished without a spire, which was only was reinstated in 1904.

MAIDSTONE

Left: High Street, Maidstone, c1930

View east up the ascent to the centre of Kent's county town. The number of motor vehicles is a portent of things to come and the timbered building in the middle of the broad street is emblazoned with Rootes Garage – buy British Cars. The building has disappeared in the same way as Rootes and has been replaced by a modern office and retail block.

East Sussex

BRIGHTON

Left: Kings Road, c1900
View looking west over the Lower Esplanade towards the Metropole Hotel and the rectangular towers of the Grand to its right. Bolla & Biucchi's establishment at 149 Kings Road Arches offered dining, tea and ice cream. Of Swiss Italian origin, Domenico Bolla and Abram Biucchi were part of a substantial migration, initially to London, in the second half of the 19th century. With large tourist numbers visiting Brighton, these emigrés ran numerous successful businesses that met the needs of the crowds on the south coast promenades. The shingle beach is a hive of activity; the pillars visible in the photograph are capstans for hauling boats and bathing huts up above the tideline.

Left middle: Kings Road, c1900
View looking east over Kings Road towards the Metropole Hotel. The huge seafront hotel, designed by Alfred Waterhouse, opened its 700 bedrooms in 1890. The grand opening attracted over 1,500 special guests, many from London, for whom extra trains were laid on with luxury accommodation. Red sand scattered on Kings Road offered a red carpet welcome. The enduring grandeur of the hotel has made it one of the country's leading conference venues.

Left bottom: The Royal Pavilion, c1920
By 1800 Brighton was well established as a coastal resort offering the many entertainments and amenities demanded by its London clientele. In the 1780s, the 21-year-old Prince of Wales – later George IV – became infatuated with the town after visiting his uncle, the Duke of Cumberland, there. In 1787 Henry Holland extended the original lodging house to form the Marine Pavilion, which the Prince embellished with chinoiserie and French decorative art. In 1808 a vast new stable complex in Indian style, by William Porden, was added to cater for the royal passion for riding and carriage driving. John Nash was then commissioned to rebuild the Marine Pavilion as an oriental palace in an exotic, if romanticised, evocation of Indo-Islamic architecture complete with onion domes and minarets, inspired by contemporary views of India by the artists Thomas and William Daniell. Queen Victoria found it too public and in 1850 sold it to the Municipality to help fund her own retreat at Osborne House, on the Isle of Wight. Just prior to this photograph, the Pavilion was used as a hospital for Indian troops wounded during the Great War in an effort to make them feel more at home.

BRIGHTON SEA FRONT

Above: Brighton, 1900

A view east along Brighton sea front, with the main entrance and clock tower of Brighton Aquarium in the centre. Taken during the late afternoon, the rather hazy photograph shows the promenade still very active with pedestrians and horse-drawn carriages. The Aquarium, designed by Eugenius Birch and completed in 1872, was all that the wealthy visitors to the town needed it to be – ornately decorated with lavish architectural features, and allowing close encounters with sea creatures. The intricate clock tower entrance was a modification added in 1874, no doubt as a landmark for passers-by as the Aquarium was out of sight; much of it was below street level so as not to disrupt the vista along Marine Parade.

KINGS ROAD

Above left: Kings Road, Brighton, 1915

A view along the terrace at the Hotel Metropole. In the distance is what was then the Palace Pier, which opened to the paying public in 1899. The Chain Pier, built in 1823, was the first of Brighton's piers. Essentially a landing stage for cross-channel boats and coastal sailing vessels, it occupied the site of what would become the Palace Pier. After a storm washed away the bulk of the old Chain Pier, construction of the Palace Pier began in 1891; it operated successfully with many entertainments, including a theatre. Now known as Brighton Palace Pier, it remains a landmark attraction.

Left: Daily Telegraph Branch Advertisment Office, Kings Road, 1909

The Daily Telegraph Advertisement Office, designed by Joseph and Smitham and faced in Burmantofts cream terracotta, with the George Hotel on West Street immediately behind it.

LEWES

Above left: High Street, 1888
Looking north-east along the High Street from the junction with Watergate Lane with a horse-drawn carrier's cart in the foreground. Carriers' carts were used to transport goods, and sometimes people, from town to town. A system of regular services was operated by local contractors in all parts of the country.

Middle left: School Hill, c1880
Looking east over the steep descent towards the Ouse Valley and the Lewes Downs beyond. The Temperance Commercial Hotel sign can be seen middle distance on the right-hand side of the road.

Bottom left: Decorative Arch, High Street, c1860
The street is crowded with people gathered for the first review of the 4th Sussex Rifle Volunteers, formed in January 1860 as one of many volunteer corps in response to the threat of invasion by Napoleon III. Britain's small regular army was heavily committed across the Empire and poached men from the militia. Despite the shortage of men to defend the homeland, many politicians were against arming ordinary working men, who might have a different agenda. The Rifle Volunteer Corps recruited from the educated classes overseen by the county Lords Lieutenant. Arches like this were popular in the Victorian period; this one carries coats of arms and the motto of the RVC, derived from a popular song of the time by the author Martin Tupper – 'Defence not Defiance'.

Above right: North Street, 1881
Looking south along North Street from the junction with East Street showing the road and pavements covered with heavy snow. The winter of 1881 was notable for a severe blizzard, which paralysed parts of southern England.

HASTINGS

Top left: Lifeboat Station, c1905
Waves crash against the sea wall and fishing boats are drawn up on the shingle beach to the right, known as the Stade, an old Saxon term meaning 'landing place'. Behind lie the famous tall timber net-drying sheds unique to Hastings, the oldest dating from the 16th century. Beyond the beach are the sandstone cliffs of East Hill, and it is possible to make out the upper station of the funicular opened in 1903. In 1858 the RNLI established a lifeboat station in Hastings, and a new boathouse was provided in 1882 at a cost of £650.

Middle left: Hastings Beach, c1900
Holidaymakers crowd the beach surrounding the sailing boats offering pleasure trips out to sea. To the fore is *Skylark*, advertising its 10 am sailing time along its hull; the 30-ton boat was built in 1852 to meet the increasing volume of visitors to Hastings after the railway connected the town with Brighton and London. The larger pleasure yachts could accommodate over 100 passengers. A popular departure point was the beach at Denmark Place near to the Queen's Hotel. At the end of the voyage the boats were hauled back up the beach by horse-powered capstans, then turned around on a turntable, bow towards the sea, ready for the next cruise.

Bottom left: Hastings Pier, 1880
View from The Parade with groups of people walking along the promenade. Promenades and piers allowed people to walk and breathe the sea air, which was believed to be healthy and a cure for respiratory illnesses. Two three-wheeled invalid carriages – wheelchairs of their time – are pictured being pulled along by men in front of the oriental-style kiosk. The large advertisement next to the pier entrance is for a minstrel show at the end-of-pier theatre. Hastings Pier – designed by Eugenius Birch, who was also responsible for Brighton's West Pier and Eastbourne Pier – opened in 1872.

Above: Hastings Beach, c1890

The promenade and beach are crowded with holiday visitors with small rowing boats for fishing and pleasure trips in the foreground. Bathing huts line up waiting for custom with their horses standing by. The huts were primarily for ladies, who could change then slip into the sea without being seen in their swimming clothes. Although the sea air was thought to be healthy, sun-bathing was eschewed by the genteel. Pale complexions were considered fashionable, and a tan equated with the outdoor labouring classes.

THE PARADE, HASTINGS

Top left: Palace Hotel, The Parade, Hastings, c1900
The entrance to the Ladies' Baths is in the centre of the picture. Sea bathing was considered very healthy, but modest Victorian ladies were not always keen to use the sea, so often salt water baths were built near to the beach. To the right of the photograph is a Bath chair – allegedly named because of its use at Bath Spa, but also perhaps because its shape was reminiscent of the hip bath. The invalid carriage had different designs, but usually accommodated the passenger in a high-sided seat with an extendable canopy for weather protection. A handlebar was used to tow the chair.

The Palace Hotel was designed by Arthur Wells and erected in two stages as buildings were cleared for its construction. The first half was the western section, completed in 1885; this was followed a year later by the eastern half, which replaced a previous hotel. The developers, Spiers & Pond, also owned the Holborn Viaduct Hotel in London. The Palace Hotel building survives, but is now in residential use.

ST LEONARDS-ON-SEA

Above: Grand Parade, St Leonards-on-Sea, c 1890
People walk on the Grand Parade with the Palace Pier in the background; a circular granite drinking fountain is to the right. While Hastings developed from an ancient fishing port, St Leonards-on-Sea – which today appears to be a suburb of Hastings – was created from scratch by the London architect and developer James Burton in the 1820s with fine public buildings, elegant villas and gardens for the middle classes. As St Leonards expanded, the land between it and Hastings was developed gradually; in 1875 the two towns merged as the County Borough of Hastings. The Palace Pier opened in 1891 and experienced a fate similar to that of many other Victorian piers – battered by storms, and losing popularity. Cut in two during the Second World War to counter invasion, it was demolished in 1951.

Right: Gibbet Mill, Ferry Road, Rye, 1934
Gibbet smock mill seen from the opposite side of the Ashford and Hastings Railway line. The mill seen here was reconstructed in 1932, after burning down in 1930. The mill that this replaced was built in 1824 and continued working by wind power until 1912. At the time of the fire, it was a part of a working bakery. The site has been occupied by a windmill in several different incarnations since 1596.

EASTBOURNE PIER

Above: Designed by Eugenius Birch, the doyen of pier architects, Eastbourne Pier opened in 1870. Its first theatre seated 400, and cost a mere £250 to build. The ornate saloons visible along the decking were added in 1901, the year that work on the new pavilion was completed.

RYE

Right: West Street, 1888 Thomas House, the timber-framed building on the left, has been well restored, while the corner house was replaced in 1920 by the brick-and-tile-hung neo-Georgian Lloyds Bank, a most attractive building fronting the High Street.

West Sussex

CHICHESTER

Above: The Market Cross, 1890
Looking towards the elaborate 15th-century Market Cross attributed to the Bishop of Chichester, Edward Story. Sited at the junction of the four principal streets in the centre of the city, it offered covered space for market traders. In the 19th century a clock was added, facing each of the converging streets.

Opposite bottom: Tennis Court and Orangery, Crabbet Park, Worth, 1907
Neville Stephen Lytton (holding a racket) and his wife Judith Blunt Lytton, 16th Baroness Wentworth (right of Lytton), in the newly built real tennis court at Crabbet Park. Lytton was to compete in the 1908 Olympics, winning a bronze medal in the real tennis event, and was a major art collector and exhibitor. Crabbet Park, his wife's family home, was the famed meeting place of the Crabbet Club, which counted among its members prominent politicians and celebrities, such as Lord Curzon and Oscar Wilde.

CRAWLEY

Opposite top: Vanderbilt's Meteor Coach, Crawley, 1907
In 1907 the multi-millionaire and coaching enthusiast Alfred Gwynne Vanderbilt transported 26 coaching horses from his Oakland Farm in the United States to London Olympia for the first International Horse Show. His equestrian enthusiasm led to a novelty coach service from London to Brighton with Vanderbilt at the reins. The following year the service again took place, departing from St James's in London and terminating at the Metropole Hotel in Brighton. At the outbreak of war Vanderbilt returned to the US. He was on his way back to Britain in 1915 on board RMS *Lusitania* when it was torpedoed; Vanderbilt was one of the 1198 that perished in the attack.

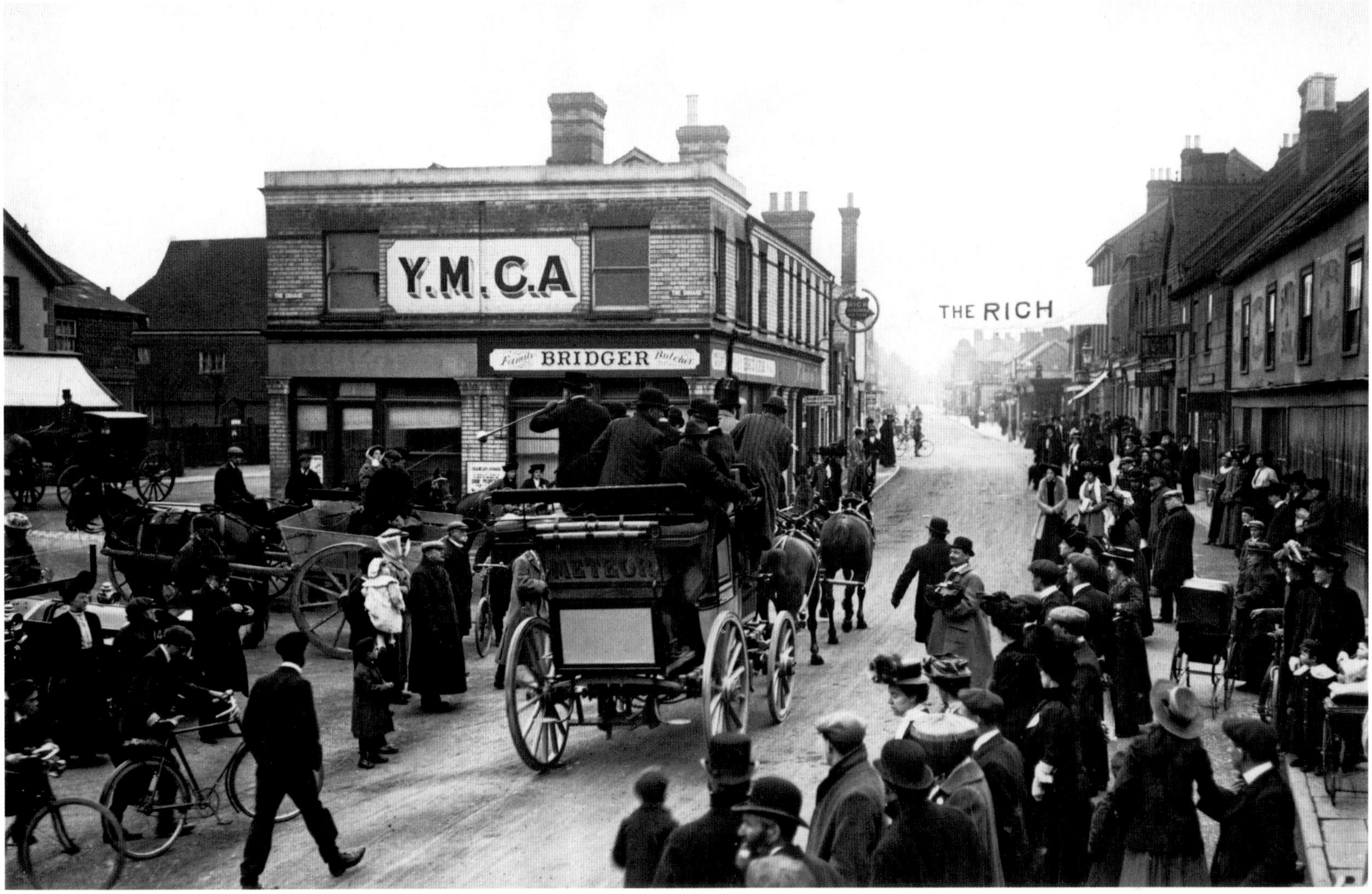
Y.M.C.A
BRIDGER
THE RICH
METEOR

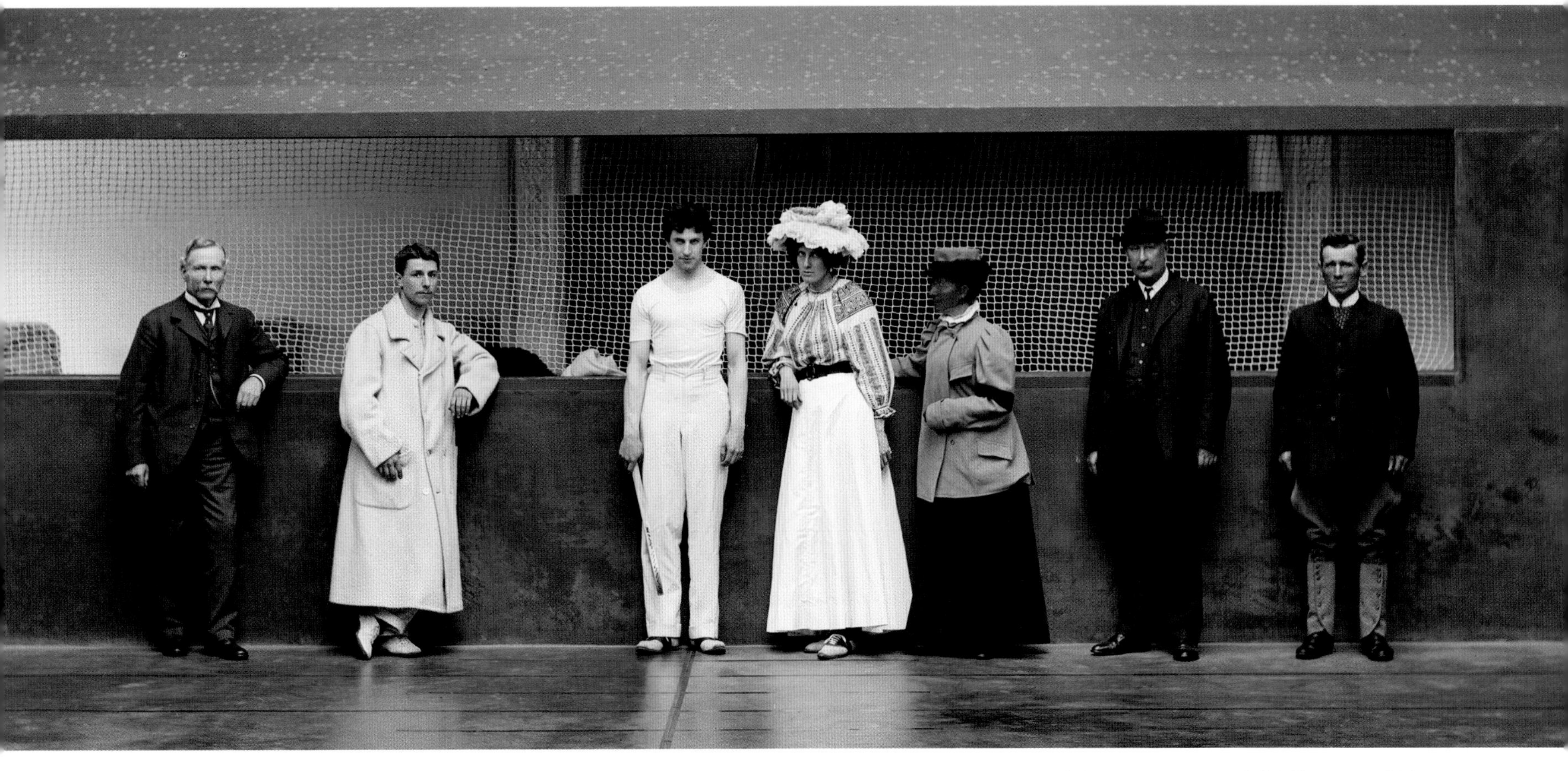

Hampshire

BASINGSTOKE

Top left: Market Place, 1878
A single gas lamp stands in the centre of the cobbled market square where a street vendor with a handcart waits for custom while people and wagons go about their business. Basingstoke began life as a Saxon village, growing into a market town as its population increased. By the 19th century it had acquired a town hall and various industries, including boot- and shoe-making and brewing, were established. The railway reached the town in the 1840s.

Middle left: Beaulieu, 1900
A view along a quiet village street. The Montagu Arms (left) was established in 1888 and named after the Montagu family of Beaulieu Abbey, not long after a baronetcy was conferred on Lord Henry Montagu Douglas Scott. Beaulieu, the family seat since 1538, has been the home of the National Motor Museum since 1972.

Bottom left: The Drummond Arms Hotel, Hythe
Looking along the main street, which connected the ferry to the town, with the Drummond Arms Hotel, a large yellow-brick building c1840, on the left.

PORTSMOUTH

Opposite top left: Portsmouth, c1899
Horse-drawn trams first operated in Portsmouth in 1865, but it was not until the Town Corporation took over the private tram system in 1898 that investment in electrification began. The tracks ran down the middle of the road with ordinary wheeled traffic on either side. A superstitious pedestrian avoids walking underneath a stepladder that leans across the pavement.

Opposite top right: Portsmouth, 1901
Overhead cables for the electrification of the Portsmouth tram system are installed in a residential street. The system was ready to open in 1901.

Opposite below: Tyrrell & Green, 136–150 Above Bar Street, Southampton, 1920
Many shops employed their own delivery teams, from shop boys on bicycles to fleets of trucks. The smart vehicles in front of Tyrrell & Green's department store, waiting to convey purchases around the city, reflect the prestige of the shop and the expectations of its customers.

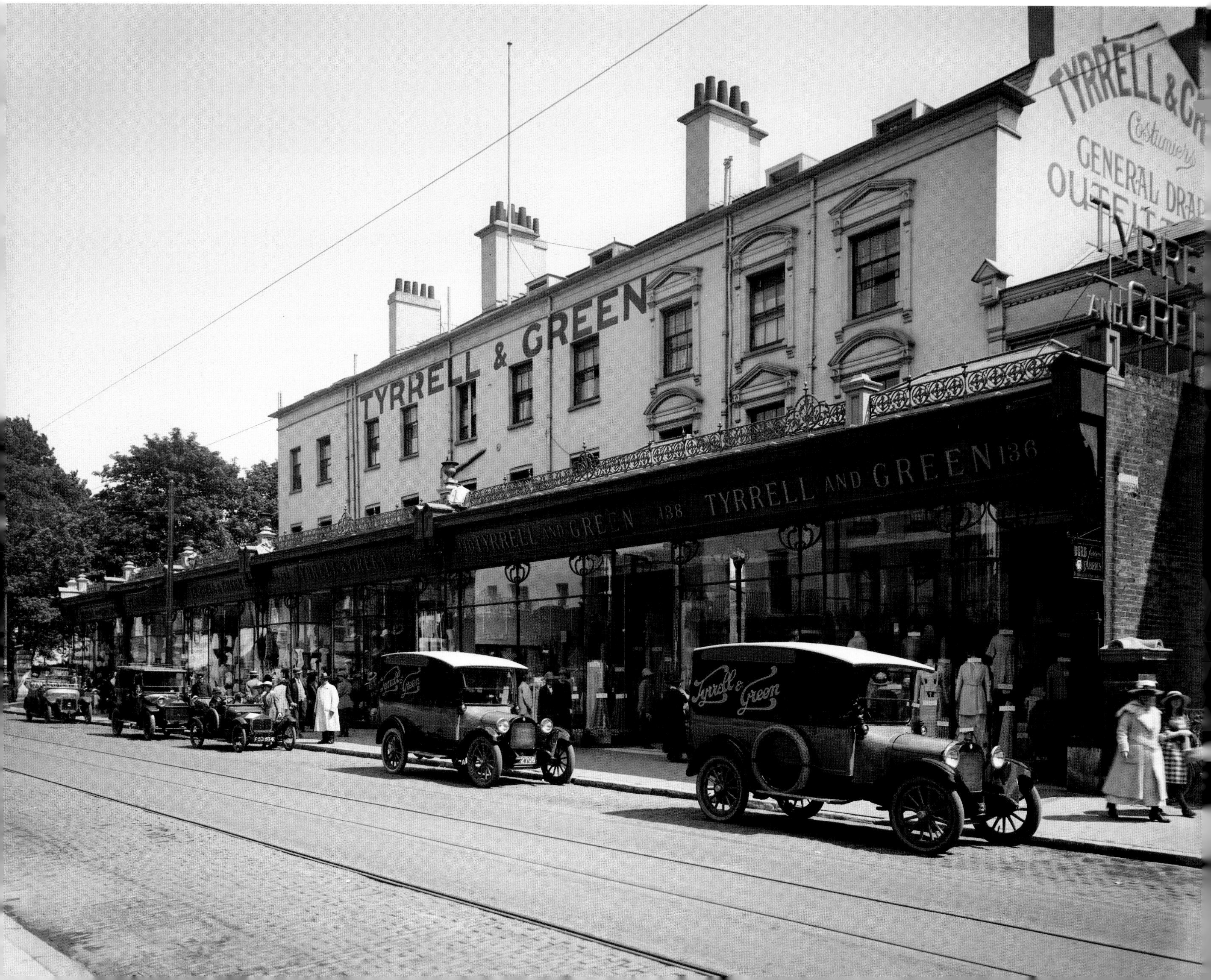

SOUTHAMPTON

Above: West Gate, 1885
Mediaeval Southampton was already an important trading port when, following an attack on the town in 1338, its fortifications were strengthened. By the end of the 14th century the town was encircled by a wall 1¼ miles long, punctuated by eight gates. The West Gate gave access to the West Quay, although it is now some distance from the sea because of land reclamation.

Above left: Bargate, Above Bar Street, c1890
Policemen and workmen pose for a photograph next to Bargate, a mediaeval gate through the town wall. Its core dating back to 1200, it was the main entrance to the town. A pedestrian arch was cut through in the 1750s.

Left: Tyrrell & Green, 136–150 Above Bar Street, 1920
This showroom displays fashionable ladies' gloves, handkerchiefs and other accessories on stands and in glass cases. Department stores began to develop in Britain in the last decades of the 19th century. A large costumier, draper and outfitters department store, Tyrrell & Green merged with the John Lewis brand in 1934.

Above left: Above Bar Street, Southampton, c1890
View looking north with Bar Gate behind the camera. This quarter of the town suffered badly from damage in the Blitz.

Above right: London Road, c1890
A view along London Road, a suburban development outside the city centre. St Paul's church (right) was originally built as a proprietary chapel in 1828 but remodelled in the Gothic style in 1863. It was destroyed in the Blitz.

Middle right: Tudor House, St Michael's Square, Bugle Street, c1880
Two men stand outside this late mediaeval building, which dates from the end of the 15th century. Tudor House was in use as a bookbinders and dyers at the time this photograph was taken. The building was restored around 1911 and presented to the town as a museum. The businesses face onto St Michael's Square, a small market place in the centre of the old French Quarter occupied in the mediaeval period by successful merchants.

Bottom right: Town Quay, 1878
Until the 19th century maritime trade was concentrated at Town Quay, just outside the town walls at the end of the High Street. Even after the first enclosed dock was built in 1842, shipping continued to use the old quay. The facilities are basic: some of the jetties are still wooden, as are some warehouses. However, the two hotels in the background, the Sun and the appropriately crenellated Castle, overlook the dock, indicating that this part of the waterfront was still bustling with activity.

THE PLATFORM, SOUTHAMPTON

Top: The Platform, Southampton, c1878
A group of children paddle and swim off a slipway beside The Platform in Queen's Park. The line of the road of the same name roughly follows the natural shoreline, although the land has since been reclaimed. A row of cannon lines the river wall, and what appears to be a light railway track runs parallel.

WINCHESTER

Opposite: The Butter Cross, High Street, 1906
Originally a 15th-century market cross and restored in 1865, the Butter Cross was sold in 1770 to Thomas Drummer, who planned to re-erect it on his estate but gave up in the face of local opposition. The timber-framed buildings clustered around the cross are mediaeval; that to the right has been dated to between 1316 and 1352. The timber-framing on the facade has been exposed and its windows restored. Its tenants, Tanner & Son, were printers and newsagents.

Above: Jacob and Johnson Printing Office, 57 High Street, 1925
This timber-framed building boasts a fine later Georgian facade, which includes two elegant bow windows. As well as accommodating a printer, this was the office of the Hampshire Chronicle, still published today.

Left: King Alfred Statue, High Street, c1910
A row of children give a sense of scale to Hamo Thorneycroft's heroic bronze statue of King Alfred with his sword held aloft, erected in 1901 to mark the millennium of the king's death.

ALLEN'S.
FOR PURE SWEETS
FOR PURE SWEETS
ALLEN'S SWEET
ICES
VELMA

WINCHESTER

Top left: West Gate, High Street, c1890
Unattended carriages wait outside a shop in the High Street. The West Gate was one of the principal entrances through the mediaeval town wall. A gateway has probably existed here since the 9th century when Alfred the Great ruled as King of Wessex, but it has been remodelled several times. The pedestrian passage was inserted in 1791; more recently the road has been diverted around the bottleneck.

Top right: Winchester, c1890
Viewed from St Giles Hill, Winchester Cathedral stands in a haze in the middle distance with the Guildhall to its right. Bridge Street, continuing the line of the High Street, runs towards the camera.

Above: The King's House, 1890
Off-duty soldiers and children stand around the parade ground of their barracks. Behind them is the unusually grand barrack block, which began life as a royal palace when Charles II commissioned Sir Christopher Wren to build on the site of the former Winchester Castle. It remained unfinished until 1792, when a new use was found for it as a barracks for soldiers. Following a major fire in 1894, it was demolished and a new barrack block built.

ISLE OF WIGHT

The choice of Osborne House at East Cowes as the summer home and rural retreat of Queen Victoria and Prince Albert made the Isle of Wight a fashionable holiday destination.

Right above: Royal Pier Hotel, Esplanade, Ryde, c1900
With its mild climate, Ryde developed into a resort early in the 19th century. The hotel, demolished in the 1930s, stood conveniently beside the entrance to Ryde Pier. The horse-drawn omnibuses are probably meeting passengers from the ferry for transport to other hotels across the island.

Right middle: Market Square, Yarmouth, c1890
The Town Hall, on the right, was built in 1763 above an open arcade to create a covered market space. St James's Church was substantially rebuilt in the early 17th century. Its distinctive attenuated tower was the result of an upward extension in 1831 by the architect Daniel Asher Alexander, the architect of the London Docks and Dartmoor Prison, who lived in the town.

HAMBLEDON

Right: The Post Office, West Street, c1905
The staff of the village Post Office pose with their equipment: a tricycle for delivering parcels, and two bicycles for letters and telegrams. The Postmaster, W E Hunt, stands next to his wife in the doorway. As well as running the shop, he was an important figure in the community. Mr Hunt was an enthusiastic photographer and 'published' a series of postcards of Hambledon and the surrounding area. This photograph was one of the series; others can be seen in the window.

ANNO DEC
VICTORIÆ REG

LONDON

Admiralty Arch, The Mall, Westminster, 1913

THE CITY

Above: Albert Buildings, 39-53 Queen Victoria Street,1899
Built in 1871 by F J Ward and occupying a triangular island site, the main elevations of Albert Buildings are formed as elegant Italian Gothic arcades, which run continuously around the bull-nosed corners. Faced in painted stone, the fifth floor central section to Queen Victoria Street forms a sheer attic storey with an elaborate machicolated cornice and parapet. The building remains much the same today with shops at street level and offices above.

Opposite top: Bank of England, Threadneedle Street, c1895
A corner view of the original Bank of England building with pedestrians and horse-drawn vehicles in the foreground. The building was constructed by Sir John Soane in 1788 on a three-and-a-half-acre site, but later extensively rebuilt between 1923-39 by Sir Herbert Baker, retaining Soane's outer perimeter screen.

Opposite below: Ludgate Circus, c1895
A busy street view of Ludgate Circus looking towards St Paul's Cathedral with horse-drawn buses in the foreground and a steam train on the bridge. The Circus was formed at the junction of Ludgate Hill and Fleet Street between 1864 and 1875.

RAIT HENDERSON & CO
PRINTERS
BOVRIL
BOVRIL
KENSINGTON HOUSE
B. BRADSHAW & CO
ADVERTISING AGENTS
THE STOCK EXCHAN
BELL & PRICHARD
AMERICAN TAILORS

BANK

Above: Union of London and Smiths Bank Limited, 1905
An elevated view from Cornhill looking west towards the head offices of the Union of London and Smiths Bank Limited at the junction of Prince's Street and Mansion House Street with the distinctive steeple of St Mary-le-Bow in the distance.

Opposite above: Mansion House Street, 1910
View along Mansion House Street towards the Royal Exchange with the side elevation of the Mansion House to the right. Between is the Royal Insurance Building, built the year this photograph was taken. The offices of the Equitable Life Assurance Society are to the left.

Opposite below right: West Gateway, Smithfield, 1915
The West Gateway, timber-framed beneath its brick facade, is visible beyond the lamp post and leads to the Church of St Bartholomew the Great, part of a priory founded in 1123. Smithfield was a place of public execution for over 400 years, and excavations outside the west doorway have uncovered the remains of people who were burned to death. The sign on the street bin in the foreground warns 'Do Not Spit'.

Opposite below left: Wood Street Buildings, Fore Street, c1899
Different businesses occupy this block of late 19th century buildings on Fore Street: shopfitters on the ground floor with Traub & Strauss, who sell fans above; Wm Hatchman Umbrellas are at the top of the building.

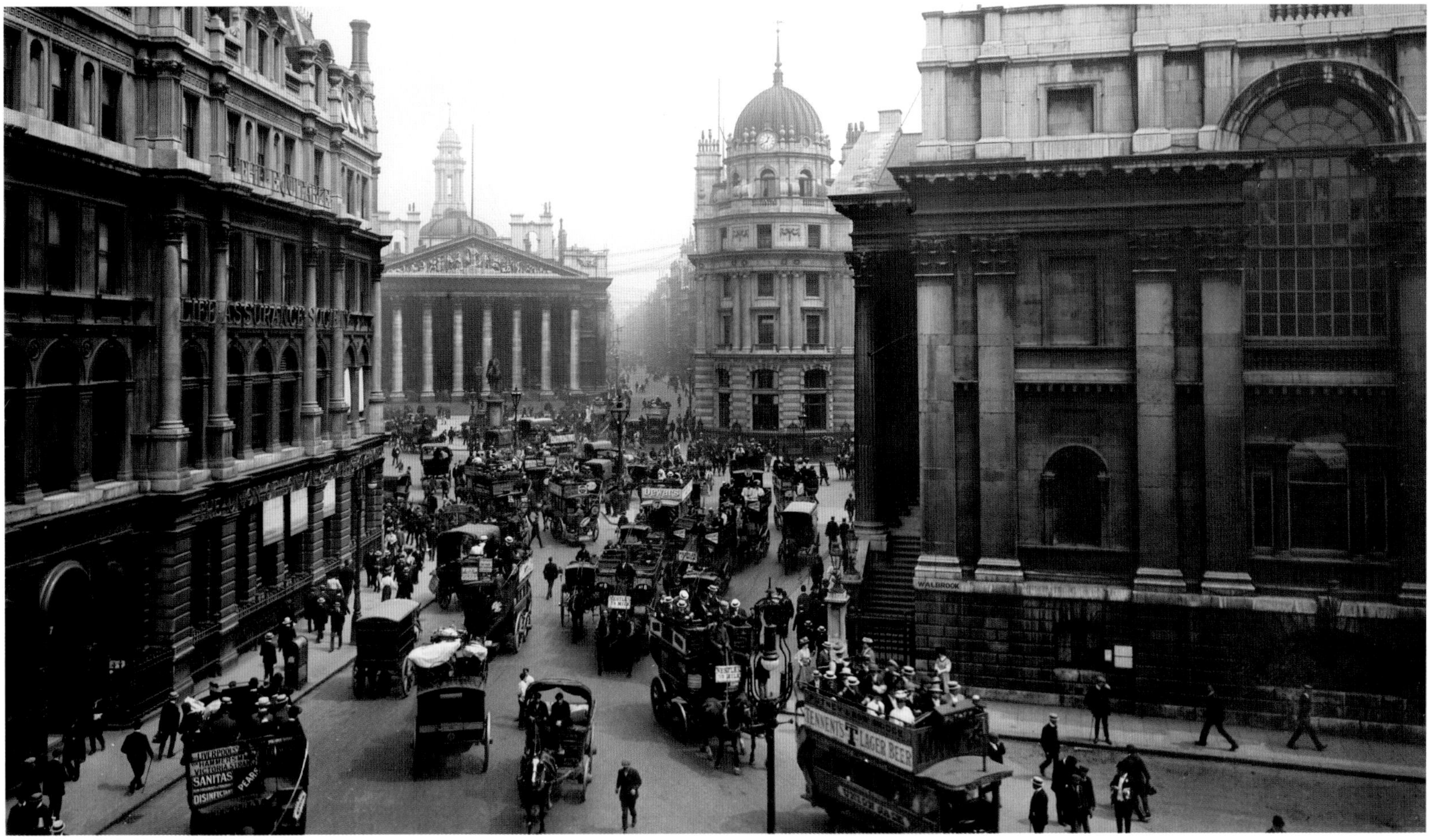

UMBRELLAS
WM HATCHMAN & Co
PEEL, WATSON & Co
W.S.THOMSON & Co LTD
CROWN PERFUMERY Co
TRAUB & STRAUSS
FAN MANUFACTURERS
JACOBSON BROS

EVANS & WITT
EVANS & WITT
57
STATIONERS & BOOKBINDERS

MIDLAND GRAND HOTEL

Above: Midland Grand Hotel, Euston Road, Camden, c1890
Designed by Sir George Gilbert Scott, and a masterpiece of Victorian Gothic architecture, the completed hotel opened in 1876, but by 1935 its reputation had declined and it was closed and used as railway offices. In one of the most ambitious and visionary conservation projects of the last 30 years, it was eventually fully restored as a five-star luxury hotel and apartments and re-opened in 2011 as the St Pancras Renaissance Hotel.

ST PANCRAS STATION

Top right: St Pancras Station, Euston Road, c1895

Heroic railway engineering. Designed by W H Barlow and R M Ordish for the Midland Railway Company, when the station opened in 1868 the span of the parabolic iron vault of the train shed was the largest in the world.

EUSTON STATION

Above right: Euston Station, Euston Road, c1895

Planned by Robert Stephenson for the London end of his London to Birmingham Railway, Euston Station opened in 1837; the first mainline terminus in a capital city anywhere in the world, its entrance triumphantly heralded by the colossal Euston Arch designed by Philip Hardwick. Despite a protracted campaign to preserve the Arch during reconstruction of the station, its demolition in 1961 and the subsequent outcry was a landmark in the development of the modern conservation movement in Britain.

MIDLAND RAILWAY
EXCURSION OFFICE
MIDLAND COMPANY
MIDLAND
BURTON

ST PANCRAS HOTEL

Opposite: Midland Grand Hotel, Euston Road, c1910
Gilbert Scott's masterpiece viewed from the east showing the iconic clock tower and figure of Britannia on the stepped gable to its right.

LIVERPOOL STREET STATION

Above: Liverpool Street Station, c1905
A view from the south-west of the station, which was completed in 1875 to the designs of Edward Wilson in a Gothic style, as the terminus of the Great Eastern Railway. The scene is a mixture of horse-drawn cabs and passengers.

CHEAPSIDE

Left: National Mutual Life Association of Australasia, 5 Cheapside, 1905
Looking west along Cheapside from Gutter Lane towards the National Mutual Life Association of Australasia offices.

Opposite above: Cheapside,1905
Flower girls congregate around the base of William Behnes' statue of Sir Robert Peel erected in 1855, with the tower and steeple of St Mary-le-Bow in the distance. The statue has been moved since several times and is now displayed outside the Metropolitan Police Training Centre in Hendon.

Above: General Post Office North, St Martin's le Grand,1903
The exterior of the General Post Office North building. Marconi made his first public radio transmission from the roof in 1896.

Opposite below: Tower of London, c1900
A view east from Tower Hill with Tower Bridge visible to the right. The Tower was built in the eleventh century on the orders of William the Conqueror and extended by future kings. The White Tower, in the centre, is flanked by outer towers. From left to right: Bowyer Tower, Flint Tower, Devereux Tower, Beauchamp Tower and Bell Tower.

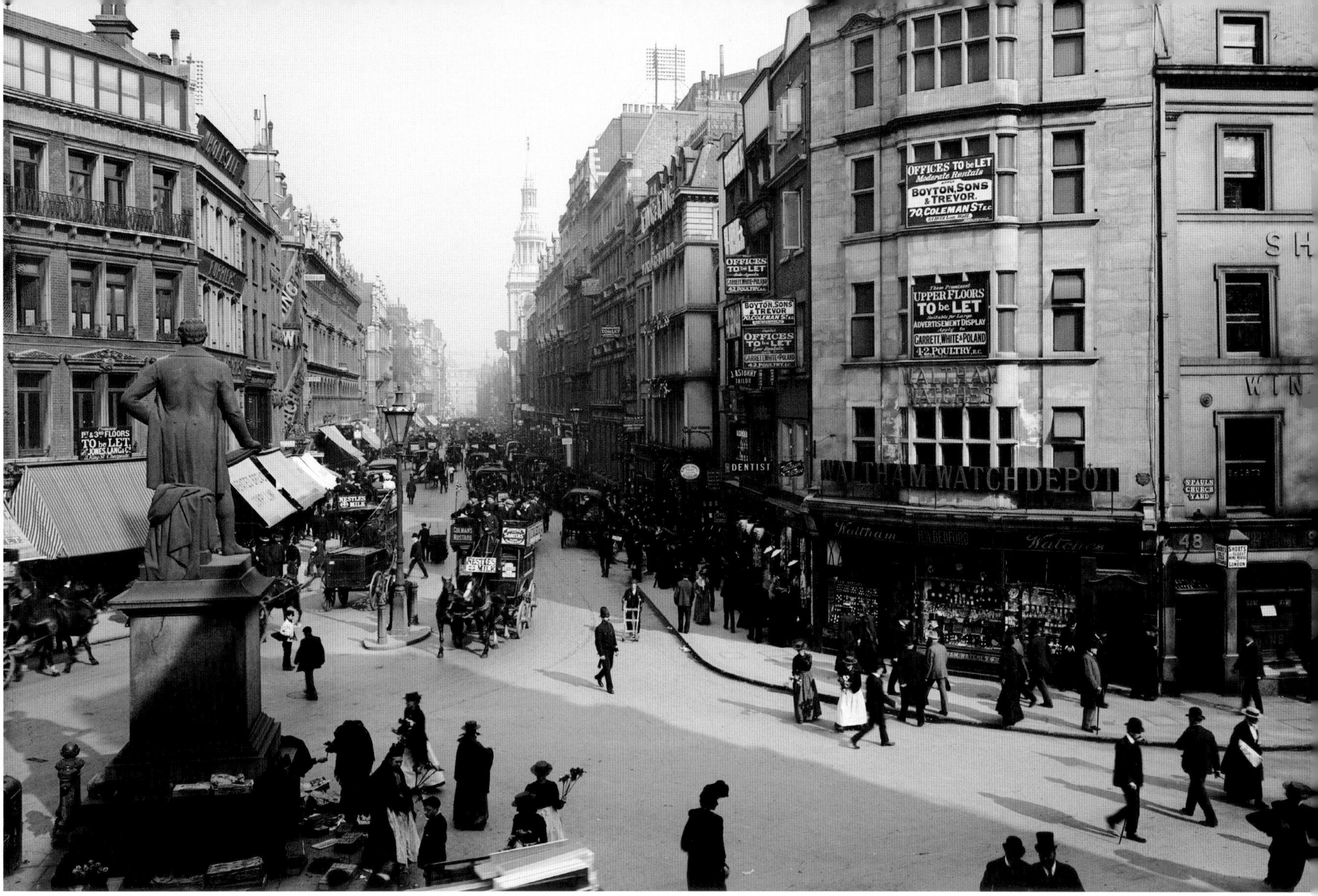
OFFICES TO be LET
Moderate Rentals
BOYTON, SONS & TREVOR.
70, COLEMAN ST. E.C.
UPPER FLOORS
TO be LET
ADVERTISEMENT DISPLAY
GARRETT, WHITE & POLAND
42, POULTRY, E.C.
WALTHAM WATCHES
WALTHAM WATCH DEPOT
DENTIST
NESTLES MILK

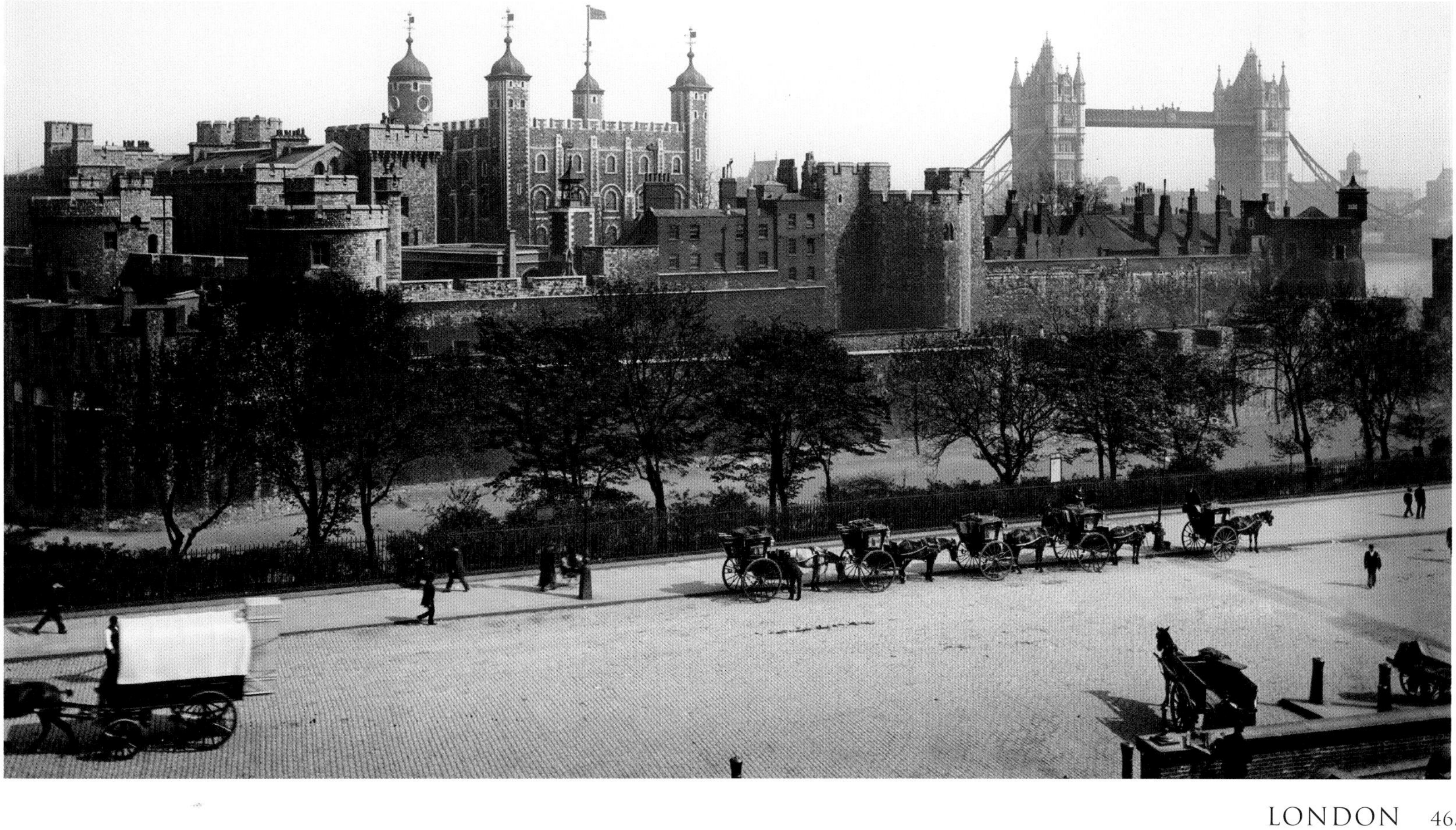

KNIGHTSBRIDGE

Above: Knightsbridge, c1900
To the left is the Hyde Park Hotel. Built in 1882 by Archer and Green, it was originally an apartment block before being converted into a hotel after a fire. Harvey Nichols department store stands opposite.

WATERLOO PLACE

Opposite below: Waterloo Place, c1900
Looking south towards the Duke of York Column on a misty winter's day. The equestrian statue of Field Marshal Napier (replaced in the 1920s by one of Edward VII) is immediately to the north and the Guards' Crimean Monument is also prominent.

Opposite above: Regent Street, 1898
View of the Regent Street frontage of East India House, the premises of Liberty & Co. and the silverware retailers, Mappin Brothers. Liberty's, opened to the public in 1875, was in the vanguard of Arts & Craft design, particularly in dress and home decoration.

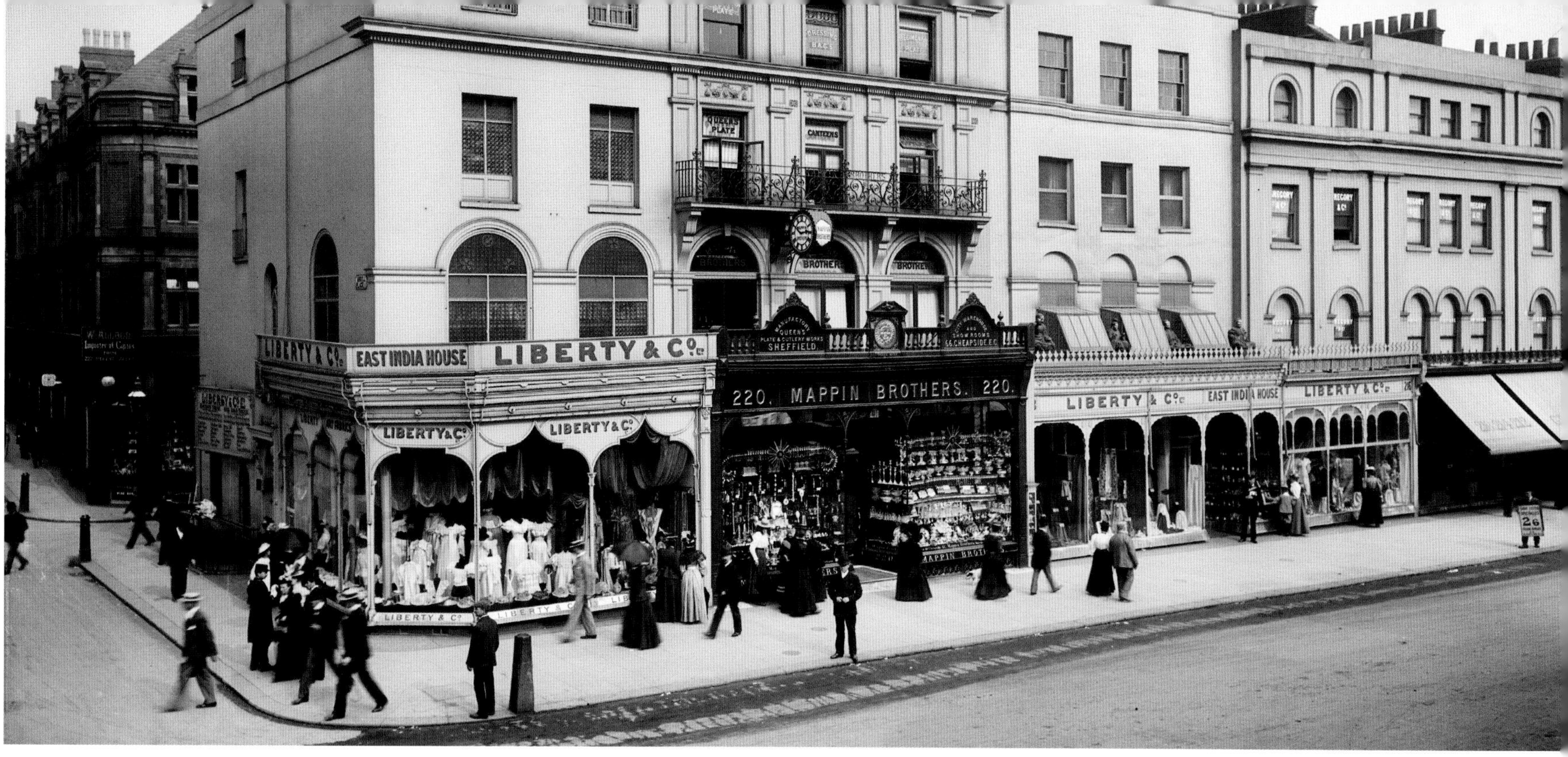
LIBERTY & Co.
EAST INDIA HOUSE
LIBERTY & Co.
LIBERTY & Co.
LIBERTY & Co.
SHEFFIELD
220. MAPPIN BROTHERS. 220.
LIBERTY & Co.
EAST INDIA HOUSE
LIBERTY & Co.

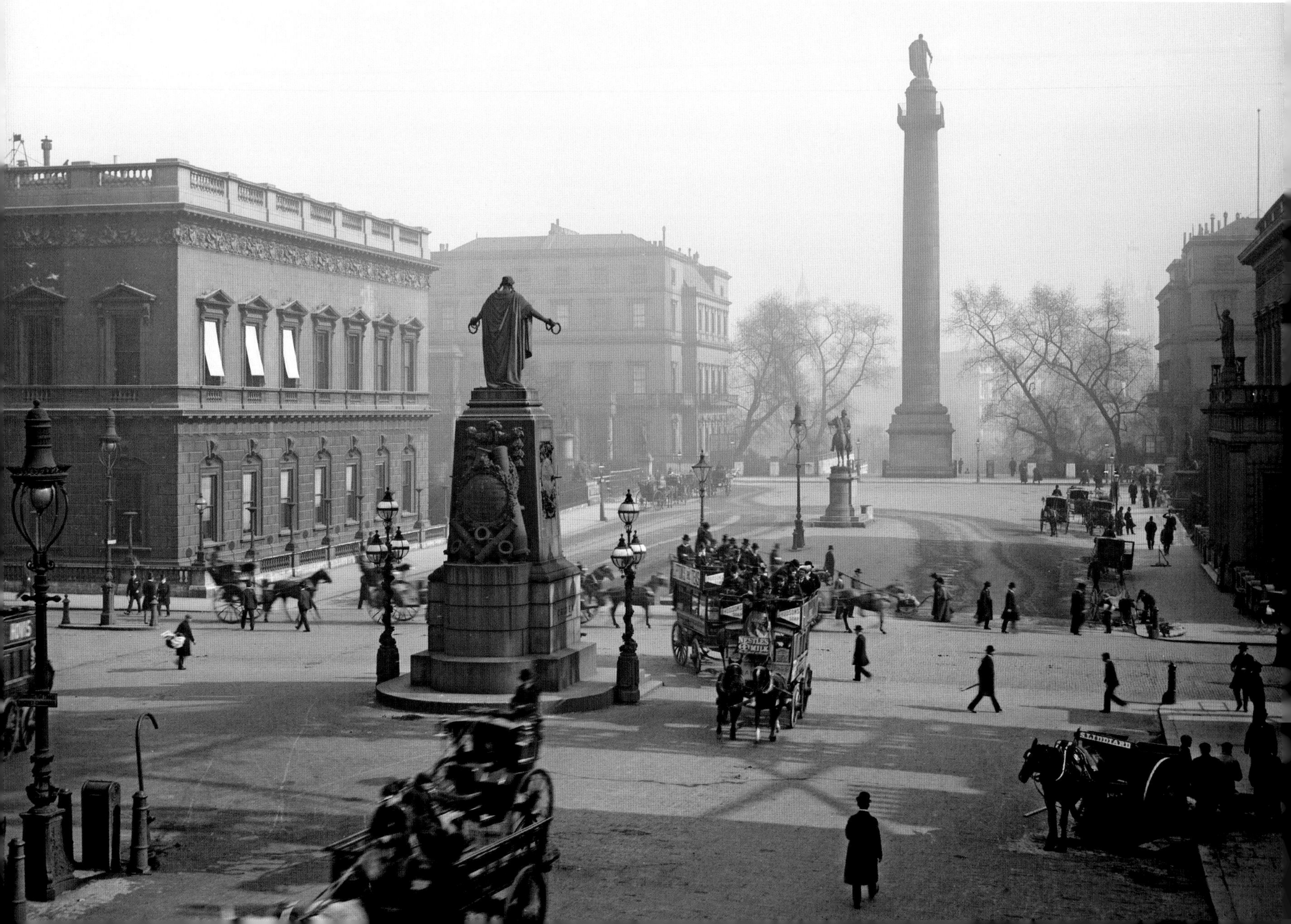

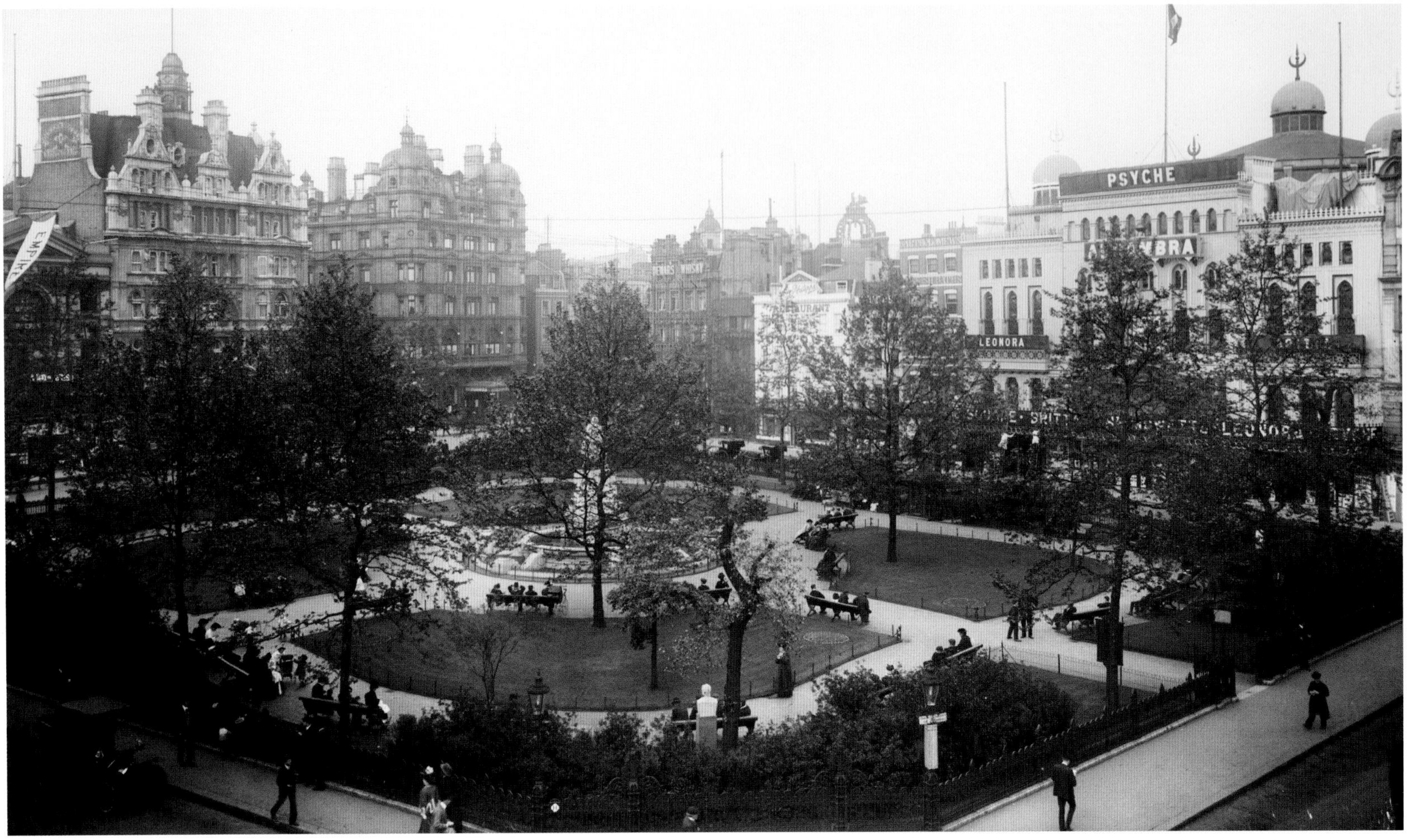
PSYCHE
LEONORA

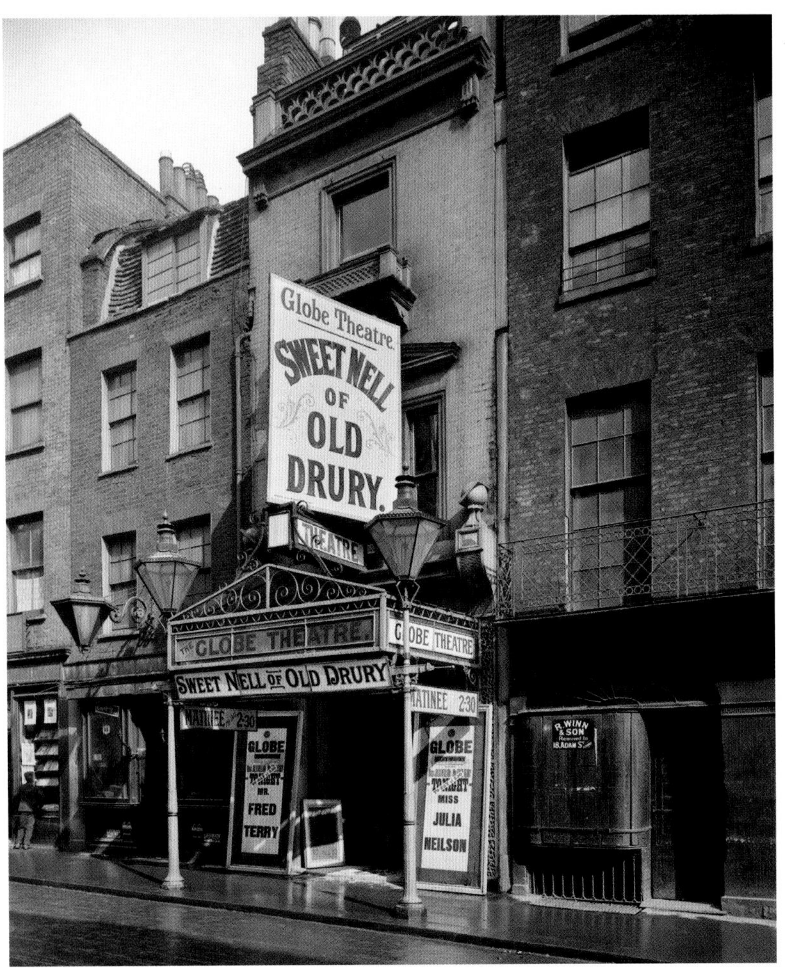

Globe Theatre.
SWEET NELL OF OLD DRURY.
THEATRE
THE GLOBE THEATRE
GLOBE THEATRE
SWEET NELL OF OLD DRURY
MATINEE 2.30
MATINEE 2.30
GLOBE
MR. FRED TERRY
GLOBE
MISS JULIA NEILSON
R. WINN & SON

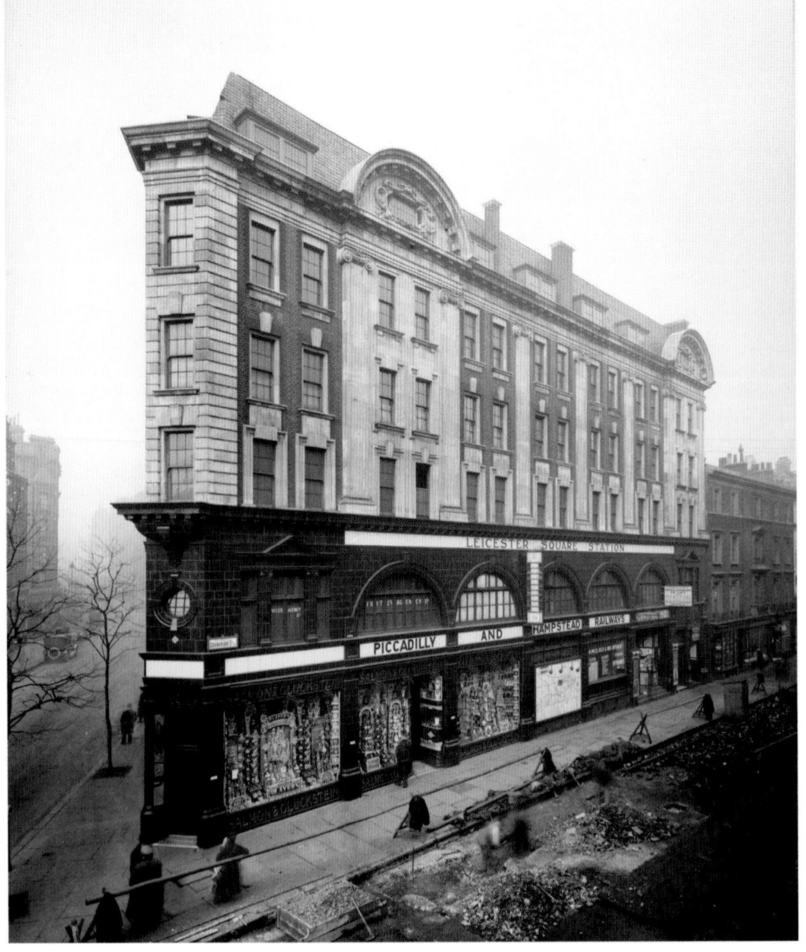

LEICESTER SQUARE STATION
PICCADILLY
AND
HAMPSTEAD
RAILWAYS

LEICESTER SQUARE

Opposite above: Leicester Square, c1910
Leicester Square is at the heart of London's theatre land; the Alhambra Theatre can be seen to the right. People relax in the public gardens at the centre of the Square around the statue of William Shakespeare.

Opposite below left: Globe Theatre, Newcastle Street, 1902
Posters advertise 'Sweet Nell of Old Drury' at the Globe Theatre. The theatre opened in 1868 and closed in 1902; it was subsequently demolished for the Holborn-Kingsway improvement scheme.

Opposite below right: Leicester Square Tube Station, Cranbourn Street, 1916
An interchange for the Piccadilly and Northern Lines (then the Hampstead Line), the building is faced in ox-blood red tiles. The corner houses the premises of Salmon & Gluckstein, tobacconists.

Right: Lyceum Theatre, 1909
A large queue outside one of London's leading theatres where Henry Irving and Ellen Terry both performed. Built in 1834, the Lyceum Theatre was substantially rebuilt between 1903 and 1904 with only the portico of the original theatre retained. After long periods of closure and the threat of redevelopment, it is now a flourishing venue for musicals.

Below: Oxford Street, c1925
A view from roof level. Designed by the American architect, Daniel Burnham, Selfridge's department store opened for business in 1909. Two large radio masts can be seen on the roof.

MAYFAIR

Top left: Dorchester House, Park Lane, Mayfair, 1905
Completed in 1857 to the designs of Lewis Vulliamy and modelled on the Palazzo della Farnesina in Rome, the house was one of the most opulent private residences in London. After use as a hospital during the Great War, it was demolished in 1929 to make way for the Dorchester Hotel.

Top right: The Royal Albert Hall, Knightsbridge, c1890
Opened in 1871 by Queen Victoria, the Royal Albert Hall was one of the key focal points in the development of Albertopolis, the cultural quarter laid out after the Great Exhibition in 1851. Measuring 20,000 square feet, at the time of its construction the roof was the largest dome without intermediate support in the world.

Above left: The Natural History Museum, South Kensington, c1900
A view of the museum from the Cromwell Road, showing its Romanesque facade. Designed by Alfred Waterhouse in grey and cream terracotta, it was opened in 1881, originally as an extension of the British Museum.

Above right: Victoria and Albert Museum, Cromwell Road, 1907
An exterior view of the central entrance and crowning lantern of the south front of the Museum designed by Sir Aston Webb and completed in 1909.

MARBLE ARCH AND HYDE PARK CORNER

Opposite above: Marble Arch, Hyde Park, c1900
Marble Arch, designed by John Nash in 1827 as the ceremonial gateway to the refurbished Buckingham Palace, was moved to its present position at the corner of Hyde Park in 1851. In 1908 a new road, Cumberland Gate, was cut across the corner of the Park leaving Marble Arch stranded on a traffic island.

Opposite below: Hyde Park Corner, c1900
A view looking towards the Wellington Arch designed by Decimus Burton. The photograph was taken in the period between the removal of the original statue of Wellington from the top of the Arch in 1883 and its replacement by the spectacular bronze by the sculptor Adrian Jones depicting the Angel of Peace descending on a chariot of war.

VICTORIA

Left top: 34-36 Parliament Street, Westminster, c1900
View of Parliament Street showing the elaborate ornamental iron railings and clusters of globe lanterns which once enclosed Parliament Square.

Left middle: Vauxhall Bridge Road, Westminster, 1907
Vauxhall Bridge, built on the site of a former ferry crossing, opened in 1906 to replace an earlier bridge. This photograph shows the view south from Victoria with the Little Ben clock tower in the centre.

Left bottom: Westminster Abbey, 1902
Westminster Abbey viewed from Broad Sanctuary with the tower of St Margaret's Church and Big Ben in the distance. The large vestibule in front of the West Door has since been demolished.

Opposite above: Houses of Parliament, c1890
A view of the Palace of Westminster, designed by Charles Barry and built between 1837 and 1858. In the foreground Parliament Square is filled with horse-drawn traffic. On the left of the photograph the river and one of the pavilions of St Thomas's hospital can just be glimpsed beyond the clock tower.

Opposite below right: Westminster Abbey, 1890
A view from Broad Sanctuary showing the abbey porch encased in scaffolding during restoration work.

Opposite below left: 10 Downing Street, Westminster, c1890
Given to Sir Robert Walpole as a personal gift by George II in 1732, 10 Downing Street has been the official residence of the British Prime Minister ever since.

SHAFTESBURY AVENUE

Left: Cafe Monico, 19 Shaftesbury Avenue, 1915
View towards Piccadilly Circus from the north-east. The building was erected between 1888 and 1889 as a swanky West End restaurant and designed by the architects Christopher and White for Giacomo and Battista Monico, who also had premises at 46 Regent Street. Wartime propaganda posters cover the hoardings next door to the restaurant.

Below: London Bridge c1900
A view from the south-west, looking towards the Church of St Magnus the Martyr, with the Monument behind and to its left, and Fishmonger's Hall to the left of the bridge. All the traffic is horse drawn, while shipping is drawn up alongside the warehouses to the right.

FENCHURCH STREET

Below: Fenchurch Street Station, 1912
Designed by George Berkeley in 1854, Fenchurch Street Station was originally the terminus of the London and Blackwall Railway. The destinations served by the station are set into a frieze under the canopy. A horse-drawn carriage advertising 'summer excursions' is parked in the forecourt.

Left: Lambeth Suspension Bridge, c1865
The bridge was constructed across the River Thames between 1861 and 1862. In the foreground a crane unloads bricks from a barge onto a cart.

COVENT GARDEN

Above: Covent Garden, c1895
Covent Garden in its heyday as a bustling fruit market, with Bedford Chambers in the background. The right to hold a market on the Covent Garden site was granted by Charles II in the 1670s.

Left: Floral Hall, Covent Garden, 1913
A crowd gathers outside the premises of JB Thomas in the Floral Hall of Covent Garden for an auction of fruit from Australia. A clerk looks out from a window in the glass and cast-iron arcade, designed by Sir Joseph Paxton in 1858. The glass, arched roof and dome of the Hall was damaged by fire and replaced in 1956. The southern portico was dismantled for the extension of the Royal Opera House and rebuilt at Borough Market in 2003.

TOTTENHAM COURT ROAD

Left: Horse Shoe Brewery, 268-268 Tottenham Court Road, 1906
Looking east across Tottenham Court Road towards the Horse Shoe Brewery, the premises of Meux's Brewery Company at the corner of Tottenham Court Road and Oxford Street. The brewery was demolished in the 1920s to make way for the Dominion Theatre.

Below: Gamages Department Store and the Prudential Building, Holborn,1907
Crowds outside A W Gamage's department store in Holborn on sale day. A W Gamage started a small shop in 1878, and it became one of London's leading department stores before its final closure in 1972. Beyond is the Gothic Revival Prudential Building, designed by Alfred Waterhouse in phases from 1879.

ALDWYCH

Above: Aldwych, 1913
An oblique view looking west from St Clement Danes Church towards the vacant corner site being developed for Australia House. The development of Aldwych, begun in 1905, was still in progress, as illustrated by the empty sites. On the incomplete gable wall is an advertisement encouraging emigration to Australia.

Left: Tower Bridge, c1889
Construction began in 1887 and Tower Bridge opened in 1894, to the designs by Sir Horace Jones, the Architect and Surveyor to the City of London. It was designed as a bascule bridge, so that the central section could be raised to allow the passage of ships to and from the busy wharves of the Pool of London.

Opposite above: Holborn Viaduct, 1868
Looking west to the construction of Holborn Viaduct. Completed in 1869, it connected Holborn Street with Newgate Street. The hoarding in the foreground advertises the newly-opened St Pancras Station, opened in 1868. To the extreme right a young couple can be seen engaged in intimate conversation.

Opposite below: Madame Louise, 266-268 Regent Street, 1912
View across a quiet Oxford Circus towards the south-east corner and the milliner's shop Madame Louise, boasting the latest Paris fashions.

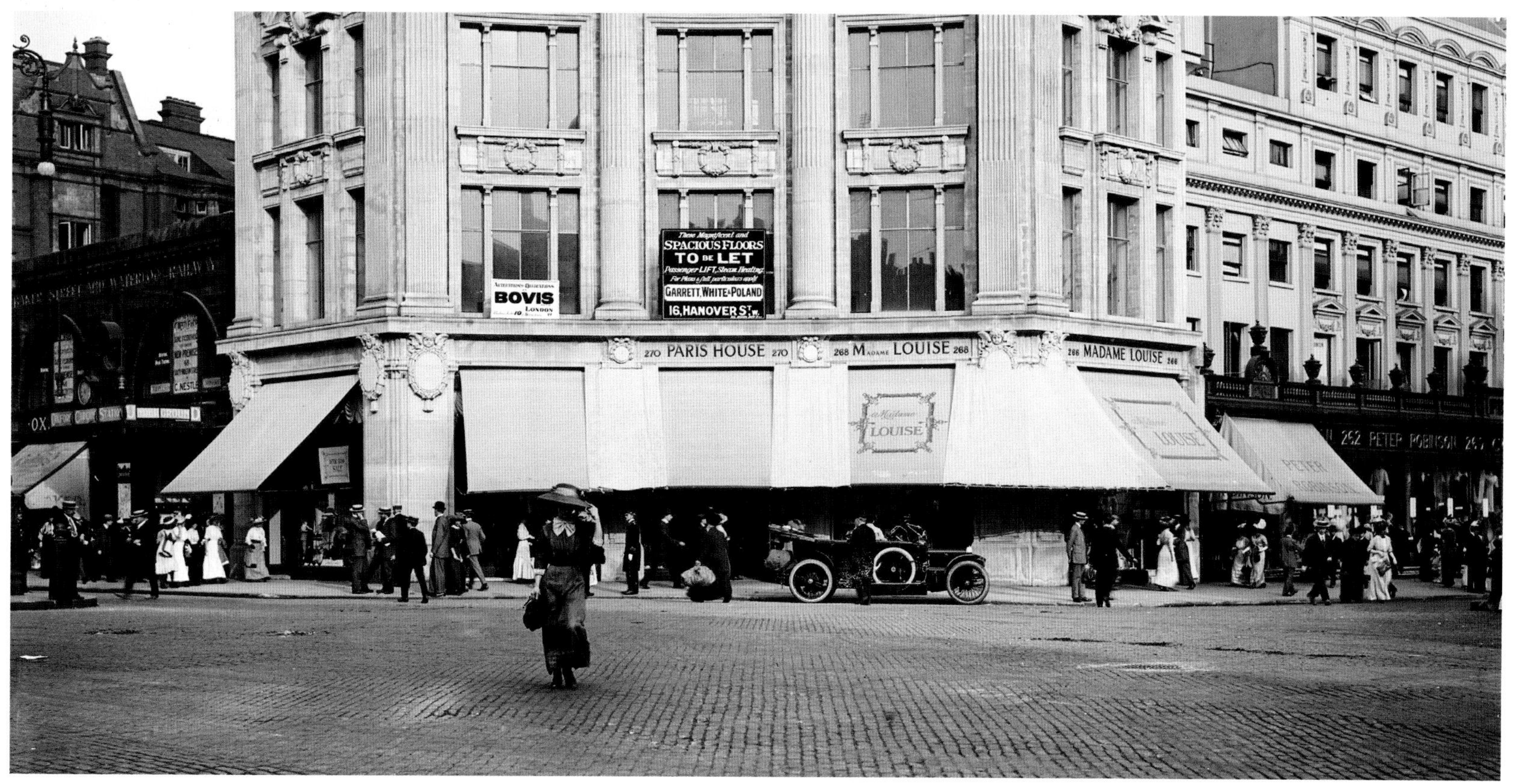

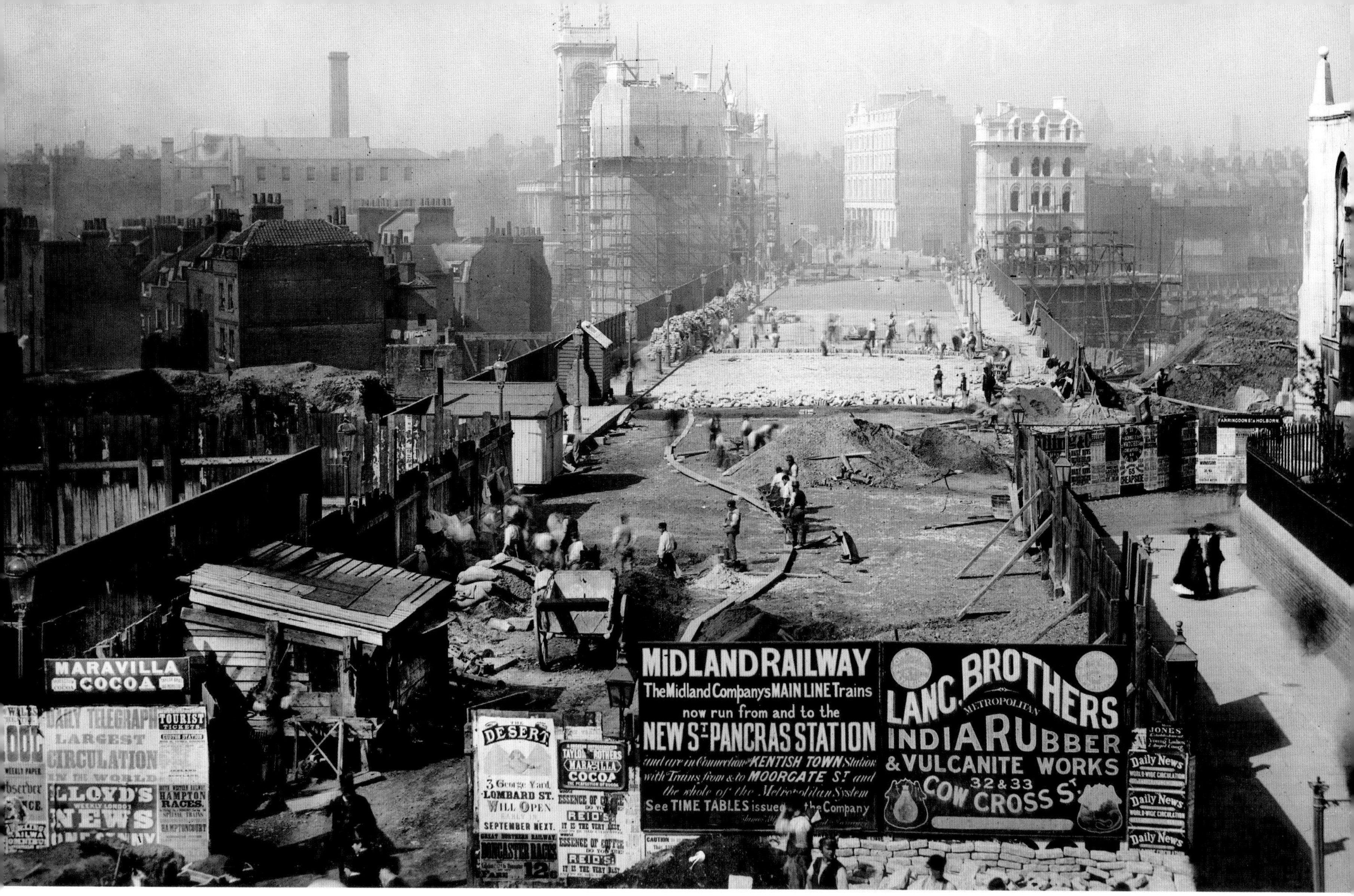
MARAVILLA COCOA
DAILY TELEGRAPH LARGEST CIRCULATION IN THE WORLD
LLOYD'S WEEKLY LONDON NEWS
TOURIST TICKETS
HAMPTON RACES
THE DESERT 3 George Yard, LOMBARD ST. WILL OPEN SEPTEMBER NEXT.
MARAVILLA COCOA
ESSENCE OF COFFEE
REID'S
DONCASTER RACES
MIDLAND RAILWAY
The Midland Company's MAIN LINE Trains now run from and to the NEW St PANCRAS STATION
and are in Connection at KENTISH TOWN Station with Trains from & to MOORGATE St and the whole of the Metropolitan System
See TIME TABLES issued by the Company
BROTHERS
METROPOLITAN
INDIA RUBBER & VULCANITE WORKS
32 & 33 COW CROSS St
Daily News
WORLD-WIDE CIRCULATION
FARRINGDON St & HOLBORN

These Magnificent and SPACIOUS FLOORS TO BE LET
GARRETT, WHITE & POLAND
16, HANOVER St W.
BOVIS
LONDON
270 PARIS HOUSE 270
268 MADAME LOUISE 268
266 MADAME LOUISE 266
LOUISE
252 PETER ROBINSON

WALDORF AND THE RITZ

Opposite above: Waldorf Hotel, 11-43 Aldwych, 1901
The building site in front of the Hotel is all that remains of Wych Street and Drury Court, cleared to make way for the new Kingsway and Aldwych developments.

Opposite below: Leather Lane, Holborn, 1891
A group of workmen standing on the pavement during the re-fit of a shop at the junction of Beauchamp Street and Leather Lane.

Right: Gaiety Theatre, Aldwych, 1911
View from the south-west of the Gaiety Theatre, decorated for the Coronation of King George V and Queen Mary, which took place on 22 June 1911, showing their initials above the entrance.

Above left: Walsingham House Hotel, Piccadilly, 1899
Walsingham House Hotel, here seen from Piccadilly, stood on the site now occupied by the Ritz Hotel. It was built in 1887 and demolished in 1904 to make way for the Ritz.

Above right: 17 Fleet Street, 1899
The north elevation of 17 Fleet Street, occupied by Carter's Hair Cutting Saloon, showing figures, including a policeman, gathered either side of the gateway to Inner Temple. This rare timber-framed survival was claimed to be the palace of Henry VIII and Cardinal Wolsey, as alleged on the advertising on the façade, but this was a popular urban myth. It was built as a tavern in 1610-11.

THAMES EMBANKMENT

Right: Thames Embankment c1890
Horse-drawn vehicles travel along the Thames Embankment on the north side of the river. Cleopatra's Needle and Waterloo Bridge can be seen in the distance, with Somerset House beyond and the river frontage of the Savoy Hotel to the left.

Right middle: 147 The Strand, c1900
View from the Gaiety Theatre showing the premises of architectural photographers Bedford Lemere and Company at number 147 The Strand. The majority of the company's surviving photographs are now held in the public archives of Historic England.

Below: The Strand, c1900
View from the balcony of 147 The Strand, looking south-west with Spiers and Pond's Gaiety Restaurant, named after the nearby Gaiety Theatre, to the right.

Opposite below: Duchy House, The Strand, 1899
Duchy House occupies a corner site on both The Strand and Wellington Street since renamed Lancaster Place. Dating from 1897, it is now used as accommodation for students of the Courtauld Institute of Art.

Opposite above: Waterloo Bridge, 1905
A view looking towards Waterloo Bridge from a window of the Arundel Hotel. The bridge shown here was built by John Rennie for the Strand Bridge Company between 1811 and 1817. Declared unsafe in 1924, it was taken down in 1937 and replaced with the current bridge designed by Giles Gilbert Scott.

CAMDEN

Top: Euston Road, Camden, 1912
View of the 'Royal Blue' horse omnibus in front of numbers 5-7 Euston Road. The omnibus carries route information and advertisements for Selfridges. The shops behind, including Boots the Chemist and the Northumberland Hotel, are also swathed in advertisements.

HAMPSTEAD

Above: Hampstead Underground Station, 1907
Hampstead Tube Station, the deepest on the network, advertised as 'now open' after the Northern Line, on which it lies, was opened by David Lloyd George in June 1907. One of Leslie Green's characteristic designs in dark maroon faience, the station has separate entrances and exits to avoid congestion during the commuter rush-hour.

EARLS COURT

Above: The Great Wheel, Earls Court, c1895
The Great Wheel, 310 feet high, was built for the Empire of India Exhibition at Earls Court and opened in 1895. It was demolished in 1907, although the entertainment grounds beneath it remained in use until 1914.

Top: Mabie, Todd and Company, 319-329 Weston Street, Southwark,1913
A view of workers standing outside the warehouse at Mabie, Todd and Company, fountain pen manufacturers. This American firm became established in England in the 1880s and thrived until the era of ballpoint pens when production declined and it closed at the end of the 1950s.

Right middle: Parkhill Road, Gospel Oak, 1920
A group of road workers using a Buffalo Springfield vertical-boilered, gear-drive steam roller to re-surface the street outside numbers 72-82 Parkhill Road. Although tarmac was used for road construction in the late-nineteenth century, it was not extensively introduced until cars became more common in the twentieth century.

ELTHAM HIGH STREET

Above: Eltham High Street, Greenwich,1890
View along Eltham High Street, showing St John the Baptist's Church and men standing beside a horse and carriage. The photograph captures Eltham's inherent rural character, remaining a village until the first decade of the twentieth century when the railways linked it to London and suburban development accelerated.

LAMBETH

Left: St Thomas' Hospital, 1878
Originally founded by monks in the twelfth century, St Thomas' Hospital eventually relocated south of Westminster Bridge in 1871 on land reclaimed during the construction of the Albert Embankment. The pavilions were designed by Henry Currey as Nightingale wards to maximize light and ventilation to the wards and to reduce the risk of cross-infection.

Left middle: Columbia Market, Bethnal Green, 1870
The brainchild of the philanthropist, Baroness Burdett-Coutts, Columbia Market, in full Flemish Gothic style, opened in 1869, but it closed just sixteen years later, before being used as workshops by the London County Council. Sadly, this splendid landmark building was demolished in 1958

Left below: Billingsgate Market, 1905
A dockside view showing porters crowding outside the entrance to Billingsgate market. Rebuilt between 1874 and 1877 to designs by Sir Horace Jones, the the French Renaissance facade cloaked a functional interior. The market moved from its Lower Thames Street site in 1982 to a new location on the Isle of Dogs, and the old market building was converted to an exhibition and events venue.

Opposite above: Hampton's Munitions Works, Lambeth, 1916
Munitions committees were established during the First World War to find premises for making military equipment. Here military apparatus is being brought from Hamptons factory, previously used for making furniture, and loaded into vans and carts to be shipped to the front line.

Opposite below: Waterloo Station, York Road, Lambeth c1895
The exterior of Waterloo Station with horse-drawn vehicles in the foreground. Dating from 1853, the buildings seen here were demolished and the whole station re-built between 1900 and 1922.

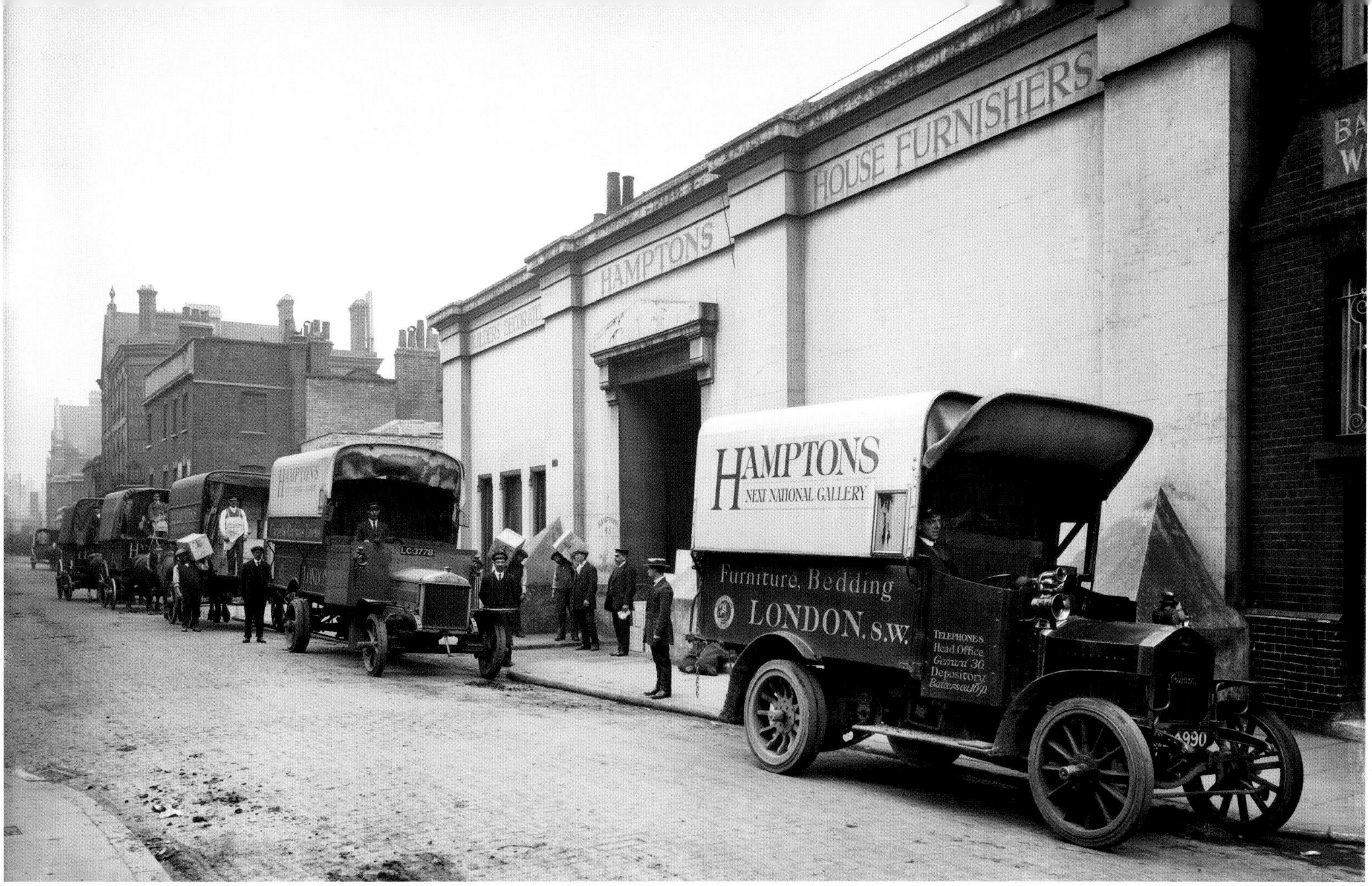
HOUSE FURNISHERS
HAMPTONS
HAMPTONS
NEXT NATIONAL GALLERY
Furniture, Bedding
LONDON, S.W.
TELEPHONES
Head Office
Gerrard 30
Depository
LC 3778

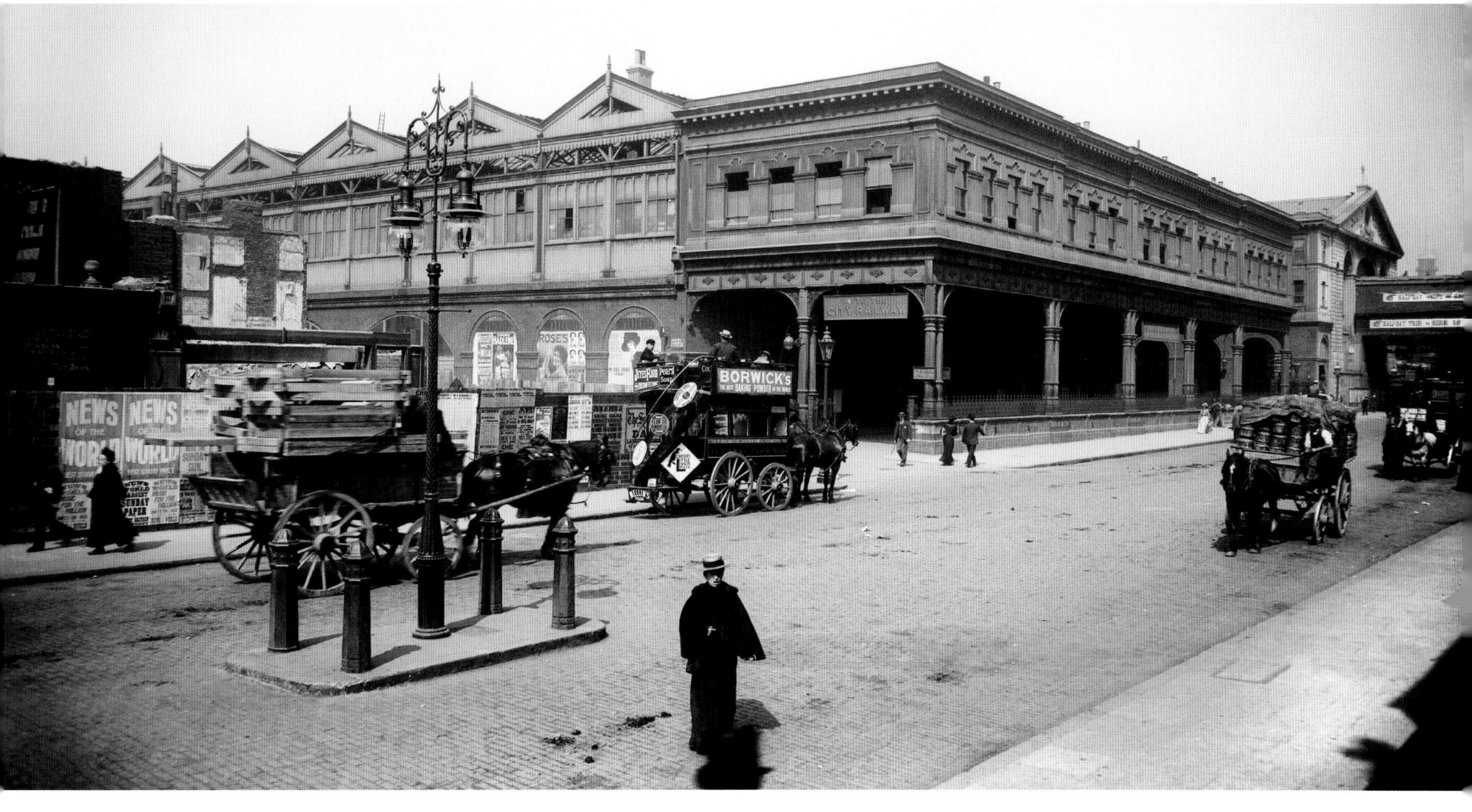
NEWS OF THE WORLD
NEWS
BORWICK'S
BAKING POWDER
CITY RAILWAY
ROSES

Gloucester Docks, 1883

SOUTH WEST

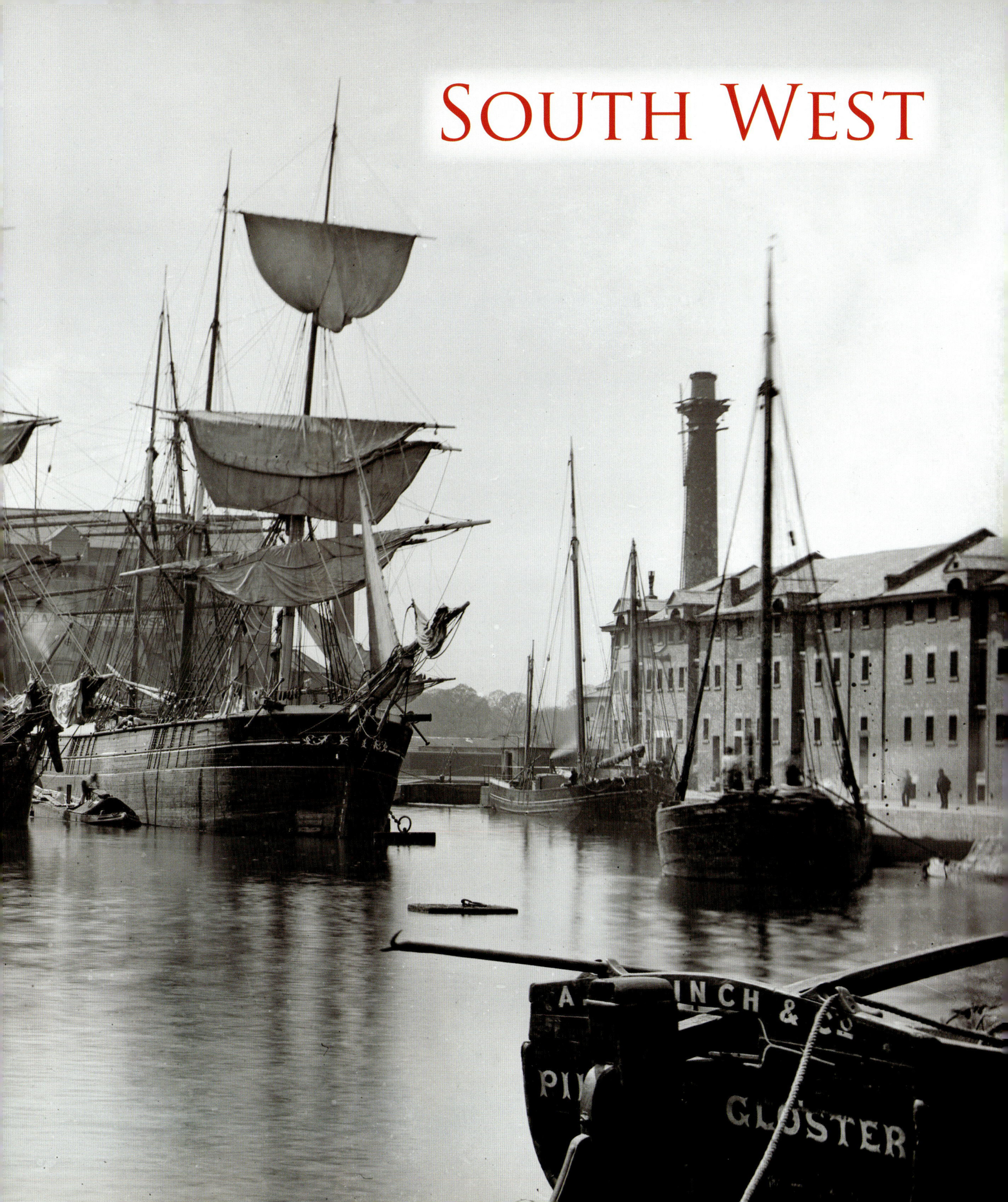

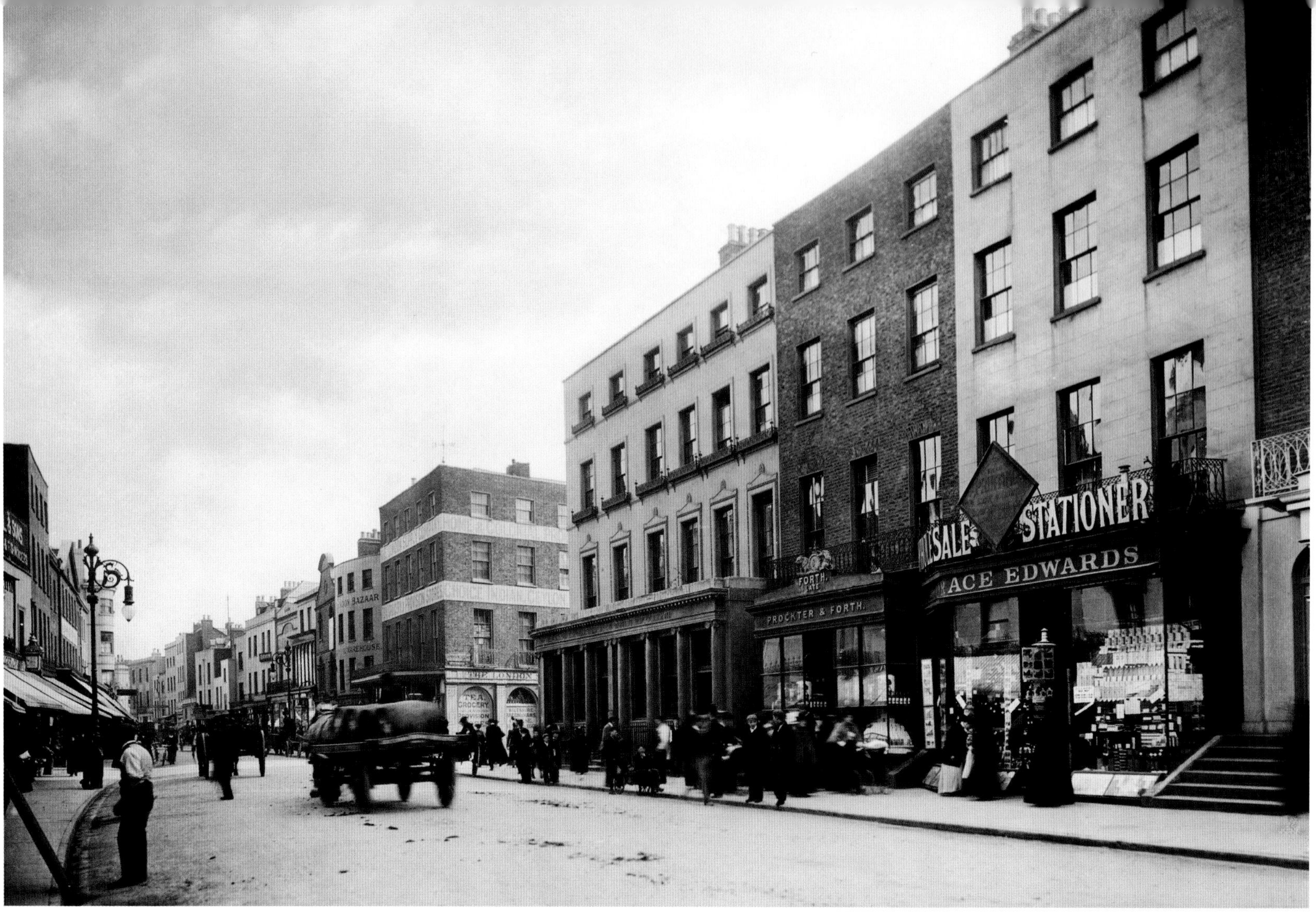
STATIONER
PROCKTER & FORTH.

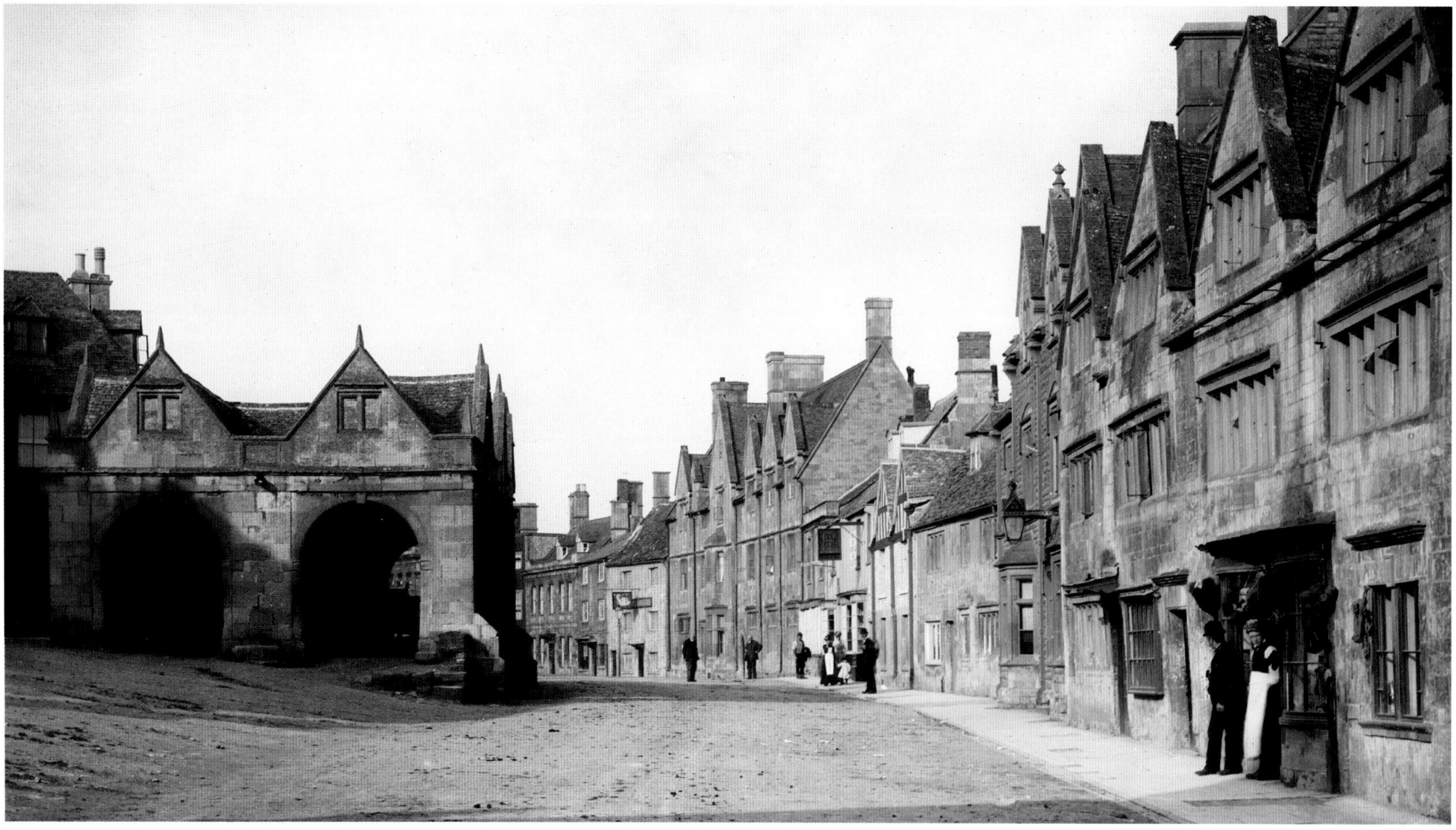

Gloucestershire

CHELTENHAM

Opposite above: High Street, Cheltenham, c1890
Cheltenham's period of prosperity began in the 18th century when it developed as a fashionable medicinal spa. This initiated a burst of building, which has given the town its distinctive character. The central area was laid out with elegant terraces, squares and crescents, and its principal street, The Promenade, was the place to be seen. The High Street was a more functional shopping street. At this point it is broad, and most of the shops occupy the ground floors of plain Georgian terraces.

Opposite below: Market Hall, Chipping Campden, 1890
The single-storey market hall backs onto the Town Hall. It was built in 1627 by Sir Baptist Hicks, first Viscount Campden and money-lender to the Crown, who owned the local Campden House.

Bottom left: High Street, Chipping Campden, 1896
The Town Hall photographed from the market place. Although it has 14th-century origins, the Town Hall was rebuilt in the 19th century.

Top left: High Street, Blockley, c1895
Residents have come out to watch the photographer Henry Taunt at work. A small boy pushes a pram, while two older boys play with a bone-shaker-style bicycle.

Middle left: Blockley, c1912
Blockley is a Cotswold town built of the local limestone. When Taunt visited, its days as a silk town were over. On the left a house with a bay window – possibly a shop – has hung a blind to keep out the sun. A laden cart without its horse stands in the road and beyond is a section of raised pavement. The imposing tower of the mediaeval church of St Peter and St Paul's catches the eye at the end of the street.

MARKET PLACE

Above: Market Place, Chipping Campden, 1895
The small market town of Chipping Campden with its main street lined with attractive 17th- and 18th-century houses built from local stone. Historically, much of its wealth came from wool, and even in 1895 the sheep market is still drawing a crowd of prospective bidders.

UNION WORKHOUSE

Left: Union Workhouse, Northleach, 1903
The Poor Law Amendment Act of 1834 established a network of new workhouses to be funded from a rate on a group (or 'union') of parishes. The new Northleach Union Workhouse was built at the east end of the town in 1836. The poor law commissioners authorised an expenditure of £3,650 on construction of the building, which was intended to accommodate up to 200 inmates.

CHIPPING CAMPDEN

Right: Chipping Campden, c1890

The Floral Festival was a big event in the town's calendar and took place at Whitsun. The Queen of the May leads the procession in an open carriage, followed by a large crowd. Her carriage has stopped beside the Market Hall for a photograph before going on to the maypole dancing. This tradition is one of many which ceased with the First World War.

STOW-ON-THE-WOLD

Below: Market Place, Stow-on-the-Wold, 1885

A corner of the pretty Cotswold market town of Stow-on-the-Wold. The 15th-century market cross, restored in 1878, is tucked behind a group of buildings at one end of the Market Place. The Perpendicular tower of St Edward's church rises behind the 17th- and 18th-century vernacular buildings.

HAMPER & FRY.
W. GRIFFITHS, CHEMIST.
HARMER'S PRINTING OFFICE.
HAMPER & FRY,
TAILORS &c.
INDER, CHEMIST.

CIRENCESTER

Opposite: St John the Baptist, Cirencester, 1885

The magnificent church of St John the Baptist commands the Market Place. The elaborately-decorated south porch, which dates from around 1500, is one of the glories of English mediaeval architecture. The 18th-century buildings adjacent have traditional apron blinds, shading both the shopfronts and the domestic windows above. The first shop, Hamper & Fry, tailor, is still trading. In the centre of the Market Place is a gas lamp and town pump.

Top left: Castle Street and Market Place, Cirencester, 1900

Wheeled traffic in the Market Place consists of two hand carts, a bicycle and a horse-drawn wagon. The narrow Castle Street, which links with the north-east corner of the Market Place, was widened in 1897. The angled shopfront on the corner is John Jefferies & Son, seed merchant, reflecting the essentially rural nature of the area.

Middle left: Market Place, Cirencester, 1883

Looking down the market place from the parish church of the capital of the Cotswolds showing the north side shop fronts with their awnings out over the pavement.

Bottom left: Market Place, Cirencester, 1890

JACKSON
H.JACKSON
H.JACKSON
22
EDGE TOOL
MAKER
CUTLER
PECKHAM

CRICKLADE STREET

Cricklade Street, Cirencester, 1903

Cricklade Street is a commercial street radiating south from the Market Place. It was widened in 1892 to allow two-way traffic. Some venerable old buildings were demolished, and Jackson the ironmonger got a new building with a half-timbered gable. Several businesses try to catch the eye with inventive forms of advertising on signs projecting over the road; Jackson's is in the form of an axe.

FAIRFORD

Above: Market Place, Fairford, 1900
A fine heterogeneous group of houses faces the triangular Market Place. Chief among them is Colston House, an 18th-century building crowned by a triangular pediment. The other buildings are of 17th- or 18th-century date. The church with its famous stained glass windows lies out of sight to the right.

Left: Castle Street, Cirencester, 1901
Castle Street is one of the main shopping streets of the town. On the left two shops are selling cane chairs, while opposite an ironmonger is displaying a range of goods. Further down is a dining room. A splendid series of buildings of different periods line the street, but unified by a sense of scale and harmony.

GLOUCESTER

Top right: New Inn, 16-20 Northgate Street, Gloucester, 1892
The New Inn, built in around 1450 by St Peter's Abbey (now the cathedral) as a hostel for pilgrims, was constructed around a central courtyard with an open gallery at first-floor level. The carriageway would have allowed access for horses and ponies. It remains a remarkably complete example of a courtyard inn.

Middle right: Gloucester Docks, c1930
Large sea-going vessels mingle here with barges and tugs; the 'workhorses' of the canals. The depth of the canal made direct links from Gloucester to the sea possible.

Bottom right: Timber yard, Gloucester Docks, c1925
Timber was imported from as far afield as Scandinavia and Canada. It was stacked in the open to dry and loaded onto railway trucks for distribution. The ancient tower of Gloucester Cathedral challenges the various industrial chimneys on the skyline.

Above: 100 Church Street (Mrs Betteridge's House), Tewkesbury, c1875
This handsome timber-framed merchant's house probably dates from the 16th century, although it was remodelled a century later and bears a date of 1664. The shop at street level is a tailor's.

LECHLADE

Left: Swan Hotel, Burford Street, Lechlade, c1900

Lechlade lies at the highest navigable point on the Thames and was the starting point of the Thames & Severn canal. It was also the site of an important ferry, and later a toll bridge. Consequently, it was a town of prosperous merchants. The Swan Hotel was built as a house in the mid-17th century. Note its elegant 18th-century bow-fronted neighbour.

MORETON-IN-MARSH

Opposite bottom: Redesdale Hall, Moreton-in-Marsh, c1887
Redesdale Hall occupies an island site in the broad High Street, part of the Fosse Way, one of the ancient roads of England. Built by Lord Redesdale in 1887, the year of Victoria's Golden Jubilee, the impressive hall on the first floor has a magnificent ceiling of exposed oak beams. The open arcade on the ground floor has since been infilled to create a second meeting hall. On the corner of Oxford Street, the small 16th-century Curfew Tower houses a bell that used to be tolled every evening. The White Hart Royal Hotel, to the right, dates from 1782.

THAMES & SEVERN CANAL

Thames & Severn Canal, Siddington, 1904
In 1783 an Act was passed for a canal to link the headwaters of the Thames with the River Severn, from Lechlade to Wallbridge, which involved crossing the Cotswolds at a cost of £200,000. It was a phenomenal feat of engineering, and opened in 1789. Here the canal is being restored before its reopening in 1904.

Top right: Labourers making puddling clay, probably in the clay pits at Blue House. This clay mix provided a watertight lining for the canal. A steam engine and temporary tramway are being used.

Top left: Work on a section of the canal at Blue House Reach.

Above left: Labourers dig clay from the large pit at Blue House.

Above right: Thames & Severn Canal, Sapperton Tunnel, Coates, 1904
The Coates portal or entrance to the tunnel, which stretches for just over 2 miles to re-emerge at Daneway Portal, Sapperton. Completed in 1789, it took five years to excavate – by hand and using explosives. A number of lives were lost during its construction.

Avon

BATH

Above left: The Cross Bath, Bath Street, c1900
Bath has long been known for its curative waters. The pocket-sized Cross Bath was constructed around a Roman pool fed by its own hot spring, and has been modified and rebuilt several times. The curved Classical portico seen here forms an attractive focus at the end of Bath Street, having outlived its therapeutic function.

Top right: Assembly Rooms, Bennett Street, 1891
The Assembly Rooms, completed in 1771, were designed by John Wood the Younger and funded by tontine subscription (in which the last surviving subscriber gains all the shares). Comprising four rooms – the Great Octagon, the Tea Room, the Ball Room and the Card Room – they proved a huge success and quickly became the centre of Bath society. This photograph shows the ballroom soon after it was redecorated by the Cotterell Brothers. The Assembly Rooms were gutted by incendiaries in 1942, but eventually restored to their 18th-century glory.

Above right: Laura Place, 1892
This impressive fountain was designed in 1877 by A S Goodridge, the son of a local Bath architect, but its superstructure was removed in 1948 leaving just the circular stone basin.

Opposite top: Milsom Street, c1900
Milsom Street climbs gently from the old town towards the residential streets around the Circus. The development is typically Georgian. Halfway along on the right the bowed facade of Somerset Buildings can be seen. Huntley, on the corner with Quiet Street, is described in *Kelly's Directory* as a 'provision merchant'.

Opposite bottom: The Guildhall, High Street, 1898
Growing civic pride was often expressed in grand public buildings, and Bath was no exception. In a city already rich in Classical-style architecture, Thomas Baldwin produced an elegant building in the Palladian style, completed in 1778. In the 1890s it was hugely enlarged by the addition of wings to either side; the southern wing had just been completed when this photograph was taken.

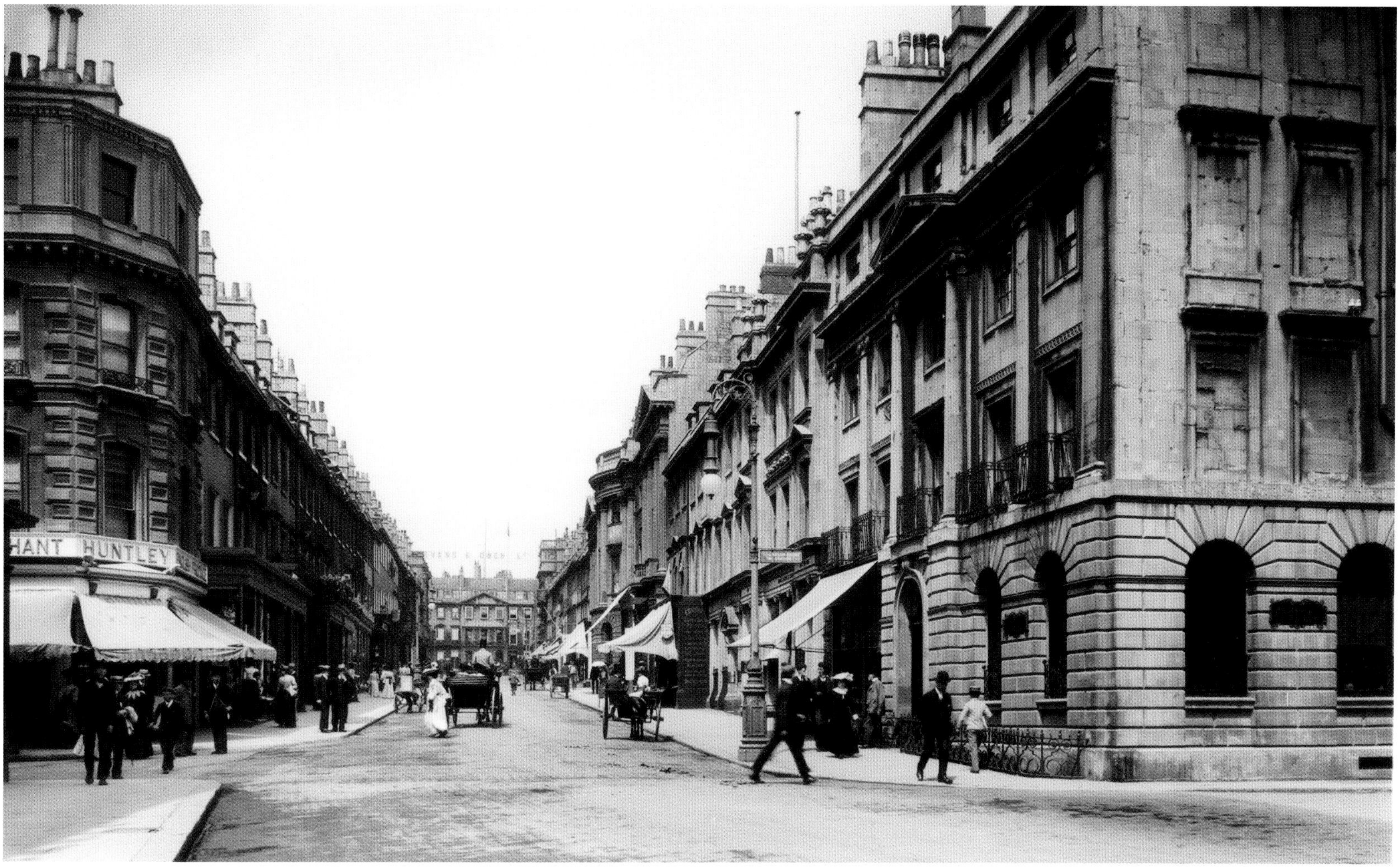
HANT HUNTLEY

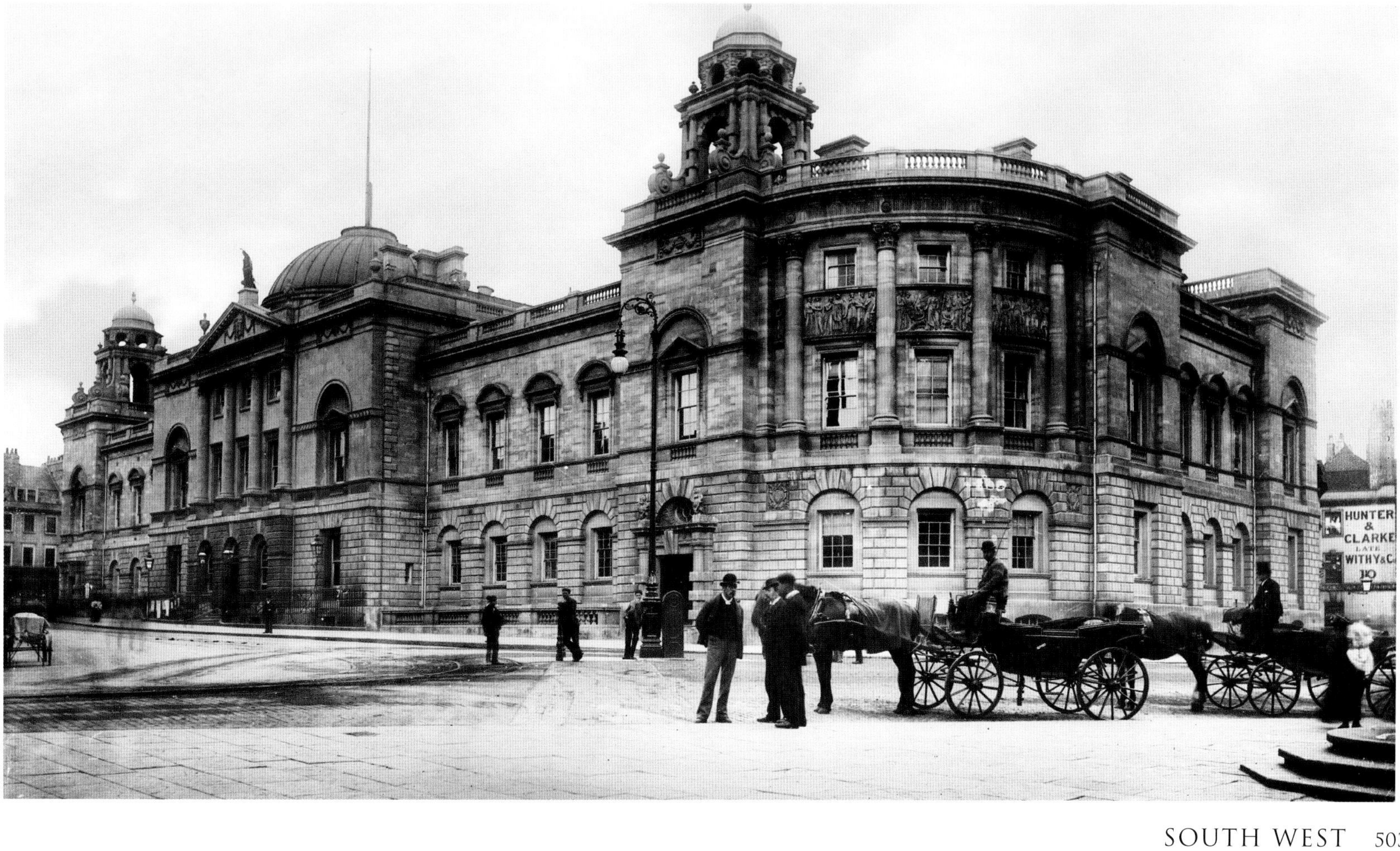
HUNTER
&
CLARKE
LATE
WITHY & C

BATH ABBEY

Above: Bath Abbey and Parade Gardens
Founded in Saxon times, the Abbey has been rebuilt and restored over the centuries. The stunning interior seen today is part of the controversial restoration work carried out by Sir George Gilbert Scott, who in 1864 began the work of transforming the Abbey in the Victorian Gothic style – most notably replacing the original ceiling over the nave with stone fan vaulting and installing the great East window by Clayton and Bell.

Left: The Royal Crescent, 1930
Designed by the architect John Wood the Younger and built between 1767 and 1775, the Crescent comprised 30 terraced houses behind a palatial facade that overlooked open countryside. Original purchasers of the leases had to conform to Wood's exterior design but were free to lay out the interiors, so no two houses are the same.

Opposite: Bath Stationery Warehouse, Old Bond Street, 1912
Three girls in pinafores stand outside Wood & Co, stationers.

TORPED
THE C
SHIPPING
AGE
PRINTERS.
WOOD & Co.
STATIONERS.
AN
PIANOFO
W.J. HALSE
STATIONERY WAREHOUSE.
W. J. HALSE
FIRST FLOOR.
WOOD
& Co
ACCOUNT
WOOD
& Co
Nº 13
FOREIGN TOURS
Arranged
OCEAN PASSAGES BOOKED
&
RAIL TICKETS TO DESTINATION
ISSUED WITHIN.
GOODS & PRIVATE EFFECTS
CONVEYED TO
ALL PARTS OF THE WORLD
NO BOOKING FEES
J&P.S
BATH ELECT
MAPS

GREAT PULTENEY STREET

Top left: Great Pulteney Street, Bath c1890
The city council instructed Thomas Baldwin to draw up a street plan that would replace the warren of mediaeval streets with more fashionable grand boulevards. Great Pulteney Street, completed in 1789, was one such example running from the east end of Pulteney Bridge to Sydney Gardens. At the junction with Henrietta Street he created a quadrangle named Laura Place, in which the fountain was erected in 1877.

Middle left: High Street, Bath, c1905
Looking north along the High Street with the Guildhall to the right. In an age largely free from traffic, an electric tram runs down the middle of the road. Electric trams were introduced into Bath in 1904 and continued to run until 1939. For four decades they were a feature of many British towns and cities, despite the fact that their tracks were a hazard to cyclists and they required a mesh of overhead cables.

Opposite above right: Edward Colston Statue, Colston Avenue, Bristol, c1895
In 1895 a statue was erected to Bristol-born merchant Edward Colston (1636-1721) who endowed several schools and almshouses in the city. Colston's legacy is now less favourably viewed because of his involvement in the slave trade.

Bottom left: 52-70 Colston Street, Bristol, 1930
Also named after Edward Colston, many of these modest vernacular buildings were 17th or 18th century in origin, but of immense character with an irregular roofline of tiled gables and robust chimneys, At ground level is a group of local shops – butcher, grocer, fishmonger and sub-post office. The shop with the sunblind is William C Wescombe, a fruiterer.

BRISTOL

Right: The junction of Steep Street and Trenchard Street, Bristol, 1866
In the Middle Ages the aptly named Steep Street formed part of the main road from Bristol to Gloucester, but in the 1880s it was demolished. Publishers Frost & Reed issued this wonderfully evocative view of this scene in 1891, a few years after the street had disappeared.

Above left: Clifton Suspension Bridge, c1900
The bridge, which spans the majestic Avon Gorge, was one of Brunel's many engineering masterpieces with a width of 702ft (214m) and its deck 245ft (75m) above the river. The huge volume of shipping using the important Bristol docks had to pass beneath this bridge. At the time of this photograph, sail and steam were still competing for trade.

R.T. PLUM,
CUTLER.
EAGLE-RANGE
SHOW ROOMS.
Nº 8
5
CRITERION
CIGAR STORES
HAIR-CUTTING & SHAVING
PLUM, CUTLER
STORES
THE BRISTOL INDUSTRIAL & FINE ART EXHIBITION

ST AUGUSTINE'S REACH

Left: St Augustine's Reach and the Industrial and Fine Art Exhibition, Bristol, 1893
A temporary exhibition hall of steel and timber housed the Bristol Industrial and Fine Art Exhibition. It was erected on new ground created when the River Frome was culverted and the new St Augustine's Bridge formed a terminus to St Augustine's Reach, part of the docks. Half a million people visited the exhibition in the summer of 1893. To the right, the 15th-century tower of St Stephen's church rises over the shops and offices. Some of the buildings (left) along Anchor Road survive as modern shops.

CLIFTON

Left: Clifton, Bristol, c1920
An oblique aerial view looking along the Avon Gorge towards the Bristol Channel. The Clifton Suspension Bridge can be seen clearly along with the Observatory (on the hilltop). The many streets of Georgian housing, including Royal York Crescent, remain a distinctive feature of this area of Bristol.

BRISTOL TRAMWAYS CENTRE

Above: Bristol Tramways Centre, 1904
The Tramways Centre was laid out in 1896 around a large triangle at the head of St Augustine's Reach on the piece of ground that had been used for the temporary Exhibition hall just three years earlier. The trams are electrified, while horse-drawn cabs wait for fares at the neighbouring cab stand and a cabman wears a heavy cloak to keep out the weather.

Right: Charles Wills & Sons, Rupert Street, Bristol, 1891
Clothiers Charles Wills & Sons' factory was constructed in 1890 to designs by the Bristol architect Henry Williams.

Opposite top: The church of St Nicholas and Bristol Bridge, Bristol, c1904
The mediaeval church of St Nicholas which stood on the approach to Bristol Bridge was rebuilt in the 18th century and again following bomb damage in 1940. The High Street runs past its east end towards the elegant spire of Christ Church, which faces Baldwin Street to the south. Bristol Bridge was for a long time the only bridge south-east across the River Avon, making it an important focus for the town. In this photograph the High Street is lined with shops. The corner building is swathed in popular commercial advertising.

THE
GEORGE
HOTEL
L.VINCENT
FRISBY.
STORES

GENERAL WAREHOUSE

Somerset

TAUNTON

Above: Hammet Street, Taunton, 1901
In 1788 a network of old streets was cleared and Hammet Street was laid out to provide homes for 'genteel' families. The street was designed to focus on the church of St Mary Magdalene, although the disproportionately tall tower seen here is a rebuild of 1862. During the 19th century the canals and railway linked Taunton with Bristol and Exeter and the population grew rapidly, from less than 6,000 in 1801 – still a reasonable size town of the period – to 19,000 by 1901. With the rise in population, the town developed: the hospital, Queen's and King's Colleges and Vivary Park were all founded during this period of growth.

YEOVIL

Opposite above: Middle Street, Yeovil, 1900
Situated on the main road between London and the West Country, the timber-framed and jettied George Hotel, previously known as the George Inn, was built as a private dwelling in the early 1400s. It was scandalously demolished in 1965 for a road widening scheme, which never progressed, as the Council subsequently discovered that it did not own the land. Shortly after, the street was pedestrianised. The building on the right, Olivers, 'The Largest Retailer of Boots in the World' remains.

Opposite below: Yarn Market, Dunster, c1910
This fine 17th-century timber-framed octagonal market hall is a monument to Dunster's once-flourishing wool and cloth trade. In the foreground, an artist has set up his easel to record the picturesque scene. Dunster Castle can be seen on the Tor beyond.

BEAR
HOTEL
THE BEAR HOTEL

Wiltshire

Opposite top left: Ramsbury, c 1890
A dilapidated thatched cottage with its inhabitants standing outside.

Opposite middle left: Porch House and Porch House Cottages, High Street, Potterne, 1914
The timber-framed Porch House dates from the late 15th century, while its jettied neighbours further up the High Street were built around 1600. After being used successively as a house, brewery, bakehouse, barracks, public house and tenements, they were restored by the architect Ewan Christian in 1872-76 as a dwelling for the portrait painter George Richmond.

Opposite bottom left: The Bear Hotel in Devizes, c1920
Dating from the mid-16th century, the Bear Hotel was a coaching inn – one of four stopovers on the main route between London and West Wales.

STONEHENGE

Opposite top right: Stonehenge, 1867
Colonel Sir Henry James photographed at the ancient site. At the time he was Director General of the Ordnance Survey which published its complete survey of Great Britain in 1870.

Opposite middle right: Stonehenge, 1901
In 1900 one of the huge sarsen stones collapsed, precipitating a restoration campaign to make the monument safe. Professor William Gowland was chosen to direct the project the following year. A small excavation took place before the massive sarsen was re-erected and set in a concrete socket. For the first time it was possible to demonstrate that the stone circle was much older than had been widely supposed, and a date of 1800 BC was suggested.

Opposite bottom right and above: Stonehenge, 1919
Public safety remained an issue, with some stones supported on timber props. A new campaign of excavation and restoration began in 1919, led by Colonel William Hawley, concentrating on three pairs of sarsen stones that were twisting under the weight of their lintels. Each 10-ton lintel was removed and the supporting stones were eased back into the vertical before being set in concrete. The lintels were then replaced (above). This was a major task for early 20th-century technology, underlining the extraordinary achievement of its prehistoric builders.

ALDBOURNE

Above: Windmill, Aldbourne, c1900
There had been a windmill for grinding corn in Aldbourne since at least the 14th century, although the mill seen here is probably Victorian. When it was demolished, the local community seems to have turned out to watch the fun. Here a group of workmen, together with some villagers and the local policeman, pose for the camera.

CRICKLADE

Bottom: The High Street, Cricklade, c1895
Cricklade, one of a chain of 'burghs' fortified by King Alfred the Great to defend Wessex, is now a quiet country town. Shops and houses line the High Street, and a public water pump is a reminder of domestic life before mains supply.

Below: Market Cross, Malmesbury, c1880
A group of men stand around the Market Cross dating from around 1500. The Abbey gate is hidden behind the cross. The spire of St Paul's Church stands as a landmark although the body of the church has been demolished.

Right: The Poultry Cross, Silver Street, Salisbury, c1920
A cross is known to have existed here since 1307, although this one dates mainly from the 15th century. The top part was restored in a mediaeval style in 1853, replacing a single pillar carrying a sundial and ball that had been added during repairs in 1771.

SALISBURY

Right: North Gate, High Street, Salisbury, c1895
Looking through the North Gate from the High Street into the Cathedral Close. The Gate was built in the 1330s, when the Close was walled for security, although an earlier gate probably existed. The two bricked-in windows above the archway have since been re-opened.

Above: Burdett Street, Ramsbury c1910
Women and children pose in the village street outside a row of thatched and half-timbered cottages – this was before the days of popular camera ownership, and the appearance of a photographer with his equipment was an event. Two wheels of a tricycle can be seen on the right, possibly belonging to the photographer, Frederick Ault.

Opposite above left and right: Men's bath, Church Street, Westbury, 1892
The changing cubicles on the left provided little privacy! The swimming pool was unheated, and in the winter months it was drained and covered by a suspended dance floor. Built in 1887 by local mill owner William Laverton in celebration of Queen Victoria's Golden Jubilee, there were also male and female washing facilities at a time when internal plumbing was rare.

Opposite below: Cellular Clothing Company Ltd, Morris Street, Swindon, 1902
Mass production in the clothing industry. Clerestory windows provide natural light for the workers. The Cellular Clothing Co Ltd was established in 1888 by Lewis Haslam, the inventor of 'Aertex' fabric.

Dorset

BOURNEMOUTH

Top left: Pier Approach, Bournemouth, c1890
The Pleasure Gardens provide a pleasant walking route alongside the Bourne Brook from the town to the pier, while the promenade continues beside the beach. The pier with its elegant entrance building, designed by Eugenius Birch, was opened in 1880.

Left middle: East Cliff, Bournemouth, c1880
The pier and beach are seen here from East Cliff. In this photograph the shelters at the seaward end have not yet been built, although the pier does seem to be being used by a passenger steamer. Rows of bathing machines on the beach also suggest an earlier date.

Below: Pier, Bournemouth, 1921
The elegant entrance building to the pier is shown here, as well as the more functional shelters at the pier head. At this date it seems to have served primarily as a deck for promenading with an admission price of 2d. A paddle steamer is disembarking, and a second is moored on the far side, underlining its importance as a landing jetty. Donkey carts wait for fares outside the gates, while rowing boats on the beach lend a picturesque air.

PROMENADE

Above: The Promenade, Bournemouth, c1900
The promenade is crowded with people walking, taking in the sea air and the view. A line of carriages for hire are ready to deliver those who have over-exerted themselves back to their hotels. The shop on the corner of the promenade sells the usual holiday souvenirs. Behind it is what was probably a sea-water bath for discreet medicinal bathers, who preferred not to use the sea itself.

Right: East Cliff, Bournemouth, 1921
The rowing boats in the foreground are probably for hire, while the motorised Skylark boat offers trips around the bay. Its mobile jetty is a practical solution to the changing tide. Bathing huts stretch into the distance at the base of the cliff, while the East Beach Café caters for refreshment-seekers. Guest houses and hotels line the East Cliff Promenade, commanding spectacular sea views.

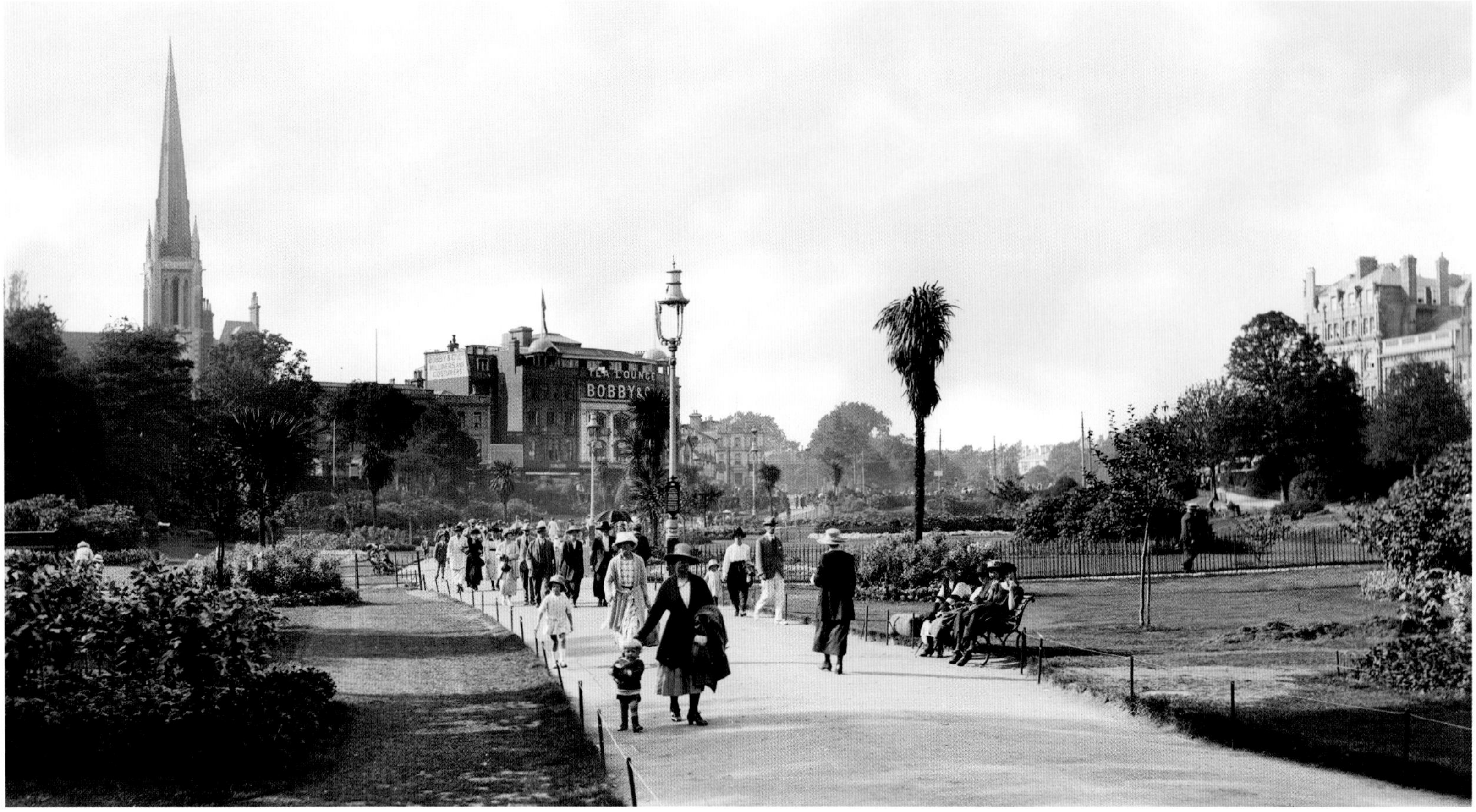

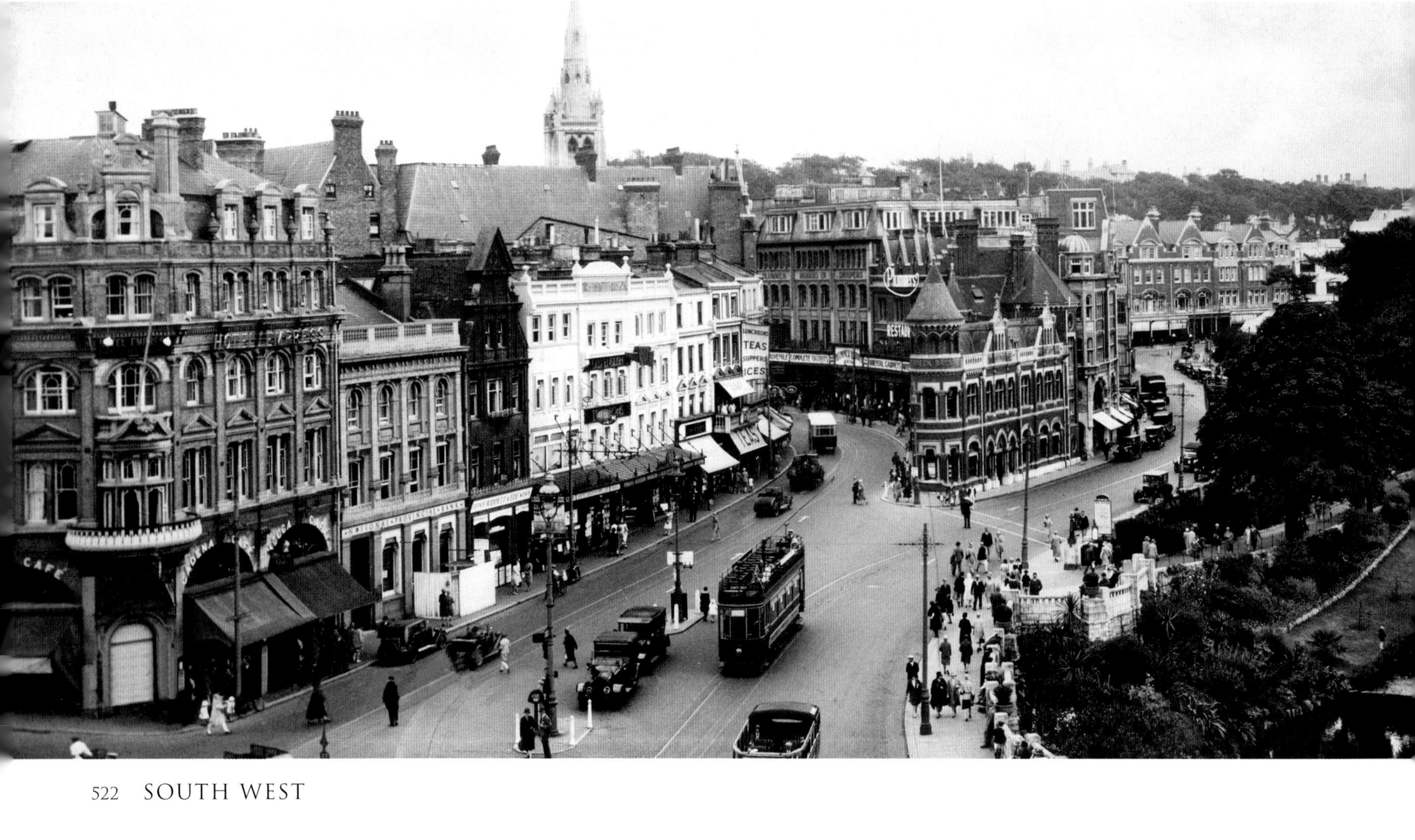
CAFÉ
TEAS
SUPPERS
ICES
TEAS

BOURNEMOUTH PLEASURE GARDENS

Right: 1891-1900
The Pleasure Gardens follow the Bourne Brook as it meanders through the town to the sea near the pier.

Opposite above: 1921
Providing a leisurely walking route, the Pleasure Gardens sit between the town and the Pier Approach. The spire of St Andrew's Presbyterian Church is a landmark, while the Tea Lounge at Bobby & Co department store advertises its pleasures to families wearily returning from the beach. The gardens were laid out by the town in the 1870s and contain many attractions including a bandstand, tennis courts and a putting green.

Opposite below: The Square, Bournemouth, c1930
Central square of Bournemouth, including the Hotel Empress, Plummers Department Store and the pleasure gardens.

Below right : Pleasure Gardens, Bournemouth, c1900
A view of adults and children enjoying the walkway running along side the River Bourne. Originally a series of garden walks, the Pleasure Gardens were created in the fields of the owners of the Branksome Estate in the 1860s. By the 1870s the fields had been leased to the Bournemouth Commissioners.

CORFE CASTLE

Above right: Corfe Castle, c1890

The famous hilltop castle dates from soon after the Norman Conquest, but it was reduced to ruins in the Civil War by Parliamentary forces following a prolonged siege during which it was defended by the formidable Lady Banks. The quiet village (technically a small town), with traditional cottages at its foot was made prosperous by the Purbeck marble industry. It received another boost when the railway arrived in 1885 bringing tourists to see the castle. A new railway bridge and embankment can be seen in the distance.

Top left: Beach & Company, East Street, Bridport c1920

The chemist, Beach & Company, is a survivor boasting an eccentric Georgian façade concealing a much older timber-framed building behind. The fine semi-circular window bays with Gothic glazing bars have lead crenellations above. The wording over the first floor windows claims: 'The Old George Inn, King Charles II came here September 23 1651'. Although trading under a different name, the building still operates as a dispensing chemist.

Middle left: High West Street, Dorchester, 1913

The Queen's Own Dorset Yeomanry was one of a number of volunteer militias formed in response to the threat of Napoleonic invasion. It saw service in the Boer War and again in the First World War . The occasion of this parade is not clear, but Union Jacks are being flown.

Bottom left: Weymouth Harbour, 1895

Four tall ships moored in Weymouth harbour demonstrate that the era of sail was not yet over. In the background the harbour is spanned by Town Bridge through which a central cast-iron swing section allowed shipping to pass into the inner harbour. The bridge is seen here following the modifications of 1881: it was subsequently redesigned in the 1920s.

DORCHESTER

Above right: Parson's Store, South Street c1940

Parson's is part of a terrace of 18th-century buildings and still preserves an early shop front. The hairdresser on the first floor has invested in a swanky neon sign. This wartime photograph shows some of the windows taped against the risk of flying glass in the event of bomb damage.

Bottom right: High East Street, c1890

At the top of the hill the clock tower of the Corn Exchange can be seen, as well as the tower of St Peter's Church and the spire of All Saint's Church. There is an advert for R B Brown 'Manufacturer of marquees, tents, rick-clothes & india-rubber and waterproof goods'. *Kelly's Directory* for 1895 lists Robert Bullen Brown as a Tent and Marquee-maker with shops at 52 High East Street and 8 High West Street.

THE ESPLANADE

Above: The Esplanade, Weymouth, c1890
Weymouth became George III's favourite resort, and his presence brought royal prestige to the town. Elegant Georgian terraces face Weymouth Bay across the Esplanade, where shelters allowed visitors to take the air and enjoy the view; a row of invalid chairs look like they may be available for hire.

Below: Highcliffe, c1890
Women and children bathe in the sea below the cliffs at Highcliffe. Beyond, bathing huts line the shore. A common sight at English seaside resorts in the 19th century, these machines were often set far apart from the bathing places reserved for men. Once they had been wheeled into the water, they allowed the female bather to enjoy the delights of sea-bathing without sacrificing her modesty.

WEYMOUTH

Opposite above: Custom House Quay, Weymouth, c1900
Arriving in Weymouth in the 1850s, the railways brought the tourist trade to the town; the Quay station was opened a few years later and provided a vital link with the harbour, both for pedestrians and cargo. Here a train meets a passenger ferry while several cabs wait hopefully for fares. The kiosk to the left is topped with a flagpole and a crown, proudly signifying the royal associations of the town. In the foreground, assorted harbour equipment has been left lying beside a gas lamp. Weymouth Quay station has not been used for passenger traffic since 1987.

Opposite below: St Edmund Street, Weymouth, c1890
Many shops have put out their awnings on this sunny day. The tricycle delivery cart of Waterman the ironmonger is parked by the kerb, while on the left is Alfred Dennis & Sons, linen drapers, and Baunton & Sons, butchers. The Classical portico on the right at the end of the street is that of the Guildhall built between 1836 and 1837 on the site of the former town hall of Melcombe Regis. The Wesleyan Chapel on Maiden Street closes the vista.

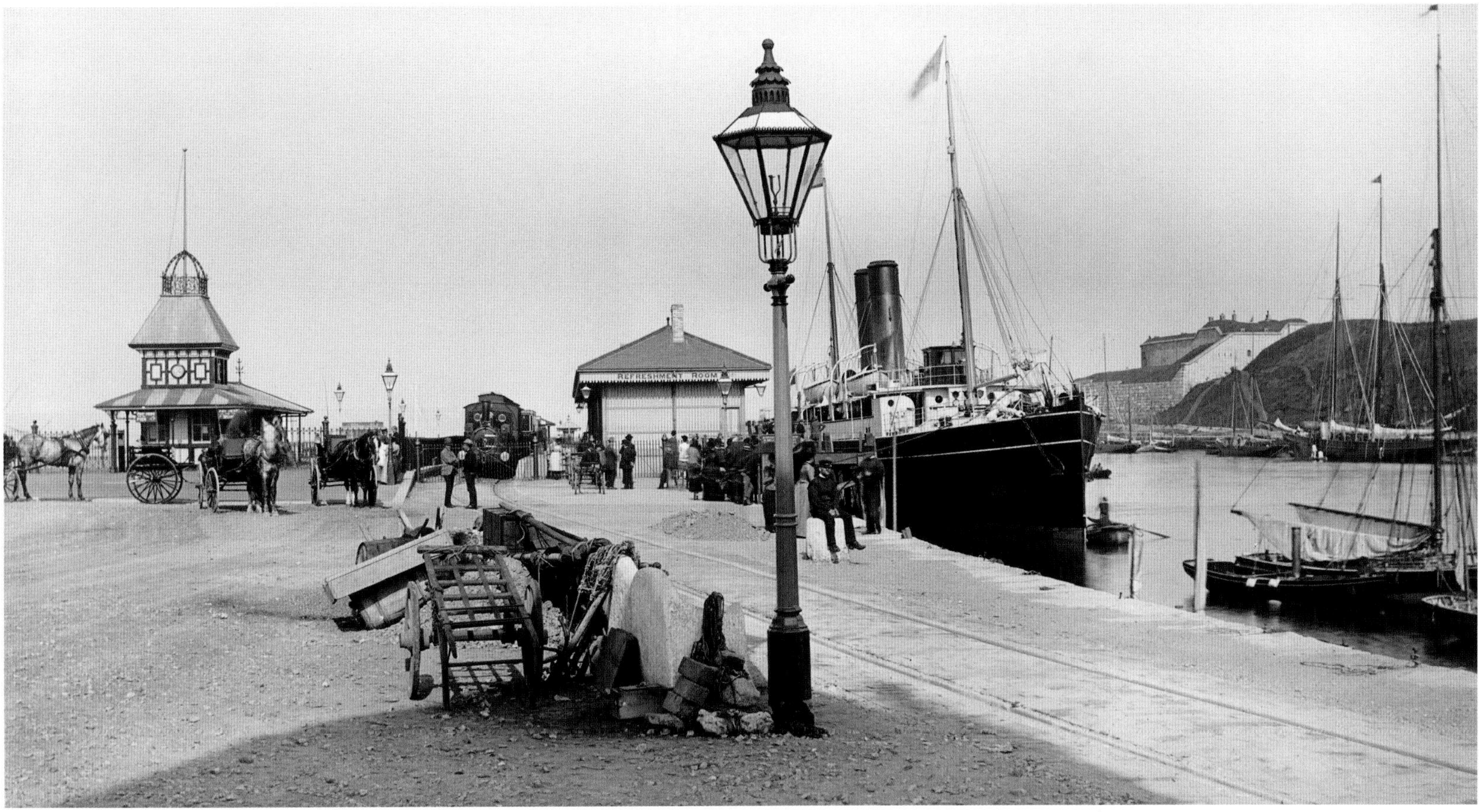
REFRESHMENT ROOM

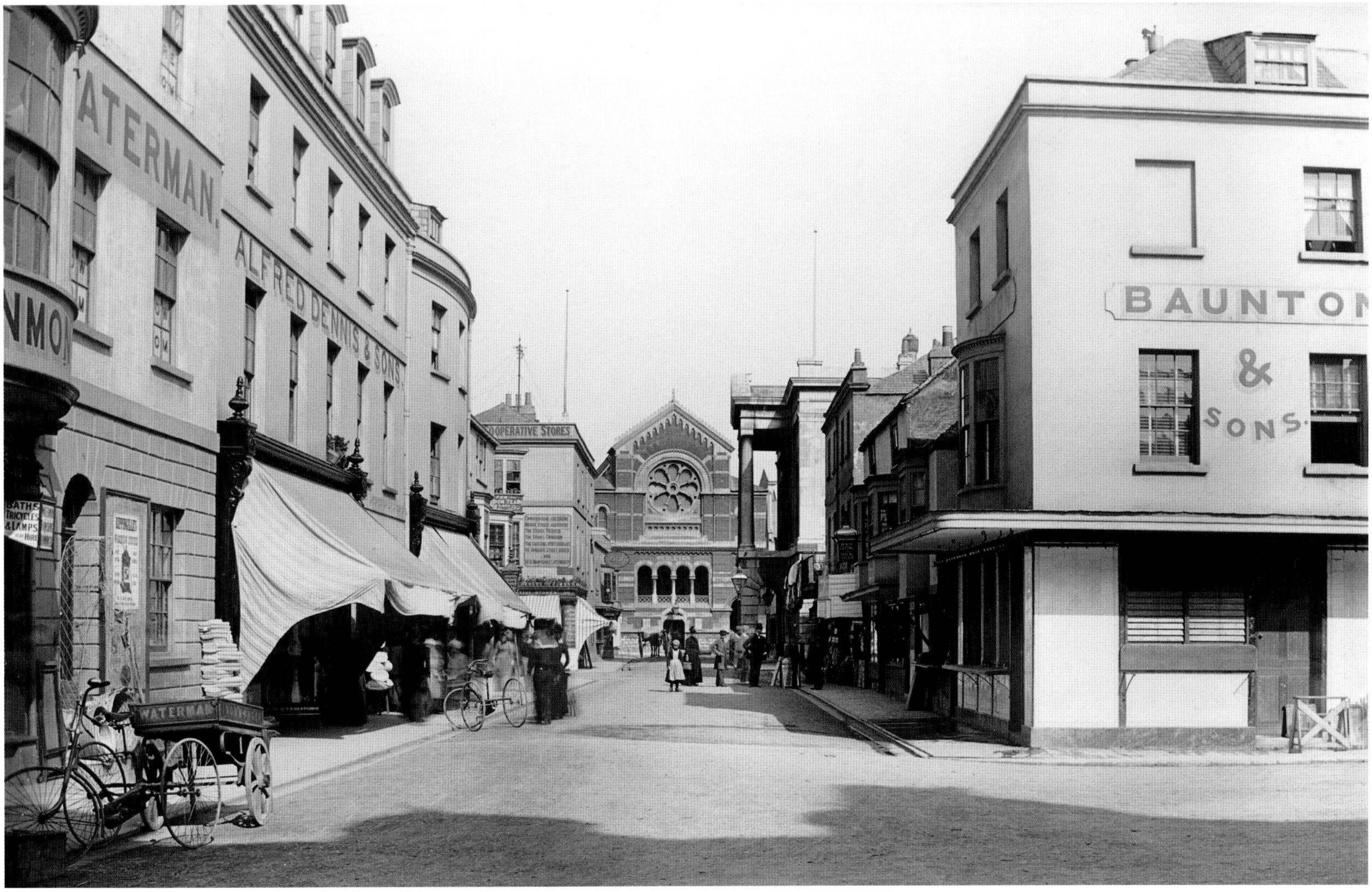
WATERMAN
ALFRED DENNIS & SONS
OPERATIVE STORES
& SONS
WATERMAN

Above: High West Street, Weymouth, c1895
Carts wait in the street, while two delivery boys with a trolley are more interested in the photographer than their work. The Old Town Hall at the head of the street is an unpretentious building largely rebuilt in 1774. The terrace of houses with curved bays is of 18th century origin, while the Belvedere dates from the early 19th century.

Left: High East Street, Dorchester c1880
St Peter's Church, built around 1420 and with a striking castellated tower, is in the centre of the photograph. To the left is the Dorset County Museum which was founded in 1845.

SHERBORNE

Right: St John's Almshouses, Half Moon Street, Sherborne, c.1895

An elderly man, possibly a resident, stands outside the door to the almshouses. Until the 19th century, social welfare was largely left to philanthropists. St John's Almshouses were founded for twelve poor men and four poor women, whose purpose was to pray for the soul of the founder. Completed in 1448, the building consisted of a chapel, dining room, kitchen and dormitories. The dormitories have since been replaced by individual rooms, but the charity continues.

Below: Sherborne Abbey, c1905

After the Dissolution of the Monasteries, Sherborne Abbey became the parish church and it still towers above the town. The Conduit, on the west side of Cheap Street, seen here in the centre of the photograph, is another remnant of the original Abbey. It was set up in the cloister in the early 16th century by Abbot Mere as a lavatorium – a place where monks could wash their hands – before it was moved to become the Market Cross. It has since been restored as a fountain.

Devon

Top left: The Butterwalk, Duke Street, Dartmouth, 1901
The Butterwalk, in the heart of the town near the quay, consists of four timber-framed houses built around 1628 to 1640. The pillars that support the projecting upper floors are made of granite. Once the high-quality houses of wealthy merchants, they now incorporate shops on the ground floor. The building was restored following war damage in 1943.

Middle left: Trinity Square, Axminster, c1895
Axminster is an ancient town made prosperous by carpet manufacturing, which commenced in the mid 18th century. The square is busy with men milling around, which suggests it may be market day.

Bottom left: The Barbican, Plymouth, c1880
A crowd gathered on the harbour front for the open-air fish market. From 1849 the railway enabled the catch to be in London that same day.

Opposite above: Clovelly, c1910
Artists and writers were quick to popularise this picturesque village. Shackson's Refreshment Rooms competes with the older New Inn and offers beds for those who want to prolong their stay. The village has become a busy tourist attraction, with sightseers ambling up and down the steep, cobbled streets leading to the harbour.

Opposite below: Exeter Cathedral, c1930
The west front of the Cathedral showing its superb 14th-century screen of sculpted figures, which bear eloquent testimony to the skill and craftsmanship of the mediaeval stonemasons. They are among the best of their kind in England, and fortunately survived the Baedeker raid on 4 May 1941 when the cathedral received a direct hit. Founded in 1133 and built of local stone, Exeter Cathedral has the longest uninterrupted mediaeval vaulted ceiling in the world.

SHACKSON'S
REFRESHMENT ROOMS
Teas & Luncheons
Fruit & Cream.
BEDS.
NEW

Top left: Mol's Coffee House, Cathedral Close, Exeter, c1900
The Cathedral Precinct was a peaceful world shut away from the bustle of the city. Mol's Coffee House was part of a timber-framed building of around 1529 given a flamboyant new façade when the Dutch gable was added in about 1885. Next door is the church of St Martin, consecrated in 1065.

Middle left: Okehampton Street, Exeter, 1901
A group of workers pose with crates outside the Beer & Patten Works, manufacturers of ginger beer.

Bottom left: Victoria Pavilion, Wilder Road, Ilfracombe, c1895
The winter garden in Jubilee Gardens. Winter gardens allowed the season to be extended beyond the all-too-brief British summer. They began as glasshouses for gardeners, but as technology developed they became huge structures that might include facilities such as a dance floor, a concert hall or refreshment rooms, as well as exotic plants.

Opposite top left: Plymouth, c.1890
Behind the pier is Plymouth Hoe made famous by Sir Francis Drake who is reputed to have coolly finished a game of bowls there before leaving to defeat the Spanish Armada. Smeaton's Tower lighthouse, on the horizon, was relocated from Eddystone Rocks in 1882.

Opposite top right: Ilfracombe, c1900
Ilfracombe was a fishing village until the railway reached it in 1874, and it became the most popular holiday resort on the north Devon coast. Steamers brought passengers from as far afield as Bristol, Swansea and Liverpool.

Opposite upper middle left: HMS *Impregnable*, The Hamoaze, Plymouth, c1885
The former HMS *Howe*, re-named HMS *Impregnable*, a training ship. It was broken up in February 1921 and the timbers used in the construction of the Liberty's department store in London.

Opposite lower middle left: Prysten House, Finewell Street, Plymouth, c1890
This fine example of a late mediaeval merchant's house was renamed Yogge's House after the merchant Thomas Yogge who built it soon after 1498. The older name of Prysten refers to the mistaken belief that it was a priest's house.

Opposite middle right: Beacon Tower, Lynmouth, c1900
The Rhenish Tower on Lynmouth pier was built around 1860 and carried a flaming beacon – later an electric light – to guide vessels into the small harbour. It was rebuilt following the catastrophic flash flood of 1952.

Opposite bottom right: Courtenay Street, Newton Abbot, 1901

Opposite bottom left: The Strand, Dawlish, c1900
View looking west towards Hannaford grocery store on the left and Dawlish United Reform church visible in the distance.

HANNAFORD
TEA & COFFEE DEALER
PROVISION MERCHANT
W & A GILBEY'S
Wine & Spirit Depot

ISTIE & BENNETT.

PLYMOUTH

Above: Athenaeum, George Street, Plymouth, 1893
George Street was a busy thoroughfare. An omnibus has pulled up outside the Athenaeum, while a cab rank occupies the middle of the road with its cabmen's shelter. Another cab waits by a gas lamp. Tracks show the route of a horse tram operated by the Corporation. The Athenaeum, with is huge Classical portico, was founded in 1812 and designed by John Foulston to house the meeting rooms of the Plymouth Institution. The grand Wilts & Dorset Bank stands at the head of the street next to the slender Victorian clock tower.

Left: The Coastguard, Hartland Point, c1910
A coastguard keeping watch on the clifftop above the lighthouse, which was built in 1874.

THE SQUARE, TORQUAY

Below: The Square, Torquay, 1922

Torquay's mild climate made it an attractive winter resort, especially for those who suffered ill health. The railways reached the town in the 1840s bringing visitors and prosperity and by the end of the century it was transformed into one of the West Country's most popular holiday resorts. The Mallock Memorial, designed by John Donkin, was built in 1902 to commemorate the owner of nearby Cockington village, who had died two years earlier.

Right: St Andrew's Church & Municipal Buildings, Catherine Street, Plymouth, c1900

This imposing group of buildings created a civic focus for the town. St Andrew's church was the mediaeval parish church of Plymouth. Next to it, the Gothic-style Guildhall was begun in 1870. In front of that, the Municipal Offices in French Gothic style were of the same date. The docks made Plymouth a key military target during the Second World War and all these buildings were gutted in the air raids of March 1941. The church and Guildhall were restored, but the Municipal Offices succumbed to a road scheme in 1947.

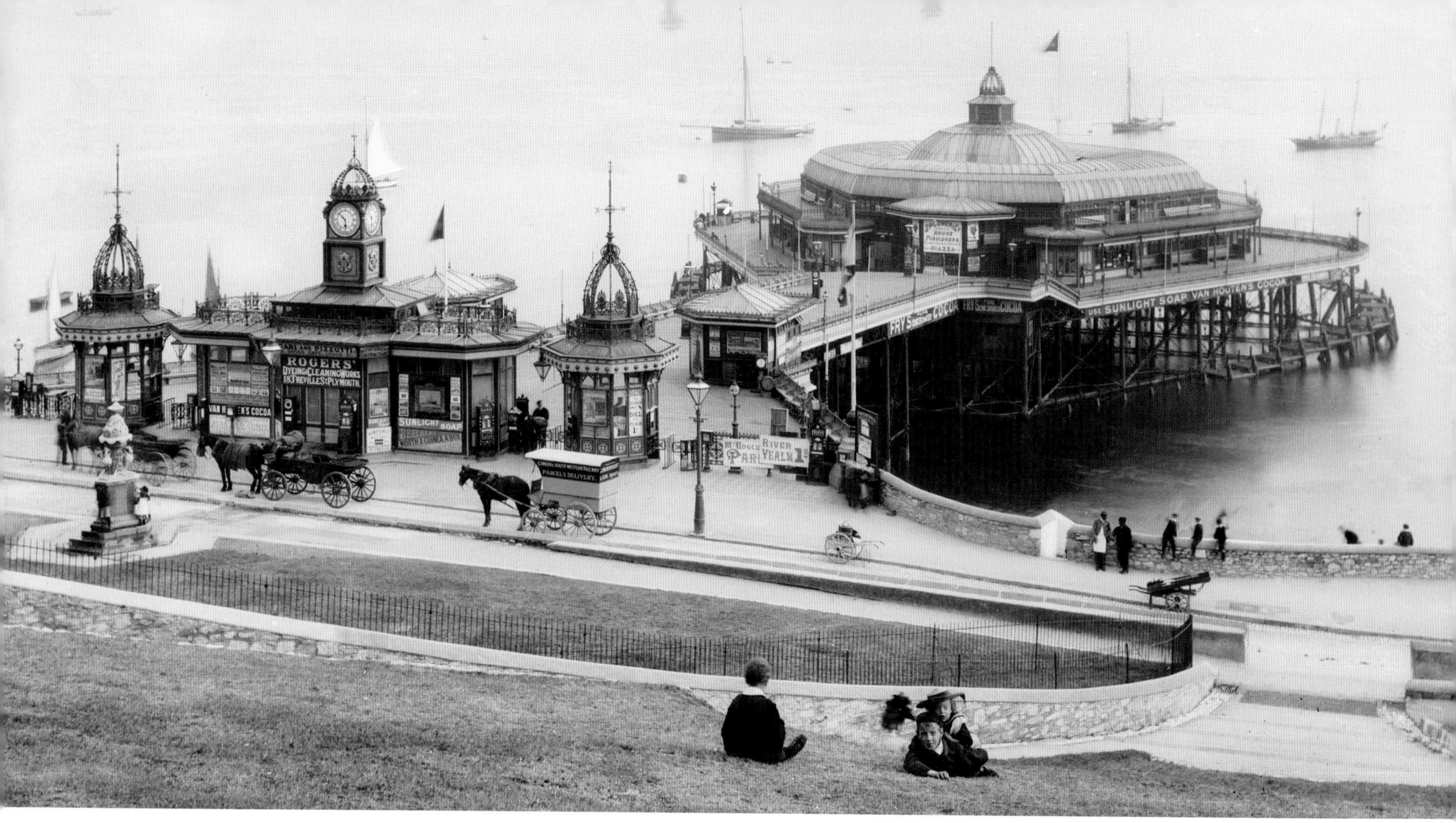

ROGERS'
DYEING & CLEANING WORKS
18 TREVILLE ST PLYMOUTH
SUNLIGHT SOAP
FRY'S COCOA
SUNLIGHT SOAP VAN HOUTEN'S COCOA
PARCELS DELIVERY
RIVER YEALM 1s
PIAZZA

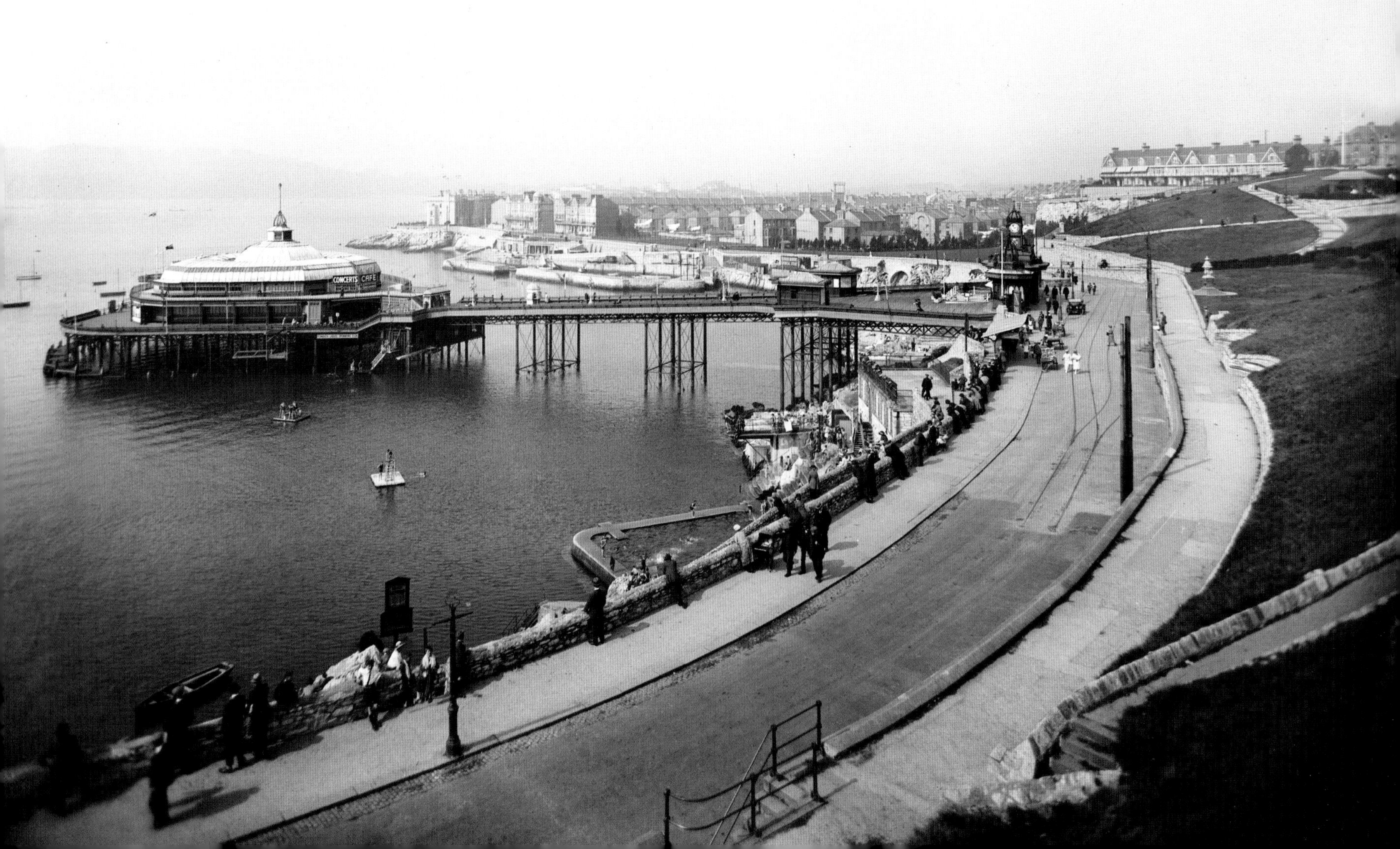

CONCERTS CAFE

PLYMOUTH PIER

Opposite above: Plymouth Pier, 1893
The ornate kiosks and entrance pavilion to Plymouth Pier, short at only 465 feet in length, is covered with advertisements for everyday products such as Sunlight Soap and Fry's Cocoa, as well as Roger's Dyeing and Cleaning Works. The admission charge of 1d kept out unaccompanied children and beggars. Damaged by enemy action in 1941, the pier was finally demolished in 1954.

Opposite below: Plymouth Pier, c1890
Holidaymakers use the two swimming platforms anchored between the Pier and the coast; a small swimming pool has been created beside the sea. Tram tracks have been laid along Hoe Road to make it easier for visitors to get from the town centre to the Pier and the promenade.

Top left: Teignmouth, c1890
Holidaymakers relax on the beach on a busy day in summer. The row of bathing machines advertising Beecham's Pills indicate that this was a favoured place for swimming and are perhaps a reminder of the medicinal origins of sea bathing. No-one is wearing beach clothing, the children having just rolled up their trousers to paddle.

SEATON AND TOTNES

Top right: Harbour Road, Seaton, c1905
A small fishing settlement, Seaton developed as a resort in the mid 19th century when terraces of Victorian houses sprang up. The Royal Clarence Family & Commercial Hotel is attempting to appeal to a genteel clientele.

Above right: Abbey Place, Tavistock, c1885
Mediaeval Tavistock was dominated by an important Benedictine abbey. By the mid 18th century it had fallen into disrepair and a road was cut through its precinct to create a new town centre. Most of the Abbey buildings have disappeared, but the Gatehouse, which still survives, was adapted to form, among other things, the town library. The tower of the parish church of St Eustace rises behind. Adjacent is the Guildhall and magistrates' court of 1848.

Above left: High Street, Totnes, c1890
Looking down the High Street towards the East Gate from the Market Place. Many of these buildings date from the 16th century, their tiled and weatherboarded projecting upper stories creating an elegant arcade beneath.

CARY PARADE, TORQUAY

Below: Cary Parade, c1890

The evidence of Torquay's origins as an elegant Georgian seaside resort is clearly visible. The parish church of St John the Evangelist in Montpellier Road, with its striking west tower, was designed by George Edmund Street and completed in 1885 by his son to his father's designs. Nearby, an urbane terrace of Georgian houses commands a fine view over the bay. A line of carriages awaits fares beside the park.

Left: High Street, Totnes, 1901

Totnes, on the estuary of the River Dart and complete with a Norman castle, has long been a prosperous market town. The iconic East Gate probably marks the site of a gateway through the defences of the Saxon burgh, though it was rebuilt in the 16th century. To either side are refined Georgian houses and shops, some of which are timber-clad. The East Gate and surrounding buildings were destroyed by a major fire on the night of 14 September 1990, but have since been authentically rebuilt.

PAIGNTON

Right: Victoria Street, Paignton, c1910
The success of Paignton as a tourist resort was closely linked to that of its neighbours, Torquay and Torbay, known together as the English Riviera because of their mild climate. The arrival of the railway in the 1850s allowed the town to develop, and a pier was opened in 1879. The buildings in Victoria Street were designed and built as a single composition.

Above: Town Hall, Torquay, 1900
The Old Town Hall was squeezed onto a narrow corner site between Union Street and Abbey Road. Built between 1851 and 1852 to designs by the town surveyor, its most striking feature is its Italianate clock tower. A new, grander town hall was built in 1911. The area has since been redeveloped, though the Old Town Hall survives and is now in residential use.

Cornwall

BOSCASTLE

Top left: Boscastle, c1895
A traditional small fishing village on the north coast of Cornwall, Boscastle sits in a tight valley carved out by the River Valency. Its harbour is protected from storms by two moles, the inner of which dates from the 16th century. A local lime kiln converted imported limestone into lime to reduce the acidity of the agricultural soils. Inland the landscape appears bleak with scrub on the steeper slopes and pasture on the windy summits.

Top right: Coverack, c1900
Another small fishing village, Coverack is on the Lizard Peninsula. Before intrusive modern development, many similar settlements could be found around the Cornish coast. A single fishing boat is moored in the shelter of the pier. Several of the village's whitewashed vernacular cottages are thatched despite the exposed coastal location.

FALMOUTH

Opposite middle right: Mrs Bailey's Pie Shop, 15 Webber Street, Falmouth, 1907
A notice in the window is the only sign advertising this shop and its wares, though Mrs Bailey is framed in the doorway making pies and the tempting aroma can only be imagined. Given the location, they may be Cornish pasties. Many working people lacked the time and the fuel to cook, and this niche was filled by bakers and other 'fast food' vendors, such as Mrs Bailey. Another notice indicates she augmented her living by taking lodgers.

Opposite middle left: Bodmin Road Station, 1901
The Cornwall Railway opened to passengers as far as Truro in 1859, with Bodmin being served by a branch line. By 1889 the company was forced to sell to the Great Western Railway. Four GWR platelayers near Bodmin Road Station appear to be digging out rotten sleepers.

Opposite bottom: Falmouth, 1907
Young children sit listlessly in a lane outside a factory gate, perhaps waiting for a parent to leave work.

Above: Cross Lanes, Cury, 1910
The Temperance Hotel and the Wheel Inn face each other across the village street. A heavy cart, possibly that of the coal man, is making deliveries. The Temperance Movement developed throughout the 19th century as alcohol was equated with moral turpitude and seen as a major social ill. Temperance went hand-in-hand with wider issues of social reform, wholesome outdoor activities like gardening, and the supply of free, fresh drinking water. Temperance hotels, which did not serve alcohol, were popular institutions. Note the white-painted, rustic timber signpost in the background.

FALMOUTH PIER

Above: Falmouth Pier, c1900
Falmouth has the deepest harbour in western Europe, and until the era of steamships it was the primary port for packet-ships carrying mail from the outposts of Empire. Vessels returning to Britain from distant parts made Falmouth their first port of call to notify their arrival and to collect their orders for the port at which to unload. In the background the distinctive Falmouth Quay Punts that ferried the officers of square riggers to the Custom House can be seen.

Left: Fish Market, c1895
A view of the Fish Market with barrels and baskets of fish being sold.

ARWENACK STREET

Above: Arwenack Street, Falmouth, 1907
A view along Arwenack Street from its junction with Swanpool Street on a sunny day reveals a main shopping street largely free of traffic. Two horse-drawn carts plod quietly along, while pedestrians walk in the road. The better quality shops employed a delivery boy to save customers having to carry their own purchases. The bicycle of the delivery boy for the chemist A Stevens is propped against the kerb. The ship's chandler on the corner of Swanpool Street, proprietor Nathan Vos, is a reminder that Falmouth was an active port.

Right: Shipwrights Hotel, Helford, 1900
A group stand in the cobbled yard of the hotel, which dates from the 18th century.

Above: Falmouth, c1905

The railways were a major employer of horses, as company carriers delivered goods between the station and the customer. This cart, badged for the Great Western Railway, takes a rest beside a railway bridge. On the bridge over the road is an advertisement for R Clarke & Co, tailors.

Left: Chyandour Smelting Works, Chyandour, Penzance, c1907

Five labourers pose outside a shed at the Chyandour Smelting Works. In the 18th and 19th centuries Cornwall was a major international producer of tin. At the height of its prosperity, smelting works such as this one at Chyandour, Penzance, converted the ore into ingots ready for export. These functional buildings, without architectural pretension, were well-suited to their role. This smelting works closed not long after the photograph was taken. The last Cornish tin mine shut at the end of the 20th century bringing to an end 4,000 years of tin mining in Cornwall.

HELSTON

Above: Coinagehall Street, 1901

A coach waits outside the Angel Hotel (far left) in Coinagehall Street. Helston has been a prosperous town since mediaeval times, and Coinagehall Street, its grandest thoroughfare, is lined with elegant 18th- and 19th- century buildings, some of which conceal an earlier core. The Angel Hotel on the left still survives, and is reputedly the 16th-century town house of the local Godolphin family, though it has been adapted and extended.

Right: Newlyn, Cornwall, 1907

The quaint fishing village of Newlyn frequently depicted by the Newlyn 'school' of artists, developed as a notable fishing port long before this photograph was taken. A street of traditional fishermen's cottages, a remnant of the old fishing settlement, runs down to the harbour where several fishing boats ride at anchor. The women and girls standing outside their doors are almost certainly fishermen's families, while a returning man carries some of that day's catch.

NEWLYN HARBOUR

Above: Newlyn Harbour, 1907
Long before mains supply, a waterman sells water around the harbour at Newlyn. His barrels do not look large enough to fill all the buckets and churns which are waiting.

Opposite below: St Keverne, c1910
St Keverne, a prosperous village a mile inland from the coast, served as a centre for the surrounding communities. This view looks along Commercial Road towards the mediaeval church of St Akeveranus – shortened to St Keverne – with the Post Office, which looks as though it might have been built as a nonconformist chapel with a recently-added porch, to the left, and shops to the right including a general store.

Opposite top left: Newlyn, 1907
A view down to the harbour in the old fishing settlement of Newlyn. Such places seem idyllic, but life was unremittingly hard in such coastal communities; the group of six children with their teenage guardian look like a single family who might have lived in the first-floor rooms at the top of the steps.

Opposite top right: Kerrier, 1901
A postwoman, emptying a Victorian wall box post-box at a remote country location in Kerrier, wears a dress and coat with a uniform cap. It was relatively unusual for women to hold such positions at the turn of the century, but working women were starting to campaign for equality and the vote through movements such as the suffragettes. Women over the age of 21 did not achieve the vote until 1928.

ROYAL ALBERT BRIDGE

Top left: Royal Albert Bridge, Saltash, 1928
The Royal Albert Bridge carries the main line over the steep valley of the River Tamar. Isambard Kingdom Brunel was commissioned to design and build the bridge, which was completed in 1859. As the location was unsuitable for a conventional suspension bridge, Brunel devised an innovative design based on a wrought iron tubular arch. As an economy measure, the bridge was only built for single-line working.

Top right: Royal Albert Bridge, Saltash 1928
Here a crew carry out renewal work on the bridge using a mobile adjustable hoist to lift the heavy iron girders and rails into place. Even so, this looks labour-intensive. The workmen all wear caps or hats and waistcoats, which was normal working apparel at the time.

WESTERN PROMENADE

Above left: Western Promenade Road, Penzance, 1890
With the arrival of a direct railway link to London in 1859, Penzance began to benefit from seaside tourism and the town slowly developed as a resort. This late Victorian terrace consisted mostly of hotels and apartments to accommodate the visitors, while the promenade offered health-giving walks. A horse-drawn charabanc stands outside the Mount's Bay Hotel, presumably ready to take guests on an excursion. Further along the promenade is Drew's Serpentine Works, which sold ornamental items made from local stone from the Lizard Peninsula.

Above right: Mrs Penrose's Refreshment House, Lamorna, St Buryan, 1901
A view of a row of houses at Lamorna in the parish of St Buryan. The occupants are taking the opportunity to have their photographs taken. In the foreground, Mrs Penrose is selling mineral water.

Above: High Street, Helston, c1900
This photograph was one of a series taken to advertise holidays in Cornwall at locations served by the Great Western Railway. Photographs like this were often displayed inside railway carriages. By the 1920s Cornwall had become a popular holiday destination.

Left: Truro Cathedral, c1900
Inspired by Lincoln Cathedral and built between 1880 and 1910 to a Gothic Revival design by John Loughborough Pearson, Truro is unusual in having three spires. It occupies the site of the parish church of St Mary which dated from the 13th century, parts of which were incorporated into the new building.

Opposite above: Treskinnock Cross, Poundstock, 1911
The village blacksmith is seen shoeing a horse. Blacksmiths would also have been responsible for making and maintaining the agricultural implements of the village. In larger areas the shoeing of horses was left exclusively to farriers.

Opposite bottom: High Street, Helston, c1900
A young man, holding on to two bicycles, gazes at the camera in the middle of the High Street, as a horse and cart approaches from behind the Blackwells Angel hotel. Two advertisement boards for transatlantic shipping lines can be seen propped up on the opposite side of the street outside the Prince's Hotel.

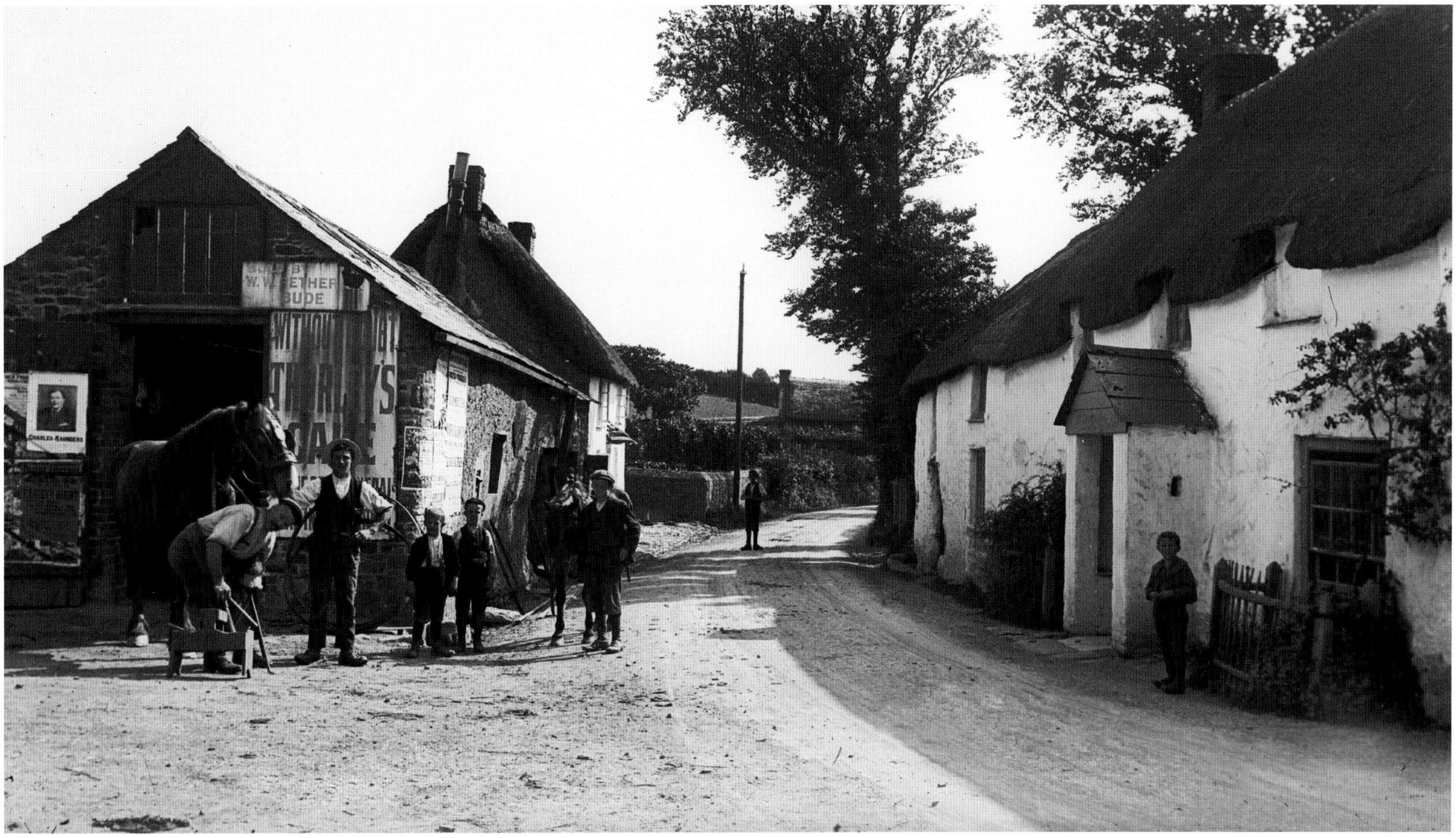
BUDE

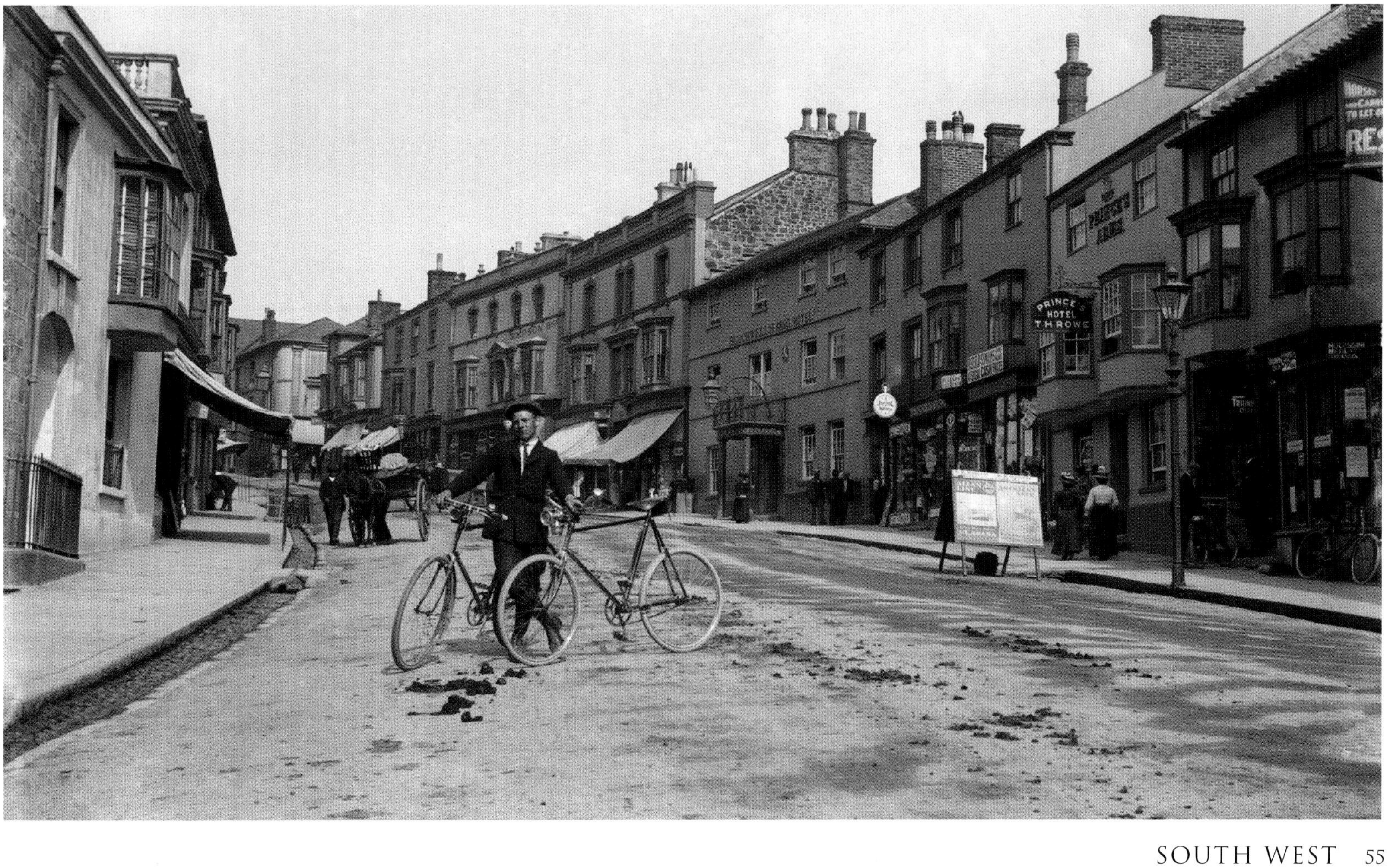
PRINCE'S
HOTEL
THROWE

OPERA HOUSE

INDEX OF PLACE NAMES

FOOTNOTES

1 Ruskin, John: *The Seven Lamps of Architecture*, 1849 (Dover Publications,1989)

2 Bell, Colin and Rose: *City Fathers*, p.186 (Penguin Books, 1972)

3 Briggs, Asa: *Victorian Cities*, p.147 (Penguin Books, 1990)

4 Winchester: *Clarence: A Lovely Land*; *Forever England* p.28 (Cassell, 1943)

5 Ruskin, John: *Cestus of Aglaia* Chapter VI Section 72. 1865-66 (JM Dent, 1908)

6 Rolt, LTC: *Victorian Engineering*, p.23 (Penguin Books, 1970)

7 Bell, Colin and Rose: *City Fathers*, p.197 (Penguin Books, 1970)

8 De Tocqueville, Alexis: *Journeys to England and Ireland*, (Yale University Press, 1958)

9 Faucher, Leon: *Etudes sur l'Angleterre* (2 vols) (Gillaumin, 1845)

10 Acworth, WM: *The Manchester Ship Canal* (Murray's Magazine, June 1889)

11 *Bristol Times and Mirror*, August 1869

12 *Bristol Times and Mirror*, March 1870

13 Dawson, George: *Address at opening of Reference Library*, 6 Sept 1865

14 Briggs, Asa: *Victorian Cities*, p.206 (Penguin Books, 1990)

15 Chamberlain, Joseph: *The Forum*, p.269 (1892)

16 Cadbury, George: *Bournville Village Trust Deed* 1900

17 Nasmyth, James: *Autobiography*, ed. Smiles S (John Murray, 1883)

18 Rolt, LTC: *Victorian Engineering*, p.123 (Penguin Books, 1970)

19 Briggs, Asa: *Victorian Cities*, p.368 (Penguin Books, 1990)

20 Gilbert Scott, George: *Secular and Domestic Architecture, Present and Future*, pp.140-142 (John Murray, 1857)

21 Trollope, Anthony: *The Vicar of Bullhampton* (Bradbury and Evans, 1870)

22 Blatchford, Robert: *Modern Athens. A City of Slums, Sunday Chronicle* (5 May 1889)

23 Chesney, Kellow: *The Victorian Underworld*, p.104 (Purnell, 1970)

24 Dickens, Charles: *Dombey & Son* (Bradbury and Evans, 1848)

25 Smith, Southwood: *The Royal Commission on the State of Large Towns and Populous Districts* (1844)

26 Booth, William: *In Darkest England and the Way Out*, p.20 (Funk and Wagnalls, 1890)

27 Sims, George: *How the Poor Live* (Chatto & Windus, 1883)

28 Winder, Robert: *Bloody Foreigners*, p.140 (Little, Brown, 2004)

29 Briggs, Asa: *Victorian Cities*, p. 371 (Penguin Books, 1990)

30 *Some London Clearings: Soho,* All The Year Round, 13 June 1885

31 Martin, Christopher: *A Glimpse of Heaven*, p.65 (English Heritage, 2006)

32 Conan Doyle, Arthur: *The Naval Treaty: The Memoirs of Sherlock Holmes* (George Newnes, 1894)

33 Booth, William: *In Darkest England and the Way Out*, p.47 (Funk and Wagnalls, 1890)

34 Booth, William: *In Darkest England and the Way Out*, p.55 (Funk andWagnalls, 1890)

35 Borsa, Mario: *England and Her Critics* (Fisher Unwin, 1917)

36 Hartley, LP: *The Go Between*, p.1 (Hamish Hamilton, 1953)

SELECT BIBLIOGRAPHY

The Buildings of England volumes, founded by Sir Nikolaus Pevsner, and the *Pevsner Architectural Guides* have proved invaluable for reference, in particular the City Guides for Bristol, Sheffield, Nottingham, Birmingham, Liverpool, Newcastle and Gateshead, Leeds and Manchester.

Journals

Building News

Economic History Review

Oxford Economic Papers

Past and Present

Sunday Chronicle

The Bristol Times and Mirror

The Builder

The Forum

The Graphic

The Illustrated London News

The Times

Secondary Sources

Aldcroft, Derek H. & Richardson, Harry W: T*he British Economy 1870-1939*, Macmillan 1969

Allen, Michelle: *Cleansing the City, Sanitary Geographies in Victorian London*, Ohio University Press 2008

Ashton, TS: *The Industrial Revolution 1760-1830*, Oxford 1968

Bell, Colin and Rose: *City Fathers: The Early History of Town Planning in Britain*, Penguin Books 1972

Booth, William: *In Darkest England and the Way Out*, Funk and Wagnalls, 1890

Borsa, Mario: *England and Her Critics,* Fisher Unwin 1917

Briggs, Asa: *Victorian Cities*, Penguin Books 1990

Brodie, Alan & Winter, Gary: *England's Seaside Resorts*, English Heritage 2007

Chambers, JD; *The Workshop of the World*, Oxford 1968

Chambers, JD & Mingay, GE: *The Agricultural Revolution 1750-1880*, Batsford 1968

Chesney, Kellow: *The Victorian Underworld*, Purnell 1970

Chinn, Carl: *Poverty Amidst Prosperity: The Urban Poor in England 1834-1914*, Carnegie Publishing 2006

Conan Doyle, Arthur: *The Naval Treaty: The Memoirs of Sherlock Holmes*, George Newnes 1894

Conway, Hazel: *People's Parks*, Cambridge University Press 1991

Cunningham, Colin: *Victorian and Edwardian Town Halls*, Routledge and Kegan Paul 1981

Darley, Gillian: *Villages of Vision*, Granada 1978

Davies, Philip: *Troughs and Drinking Fountains*, Chatto & Windus 1989

Davies, Philip: *Lost London 1870-1945*, Trans-Atlantic Publishing 2009

Deane, Phyllis: *The Industrial Revolution in England 1700-1914*, Fontana 1969

Deane, Phyllis & Cole, W.A: *British Economic Growth 1688-1959*, Cambridge University Press 1969

Dennis, Richard: *English Industrial Cities of the Nineteenth Century,* Cambridge University Press *1986*

De Tocqueville, Alexis: *Journeys to England and Ireland*, Yale University Press 1958

Dickens, *Charles: Dombey & Son*, Bradbury and Evans 1848

Dixon, Roger& Muthesius, Stefan: *Victorian Architecture*, Thames and Hudson 1978

Douet, James: *British Barracks 1600-1914*, English Heritage 1998

Faucher, Leon: *Etudes sur l'Angleterre*, Gillaumin 1845

Flanders, Judith: *The Victorian City. Everyday Life in Dickens' London*, Atlantic Books 2012

Flinn, MW: *British Population Growth 1700-1850*, Macmillan 1970

Floud, Roderick and McCloskey, Donald: *The Economic History of Britain since 1700, Volume 2.1860 to the 1970*s, Cambridge University Press 1981

Ford, Colin & Harrison, Brian: *A Hundred Years Ago*, Bloomsbury 1994

Gilbert Scott, George: *Secular and Domestic Architecture, Present and Future*, John Murray 1857

Girouard, Mark: *Victorian Pubs*, Studio Vista 1975

Girouard, Mark: *The Victorian Country House*, Yale 1979

Hall, AR: *The Export of Capital from Britain 1870-1914*, Methuen 1968

Harrison, Fraser: *The Dark Angel: Aspects of Victorian Sexuality*, Sheldon Press 1977

Hartley, LP: *The Go-Between*, Hamish Hamilton 1953

Hobsbawm, Eric J: *Industry and Empire*, Penguin 1968

Hoppen, K Theodore: *The Mid-Victorian Generation*, Oxford 1998

Hunt, Tristram: *Building Jerusalem: The Rise and Fall of the Victorian City*, Phoenix 2005

Hubbard, Edward & Shippobottom, Michael: A *Guide to Port Sunlight Village*, Liverpool University Press, 1990

Hylton, Stuart: *A History of Manchester*, Phillimore 2003

Jones, EL: *The Development of English Agriculture 1815-1873*, Macmillan 1968

Kitson Clark, G: *The Making of Victorian England*, Routledge 1985

Knox, Collie: *Forever England*, Cassell 1943

Marshall, JD: *The Old Poor Law 1795-1834*, Macmillan 1968

Martin, Christopher: *A Glimpse of Heaven*, English Heritage 2006

Morris, RJ & Rodger, Richard: *The Victorian City 1820-1914*, Longman 1993

Nasmyth, James: Autobiography, John Murray 1883

Paterson, Michael: *Life in Victorian Britain*, Constable and Robinson 2008

Pelling, Henry: *Modern Britain 1885-1955*, Sphere 1969

Rackham, Oliver: *The History of the Countryside*, J M Dent 1986

RCHME: *English Hospitals 1660-1948*, RCHME 1998

Rolt, LTC: *Victorian Engineering*, Pelican Books 1974

Royston Pike, E: *Human Documents of the Industrial Revolution in Britain*, George Allen & Unwin 1970

Royston Pike, E: *Human Documents of the Victorian Golden Age*, George Allen & Unwin 1967

Royston Pike, E: *Human Documents of the Age of the Forsytes*, George Allen & Unwin 1969

Ruskin, John: *The Seven Lamps of Architecture*, Dover Publications 1989

Ruskin, John: *The Cestus of Aglaia,* J. M. Dent 1908

Saint, Andrew: *Richard Norman Shaw*, Yale, 1977

Saul, SB: *The Myth of the Great Depression* 1873-1896, Macmillan 1969

Sayers, RS: *A History of Economic Change in England 1880-1939*, Oxford 1967

Service, Alastair: *London 1900*, Granada 1979

Sims, George: *How the Poor Live*, Chatto & Windus 1883

Stamp, Gavin: *Britain's Lost Cities*, Aurum 2010

Stamp, Gavin: *Lost Victorian Britain*, Aurum 2010

Steinbach, Susie L: *Understanding the Victorians: Politics, Culture and Society in Nineteenth Century Britain*, Routledge 2012

Stuart Gray, A: *Edwardian Architecture*, Wordsworth 1985

Trollope, Anthony: *The Vicar of Bullhampton*, Bradbury and Evans 1870

Upton, Chris: *The History of Birmingham*, Phillimore 2011

White, Jerry: *London in the 20th Century*, Vintage 2008

Winder, Robert: *Bloody Foreigners: The Story of Immigration to Britain*, Little, Brown 2004

Young, GM: *Victorian England, Portrait of an Age*, Oxford 1969

Ziegler, Philip: *Britain Then & Now*, Weidenfeld and Nicholson 1999

PHOTOGRAPHIC CREDITS AND ACKNOWLEDGEMENTS

Photographs in this book © Historic England.
Additional photographs courtesy of the following archives:

© Getty Images:
54; 55 t; 56 top right; 68; 70 t; 71; 74; 75 b; 82 bottom right; 92; 107; 123 b; 124 t; 144; 145 b; 146; 147 t; 148; 153 b; 156 b; 176 t; 178 t&b; 179; 191 t; 200 t; 201; 202 b; 203; 224 t; 225 t; 226; 227 t; 234 above and below left; 241 t; 243 t; 245 middle left; 245 t; 253 t; 254 top left; 259 t right; 271 top & b; 273 t right; 283 top; 303 middle; 306 b; 311 t & b; 321 b; 325 b; 328 t&b; 336 b; 337 t; 348 t&b; 349 t; 352 b; 353; 418 t; 419 b; 419 t; 422 middle; 432 t right; 433 t; 435 b; 437; 445 t; 447 t right & t left; 490 t; 503 t; 506 t&b; 508 b; 510 t; 511 t; 514 b; 514 t; 517 top right; 522 b; 526 b; 535 b; 536 b; 539 b; 539 t; 548 t; 550 t; 551 b.

© Heritage Photographic Resources:
(Francis Frith Collection)
96 b; 105 t&b; 106 t&b; 110 t; 115 t&b; 118; 119 t&b; 129 b; 129 t; 143 b; 155 b; 155t; 157 b; 157 t; 169 t&b; 174 t; 176 b; 199 b; 202 b; 214b; 218 b; 244 b; 246 t; 247 t&b; 248 b; 249 t; 294 t; 299 t; 300 b; 301 b; 302 t&b; 304 b; 304 t; 305 t&b; 307 t; 310 t; 313 b; 340 t&b; 341 t&b; 345 b; 346 t&b; 347 b; 355 t; 356 b; 357 b; 362 b.

© Newcastle City Library:
34; 161 bottom left & right; 170; 171 all 4; 173 t&b;

© Manchester Central Library:
108 t &b; 109 t& bl & br; 111; 110 b; 97; 104.

© Oxfordshire County Council, Oxfordshire History Centre:
(Henry W Taunt photographs)
403 t; 415 b; 446 t; 381 t; 412 t; 381 b; 416 top left; 412 b; 366 t; 408 b; 446 middle; 321 top left; 320 top and bottom.

© Harry Chambers: 364/365

© Library of Birmingham:
9; 254 middle and b; 255 t; 262 b; 263 b; 272 middle; 288 t&b; 289 t&b ; 290 b; 291 b.

Courtesy Library of Birmingham:
262 b; 263 tr, tl; 272 t, b; 290 t; 291 t.

Every effort has been made to ensure that the copyright details shown are correct, but if there are any inaccuracies, please contact the publisher.

Thanks to the following for their help:
Julia Skinner, Francis Frith Collection
Amba Horton, Toby Hopkins, Getty Images
Geoff Burns, Library of Birmingham
Jane Hodkinson and Jane Parr, Manchester Central Library
Sarah Mulligan, City Library, Newcastle
Mark Lawrence and Helen Drury, Oxford History Centre
Harry Chambers Photography

Thanks to the editorial and production team:
Tim Hill, Wendy Toole, Lyn Mellor, Cliff Salter.

Thanks also to historian Carl Chinn for his help.